GOING PLACES IN THE SPIRIT

MAPONGA JOSHUA III

redOystor

London | Johannesburg | New York

Published by RedOystor Books; 2017
        an Imprint of RedOystor Media (Pty) Ltd

Published by RedOystor Books
an imprint of RedOystor Media (Pty) Ltd
    Ground Floor, Lakeview Building,
    1277 Mike Crawford Avenue, Centurion, 0157

www.redoystor.com/going-places-in-the-spirit
www.facebook.com/FarmersOfThough
www.farmersofthought.com

Cover Design & Layout by
RedOystor Media (Pty) Ltd
        Cover Design © Mpho Maja
        Edited By Kelebogile Kekana

Also available on Amazon.com
Available on Kindle and other retail outlets

    ISBN: 978-0-6399789-8-7 (Print)
                978-0-6399789-9-4 (epub)

Reviews

A must read book that will redirect your mental faculties to something more fulfilling and meaningful. Christianity as read and understood from the book of Acts, is a Spirit filled movement that is contrary to the Christianity of the missionaries, which put emphasis on the physical appearance, forms and schedules, protocols and manuals, at the expense of the core of a human being, his spirit. This mechanical form of Christianity by missionaries starves the Spirit and feeds the flesh.

It is possible to reconnect, and relive the book of Acts in present day is all the book seeks to address among other interesting issues that are hardly addressed on your church pulpits.

Sangomas connect with their spiritual realm at the twinkling of an eye, yet professed Godly Worshipers of YHWH seem to be calling on a being who have been, like the mount Carmel experience, gone on holiday.

The book addresses key issues on how to connect in the spirit with YHWH because those that worship Him must do so in Spirit and in truth.... Get your own copy and thank me later.

Mossiah Mossiah
- Founder of He is Coming Series Concerts by Commission Music Group

The Gospel in the hands of the enslaver, the colonizer can only be used as a tool to tame Africans and steal their land. Christianity in the hand Imperial Eurocentrism makes the African Christian to become a *Mephibosheth*.

This book has the power to rescue us and lead us to the Savior.

The twenty first century writers and preachers must be honest and never fall into the trap to write and preach like the oppressor. Remember the songs "Take the world and give me Jesus", I'll rather have Jesus than silver and gold, Africa! you can have both.

The message from those who need something from you might not be the true Gospel because their need breeds desperation and greed. While they're sharing and teaching you they will empowered and enlightened but drop that you remain dependent and feeling incomplete without their systems. The cry to share what you know you don't have to condemn, degrade and demonize me nor culture me and my traditions.

Thulani Thabethe
TTMWELLS at Divine Growth Center Witbank-RSA, Counseller and Minister

Gye Nyame
God Reigns Supreme

Revered as one of highest Akan spiritual symbols. It is a symbol that has many interpretations.

"Except God" simply means that one recognizes the supremacy of God and, in essence, one is not afraid of anything-except the Supreme Being.

Contents

Dedication   i

Disclaimer   ii

Epilogue   1

FAQ   3

Foreword   7

Why Write this Book?   11

An Introduction   15

Being yourself   25

Re-colonized   41

Africa Arise   45

Our Moral Debt   55

A Divided Worship   71

Real Ministry   93

Melchizedek   131

In Prayer   153

God's Presence   167

Master Servant   215

A foreign God   247

Music and Worship   257

Worship and Music   279

Your Presence   307

God Facing   337

Revelations   353

Glossary   365

Music Notes   373

References   379

About the Author   387

Dedication

I Dedicate this book:

To the Black nation, to sons of Ham, the Edenites

To those who want to "go places in the spirit"!

To all the seekers of truth,

To all who desire to move to the higher world of the Spirit?

To all who want more out their Spirituality?

To those who want to challenge white-thinking for indigenous faith and knowledge!

To those who want to eat the bread and throw away the plastic!

To the body of Yashua: to all who can hear the Voice saying, "Come up here" [1]

---

1. Revelation 4

Disclaimer

"Going Places in the Spirit"

Disclaimer: The author does not represent any official position of a church or political entity but desires to experience the reality of living Spiritual life: this entire work is based on limited spiritual experience but questions and assumes to drive people towards a deeper desire to be supernatural so as to control the physical.

Decolonizing Christianity

Other books written by Maponga Joshua III:

So you want to be the Master!
Shopping Skills
Women in the Kitchen
Going Places in the Spirit
12 keys to Infinite Possibilities
For our Children
Gems for Corporate
Dare you Cross the River
Preaching Dynamics
Models of Manhood
8 in One (wife fit for a king)

Whiteman "lets control" Chinese man "lets create" Jewish man "lets invest", Blackman "lets pray that God does it all for us" [1]

---

1. Dr Umar Johnson

Epilogue

The spiritual church is under siege from false western teachings (Euro-Christianity) that introduced us to other false gods foreign to our land.

Our wayward teachings away from spirituality to Christianity, from the Torah to catechism, from Scripture to church manuals, from the bible to denominational doctrines and declarations, from faith healing to commercial healing ministries, from "thus says the Lord" to prophetic movements is a shame, all these shall burn in the lowest parts of hell.

The television ministries champion these "new movements" in the spiritual realm. There is a multiplicity of fake miracles and fake happenings to mislead the souls that are seeking.

In some cases worship has become a display of magic and gimmicks, "show time", entertainment that has no YHWH as a Subject or Object of worship. "

Demons have the nature to walk into our congregations and we are instilled with fear to run away from things that God has given us power over.

While we clap our hands our hearts are crippled, and the spirit cannot move when the hearts are locked in anger, for anger contaminates the aura and passage of the spirit.

This fake Eurocentric Christianity experience has produced religious paraplegics. While the "Jews/whites" are inside the temple enjoying the blessing of YHWH the rest of the Christians world communities sit to beg for hand outs at the door of this Hebrew based faith.

The time of refreshing is now.

It is when it rains that mental plants will bud in the beauty of spring and will we sing free at last. Free from lies and oppression, free from these white demons some of them in black skins.

The Christian community needs cleansing.

This Euro-Christianity is committing suicide and harlotry with democracy, and the African churches have become a brothel of faith.

Who will dare ask or challenge the status quo? Church has become a league match of demons and devils with pastors as clowns and idiots on the circus stage of faith.

The farmer of thought must secure new land for fresh crop and a bumper harvest. Our hunger for figs can't make us eat the fig leaves.

Maponga Joshua III
CEO - **Farmers of Thought**

FAQ
(Frequently Asked Questions)

"Start by asking the right questions"[1]

When wisdom is given to the chosen they will live and not do wrong again withering through forgetfulness, or through pride, but those who possess wisdom will be humble... and complete the number of the days of their life." [2]

- o Black Question - what is worship?
- o Black History - where are we coming from?
- o Black problem - what is the black problem?
- o Black fakes - whose voice is it... and whose hands?
- o Black pool - tradition versus experience
- o Black worship - black God or a white God?
- o Black spirituality - physical or spiritual?

1. Dennis Healey; English Politician born in 1917. Chambers Book of Great Speeches, Edited by Andrew Burnet, Chambers Harp Publishers Ltd 2006, 2013.
2. The Book of Enoch: A modern translation of the Ethiopian Book of Enoch: SOAS Library at the University of London. Pp 13

- o Black Politics - who drives our political bus?
- o Black heart - theology and practice
- o Black covenant - Are Africans Hebraic?
- o Black reality - what is in the Realms?
- o Black sin - immorality and spirituality
- o Black music - do we sing to the soul or to the mind?
- o Black presence - what is the Black Experience?
- o Black Hebrews - Are blacks Hebrews?

Why fight with the system of Christianity? Who is benefiting from this present system? What are the possible solutions?

PURPOSE OF THIS BOOK: WHY WRITE THIS BOOK?

Why do white people want us to be white before God can accept us? Is it *okay* for a black woman to make tea for a whiteman? Is it *okay* for a white woman to make tea for a Blackman?

Who runs the physical? (Spirituality or Christianity? What is a worship experience? Where does Genesis begin here Africa or Europe? Who is this God to the African nation?

How do we use the sacrifices to access the spiritual dimension? What is the genealogical and anthropological connection between Africans and Hebrews? What is the significance of water, wine and blood (animal sacrifices)?

Why worship at a distance? What stops us? What is worship? And what hinders honest worship?

Why lean on gold while begging for Gold? What is acceptable worship, how do we approach? What are the key demands of worship?

How do you worship a God who has cursed you? How do worshippers cleanse themselves? How do we claim this victory over such oppression? Why bring tradition to worship?

What is worship?

Where is the venue of worship? How do we prepare for worship? Who occupies the heart of the worshipper?

What is in the name?

How do we celebrate our being? How far should worship take you?

Where does worship take place, on which realm does worship take place?

What is the demon that occupies many worshippers?

What is African worship? How much damage did colonialism do to the African people? How deep are the scares of poverty on the canvas of the soul of the Blackman? What is the psychology of worship and colonization of Jesus?

Who needs deliverance? How does the African enter the presence of deity? What is the power of the worshippers? What type of music reaches the spirit and soul of man? How do we reach the meaningful spiritual depth?

What are the five key questions that enhance worship? What are the key elements of worship?

How do we relate to scripture to find our experience?

Foreword

This book clearly presents evidence that we need to use now, not later, but now.

Bishop Maponga Joshua III tears apart and puts together the political, sociological, psychological and religious fabric of the current African modern culture.

The former enslavers, colonizers, and oppressors have written and taught the Africa our entire history. To us everything that we've been taught are fabrication and *false truths* rewritten to favor *them* to control the African child. When the oppressor and the oppressed both share the same Savior, there's something wrong with the equation. Religion is seen as another imperial military tool of oppression and power.

The religious mythology, symbolism and nature of Capitalistic Europeans are shown to be totally separate from the African experience. Worship is a spiritual journey, which takes you from one dimension into another. Religion from the Latin verb *religare*: "to tie back; to hold back; to thwart from forward progress; to bind".

Religion is a system of control based on unchallenged, dogmatic beliefs, which hold back the progress of consciousness.

This book breaks down the molds of religion and releases us to spirituality. The African, in an attempt to see European's religious psychosis must reduce the African vocabulary and eliminate 90% of the words.

Words represent intelligence; therefore, the African must reduce 90% of their knowledge of self to get near the European mind. This book is an African language about spirituality, and worship of the true and living God - the Creator.

Bishop Joshua Maponga vividly lambastes the effects of colonization on the African's psyche. The tragedy of colonization is that it not only colonized the land of African people, but their perception of God as well.

During the enslavement of Africans they were given a Christian religion that taught them to believe in a white *God*, white *Messiah*, white *Angels* and white *Prophets*.

These depictions of "white only" deities were deliberately done to subconsciously indoctrinate the false belief of white divinity [and therefore superiority] upon the minds of the African slaves. The slaves believe in white gods and it makes them subconsciously believe that the slave masters, also being white are closer to God or god like.

To protect their positions of white dominance they believe it was necessary to instill the belief of white superiority into the minds of the African slaves.

The 'white idolizing religious indoctrination' process was also used to make the African slaves more loyal to their masters. From the perspective of the slave masters, it made them better slaves.

The effects of that brainwashing scheme initially implemented more than four hundred years ago still continues upon the mind of millions of Africans. It is the reason why you can presently visit many black churches and find its walls stubbornly adorned with pictures of only white deities. This conditioning has been left uncorrected and *un-removed* for generation.

This book is an attempt to correct this evil and its effect on the African people. In this book you will learn that nobody brought God to Africa, He was already here.

That darkness is the womb of the creative genesis process; the African must speak "let there be". No matter how dark the night has been, soon daybreak will reveal the evils of the night. The Spirit of the worshipper must go and unite with its Maker, not colonized and devoid of the imported *Eurocentric* faith, which destroys dignity and perpetuates slavery and poverty.

Most Africans are unaware that their spiritual experiences of trance shaking when feeling a spiritual connection with their Creator, and speaking in tongues has nothing to do with Christianity, but a natural sensitivity of the spiritual world.

In fact when early African slaves displayed such behavior. Their masters often expressed feelings of shock because they found the displayed behavior to be strange and alien to the Christian religion they were teaching the slaves.

This is because these expressions of spirituality (that we now perceive as Christianity) are in fact totally African expressions. Many African Americans believe that it's the power of Christianity, a white Jesus that they're feeling but this same behavior may be found in the deepest parts of Africa by Africans celebrating their ancient religion?

Maponga teaches that the people presently known as Africans and or as Black have had a deep relationship with their Creator/The Most High/ God, long before the European stepped foot on this continent. That if your ancestors are demons, then what are you?

This book is a liberating tool, and antidote of walking around as a white "coconut" godless zombie trapped in black skin. Our relationship with the Creator was established long before the names of Mohammed or even Buddha were ever uttered.

Through Bishop Maponga's teaching and research about worship you will learn that the way we connected to our Most High was originally done in a more organic and spiritual manner. Not through organized religion but through a personal oneness between the inner mind and that which we now know as God through Christ.

No two individuals may verbalize their 'being' experience in the same manner. Some say that He speaks from above, some say He comes from within. Some may also say that He comes through the mind, while others say the heart is the center, or the soul being the receptor of divine presence.

It doesn't matter because in our true belief system they are all correct.

It is their own individual oneness with The Most High that punctuates their expression! It is these man made religions that often perverts the truth confuse men and justify wars that enslave millions into spiritual coloni-zation.

Bishop Maponga's book is a holistic fusion of the past, present and future. We can see the African's past connect to his future.

This book may shock you, but it will awaken you to the reality we must face. It is a masterpiece that is highly valuable to our race.

Pastor Vincent Mafu

"If cattle and horses, or lions, had hands, or were able to draw with their feet and produce the works which men do, horses would draw the forms of gods like horses, and god like cattle, and they would make the gods' bodies the same shape as their own." [1]

---

1. Xenophanes of Colophon was a Greek philosopher, theologian, poet, and social and religious critic. Xenophanes lived a life of travel, having left Ionia at the age of 25 and continuing to travel throughout the Greek world for another 67 years

Why Write this Book?

Purpose of this book is therefore

TO FIND THE HEART OF THE WORSHIPPER

- o To prepare the leader as a worthy vessel of worship
- o To introduce the worshipper to the worshippers
- o To unsettle those complacence and recycled in their faith
- o To explore the parallel of African and European Worship

TO OBSERVE THE SPIRITUAL MUSIC AND ENTERTAINMENT MUSIC

TO EXPLORE THE ROOTS OF REAL WORSHIP AND ADD UNDERSTANDING TO MYSTERY

TO CALL FOR A CHANGE IN THE LIFE OF THE WORSHIPPER AND WORSHIP LEADER

- To rebuild meaningful worship services
- To assist the seeker to access an honest faith platform
- To build churches that are effective
- To unmask the hypocrite and search for genuine
- To improve spiritual connections of African Worshippers
- To challenge the traditional forms of Eurocentric worship forms
- To select the correct type of music for right kind of impact
- To share an experience and guide the young theologians
- To ask questions which are a no go area for many theologians

TO CREATE AN ENVIRONMENT WHERE THE HOLY SPIRIT CAN MANIFEST

- To introduce the worshipper to the Almighty during worship
- To use music and worship as a passage into the very Presence of God

TO CREATE DIALOGUE BETWEEN CREATOR AND CREATURE DURING THE MOMENT OF WORSHIP

- To initiate a robust debate in the Christian community
- To bridge the gap between Western theologians and African theologians

TO PUSH PEOPLE TO DEMAND, REQUIRE AND EXPECT MORE AT THE HOUR OF WORSHIP

TO ASSIST THE EUROPEAN TO APPRECIATE AFRICAN THEOLOGY

"The learning and knowledge that we have is, at the most, but little compared with that of which we are ignorant. " [1]

"Life is not a problem to be solved but a reality to be experienced. Just as in earthly reality life lovers long for a moment when they are able to breath forth their love for each other to let their souls blend in a soft whisper, so the mystic longs for the moment when in prayer he can as it were creep into God" [2]

And *"without music life would be a mistake"* [3]

1. Plato: the Greek Philosopher 427 B.C
2. Screen Kierkegaard, Dannish Philospher born 1813
3. Friedrich Nietzsche: German Philosopher 1844

An Intro-duction

In the Beginning

Institutions of religion "cannot do without spirituality, but spirituality can flourish without religion abound to traditions."1

Worship is spiritual. Music is a venue for spiritual interaction, the permanent residence of the spirits, the act that joins to tango the soul of mankind with the supernatural hosts.

*Uma ungesona isa**ngoma**, wenzani, ufanani Engomeni?* [2] (If you are not a

1 Paul Post, Phillip Nel and Walteer; Van Beek, Sacred and contested Identities (space and ritual dynamics in Europe and Africa p 4
2 Gcina Nhlapo, 29 March 2016 Interview on Music. He is a musician and Worship leader as Cities of Refuge Johannesburg. The power of African worship and praise is in their experiences, which they have not been allowed to express fully.

medium what are you doing with the song?). The "*sa-ngoma*" is a master of song and the drum, a mediator of spirituality. Even in silence the song is still heard, it awaits, music is spiritual, for us in Africa, it is a language of the soul to connect with the spirit. Alas they said " To win a people for Christ, it is necessary to Europeanize them.

Behind all systems of administration lies the fundamental question of "**WHAT WE INTENDED TO DO WITH THE AFRICAN**,"[3] the Caucasian question. To us Christianity is a religion; to them it's a management strategy to systematically fragment African society.

The African anger has been castrated by religion to a toothless dog on the leash of white economics. Going places in the Spirit seeks to liberate the young and experienced Christians who seek to move beyond the ordinary to the supernatural. Seeking for depth during the moment of praise, worship and silence in the presence of God.

The witches and wizards make mockery of our ignorance in this regard of spiritual education and encounter with the supernatural. They move in and out of the physical and the spiritual realm with ease and cause things to happen. They fly in the night in the spirit, have control over forces of gravity, and elements. Why because they fight with the principalities, and the *Euro-christianity* has no education or transport into the spiritual realm?

The indignity of African churches has been bombarded by the "fear of bringing back "*pagan*" elements in the church life, which eventually resulted in the introduction of drums (*Ngoma*) in church services."[4]

Thousands of Black people in Rhodesia and Portuguese east Africa attribute godlike and terrible powers to white people. They believe that white people are the sons of the living flowers that grows somewhere under the restless cold passionate seas and that blond Europeans are half-human and half plant (because they argue, who ever saw yellow hair on a human head, yellow hair like that one sees on the head of a mealie cob'

As Vaclav Havel would say "*We live in contaminated moral environment… our country is not flourishing. The enormous creative and spiritual potential of our nation is not being used sensibly.*"

"Entire branches of industry are producing goods that are of no interest to anyone, while we are lacking in the things we need. A state which calls

3. Edwin W Smith: the Christianity of Africa in the golden stool, Hilbron Publishing House, p 173
4. Paul Post, Phillip Nel and Walteer Van Beek, Sacred and contested Identities (space and ritual dynamics in Europe and Africa p 43

itself a workers state humiliates and exploits workers."[5] The African nation needs to take responsibility for the exploitation we have suffered, it has been self-inflicted. A continent that houses great knowledge and civility now reduced to slavery, polluted ground, deforestation, hunger, disease, a basket continent and a charity case run by puppet leaders and thoughtless theologians that push people into the hole of meaninglessness.

Is it possible that the African child has been used so much that when he looks at this system he sees it as *"totalitarian system and accepts it as an unchangeable fact and thus helps to perpetrate it."*[6]

So great is the lack of understanding between black and white in Africa that there are whites who refuse to accept the fact that a blackman is a human being like the Indian, the Colored, the Chinese and the European himself. These people believe nothing else about Africans but that they are lazy, stupid, stubborn creatures, something between an ape and a human being. "You can not fight an evil disease with sweet medicine,"[7] or liberate a nation with caged leaders. The one who feels the stones in the shoes must take it off to compete with the best. We will not sit while the whiteman pees in our wells of fresh water.

Look at the image on the following page (**Fig1.1**)below at the chart and measure your competence levels. This subject will anger and unsettle many who thrive on African ignorance and use Christianity as flee market of cheap second hand experiences of white missionaries rather mercenaries.

The African sits to reminisce the sentiments of white ferry stolen stories from the black nation. Africa must move from unconscious incompetence to conscious competence. The hub of world religions, the cradle of mankind cannot be a dump-site of ideological decay from the whiteman. Our people need to think of solutions not strategies to uphold oppressive ideologies.

Consider the frames:

Boxes of thought shows us three types of people:

1. **Those who think inside the box:** limited and closed conformists, who are drunk with the wine of traditions and will kill to keep the system and status quo, under lock and key

---

5. Vaclav Havel: 1990 Television and Radio interview from Prague, Czechoslovakia. "The contamination as a sin we committed against ourselves".

6. Ibid

7. Credo Vusamazulu Mutwa, Indaba, My Children (AfricanTribal History, legends, customs and religious beliefs) Blue Crane Books, 1964

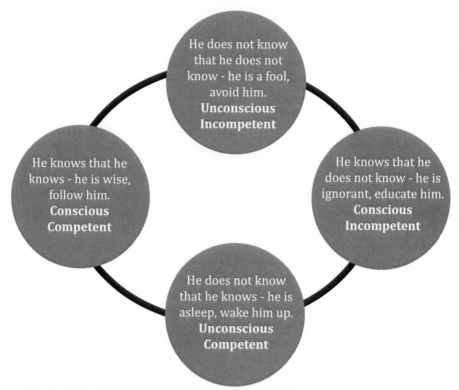

He does not know that he does not know - he is a fool, avoid him. **Unconscious Incompetent**

He knows that he knows - he is wise, follow him. **Conscious Competent**

He knows that he does not know - he is ignorant, educate him. **Conscious Incompetent**

He does not know that he knows - he is asleep, wake him up. **Unconscious Competent**

Fig 1.1: Consciousness

2. **Those who think outside the box**: their reference is still the box. They dare to move out and try new things but will not go very far for they still need to be accepted by the multitudes in the box.

3. **Those who "break the box and think"**[8]: my kind of group, free and open to explore the world, like infants they ask questions on everything and further question the questions, a quest for answers, solutions and meaning.

Those who have bought the t-shirt and its torn, maturity has forced them to be real and like the leapers of the books of Kings when confronted with death on either side *'leaper-logic'* kicks in.

"If we stay here in the camp we will die of hunger. If we go to the city we will die, better we die in pursuit of help."

Their resolute mind was confronted with the divine intervention, for the angel host had moved at their decision to a sound of rushing wind in the sky, and the enemy thought help had been summoned.

---

8. Richard Sauta: Brigadier General an independent thinker and military strategist (special forces)

The African has to understand that it is death either way. This *fake* white Jesus will kill us if we continue to stay and if we move away we are branded as rebellious. I suggest that rather we die in pursuit of the Savior, than rot in this leprosy of insignificance.

In the absence of thinking religion is worse than witchcraft.

Religion is changing its shape for spirituality, and it is not returning – it has never gone away. But as is widely acknowledged by now, the secular-ization process itself must also be nuanced and reinterpreted…central perspective of cultural dynamics. [9]

Faith has become a lucrative industry, in the face of *"imperial civilization"*.

"We have become like empty shells as we seek to fill our hearts with the toxins of modern materialism and technology. In vain we spend only to sink in debt and die lonely."

The truth is *"the people are the antagonist of industrial society. The principle of the people against the principle of industrial society."*

This story has not been played out, but the tide is raising in the village against the industrial city…the people and the earth shall rise up as it were against abstracts, non-committed, inhuman system of industrial society. Man and earth will find each other again. [10]

People are real and not an industry of zombies who must conform to nonsensical norms. If religion and Christianity says it is what it is, then it must bring practical solutions to human plight and not put cotton wool on the face of the masses to manage them and keep them in bondage.

The masses seek an experience with God, the industry seeks money to expand business, conflict is brewing and truth will triumph. Profit is secondary people are primary.

The African, through worship hopes for a solution in the now and a better life hereafter. The *colonial whiteman* uses faith as a management tool to oppress the conscience of the commoner; (the black person) this is coming to an end as the monster called *'imperial Christianity'* is finally being proved to be an industry instead of a spiritual pedestal it has deserted.

This is a wolf in a sheepskin that feeds on the African lamb, a perpetual parasite that feeds on the conscience of the gullible. The principles enshrined in the creed are by far not the desire of the Christian movement *'do unto others, as you want them to do unto you.'*

9. Paul Post, Phillip Nel and Walteer Van Beek, Sacred and contested Identities (space and ritual dynamics in Europe and Africa p 5
10. Juegen Moltmann, Theology of Hope, Fortress Press, 1993, pp 319

Will the whiteman want me to treat him the way he has treated me?

When the black man talks revenge he is evil, while the Whiteman perpetuates oppression its called civilization. The black man pays with his life and soul to be "*civilized*".

How will the whiteman deal with the justice of YHWH? When the whiteman prays what does he tell God? Is it civil to refuse another man a glass of water? Why put a fence around a river and prohibit the poor a drink?

People want to meet this God whom the whiteman says is a savior.

Why is the whiteman not saved by his own savior?

The church cannot lock (Jesus) *Yashua* in prison like Pilate for private amusement or summon him for a miracle showdown like Herod.

I prefer to use the Hebrew name **YaHshua**, instead of His Gentile nickname *Jesus*.

Does it matter what we call him?

If it does not matter why bother people who call him other names and worship him in different forms?

Is it possible that Christianity has created an idol called Jesus and we are all forced to worship this evil white Caucasian pagan idol?

To weave our African people together there has to be a teacher and a student. The Teacher is the needle and the student is the thread.[11] Let the nation build its industries and sell its produce but let it never be that we make tools and sell our brains.

The value of material is replaceable but our minds cannot be auctioned for a potash of soup. The mental faculties of a nation cannot be contaminated by so much bacteria that a nation would hate itself and try to become another. To abandon even our skin, hair, language, diet all for a cup of tea and a white name. Sadly anybody who challenges these norms is deemed as motivated by demons.

"*If you see things differently, you are either ignorant, stupid, arrogant or evil. Wickedness is a crime against peace not a crime against truth*"[12]

---

11. Miyamoto Musashi, The Book of the Five Rings, Bantam Books 1982, pp 9 the master must guide the student as the outcome is on him changing into enlightenment The student must understand that he is the object and primary beneficiary of education.

12. Twitter: @giles_fraser http://www.theguardian.com/commentisfree/belief/2013/may/31/wickedness-allied-truth-religious-belief-heinous

Eggs do not hatch at the same time. Studies and history will shock you to your boots, yet to fully appreciate the scene lets visit the slave fields and see how the white oppressor thinks. To kill a white-man is treason, to tear a blackman apart using horses is called breaking the nigger for economic benefit.

Read carefully and see how the church of *Eurocentric Christianity* has the gene of its master, the whteman. This strategy to abuse blacks and press them into social re-engineering models has been thought through by imperialist, one of the champions Lynch outlined some critical information that we need to consider.

The quotations below are extracts from their scientific program to break black slaves.

He goes to length to share his "*methods*" for control of slaves.

"A FULL PROOF METHOD FOR CONTROLLING YOUR BLACK SLAVES. I guarantee every one of you that, if installed correctly, **IT WILL CONTROL THE SLAVES FOR AT LEAST 300 HUNDREDS YEARS."** In his program are three tools that he prides himself with **FEAR, DISTRUST AND ENVY FOR CONTROL PURPOSES."**

It is build into the Eurocentric Christianity that the church breeds people it can not trust and according to Lynch **"DISTRUST IS STRONGER THAN TRUST AND ENVY STRONGER THAN ADULATION, RESPECT OR ADMIRATION**.

"The Black slaves after receiving this indoctrination shall carry on and will become self-refueling and self-generating for **HUNDREDS** of years, maybe **THOUSANDS."**

A close look at the strategy will reveal the pitch to destroy the fiber of the community. The target was to break apart African social structures of thinking, and create war between the old and young, the light skin and the dark skin and ultimately *'pitch havoc'* between males and females. **"LET'S MAKE A SLAVE".**

Frederick Douglas an evil man also came up with satanic statement **"LET'S MAKE A SLAVE"** the scripture teaches **"LET US MAKE MAN".**

This study is a scientific process of man-breaking and slave-making, black people are classified with beast and horses.

It describes the rationale and results of the Anglo Saxons' ideas and methods of insuring the master/slave relationship. "So evil was the method that the slave traders would select males and females to breed, the same as they breed horses.

The purpose was to break them from one form of life, "*Ubuntu*" to another, "*coconuts*"; black outside white inside, and reduce the human beings from their natural state into tools for hard labor.

Whereas nature provides them with the natural capacity to take care of their offspring, we break that natural string of independence from them and thereby create a dependency status, so that we may be able to get from them useful production for our business and pleasure.

"Both horse and niggers [are] no good to the economy in the wild or natural state...both a wild horse and a wild or natur[al] nigger is dangerous even if captured.

Both must be **BROKEN** and **TIED** together for orderly production."

The plan would prove effective if the slave owner would be able to allow the nigger to "**KEEP THE BODY**"... and the slave owners "**TAKE THE MIND**! In other words, break the will to resist. Train the female horse whereby she will eat out of your hand, and she will in turn train the infant horse to eat out of your hand, also.

"When it comes to breaking the uncivilized nigger, use the same process, but vary the degree and step up the pressure, so as to do a complete reversal of the mind."

"Take the meanest and most restless nigger, strip him of his clothes in front of the remaining male niggers, the female, and the nigger infant, tar and feather him, tie each leg to a different horse faced in opposite directions, set him afire and beat both horses to pull him apart in front of the remaining niggers.

The next step is to take a bull-whip and beat the remaining nigger males to the point of death, in front of the female and the infant."

Don't kill him, but **PUT THE FEAR OF GOD IN HIM**, "for he can be useful for future breeding." It is clear on the process above that the white barbarian under the guise of civilization is calling himself "*god*" to the oppressed black race.

They would go to church on Sunday and read "slaves obey your master."

The African woman was forced and broken into submission that *she* in turn will *"train her offspring in the early years to submit to labor when they become of age."*

It is clear that even the single parent phenomenon we now experience was thought through to remove the male image and psychologically make the women seem independent and in front of the scared male uneducated nigger and *"mentally weak"* male, the female was the insulation tape.

Empowerment deals and women affirmation can not be taught to us by white imperialist our women have always been queens and this *Eurocentric Christianity* is a feminine religion that is not biblical as it seeks to destroy and remove value and responsibility of male black species.

Male are not as useful as except for their sperm and power to labor, the minds of black males are not respected at all.

Simply put black woman would stand guard to the white imperialist while he sleeps, used against each other to protect the enemy.

Religion has the best picture as our women are more "Christian" than man and entrench this white poison into the minds of the young black children who grow up to be slaves of the same devil who killed their parents.

In summary the process would break the *'uncivilized savage niggers'*, place the *'female savage into a frozen psychological state of independence'* kill the protective *'male image'*, create a submissive dependent mind of the nigger male slave and so doing *'we have created an orbiting cycle that turns on its own axis forever…'*

It is therefore true that to fulfill this mission they tempered with our minds to confuse our "mental history and create a multiplicity of phenomena illusions, so that each illusion will twirl in its own orbit, something similar to floating balls in a vacuum."

It is a fact that Christianity is one of the balls in this vacuum of meaningless floatation.

Of interest to imperialist is the deliberate intention that **"WE MUST COMPLETELY ANNIHILATE THE MOTHER TONGUE"** …

BEING A FOOL IS ONE OF THE BASIC INGREDIENTS OF ANY INCIDENTS TO THE MAINTENANCE OF THE SLAVERY SYSTEM."

This civilization that we have been given is a hog pen.

The question I still ask is why has the black man not stood up to clean up the mess the whiteman has caused.

Primarily to kick the whiteman off his land, the answer is "if you put a slave in a hog pen and train him to live there and incorporate in him to value it as a way of life completely, the biggest problem you would have out of him is that he would worry you about provisions to keep the hog pen clean"[13]

The scientific process above has birthed the modern African elite class of the civilized. We have today those who are comfortable to sleep in a hog pan and have no desire to break rank and build a palace.

So deem is the picture that our children are on death row with the piglets.

---

13. Willie Lynch letter: The Making of a Slave: This speech was delivered by Willie Lynch on the bank of the James River in the colony of Virginia in 1712. Lynch was a British slave owner in the West Indies. He was invited to the colony of Virginia in 1712 to teach his methods to slave owners there. The term "lynching" is derived from his last name. Additional Note: "Henty Berry, speaking in the Virginia House of Delegates in 1832, described the situation as it existed in many parts of the South at this time: "We have, as far as possible, closed every avenue by which light may enter their (the slaves) minds. If we could extinguish the capacity to see the light, our work would be complete; they would then be on a level with the beasts of the field and we should be safe. I am not certain that we would not do it, if we could find out the process and that on the plea of necessity." From Brown America, The story of a New Race by Edwin R. Embree. 1931 The Viking Press.

Being yourself

Created in the Image of GOD

Being your self is simple. Hold a fruit while you talk to the tree and prepare the seed. You are but a fruit. The past…your roots…the future your seeds. All are connected in you.

Be comfortable of what the Lord has done in you and let no man make you feel less than you are! Our history is our pride. Our future our hope but today is our duty and labor. We cannot fold hands and pray. Rather let us roll sleeves and work at our eroded self-esteem.

Let's eat our food in a "primitive" way, drink our water and have a relationship with our real mother... the land.

We have lost more than we have gained!

Civilization has made us uncivilized.

We are educated but have become stupid and zombies on our land.

We don't even remember how to dig a well, or follow a bird that knows where honey is in the forest. We can no longer preserve food without a fridge or treat a wound without a chemist. Some of these plastic clothes, when we sweat draw chemicals into our bodies, which cause cancer...

I call for skins and Cotton;

I call the African soul back to our Creator.

I call the past and the future to meet in the present.

I call for an awakening of the African Nation.

I call for the Spirit and the Soul of the *'African to Arise'* from ashes.

Dry bones, dry bones hear the word of the Lord.

Jo Thobeka Wreford: Working with Spirit (experiencing Iza*Ngoma* Healing in contemporary South Africa, epistemologist of healing) raises a number of pointers that shed light on the subject of *African Spirituality.*

Isa*Ngoma* is a person who works to heal using spiritual connections and indigenous plants and herbs. Spiritual tutelage is vital for life.

Ngoma: a. The song that is sung with purpose to nourish the soul, an emotive expression of praise, worship, or celebration (*ingoma*- a song)

Ngoma: b. The process of healing and initiation into the spiritual realm to function and operate as a medium between the spirits and the living.

Ubungoma: the art of healing consultation with the spirit.

Ngoma: c. a traditional drum used in the processions and rituals, services of *twasa*, to enhance the music, the rhythm of song. The initiate must first be trained and (*twasa*) a rigorous process of preparation, through mimetic, observation of nature and self. Every African community has a drum.

Ngoma is an institution, which "contributes to the well-being of the community, by enhancing the renewal and reproduction of social networks...the locus of social contest."[1] It's a communication tool for horizontal and vertical use. The whiteman is selfish and evil to advance his cause. "Selfishness is not living as one wishes to live, it is asking others to live as one wishes to live. And unselfishness is letting other people's lives alone, not interfering with them.

---

1. Rijk van Dijk, Ria Reis and Marja Spierenburg, Ngoma, The quest for fruition therough Ngoma, p 39

Selfishness always aims at creating around it an absolute uniformity of type. Unselfishness recognizes infinite variety of type as a delightful thing, accepts it, acquiesces in it (and) enjoys it. It is not selfish to think for oneself.

A man who does not think (for himself) does not think at all. It is grossly selfish to require of one's neighbor that he should think in the same way, and hold the same opinions.

Why should he?

If he can think, he will probably think differently. If he cannot think, it is monstrous to require thought of any kind from him. A red rose is not selfish because it wants to be a red rose. It would be horribly selfish if it wanted all the other flowers in the garden to be both red and roses."[2]

The African Christian has been made to believe that his culture and past are irrelevant, dark, evil, devilish and to look civilized he has to be Christianized and divorce himself from the primitive, "barbaric" ways to (*of*) his ancestors. A study of anthropology will reveal that there is a cultural migration from Africans to become European.

The African should not divorce himself from the spirit world, for he already found the path to **YHWH** that the west still struggles to build.

The anthropologists of the west will call this magic, sorcery, enchantments which challenges science, a frightening space (p 3) in pursuit of his spirituality the African has a plethora of sensations, emotions, experiences that inform his response to his God. The praxis of this discourse intends to not only expose the deficiency of *Eurocentric Christianity*, but hypocrisy of 'Christian' spiritual connectivity.

It is clear that the white God does not hear black prayers or identify with the so called 'uncivilized'. This white God cannot accept the African as he is – but seeks to change him from 'beast' to become "white human".

Millions of our people are locked in these stonewalls with life imprisonment without parole. The chapters that follow will expand more on the evils of this Eurocentric Christianity, which has made Europe pagan while Africans are intoxicated with this diabolic caricature called Christianity and Protestantism.

The church, heart and institutions must start teaching spirituality, than doctrine. The language of the spirit is foreign to the worshipper (p21).

2. Oscar Wilde, The Soul of Man and Prison Writings: The Soul of Man Under Socialism, and Selected Critical Prose, Oscar Final O'Flahertie Wills Wilde, October 16, 1854, Dublin, Ireland Irish.

Real life must be experiential anthropology, uncomfortable reflexivity.

Practitioners must be ethnographic not as observers but participants, *"take off their shoes"* as they approach the intricate cultural tapestry of African spirituality. It may look *mimetic and primitive* yet its praxis holds the people to a deep connections with mysteries of human existence that science is foreign to. Religion and science need a laboratory to investigate the DNA of worship as it is a door into the wisdom of the past and has keys to the future.

There is *"contamination"* (p24) and pollution and sickness in the soul of men that needs healing. Materials and commercialization of religion does not reach the human spirit, instead *European Religion* keeps people in intellectual shackles and chains them to subservience.

'The meek will inherit the earth' because they can't afford better coffins to keep the earth out. Religion is the greatest form of nation control ever invented. With its authoritarian hierarchies it creates mindless sheep who doubt their own intellect and put their lives in the hands of external entities."[3]

Priests, Pastors, Bishops, Imams, Fathers, have gained ground to own the conscience of the people, and have built an evil prison of the soul of many.

"Bring me out of prison so I can thank you, the godly will crowd around me, for you will deal bountifully with me."[4]

This pluralist work advocates for mutual respect of spiritual education across the terrain of human existence instead the one who brings a religious belief will bully, bulldoze, kill and dominate other beliefs to assert their own. Africa can attest to this reality, and has become a slave of European religion called *Eurocentric Christianity* in exchange to spirituality, land and indignity.

FOUR STEPS TO DIAGNOSE THE SICKNESS OF THIS (*EURO-CENTRIC CHRISTIANITY*) RELIGION:

We ask questions not because we have answers but to activate a nation to think and look for solutions. As in medicine the condition of our people has to be diagnosed as *Euro-christianity syndrome*, which manifests itself with withdrawal from family and local culture as one migrates to white culture.

3. http://www.rantlifestyle.com/2014/08/13/21-reasons-why-religion-is-wrong/
4. Psalm 142:7

In some cases its followers speak in languages they don't understand and collapse in convulsions under the spell of the 'holy spirit'. Some donate their entire wealth and time to this faith, to build churches while their own homes and families struggle with livelihood.

- ○ **The construction of this illness:** (euro-christianity syndrome). Is it man made or god made, a curse or blessing to the African? Who came up with it? Who are the masterminds behind this hideous religious system? Why did they design this system of worship? How does it benefit them? Why is it being marketed as the best form of life? How do people look at themselves in their new status of faith? Does it produce better people, better citizenry? Is this religion or politics?

- ○ **Causes of disease:** (dysfunction) what are the symptomatic manifestation? What are the clear signs that show its failure? Does it liberate people or oppress them? Does it teach truth of white culture? Do the members love God more than each other? How will they love what they have not seen, when they cannot put up with they can see? Is the *Eurocentric Christian* community healthy mentally? How come they eat snakes, drink Jeyes fluid and *Doom* each other to cast away spirits? Why do people say they have heard from the Lord when the Lord has not spoken? Does the Lord eat the tithe, or it's the MOGs (Man of God/goods)

- ○ **Medication and healing:** (how do we connect) what kind of medication is required? Is the African nation *aware* that she is sick and needs immediate healing? How do we begin to detox our nation of this poison that has settled in our loins? What types of programs do we need to develop to heal the nation? What systems must we destroy to reinstate the dignity and value of our people? How do we find our God and where is He?

- ○ **Lifestyle and maintenance:** (sustainability) how do you maintain health of a nation after treatment? What is the diet that will be introduced to avoid withdrawal syndromes once a person is wined from this addiction?

Who are the new champions of social re-engineering to construct continental mental exodus to sanity?

This *Eurocentric Christianity* system of worship as a religion is sick because it does not function to deal with root problems of poverty and equity.

This wicked *European Christianity* is tool in instrumental conditioning.

It is used weekly to drug the poor and ignorant. It does not connect people to God but to itself. This model is not sustainable for it does not connect with the soul of the African – but steals the resources from the natives to enrich the white capitalist and stakeholders. If it was such a perfect system of social order how come Europe is now pagan while Africa is moving to become a Christian continent?

Why are churches up for sale in Europe and being converted into movie-houses, clubs and libraries? Where are the Europeans on Sundays? Has sport not become a better form of church? The whiteman got here after two centuries, and we have started.

Religion must become familiar with the science of healing and human psychology so that it can render an honest ethnographic holism approach to religious practices and not force or colonize worship.

There "aspects of non-reciprocity, arguably far more important for being more intractable, concerns the lack of intellectual appreciation and respect given by biomedical professionals to traditional healers."

Fig 1.2: Unknown

"**IzaNgoma** operate from the spirit empowered base."[5]

What is Christianity if it does not tap into the spirit and souls of man and plug them into the realm of divine solutions? Christianity operates on the lower level, the mind, facts and reason – it theologies and spiritualizes what is meant to be pragmatic spiritual encounters. This work is a **Christological experiential anthropology** which seeks to find the language of the spirit (implicit blackness and the operative of effective worship in the spirit, with the spirit this should be a daily reportage. The worshippers must *"go native"* and invite opprobrium and a suspicion of somehow letting the side down) **p 33**.

This is a *reflection* of my Christian education which may now come into question. It is safe to acknowledge that *Eurocentric Christianity* is not holistic but mechanical intellectualism of ceremonial dogmatics. In line with ethnological anthropology African spirituality has been colonized and deemed primitive, "as if they accept the hegemony of the other cultural practices while being initiated" **p 35**

Often blackness is stereotyped as not good enough, unclean sub civilization. You can't colonize worship and teach lifeless mimic of western traditions "menacing capricious" expectations. African worship can not be "a colonial mirroring of otherness that reflect back to colonizer the barbarity of their own self reflection" in a nut shell the church has build the "desire to own the colonizer's world." **p 43**

What we call church programs are school and training grounds of 'civility', deliberately designed to win the African from his mothers breast to a proxy white based faith and theories. The world of the spirit scares us all but it is here that the past and the future meet unlimited. Spiritual people are better connected to the spirit and to themselves and nature. Worship is life, while *Eurocentric Christianity* is a surrogate child of neo-colonial capitalism. Our churches have become an ATM (automated money machine) of western architects. Africa needs self-determination from this demon of materialism whose uniform is '*Christianity*'; a means to talk to God and have a *"better life"*, and by inference, being treated as lesser, inferior, and unworthy of the privileges that generally escort whiteness **p33**

" blinkered ethnocentric thinking in anthropology" **p39**

Do not be defined by your materials. Instead you should define your materials. Learn the spirituality of everything, and learn what spirit drives your events. Plug in today and start asking the right questions.

---

5. Ibid 29

The encapsulation of a real happenstance means the divine and the human must congregate in the spiritual zone, the space many religious protagonists are afraid of and preach against. These respected spiritual leaders have never been in the zone of the spirit or spoken to God to lead people into a terrestrial they do not know. It is a story of blind mice that lead each other into a trap. To be a worshipper the feelings, the body, the visions, the experience, has to go through you to influence the people. You are a channel through which healing reaches the populaces. Look at our spiritual service of worship ruminate on it a little bit. Focus on the word "*spiritual*," logikos, it simply means in the realm of the soul.

When we talk about worship, we're talking about something that originates in the soul, in the inner person. The word actually could be deciphered 'reasonable', as it is in some translations it originates in the intention of reason and intelligence. "Worship is *latreia*, it is a religious worship, and it is a word used for priestly undertakings. Our worship before God, the service that we render to God in worship, it is transcendent. That is to say, it is intramural rather than external. True worship originates in the soul, it is spiritual and that is where it begins,"[6] and that is were it must end.

To worship in depth we must consider the conscious worshipper and unconscious self. Losing you in the midst of worship, going beyond the epithelium to experience the transformative experience beyond the senses. Spiritual intimacy is urbane to experience rather than dispute. One needs to know in-order to do; the convicted are deeper in search than the staunchly convinced. Worship can be indignant when the facts replace the person, truth is not doctrine but person, and relationships are not erected on paper but hearts. The worshipper therefore must find the temperament of his God.

In the presence of God the celebrant must be able to live and replicate this infancy. Until the worshipper becomes like little a child, the worshipper cannot see the kingdom of heaven, at the very core of "such reticence, reflects western ambivalence toward mimicry per se." **p43**

When the saNgomas talk they say "the ancestors are in me. When they are in me, I know that they are here. I feel them. They are happy with me and I am happy with them. I think of them always, they know that I am thinking of them."[7] **p47**

6. Grace to You: Unleashing God's Truth, One Verse at a Time The Critical Elements of True Worship Scripture: Romans 12:1-2 http://www.gty.org
7. Jo Thobeka Wreford Working with Spirit (experiencing Izangoma Healing in contemporary South Africa, epistemologies of healing)

The clarity of this relationship glares the Christian in the face.

Can the Christians say, "the Lord is in me, He lives in me, and I can feel him and work with Him? I know He is happy with me, as I am happy with Him?"

How do we tutor the "Christ in us" concept, the newborn again being new creatures? Are we possessed of God as the *saNgoma* is of the spirit? This is a white Christian question. Are we what we profess to be?

LIFE BETWEEN:

o *Between:* Fear and faith they work jointly except they are in opposition doing the same in contradiction. Fear creates the mysterious and gives life to the absent. Faith also accepts the nonexistent as present and experiences the not yet, and assures itself in the one who will accomplish.

o *Between:* Past and Future: your relationship with time. You are the present, you connect the two times, and to be cognizant, to live and experience that presence of time is worship. Silence is the door to the inner spirit of humanity, "be still and know that I am God"

o *Between the teeth*: (what you eat) your diet eating is worship. Life is found in diet and to eat is spiritual. Refuel of the flesh, without which the spiritual ultimately dies. To sustain the body in good health is a spiritual task of the living, incarnate miracle of borrowed life, "food sustains".

o *Between your hands:* labor and action - worship is labor. The discipline of labor to plant and harvest and harmony with nature, the collaboration of the human with divine resources (rain) and work the land. Working the land is a spiritual connection. Here is the solution for poverty, land and labor, not faith and prayer.

o *Between eye sight and influence*: the third eye sees with the spirit. The aptitude to see things in many dimensions is a spiritual gift, its not only what you see but what your internal eye, the third eye can perceive. There is more than what meets the eye, life is not as visible at times we have to close our eyes to see the true reality of the physical realm.

o *Between reproduction and procreation:* sex is worship. Under the new civilization this is a sport and entertainment with no sacredness, yet between the corridors of our legs is divine factory for the next generation.

○ *Between heaven (spirit) and earth (physical), spiritual and physical* - experience is worship. Then life must be lived between these two realities and movement between the two realms must be a daily activity for the living.

THEO-POLITICS 101

"The African people are politically free but economically insignificant." Colonialism in the glove of Eurocentrism had the white agenda and Africans coexisted with abuse to build western civilization. European whites came Africa and had access to more wealth, which bequeathed them more privileges, and accorded them more dominance than the local black African person who was considered as periphery. To build this imperialistic state they had to *gizmo* social injustice, income inequality and curb blacks to retain property, opportunities and utilization of their land. This was structurally designed up to date the African is still trapped in this white prison.

To perfect the system they systematically deprived the African man from having a solid family unit, as their women were taken as housemaids and concubines, leaving the man to a promiscuous lifestyle in the hostels and mines. The *whiteman* accumulated wealth undeservedly on the blood and sweat of the black African. Independence was supposed to tax a wealth tax on the whites, and build restitution funds and also "educate the whites on the injustice of apartheid" Sampie Terreblanche, one of the subject to be taught is the systematic nature exploitation used by their fathers to enslave people on their land.

The purpose of this course is:

1. To drive the whiteman not only to apologise but also consciously be prepared to share the wealth, which is the foundation of the Christian faith he came to teach the *blackman*.

2. To educate the whiteman on the damage he has made to the homestead of the *blackman*, the vegetation and natural environment that has been vandalized while digging and taking resources.

3. To show him the path of sustainable development and civilized way of investing his money without destroying the habitat.

4. To show him Christian ways of dismantling institutionalized poverty and exploitation of the Africans, which pushes global inequality.

5. To teach the whiteman the nature of greed in other lands, Australia, New Zealand, America and Canada, and how the Caucasian white males have completely exterminated the indigenous populations to transplant European cultures into these lands under the guise of "*European civilization*"

6. To show the whiteman that Europe was build on the exploitation of the Western World and show how the local whites have contributed to the demise of the local black people.

7. To reveal to the *whiteman* that there is globalized injustice and marginalization of the blacks and other indigenous people, and the whiteman is the culprit of this abuse. While he teaches democracy, he is also the tyrant of justice. Imperial Capitalism is a direct consequence of *Eurocentrism*, and is an inhuman treatment of colonized world and the usage of "*surplus expropriation*" of other parts of the world to enhance Europe. The wealth taken from the black people was used to create empires and war-making lords in Europe.

8. To teach the *whiteman* to stop using the name of the Lord in vain, as religion was the vehicle of imperialism, to inculcate white culture into the blacks and permanently remove national and cultural identity.

The machinery of western propaganda will be driven from pulpits (Christianity) and God, as faithfulness to the calling of the gospel will reward obedience. It is a simple fact to admit that the orientation of the west is Catholic and Protestant (all churches that have their headquarters in the *white land* (Europe and America) can not refuse a fact that they have a white agenda on the black people.

The introduction of religion is a for-runner to introducing imperial capitalistic economic systems that robe and destroy the indigenous culture and wealth base of the African people. Jesus is for sale to the African.

Often the success of imperial capitalism is attributed to the superiority of their religion, God and culture, and the African is presented as inferior hence he is conquered and subdued as a slave. But the fact is, the west is a permanent parasite of African resources, who exploits, steals, rapes, represses, destroys and manages his "Eco-culture satellite" colonial superiority. Europe is not a center of world history. The legal system/framework and prison would be used as a tool to enforce the new culture. The narrow minded Christian will fight, if you tell them, they worship white culture in Christianity not the Messiah of the Scriptures.

This Christianity of today is "European rationality mixed with Protestant ethics"; it does not have the gospel as a subject or the Messiah as an object of study and emulation. Jesus is a slave to European culture, colonized and whitewashed to look like them.

How does a black Jesus leave the continent and come back white with blue eyes. So that when the black man fight the whiteman there is guilt of surgency against a *superior race*, nowhere in the bible are black identified as gentiles, until Paul is in Rome and Corinth and he calls them gentiles.

White people are aggressive, ruthless, thieves, greedy, unscrupulous above all hypocrites, how dare they impose their egocentric story to write my *His-tory*.[8]

The preacher of the 21st Century has to find relevance and understand his mission field and design methods of reaching these people, breaking these walls with the good news of the gospel. The question is does the gospel relate honestly with those outside of Eurocentric culture?

Christianity finds itself trapped between these four walls. Never forget that "God is working out in the lives of men and nations a definite purpose and that purpose was good, and that the God behind all history was not only of power but also of love".[9]

- o Eastern Mysticism – with its "Plurality of gods"
- o Islam- the lifestyle and intolerance tendencies
- o African Indigenous 'Christian' faiths- viewed with suspicion by the white theologians, called idol worship and paganism
- o The Orthodox and mainstream churches- seems to be the guards at the doors of expression and freedom. They use instruments of the west to enforce the new God to us the "pagans"[10]. These walls inhibit the full growth of the spiritual person to maturity in spiritual exploits.

Behind these imaginary walls of *Eurocentric Christian* spiritual restrictions are real people and cultures that need real solutions.

Until the Christian faith shows up with practical solutions it will be difficult to sell the present generation a *pig in a bag*. The question is do we make them Christian or spiritual?

8. Sampie Terreblanche: Western Empires, Christianity and the in equalities between the west and the rest; penguin Books 2014, page xiii-18
9. Charles Forster Kent, Judaism, Sterling Innovation, 2010 pp 273
10 Apostle I.N Sithole, Oasis of Life Family Church, Daveyton Johannesburg, Interview 2015

So they asked what was your past like

I had seemingly had less and did more. Now I have more and enjoy far much less. Life gives us blessings and moments of celebrations. While the metropolitan kids are running indoors to hide behind their walls. The rural kids still find a moment to dance in the rain.

To date I still bath in the rain. Joy and happiness is not for sale but that when the human soul gets in contact with divine acts of grace. Allow your feet to touch the ground often and the rain to bath your skin – experience nature – awareness is worship.

As the rain washes the dust of a hush summer and waters the ground with hope of springs. The young jump and spring with life. In the purity of their joy they are in touch with nature and their heartbeat is in sync with the seasons. If you look at what they do not have, you may think you are rich, but if you look at what they have you can see that you are poor.

Our hands are full of things yet our hearts empty of love, life and hope. We are present in the physical yet absent in spirit. Moments of great encounter pass us by while we fantasize in the world of gadgets, movies and shadows.

What is the use of things that push joy out of our lives? We are occupied with social media, which has made us belligerent and data is the new currency of communication. Always talking to the one who is not here.

The quench of gossip has become an appetite. This reality is a demon that can't be pacified with fake prayer. Oh! For the days of old when we looked at stars and 'owned' them as they shot across the sky we knew where our wives would come from. Ancient stories that unlocked our imagination to the land of possibilities.

We slept with our feet soaked in mud and maize cobs in our hands and our pockets full of groundnuts. With a plastic school bag in one hand grandma would whip a spoon of peanut butter on the other and a sprinkle of salt. The day had started and water I would drink at break time.

On my way from school I would go via the river with the cattle from graze often to drink fresh milk with the calves as they galloped on the veld of *Bikita* at dusk, I would hear the wheels of *Matambanadzo* busses bringing us letters and parcels from those in town.

Our aunties and uncles who worked in the cities had lots to show when they came back. Some were as dark as me but due to the witchcraft of town they would come back lighter *"ambi"*. Sundays were special, as the farm would smell hair, as our aunties would share the boiled round nuts while with some hot combs they would strengthen their hair with hot stones and Vaseline. Dare you miss your hair and it touches your ear you will have a free tattoo. The evening would dine with drums in the distance as rituals that evoked the very ground to harmony.

THE AFRICAN AND HIS SOIL

This relationship is like son and his mother. He never owned his land. His land owned him. From it, he came to it he will return. He worships and beats the skin of a dead ox to melodies that join the dead and the living.

The very sound of the drum resonated with our very nature as we stomped the ground to weary the body as we prepared the arrival of the spirit.

The gospel of truth must deliberately break these walls and seek to present the Messiah with his saving power without subjecting others to colonial imperialism. The Christianity of the African has not matured to a lifestyle as it takes the African for granted that by complying the African is converted.

The European theologian has not studied or understood the African psych without passing judgment. There is lots to teach, yet Christian arrogance annihilates dialogue.

"W*hite people* have not bothered to study the African people carefully – and by this I do not mean driving around the African villages taking photographs of dancing tribesman and women asking a few questions and then going back and writing a book – a useless book full of errors, wrong impressions and just plain nonsense."[11] How can we experience a full Christian experience while suffocated by white customs and perception?

What Africans have come to deem as Christianity is not Christianity of the books of Acts, but *a recycled white ideology of white customs and practices.* The African now worships what he does not know and hopes that these foreign white practices will connect him with the God he has lost contact with.

Part of the strategy of Christianity had to do with unplugging the African from the sources of power and divine contact now clustered with meaningless euro-centric dictum.

---

11. Ibid, pp xviii.

The worship of the African is in the canopy of nature and baptized in his natural cycles of planting and harvesting celebrated with a song and a dance, that is why we have the God of rain, of creation, of nature, the "white belt that binds the entire creation together" (*Ziyenda kuenda mucheka muchena wakasunga nyika*).

The programmed faith does not work as it mounts up to hypocrisy and fear of system and human beings more than the fear of the Lord. The fact is "No race of mankind has been so misunderstood, no race has been misrepresented, more abused and misused than the black race of Africa. The Arab, the whiteman, (and now the *Afropean*) and even after three thousand years you have not changed much"[12] as the Romans crucified the Messiah, the African is on the same cross.

The Death of the Messiah on the cross surrounded by two thieves is similar to the pain of African continent surrounded by the two thieves the west and the east *"the Arab/Asian and the whiteman."* Too long the African has been discounted as lowdown, with no brains inferior subhuman to which you do anything with impunity, *Mutwa* continues.[13]

He died between two thieves: the east and the west, and Jesus dies with the black continent at the center. They all come to steal and kill like their father the devil.

---

12. Ibid, pp 534
13. Ibid pp 535

Re-colo-nized

Euro-christianity is religious colonization!

Euro-christianity, is Judeo-based faith system that does not practice Judaism.

It's a worldwide movement of divided people who believe in the same Bible with a thousand different interpretations. Everyone who holds the book claims to know it. The *Bible* been a cause of many wars and ills on the society. Through it, nations have been altered, traditions vandalized, names changed to be like *whites*.

Democracy is a surrogate child of this system whose father is the devil and imperial capitalists who want to make the world a global village and they as economic chiefs to rule the poor. The Christianity of Acts and what we have now are not the same.

Pagan Christianity under the Catholic church has a very dark history of killing its children (538-1798 AD DARK AGES) when the church sold forgiveness, made monasteries and nuns and priests who where forced into celibacy only to end up molesting children and nuns committed abortion and the church windows were kiosks to sell indulgences. Through it nations and monarchs in the west have been established.

The wealth of African was used as offerings to pay homage to the pope.

That is how Rome accumulated its wealth to become one of the richest countries in the world with control over the world economy, all in the name of Christ.

Allegiance to the system was rewarded and those who opposed it were put on the burning stakes and hunted like foxes. It's a religion that makes its worshippers slaves of those that think for them. It psychologically excludes those that ask questions of practice and ecclesiastical lethargy. It's mild form of idolatry where people have faith more in the form of worship rather than the object of worship.

Congregations are collected into religious pacifism and consciences hypnotized to compliance. People are asked to surrender their consciences to the church and a cluster of doctrines often obstructing the God they profess. It's a highly competitive space of egos, hatred, and gimmicks, and envy and complex expressionist who run on self but the say "the Lord says" when he has not said. They don't even know His voice.

In Africa they are seen on weekends dressed up in ties and jackets walking into buildings that are under utilized, most of them are locked for six days. And the day they use them they are half asleep.

Their God dwells here they say, when the real church is the heart. Christianity is a status of "social enlightenment" where those who have not accepted it are deemed primitive, demonic and uncivilized. It creates false family ties where people give more money to churches than their own parents. "But those who wont care for their relatives, especially those in their own household, have denied the faith and are worse than an unbeliever/infidel"[1]

Christianity has to come out in the open and begin to tell people the truth. Churches must stop collecting money from the poor and start to be interested in how people are making that money. It is also a religion that has removed us from our God to bring us into all forms of idolatry "Christmas, Easter holidays, Good Friday, Mother's Day, Father's Day etc it

1. 1 Timothy 5:8

has no recognition of our indigenous worship of *Yah* according to the bible "TORAH" it's a religion that speaks against the statues of *Yah* in as far as polygamy, worship of one God not the trinity. Oh hear Israel our God "*YAHUAH*" is one! Today there's multiple deities created by Christianity![2]

Why does the church collect tithe from the widows and orphans? Widows are claimed as wives of God and orphans as children then tithe is collected in the name of God.[3]

Why then does the church not give God's wife his money? Why are God's children orphans prohibited from eating from the tithe (their fathers money)? Is it acceptable for widows to return tithes?

This God that we preach must come out and show himself true to the people. I believe He is there yet we seem to fail to plug into Him.

There are three things to consider in your Christian walk to become a spiritual experience or the communist expression is fulfilled that Christianity is there to control the masses. While people become Christians, here are a few things to consider.

1.   **Walk apart:** Two minds, two agendas and saved but not redeemed from anger, poverty and hatred. Prayer is used as a tool to persuade God who does not understand or is aware of the situation. The spirit of man and his makers are not in sync, religion is practiced in venues not in the heart and life of the believer, and it's an event not lifestyle.

     This schizophrenic approach to life creates bipolar mentality as we move between the sacred and the common we assume split personalities, the church person and the secular person.

     How can two people walk together unless they are agreed? Has the African agreed with God as introduced to us by the colonialist? Are we in agreement with his love and care for us as a people? Has He been a source of comfort to us, or a center of our pain? Does he even love us?

     I mean this economic spirituality and Eurocentric Christianity does it even address our pain and give us solutions to hunger, disease and poverty? Does it teach equality, or equity, dignity, or slave submission? We walk but apart.

---

2. Nhlanhla Shabangu, an ardent student of History and Hebraic literature. Interview Johannesburg 2016. He is a heritage fundi Egyptology, Ethiopian and Kermit Continent a lover of the darker races an activist of social change.
3. Isaiah 54:4-6 for your maker is your husband

2. **Walk behind:** the one who is following, allegiance and obedience to systems and rule, "in good and regular standing". The mob followed Jesus for food and blessings. Compliance to forms and norms, a great number that know nothing more than what they are told and find themselves in meaningless rituals.

   The personal faith is replaced with group psychology, adherents to the same foolishness. "What do people say I am? The personal question is "what do you say I am?" the individual must take a personal journey into the depth of their souls and find the spiritual conversation and say, "I believe therefore I do"!

   Christian Theology is a foreign white cooked oppressive dogma, the poor African is simply told to accept and follow and not question. The whiteman has placed himself as a thinker and the Blackman is told to walk behind, not behind God, but behind the whiteman's thoughts.

3. **Walk together:** in Christ and Christ in us. Let the mind that was in Christ be in you. Not I who lives but He who lives in me. Walk in the spirit full of the deposit of the Holy Spirit and the treasure full in our souls. Worship in the spirit.

   These walk and work with the spirit of truth at work. Directed from inside in the full nature of Immanuel, God is with us, within us, agents of Grace love and functions of divine encounter. We speak as He speaks in us and move as He moves.

   Living from INSIDE to outside, the campus of our spirit must be in sync with Him. To live a spiritual life means to control the flesh from the spirit.

Africa Arise

The western imperialist think that African philosophy, "The **professional philosophy** trend argues that the whole concept of a particular way of thinking, reflecting, and reasoning is relatively **new to most of Africa**, and that African philosophy is really just starting to grow."

An example of this growth is the **Kawaida** project, created by **Maulana Karenga**, an ongoing search for African models of excellence in the **seven core areas of culture**: history, spirituality and ethics, social organization, political organization, economic organization, creative production (art, music, literature, dance, etc.) and ethos. Have we been fast asleep so long or we have our own world-view of life, which the whiteman does not know.

Would they even bother to ask or establish this as a fact, or they judge us based on their methods. The thinkers on the land are frustrated as they are misunderstood by the colonialist who want to shape the way we think like we can't think for ourselves.

Africans love wisdom and respect it. It is orally transmitted from generation to generation and the stored in the natural way of doing things, hunting medicine, astrology and many other subjects.[1]

Gyekye challenges the view that in African thought, community confers person-hood on the individual and thus the individual's identity is merely derivative of the community. He attributes this view to African philosopher Ifeanyi Menkiti, as well as socialist political figures like Ghana's Kwame Nkrumah, Senegal's Léopold Senghor, and Tanzania's Julius Nyerere.

Instead, Gyekye argues that African thought ascribes definite value to the individual. He cites an Akan proverb, "All persons are children of God; no one is a child of the earth" in support of his argument that a person is conceived as a theomorphic being, having in their nature an aspect of God. This soul (known as okra to the Akan) is described as divine and originating with God." [2]

"The double bind is posed to not only by black people but also by white critics who expect black intellectuals to be primarily agents of praxis. It is understandable for familiar reasons. The assault on black humanity makes devoting one's energy to intellectual pursuit seem much like proverbially playing violins while Rome burns"[3]

Jacob K. Olupona outlines 15 key factors of African Religion, in this book we have picked a few just to illustrate the place of African religious thought.

- o "African traditional religion refers to the indigenous or autochthonous religions of the African people.

---

1. http://www.philosophybasics.com/general_african.html
2. Kwame Gyekye (born 1939) is a Ghanaian philosopher, and an important figure in the development of modern African philosophy. Gyekye studied first at the University of Ghana, then at Harvard University, where he obtained his Ph.D. with a thesis on Græco–Arabic philosophy. He has been a Fellow of the Smithsonian Institution's Woodrow Wilson International Center for Scholars, and is a life-time Fellow of the Ghana Academy of Arts and Sciences. He was educated at Mfantsipim School
3. Lewis R. Gordon, Africana Philosophy and Philosophy in Black Lewis R. Gordon, The Black ScholarVol. 43, No. 4, The Role of Black Philosophy (Winter 2013), Published by: Taylor & Francis, Ltd.

- o It deals with their cosmology, ritual practices, symbols, arts, society, and so on. Because religion is a way of life, it relates to culture and society as they affect the world view of the African people.
- o Traditional African religions are less of faith traditions and more of lived traditions. They are less concerned with doctrines and much more so with rituals, ceremonies, and lived practices.

When addressing religion in Africa, scholars often speak of a "triple heritage," that is the triple legacy of indigenous religion, Islam, and Christianity that are often found side by side in many African societies.

Traditional African religions have gone global! The Trans-Atlantic slave trade led to the growth of African-inspired traditions in the Americas such as Candomblé in Brazil, Santería in Cuba, or Vodun in Haïti.

Furthermore, many in places like the US and the UK have converted to various traditional African religions, and the importance of the diaspora for these religions is growing rapidly.

African religions have also become a major attraction for those in the diaspora who travel to Africa on pilgrimages because of the global reach of these traditions.

- o Indigenous African religions are not based on conversion like Islam and Christianity. They tend to propagate peaceful coexistence, and they promote good relations with members of other religious traditions that surround them.
- o Today as a minority tradition, it has suffered immensely from human rights abuses.
- o Women play a key role in the practice of these traditions, and the internal gender relations and dynamics are very profound.
- o African religions to gender is one of complementarity in which a confluence of male and female forces must operate in harmony.
- o Indigenous African religions contain a great deal of wisdom and insight on how human beings can best live within and interact with the environment.
- o Given our current impending ecological crisis, indigenous African religions have a great deal to offer both African countries and the world at large.

"African indigenous religions provide strong linkages between the life of humans and the world of the ancestors. Humans are thus able to maintain constant and symbiotic relations with their ancestors who are understood

Christianity
Islam
Hinduism
Native Religions

Fig 4: Invasion of Africa

to be intimately concerned and involved in their descendants' everyday affairs."[4] "Natural objects, such as rivers, mountains, trees, and the Sun (as well as forces such as wind and rain), represent the natural spirits. Africans integrate this religious world-view into every aspect of life.

In the fifteenth century Christian missionaries became the first wave of Europeans to invade and occupy African lands. They relied on the backing of European medicinal remedies and colonial military power.

4. Jacob K. Olupona is Professor of African Religious Traditions at Harvard Divinity School, with a joint appointment as Professor of African and African American Studies in Harvard's Faculty of Arts and Sciences. A noted scholar of indigenous African religions, his books include African Religions: A Very Short Introduction, City of 201 Gods: Ilé-Ifè in Time, Space, and the Imagination, Òrìsà Devotion as World Religion: The Globalization of Yorùbá Religious Culture, co-edited with Terry Rey, and Kingship, Religion, and Rituals in a Nigerian Community: A Phenomenological Study of Ondo Yoruba Festivals. In 2007, he was awarded the Nigerian National Order of Merit, one of Nigeria's most prestigious honors.

By using local languages and converting Africans from their ancestral religions to Christianity, missionaries paved the way for early modernization and Western colonialism. Western colonialists negotiated and drafted treaties with African leaders, stripping Africans of their lands, depopulating the countryside, destabilizing their economies, overturning political rule, and uprooting cultural and lineage continuity.

By the 1900s Christianity was firmly entrenched in most of Africa."[5]

DO AFRICANS REALLY WORSHIP ANCESTORS?

The Jews believe in God of Abraham, God of Isaac, Jacob etc. These names are mentioned during prayers posthumously. Simply put they are Jewish Ancestors. Does God expect us to throw away ancestors and assume new ancestors? Will it change the biology and genes of my tribe when I claim to be a child of Abraham?

Was God not involved in my history and sought to reveal Himself to me in my generation? Is the Jewish ancestry superior to my ancestry? Why does the African refer to his ancestor as demons when the whiteman refers to his ancestors as saints? What is the role of calling on the Hebraic ancestry to access God when all nations came out of Adam? Does God get angry when he hears me call on my late fathers name as a source through which I came into this life? Where does African history end up in worship? Is recitation of my African lineage a sign of idolatry?

Why did colonialism change our names for white names?

Would a man calling his God in a foreign language be heard? Does the blood that runs in African veins respond to *Eurocentric* etiquette? Can the European dance freely to the African rhythm? Can a whiteman access his ancestors through an African Medium or a black man speak to these ancestors in English?

Dyanti suggests that "Genesis original text of chapter 2 verse 7 "*vayiytser Yahaweh Elohiym, et Adam afar ha Ad amah vayipac b'apaw nishmat chayiym wayiy adam l'nephesh chaya*", the double yod in the word (**chayiym**) meaning "life" suggests in midrash, that those who lived before continue to live through those they (*chayiym*) pass to, and the '*dam*', meaning "blood". So in those who are righteous, God sees in them "Abraham", somehow God cannot attend to our prayers because He sees our fathers and their iniquities in us, those who lived before continue to live within the parameters of our existence.

5. African Traditional Religions, Worldmark Encyclopedia of Religious Practices COPYRIGHT 2006 Thomson Gale

In the same breath if the Lord was not happy with our forefathers he would have killed them. Their blood is alive and between the creation of Adam and you that life has not been cut off.

The gene on life is as fresh as God breathed into the nostrils of grandfather Adam. In Adam we are united and in Abraham we are divided. Adam for genetic connection Abraham for religious connectivity and hence we needed a second Adam.

"The God who made the world and all things in it, since He is Lord of heaven and earth, does not dwell in temples made with hands; nor is He served by human hands, as though He needed anything, since He Himself gives to all *people* life and breathe and all things; He made from one *man* every nation of mankind to live on all the faces of the earth, having determined *their* appointed times and the boundaries of their habitation, that they would seek God, if perhaps they might grope for Him and find Him, though He is not far from each one of us; for in Him we live and move and exist, as even some of your own poets have said, 'For we also are His children.'

"Being then the children of God, we ought not to think that the Divine Nature is like gold or silver or stone, an image formed by the art and thought of man. "Therefore having overlooked the times of ignorance, God is now declaring to men that all people everywhere should repent, because He has fixed a day in which He will judge the world in righteousness through a Man whom He has appointed, having furnished proof to all men by raising Him from the dead."[6]

There are a number of issues that the book of Acts is raising
- He made all things
- He does not dwell in human man vessels and temples
- He needs nothing from mankind but gives to all
- He sets up times and seasons
- He establishes boundaries for land and habitations – He gave us land
- He purposes that in each land we should seek Him
- He is no far from any one of us
- All life exists and moves and has being in Him
- Civilization does not make us children of God we are by creation

6. Acts 17:24-31

- o Move your attention from the emblems fashioned by men or religion that is found at a price of gold and silver. Don't allow artistic impressions to cloud your mind to your true identity in divinity.

- o We must move from an age of ignorance to light. Our minds must shun darkness of mans thoughts and seek divine illumination. Look into the eyes of your God and let His understanding fill your soul with discernment.

- o Ultimately, we should turn away from that which is not divine: repent from this idolatry of human craft, or we be judged and condemned.

The African must not feel ashamed to call upon the goodness of God as he celebrates his past. African needs to start to make sense of their idioms in worship, and praise style and call on the Creator who is not far, who is connected to us through our forefathers (ancestors the people through which we are here, to celebrate them, is to realize the channel through which we have become).

While at this, as we call their names we do not stop with your ancestors that you know after your fore-fathers acknowledge your past like I do Joshua Maponga son of Lazarus, Son of Munyuki Marara, son of Muchena, Son of Nhokwara.

If I run out of names I go for the animals Shoko\Soko – Bvhudzijena- (A more comprehensive prayer format is given at end of this chapter that will include the entire Africa) it looks like in our African worship you have to identify yourself first and your tribe and your people. Then move up to identify the God you call upon, then lastly list your request and as you seek solutions.

Hevoi Shoko,
Hevoi Vhudzijena, Mukanya (the white head and majestic strides)
Hekanhi waro Mbereka (Indeed the progenitor and great ancestor)
Makwiramiti, mahomu-homu (the tree climber and caller on the mountain side)
Vanopona nekuba (he will take without asking)
Chirambakusesera (no need to wipe his back)
Vanamushamba negore (no need to bath, as He showers in the rain)
Makumbo mana muswe weshanu (he moves on four legs, but his tails is the 5th)
Hekani Soko yangu yiyi (My word and the glorious)
Vakaera mutupo umwe Nashe (the kings are related to you)
Vana VaPfumojena (the children of the white spear)

Vakabva Guruuswa (originally from the mighty grasslands)
VekuMatonjeni vanaisi vemvura (the rain makers of the Matopos)
Meso asinganiwi, mabobi-vukomba (the rain will never touch your eyes)
Shoko Mbire hwiramiti yaSvosve (the rare sight of the of Mbire or the Svosve dynasty

Vanobva Hwedza (they come from Hwedza- from the east the Wiseman of the east)
Vapfuri vemhangura naVacheri vayo (the iron monger, miners and smiths)
Chiwere shoko yembereka (those who live on the edge)
Zvaitwa matarira vari mumabwe (piping at those who are in the rocks)
Mhanimani tonodya, svosve tichobovera (feeding on scorpions and ants)
Maita zvenyu rudzi rukuru rusina chiramwa (a nation which does not give up)
Matangakugara (we sit first before we engage)
Vanopembera namachira machena (the whiteheads and those who celebrate in purity)

Vakawana ushe neuchenjeri (wisdom put them on the chair to rule monarchs)
Vakufamba hujeukidza kwandabva-mukanya (carefully looking at where they are coming from)
Pavagere rinongova jemedzanwa (the is lots of noise and celebration where they are)
Kugara hukwenya-kwenya (will not stop scratching)
Vari mawere maramba kurima (living in the rocks He refused to plant)
Vakarima vanochema newe (those who have farmed have to deal with you)
Vamazvikongonyadza kufamba hukanyaira (pride and self worth, seen in their steps)

Chibwe chitedza chinokwigwa nevanaman'a (slippery rocks you need cracked feet to walk on them: be careful when you deal with them)
Zvibwezvitedza, zvinotedzera vari kure (from a distance they are difficult)
Asi vari padyo vachitamba nazvo (when they give you their hearts they are fun to play with)
Zvaitwa Chiwere rudzi rusina chiramwa (the mountain climbers will have it hard to get them fed up)
Maita vari Makoromokwa, (living on the side rocks)
Nhanzva pamawere, (sliding on the mountains side)
Vanemhazha kumagaro (they get bold on their bums not on their heads)
Mugarandaguta, vasingadyi chakafachoga (they will only sit when they are full)
Chigaramboko kugara mashamba huda (full of options, to sit on your pumpkins or on the rocks)

Haiwa zvaonekwa BVhudzijena (the visible works of the Bvudzijena: this is how you know he is a Mbire child)

...then I JOSHUA MAPONGA join with son of Ham, who is the son of Cush, the Son of Noah, the son of Methuselah, Son of Enoch, Son of Seth, Son of Adam, **Son of God**.

In simple terms Maponga Joshua III is not a creation of evolution but a product from the hand of YHWH. It must be put on record that from the time of creation when the breathe of life was breathed into Adam I was breathed there also.

I lived in Adam's loins and I have not died till by birth. My parents into generations past are a confirmation that I was purposed to live. (Read the sample prayer at the end of the chapter)

The circle of worship is connected to the source of life. The witch-doctors lie to people when we pray and say, "talk to those that we do not know".

It is critical to correct ancestral worship and connect it to the right source that the True YHWH and not allow the umbilical cord to end before the worshipper has access to God.

The Worshipper should know the source of worship, and intentions for worship, to worship is to tap into this sacred space of history which leads to the creator and the more we go back to the source of our creation we end up in the future with Him.

Looking backward at the future, a backward glance with a forward look. To understand what He has done in the past it sees what He is doing in the future. With YHWH the past and the future are the same, for to him there is not time, as He is time.

Celebrate your past; your future is wired in your history, the DNA of all mysteries is the seed, which contains the future the past and present.

Our Moral Debt

What about Democracy?

If these oppressors were democratic why did they oppress us? Why do they deny us access into our resources? Is there democracy without colonization?

What is democracy and why is the west so obsessed with this system of governance? How does democracy deal with indigenous people? What is the rule of law in the system?

What is the moral debt of colonizers at the celebration of independence? When a country is independent what does that mean? Independent from whom and from what? Do banks and Ill-gotten money find its way to the oppressed?

Does the slave master...or will the slave master pay reparation for the damage caused? What is equality without equity? Are the oppressors civilized? What role does religion play in the equation of freedom? Are Africans improving after independence? Who has an interest in African politics?

Do we have industries that produce finished products or raw materials? Are our systems built to improve local economies or benefit the oppressors?

The only reason we stay with the oppressors is because the bible says "thou shall not kill". Religion therefore is a tool of managing black anger.

THE AFRICAN MIRACLE

Lazarus Come Forth - How to perform a miracle?

How to perform a miracle on your mind! Follow the simple steps to witness a paradigm shift and see your mind resurrect from the catacombs of the dead.

The miracle of Bethany in John 11 will be help to open up new horizons of perception.

As Lazarus was sick so Africa is sick living in the realm of death.[1] But his sickness is not unto death.

The power of the Lord will be manifested when Africa:

1. Is a friend of the Super-natural?

2. Invites YHWH to its challenges

3. Takes Him to the grave of our death and ignorance

4. Removes the stone, which is sitting on our previous knowledge intended to cage us and hold us bound to opinions and not truth. To remove limitations and to open our hearts to learning.

5. Waits for the word, the word cannot enter where the stones are blocking the entrance and effect of the word.

6. Unwraps Her miracle, begins to show an interest in the process of our liberation

7. Feed herself, not pray for a miracle we don't want to participate in. The nation must arise from death to life.

---

1. Rabbi Ralph Messer, Torah Law or Grace, Simchat Torah Beit Midrash Publishing, 2011. Pp 161 kingdom Principles to live by.

8. Takes it home, we cannot stay at the graveyard forever, soon or later we have to move from here and go home and life must be experienced not always expected.

9. Yes hope is good, but there comes a time when dreams are realized and life is lived, not a castle in the air. Freedom cannot always be advertised to be coming tomorrow.

Immanuel speaks the word that is the only miracle He performs at the resurrection of Lazarus and the human beings through his work to realize the miracle. Do not pray for a miracle you are not willing to participate in.

Most critical is to remove the stone in our minds, hearts to give entrance to the word. In this volume Going Places In the Spirit we share our African story.

THOUGHTS ON DEATH - LAZARUS AFRICA

Death does not kill for you will be dead already. Fear the things that kill, when it's cold Finger touches your mortal flesh the pain is felt by those who remain. Tell your children to run away from drugs, cheap sex guns and speed for these are the vehicles of the shadow of death.

There is no fear for no one has gone there to give us a full report of what happens in the jaws of the grave. It is an appetite that cannot be quenched, it harvests from rich and poor. It has sneaked through the windows of the mighty even the orphan is not spared from the pangs of its jaws. Yet one would still ask what is death, what is the spirit, and what is the soul? Is it the cold car with a new engine, or the new car with an old body?

If you take a range rover engine and put it in a golf body? Or you take a golf engine and put it in a range rover body? Then what is it that you now have in the event that you have a spirit in a human body or you have a body in a spirit?

Is the space of demons and angels a spiritual space in which the human character is subject to bigger powers in full operation in the land of the living?

Since the Lord taught that the dead know nothing, and in the same breath we hear that death is not death but sleep, when one sleeps can they still hear? Do ears go to sleep or they remain as antennas of safety! Who will hear the voice of the trumpet when the Lord returns with the clouds of heaven? How do they hear if they can't hear?

Death harvests talent and mischief …power and arrogance foolishness lingers in the mind of the living only to close the days with tears and mourning. It is God who kills; it is Him who gives live. Life and death are the weapons of grace that reduce the lives of the wicked.

To die is to live (we come from death) and so to live is to die and move slowly towards the grave.

As long as we eat we confirm that we are dying and that life is not inherent in us but depended on the outer to sustain. Who can say *I am*, except the things that are in us.

Death itself is a silent messenger who follows choices and garners them. To plan and worry about death is to forget to live and the worst is to die before you live.

Death is a state for those who don't know why they are here. No goals and plans for this life. Death is a state for those who don't love without faith and passion, and can't feel sorrow for human pain.

Death is the last stage into germination; the sleep between the land of mortality and the land of immortality, in silence and darkness does the seed of death rot to come up as a new fresh plants in the cycle of life.

Death is life therefore life's manure. The very ground that roots the fruit of expectations in every bosom. Death measures the longevity of our trial days and gathers all at our exit to reflect on the undertaker. Death speaks to the living and places value on life; long life is no blessing to a wicked man.

Death unites us with the very soil we come from, confirms the dust that we are we come from this earth that what we are and every time we fall we come back to the ground and at death the grave accepts us. When life sickness and disease eat your flesh then death welcomes and hugs you

Into cold hands. It is a temporary holding cell for the weary and broken bodies and rest from physical pain. A place of silence a glimpse of eternity. Death is only one night between this life and other. Time is still, all the future is but a morning away.

Death is on your shadow so in the body you must leave. When you lie down to sleep you and your shadow are together in the presence of death while you sleep. Close your eyes in the darkness of your eyelashes. There, looms the call to the grave. There are sounds of silence when you sleep every night and whispers of the spirit echo in every soul daily that remind you of the day you shall join your forefathers.

The very tears in your eyes are the blankets that cover your pain. In the midst of darkness as in Genesis 1:0 the Lord stood in the dark with water and darkness and said "let there be". Use your darkness (as you pray close your eyes there is darkness and waters, tears in your eyes, say a word "Let there be") to recreate your chaos, as there is no planning in the grave whence you go.

Cry for yourself while you live for death is a place of silence you will not return but be changed in a twinkling of an eye. To worship is to stand between the living and the dead, it is a spiritual connection with darkness and tears, to burst out as light and day. Thus worship is a creative expression and interaction with the spirit world. You as a worshipper will decide whom to worship and who to direct the people to?

THEOLOGICAL DRY BONES

Warning! Strictly for theologians and seasoned ministers as for laymen stay away or read with caution.

There are times when this *Eurocentric Christianity* does not make sense at all. These issues just don't make sense to the seeker of truth and this theology does not seem to be coherent with it. God hates human sacrifice and the bible calls it pagan. How do we reconcile the death of Jesus as sacrifice for our sins (which Adam committed by fate we are all condemned). God tested Abraham by calling for the sacrifice of Isaac human sacrifice (Gen 22.12). The Old Testament is a gallery of blood of animals to pay for sins and appease God.

The Torah teaches that Parents are not to be put to death for their children, nor children put to death for their parents; each will die for their own sin (Deut. 24:16). Jesus is the Son of God why did the Father put son to death since human sacrifice is forbidden by the same scripture?

The Bible makes it quite clear that God hates human sacrifice. The pagan nations that surrounded the Israelites practiced human sacrifice as part of the worship of false gods and such "worship" was detestable to Him and that He hates it (Deuteronomy 12:31; 18:10).

Furthermore, human sacrifice in Old Testament with evil practices such as sorcery and divination, which are also detestable to God (2Kings 21:6). So, if God hates human sacrifice, why is His sacrifice of Christ on the cross acceptable as a means of our salvation?

Who was appeased at Jesus' death, devil or God?

Modern society associates the phrase "human sacrifice" with brutal, demonic, or satanic ritual and Christianity brands as evil. In the same vein is it not true that Christianity is built on the very pagan principle of the blood of a man Jesus and his human sacrifice to appease God? It is clear that human sacrifice can usually be related to the recognition of human blood as the sacred life force.

Is Christianity not pagan in practice by accepting blood sacrifice, by definition of the same book the bible?

Why kill the innocent while the criminal is watching?

Christianity has to answer why it glories itself. Is it not the highest form of witchcraft to have the blood of a man in your hands for power and grace! If this is so, what power and access to God do we have? *Bushido"*, aka. '*The way of the warrior*'. It consisted of a semi-suicidal ritual in which the warrior was required to cut himself. Is the death of neither Jesus nor Bushido? Since he is God and can not die?

Did the Phoenician and Carthaginian civilization, the people of these groups religiously sacrificed children and bury servants with their masters? Same with the Pharaohs and so was *Shaka Zulu's* mother Nandi buried with a dozen maidens with his mother. If Adam sinned and we all sinned did we have a choice? In Romans 5, the second Adam gives life while first Adam brings death. Why must we now chose life when we did not chose death? Death to all, must we not all under the new covenant. Is death stronger than life?

The *Eurocentric Christianity* has been a breeding ground of vicious dogs and the enemy of our souls knows when you have dogs, greedy dogs, give them bones and you can eat all the meat.

THOUGHTS ON MONEY

"Then they asked "tell us about money:" Money can be made by people but it does not make people. It is a visitor who is here today and away from you tomorrow, like a prostitute she goes and never looks back. Money has a spirit of its own and brings voices and friends you don't know.

If churches are built on money they have no relationship with their members, but the wallets of the congregation. The more money you have the greater the population of open mouths that want to eat it.

It has troubles of its own and its pain is felt when it's gone. The love of it is the root of all-evil yet the absence of it also. He, who started it, does not have it too. Kings attract gold and they become powerful. It is a means to an end not an end in itself.

From the ground it comes to the ground it takes us, and from the same ground we also come. Our affinity to it is looking for that which is like us as it is in us.

To transact money moves as goods and services are exchanged for it.

The black book says we must eat from the ground and our sweat must be paid in gold. If you sweat and you are not eating someone has eaten or is eating. It is the pain of the wicked that God makes them gather money only to give it to those that fear the Lord. Money is a subject for politics, economics and now religion and it has become the currency to access divine favor.

Money is now the very plasma of human operation, goodness and evil.

Time in hours, work is all measured in money. Have a good relationship with money. It is not equal to buying power, but make a deal keep her in your house, look at her and don't fight with her. Cure your fear and smell her presence. So I saw a man walking who had money and the other who did not. The spring on their heel showed me who had options. Poverty reduces the quality of life, freedom is to live without fear of loss of your substance.

Therefore money is a means to options. Better is a little to a sinner than much, for in the abundance of religious money there is plurality and appetite for evil. Once it is too much it makes the owner uneasy. Maybe it is for that reason that in heaven, streets are paved with gold so as to correct human poverty that which we suffered for on earth we must walk on in glory.

So you can buy things with it but not dignity. You either have things or things have you. You can transfer money but you cannot transfer respect and dignity. You can pay in petty cash, cheque cash or stolen cash but still cash is king. Your relationship must be with the maker of the material and not the material. Real value is in a smile and a warm hand of fellowship.

The best things in life are free so that money cannot be used to buy happiness or religious favor with God. Yet without it the modern society cannot find happiness. Many religious organizations have poisoned themselves as access points to financial freedom/free-doom.

Faith has been assigned to look for money and churches are used to pray for it, only for it to vaporize in the hands of the believer. To believe or become Christian while poor is to make God a cash machine.

In the abundance of goods and money it is easy to seek and come back to God with your substance: if you can then you are a true worshipper come in and praise the Lord. Until you have your own money you will never know who you are.

Spare a thought for Democracy

Democracy is an illegitimate child of Eurocentric Christianity whose real mother is the devil. *Eurocentric Christianity* is the deacon at the door of this mental slavery. She has paraded her nakedness as an evil woman who teaches gods as having favorites and some of us being less human and undesired by them and their God.

Democracy is committing suicide before our very eyes, and soon it will be buried and Africa will be free from this tyrant. African politics and religion is at the mercy of white dominance. Is democracy a gift from God? What rights does democracy promote when she speaks looks like a lamb but speaks like the dragon? What is the right form of governance democracy or theocracy?

Democracy is a hollow pie, with promises of freedom, which only comes as polished capitalism with results of social oppression worse than our kings of the past. Even in the west it has proved that it can be bought, democracy is a political system for the rich where the poor are bribed to think they matter, when in fact it is voluntary oppression and exploitation.

Democracy is a theory on the bus of capitalism, a passive passenger of mass control. We are "given" freedom, power and parliament; we spend our attention and days arguing about rights, democracy and policies to protect western industrialists and their multinational companies. We gnaw bones while they eat meat.

When you live in Australia. What are you? An Australian?

When you live in America what are you? An American?

When you live in Europe as a black man what are you? European?

Then what do we call the whites who live in Africa? What is a nation and how can we access God who cares for local nationals? Does this God only speak and answer the prayers of the civilized?

What is the use of democracy if black nations are sinking deeper into debt and poverty? Of what use is the freedom charter if the quality of life is deteriorating?

Religion therefore is a tool of managing black anger. What's the use of a government if:

- It does not have a bank to control its own interest?
- It has no industry to manufacture its own cars and weapons ?
- It has no schools and curriculum to teach its own children their pride and history?
- Its schools become factories of slavery African slaves on the white market?
- It has no land to plant its own food or mine its own minerals and give land to its own citizens .
- It has no political will to change or upset the status quo of oppression?
- It's a chat room powering a talk show of political lingo and quotations of Marxism and Che Guevara?
- Its children cannot see the future?
- The majority economically sodomized by the minority (the whiteman)? Has Christianity not been the deacon who presses the blackman down while capitalisms sodomize the Africans?

Has the African lost all sense of being and will to change while under this curse of *Eurocentric Christianity*? Has our appetite of coffee and sugar sealed our taste buds to our social health and national pride? Flights and parliamentary debate have become entertainment to rebuke and jest to our struggle as a nation.

An African child, who watches, has lost respect. We have a broken spirit as a people. We cannot blame the whiteman as this has now become voluntary slavery! Who do we blame now? If you have dogs, give them bones, while you eat the meat. I appeal to all let us eat meat let us give them bones!

Instead of looking to *Eurocentric Christianity* for solutions the African must go back to Eden (the very soil on which you are standing on African is Eden) and learn that all herbs are for food. Go back to the ground African man and put your ear on the belly of your mother earth, and when you hear someone insult your mother let the raw anger row.

The Torah teaches us to consume every herb yielded from the grass, trees and nature. Weed is also a herb could be one of the purest forms of the herbs, lets find ways to harvest this knowledge into a science.

Back to our roots and herbs not clinics and hospitals and deliverance nights with demon possessed ministers who are after your money. We worship imposed ancestors who are in pharmaceuticals branded packages, to kill us and destroy us, we don't even see it but have accepted it as gospel truth.

Our nation is under a spell of idol worshippers. Our people now think that things they ask for will fall from heaven. We now cut a tree to make an idol and worship the dead wood of your crafting skills. The fool should have kept the tree and keep praying to a living God to water it for him to continue eating the fruit and have shade in the heat of summer. Now you have an idol, no fruit, no shelter, no clean air: now we have churches, but no houses or safety or health.

The next prayer night will be to pray for what you destroyed and ask the idol to give you fruit and shade. What a paradox of stupidity with economics on the table of *Eurocentric Christianity:* this is in bed with politics that destroy the ecosystem.

Is it not prudent to rather pray to the living tree than deadwood? When the Axe entered into the forest and the trees said, "Look! The handle is one of us". How dare we call those who cut trees civilized? Then set up funds to plant trees and fight carbon emissions. Those who live with nature are primitive they need the whiteman to enlighten them on how to destroy their habitat.

Those who kill elephants and rhinos are civilized as they use horns for potency instead of herbs.

The black man in a skin is nude and uncivilized so they think and a white person stark naked in a 'nude restaurant' is liberated. . Who told you that you are naked? The book of Genesis asks the question. Then after he has convinced you that you are naked, he comes and sells you clothes to cover your shame that is his sport.

The liberation of Africa demands a look back to the past and to look ahead. The wealth of our nature and it's resource a will be plundered and we will remain with holes in the ground and mines and toxic arsenic ground from dumps. These white people are here to mine our gold, diamonds minerals and leave us poor while they cut our trees and build us prisons? Why put us on contraception and introduce same sex policies?

Why build towns and take away land, whose economy is it?

Who benefits from this social vandalism?

Why cut our trees and force us to worship your idols? Africa arise! The one who gives you food will rule over you. It is safe to plant your trees and eat from them. Breed your animals and till your land. The rain will fall and rivers will flow again. Your bank is calves and seeds in your bans. Poverty is not lack of gold but absence of dignity and self-respect.

Why do we have to deal with puppet governments which are run by parrot capitalists. They continue to rape our economies and push us into the Abyss of self-hate? How rich is a millionaire whose mother still lives in a shack and the road to his palace is sort and has potholes. How loving is God who keeps the locals in poverty while the white-man oppresses him?

How rich is a man whose school children sit on the floor and pit latrines are a norm. You can have money without a spirit of love, empowerment and giving your wealth is but a donation to the system of disgrace.

Why cut a fruit tree and then pray for fruit and food? Murder is to reduce the access to resources and using religion as a begging station. The truth is this "white god" will never answer our prayers. This dead wood called democracy will leave us poor and infested with self-hate.

This idol, *Eurochristianity*, will take us to mental institutions and castrate us to eunuchs. Our land will become a museum of ghost towns. The true Christianity of Acts and old testament teaches us to plant trees and allow us to eat their fruits in peace.

Do not despair there is a future, the death of this white Jesus and his democratic angels, there the sun will shine bright again. My people will plough and animals will graze on land, the black man will be free from oppression, the Creator will look at us and smile again. Hold on a little while longer it won't be long that our shadows will touch the waters and melt into dreams of expectation. The future is coming to meet our pain at the junction of destiny we will know we are in the image of YAH.

Fear not and do not despair these are tears of a woman in labor, it's for a moment, the smiles of an infant will melt the sorrows of the night, once we have hope all is possible... the sweat of our pain will yield its fruit and rewards of glory.

I see a bright future for my people. I see us looking back to see ahead, the night has whispered wisdom to the day. I look ahead I see honor and reward for our patience. Had it not been for the religion our hands will be full of blood of fools. Come stand with me the *Sons of Cush*. The mighty tribe of the *Hamites* you are great as you were once great. History will dine with your future.

I go for a while to the land of my fathers...now you see me for a while ... then no more. Grace will return to you and you will believe. Too long we have given ear to the hogwash of oppression that pacified our indigenous knowledge. We have worshiped the redundancy of imperialism. Arise my people and look at the sunrise, glance across the horizon and waters of despair, the tree was not uprooted but pruned.

There shall be showers of blessings. There shall be a season of refreshing. It will shoot again and the birds and beasts will return to the meadows of pride. I see the grand entrance and return the restoration of Africa, her glory is like Gold in dust.

Africa arise! It's not where you are but who you are.

HERE IS HOW AFRICAN KINGS BECAME IDOLATER IN CHRISTIANITY

How to take away power from the people?

How to convert a king to slave? The retard is the African who has become white in a bid to seek for favor, like a tree uprooted and roots exposed it can only live but for a little while.

"Many strange things have happened in Africa that have puzzled and shocked the world, no explanation to the rest of humanity the strange work of the African mind".[2]

Read Daniel chapter one and think: progressive colonization

1. Besiege a people, shut them in, and lock them in their walls. Control what goes in and out. In due time they will submit and bow down and submit when resources are depleted; besiege them through immigration laws and identity cards.

2. Determine with whom they must interact. This is not physically, but economically, spiritual besiege, our political and social and cultural is under siege. "To know the enemy, know yourself".[3] Only in this introspection will you see if you are what you are or what he wants you to be.

2. Credo Vusamazulu Mutwa, Indaba, My Children; Blue Crane Books 1964 pp xvii
3. Miyamoto Musashi, The Book of the Five Rings, Bantam Books 1982, pp xix

3. Africa must ask itself the question "are we becoming better Africans or we becoming bastard kids at the European Kindergarten of "civility". It is reason to worship another human being "YHWH is the only one whom we may serve and praise. We may sing only to his greatness and obey only his commands. We may not act in this way towards anything beneath Him. Whether it be an angel, a star, one of the elements, or any combination of them." [4]

4. Take away symbols of their faith and make ridicule of their history. Distort their confidence in the faith of their fathers. Parade the weakness of their God and they will bow to a superior deity you give them. There is no way you can be a slave and your God is free. When a nation is captured or "under capture" it is their God who is captured.

So take some of the vessels of the house of God; and he took them away into the land of the colonial house of his God; and he put the vessels into the storehouse of his God.

By rendering the God of the land powerless to protect his own citizens. The oppressor is at liberty to abuse the slave with the permission of his god.

5. Separate the slave from each other break the social structure and cultural respect lines. You will have a group that is alive with no structure. Those who do not know where they are coming from don't know where they go.

6. Give some of them positions of influence in the ranks of the oppressor and all slaves will start to compete for "upward mobility". Look at black churches in the absence of the white-man; they are whiter than the whites.

7. When a Blackman takes position in a '*kings house*' oppresses other blacks more than the whiteman. "Colonial rhetoric did much to whip up regional sentiments and in the process politically seriously divided the African community."[5]

8. Take away their language and have them trained in the writing and language of oppression. For in language there is passing on of traditions with stories and the DNA of the past is distorted and

4. Aryeh Kaplan, Maimonides's Principles (fundamentals of Jewish Faith), Olive stone Publishing Services 1984, pp 37
5. Aneneas Chigwedere, The Mutasa Manyika Dynasty 1695-2000, Mutapa Publishing House 2015, pp 159

obliterated when language is taken away! Where are our languages?

9. Change their diet, with a regular amount of food and wine every day from the king's table was ordered for them by the king; make them live on hand outs. Make them depend on the system. Take away freedom and create perpetual dependency on salary... Welfare.

10. Inversely this builds fear in the slaves to go independently. It reduces the slaves appetite for risk for predictability creates false comfort, like crabs waiting to be cooked in a controlled fish tank, life is good until they are put in the pressure cooker! Our food made us strong. 'A good life is fast foods full of cancer'. Now we have a good life, but we are weak. We used to walk and work in the fields now we drive and die faster!

11. Create a path for them through which they develop to become informed slaves. They will go to school and study to be cared for three years so that at the end of that time they might take their places in the establishment of the oppressors.

12. And among these there were, the children of *Judah, Daniel, Hananiah, Mishael, and Azariah*. Change their names. Remove their sense of cultural names, replace them with the white names of their *slave masters,* for in a name there is character!

13. Change their geography; dispossess them of their land and remove their sense of land and geography and address. Pull them away from their roots and they will have no reference to run away to.

14. Change their clothes, for these have identity and social status. The culture of the oppressor will show the fantasy of the oppressor. Breasts were never sacred to blacks until the Whiteman came. Now our women would rather breast-feed their man than their children. Breasts have become a center of cosmetic than primary health care center for infants.

15. The call to the black nation is in verse 8 verse and Daniel had come to the decision that he would not make himself unclean with the king's food or wine; so he made a request to the captain of the un-sexed servants that he might not make himself unclean.

From this story the African can learn a few things from Daniel the statesman.

We make decisions: decide, and have a purpose at heart

i. Keep it true and pure from colonial contamination;

ii. Go back to basics, keep life simple. Be a healthy nation and keep the corridors of thinking clear

iii. Keep it clean. Cleanliness of the soul and identity must be maintained and all the slaves must keep their channels of divine communications clear from Eurocentric contamination.

The world has lost respect of the person. The uniqueness of character tribe and nation is always viewed from the global uniformity under filthy cloth of democracy.

Ethnic tribes that have lived under their technologies are disregarded for the western measuring yard. Life cannot only be viewed through the lenses of the Caucasian.

Imperialism is when western technology and its developments harass and abuse locals around the world as they drive the propaganda of their economics, their politics, their religion, their food, their family structures and their culture. This is not negotiable but social imperialism, which seeks to totally remove all diversity into surrogacy of white supremacy.

The African needs to find his soul and identify those critical non-negotiable traditions and traits that must be retained in trade of tea and creamer.

What is your purpose in your heart? What contamination has clouded your soul? How do you look at fellow blacks? How do you worship? Who do you call upon in the day of your trouble? How far is your God from your trouble?

What do you do to please Him?

Do you feel you have become a better slave than the primitive ones who can't speak and write English? How do you feel when you look at your own culture? Your language, culture and clothes are not barbaric.

When last did you go home to your village and not try to change them but experience life as it is?

Where are your vessels of worship? In which house are they locked up? In which language do you pray? Which clothes does your God accept into the church and why? Do you have an alter for your God?

Which songs bring you closer to the Lord? How and when did you lose your soul to colonial forms?

Who are you my African brother?

Who are you my African sister?

A Divided Worship

Racism and its impact on African worship

Racism is white-based segregation. And the "White race is the most aggressive genetic group of humanity"

"Nuclear war, environment pollution, resource rape, all are primary threats to survival and all are the results of peculiarly Caucasoid behavior. Their values and psychology are far from global but local to their intent."

"The major problem of this world is white men"[1] The gospel that the African received was designed for the poor and never to allow for equality between whites and blacks.

---

1. Michael Bradley: Chosen People from the Caucasus. (Jewish Origins Delusions, Deceptions and Historical Role in the salve Trade, Genocide and Cultural Colonization.) Third world Press, Chicago, 1992

How did African Jews of North Africa end up being whites of Europe? How long did it take a black Pharaoh to notice a white Moses? Had Joseph been white how come his brother's could not recognize him amongst the Egyptians? When did the European Jews convert to Judaism? What is the difference between Jews and Hebrews?

The black race (Hebrew) had direct contact with YHWH prior to "colonialism" as the Jews direct contact prior to new dispensation and diaspora. It is a clear fact that the two nations know that there is something missing in our worship service that seems not to reach the desire of the human soul. The Jews cry at the wall of David for the Messiah must show up and fulfill his promises for Israel. The African church has been given a powerless religion that has become a social gospel that makes them function in the realm of slaves and not masters.

Observation reveals that we have lost the very ingredient that made us a people of power. The Pyramids, the ruins of Timbuktu, the rivers, and mountains all were connecting centers of spirituality. The African land was a basic shrine of spiritual manifestation and morality was enforced from a spiritual platform not judicial.

This is a personal spiritual journey in search of answers and in pursuit of connectivity with the supernatural. This work comes out of observation and interaction and dissatisfaction with insulated worship services.

To ask basic questions "what happened to the God of Africa? Did we know him prior to the white-god? Was our God captured by the whites?

Does this new God know us and can he answer our prayers? If he is there, can he perform? How do we access him and call on him?

After 30 years of pastoral work I stand here and ask where is the power of the gospel? Is this all that we have, rituals and doctrines that make us dogs under the master's table?

Who does God identify with the oppressed or the oppressor? Then prayer becomes a dangerous thing to do "for it reminds the oppressed of the Christ who identified with the rejected to the point of giving up his life for the liberation of mankind" especially for the oppressed."2

Will Western religions ever respect or even consult the native Africans when designing and formulating doctrines?

It's so naive that even in hot weather, simple climatic changes around the world, we are all forced to be in ties and jackets in the heat of Africa!

2. Desmond Mpilo Tutu, Hope and Suffering, Skotaville Publishers, 1983, pp x

Will Africa ever be free to get some fresh air than sit in ovens and dressed in hot apparel while singing some old hymn of the oppressor? If Africa will call on the name of the Lord will He not hear? Can we evoke the spiritual powers to solve our human issues? Then the doctrine must be a tool for the mind not a master of it.

SPIRITUALITY

Scriptures cannot be reduced to dogmatics, but a gateway into the spiritual realm. A close look at the word will inform us that the divine does not reside in the natural and that the human body is by creation spiritual and when placed in a conducive environment it can operate at the spiritual level.

To begin with child birth, after nine months of in under water in the mother's womb without an oxygen mask shows the complexity of spirituality shared by a *saNgoma* in their initiation and the Christians at their baptism. What we see as miracles in the scriptures must then be understood as the invasion of the spirit in the affairs of the living. We need to ask, what powers operate in the spiritual realm, which is very active with witchcraft, and sacred cultural expression?

If they can call on their God quickly why is our righteous one so distant and need lots of music, money, to be caused to move? Are our prayers directed at God or at the door of the white-man that holds our resources?

Is there a true Christian who is poor?

Has poverty made God an ATM and the prayers a begging session for poverty alleviation? Is the service directed at a spiritual connection of physical deficiencies? Is it impossible for the human being to interact with the spiritual If these things that the people are praying for are met will people still come here to pray? Why do people come to church?

What is the greatest need for the human soul?

Is the purpose of the gospel not to place the hand of the sinner into the hands of his maker? When this relationship is consummated in the spiritual life, of what function is the human being? Is it not natural to be spiritual?

Does Christianity teach God as untouchable?

How far is YHWH from human beings, or it must teach his proximity and direct his dwelling into the fiber of our own DNA and lives. What is the one thing that we lack in our worship services?

Like a woman at the well what is the deep desire of the African Christian? Do people pray to access materials that "civilization" has brought or to find his spiritual self?

What will be best solution, to give the African fish (god in a package) or show him how to fish for his Creator? Has our desire for heaven overshadowed our function on earth? If God wanted us in heaven then why did he create us on earth?? Has the true gospel "occupy till I come" been replaced with escapism based on an ineffective doctrine of master and slave?

Is this gospel interested in making us spiritual or servants? Is it a gospel for masters or for slaves? If slaves will be masters then what will the masters be? When a person has attained awareness and enlightenment and operates in the spiritual zone what will be the use of the physical structure? Who can deal with a spiritual person?

What is the full potential of the African Christian? Given the right tools can we call Him into our worship services and experience the power? What causes people of our time to fill up halls and stadium looking for this new God to manifest? These questions refuse to leave my heart and cause the searcher to look deeper into the gimmicks, magical ceremonies and indoctrination of the people for maintenance and not for full spiritual operation.

The farmer of thought has to farm the ground – the season is now.

The key driver of this work is the need for the real as of old, people went into this zone and came back with answers. There is a journey every living human being must travel, not only physically but spiritually: hence the title "*Going Places In the Spirit*".

It's a call that our newly found faith must take us to the very presence of the Lord we profess and anything less than our arrival in the Presence of our Creator is idolatry.

The dualistic nature of man must seek for meaning in rituals. It will be glory when the reader can appreciate that there are two layers to worship all these ordinances have a "historical and spiritual agricultural meaning; the mystic delve beyond these into layers of hidden inner meaning"[3]

The saints of old as our ancestors went places in the spirit:

The ark floated while the world drowned in water
Barren wombs were opened after passing death and age

---

3. Norman Solomon, Judaism, Oxford University Press, 1996, pp 59.

The burning bushes without burning
The miracles of Moses to Egypt

The tempering with natural elements and the supernatural transportation of the Israelites from Egypt to Canaan starting with the parting of the Red sea, the bitter waters, shacking of Mount Sinai, feeding with manna, water from the Rock and the roll away of Jordan.

The collapse of the city of Jericho the wars that were fought by the supernatural, when the nation was in harmony with YHWH you could see the divine daily involved in the success of the nation.

Stand with the Samson and see the power of the Holy spirit when in operation in the human body, Elijah's presence and the provisions and resurrection of children and there is an art to stop rain and to call rain.

Elisha is said to have been able to see things before they happened even had access to the private bedroom of the *Aramean King*. These are all not foreign to African spiritualist and *saNgoma*.

In our Christianity we have lost the science of relevance, secrets to the very ground we stand on, the air around us has gone silent in the business of life, hence the result is our depressed lives of emptiness.

To "*go places in the spirit*", and stand me in the furnace with the Hebrew boys, fire has no power over a spiritual body. What does it mean to be like *Yashua*, walk on the water, multiply food, call fish into nets, address demons in the possessed, walk through walls, speak to the winds and the waves and they obey. Is this not the ministry of the disciples? Phillip flew to Ethiopia on a cloud of mystery, what witches do at night the Lord does in the day.

Clothes were carried to the sick and they were healed, the shadows of the spiritual disciple touched the halt and the lame to be healed. Paul and Silas, at midnight we can call on the Lord and the presence of the divine enter to break chains and open doors. Imagine the amount of power the supernatural brings into the heart of faith to transform the human body into powerful agent of change.

The gospel that focuses on sin only limits the capacity to explore function in the hand of the divine, that is heretic and evil to push people into guilt rather than function in the spirit. The battle is not physical but spiritual, teach the people to rule the physical from the spiritual. Now more than ever we need spiritual tools to deal with the physical problem, the material world must be brought into subjection of the spiritual realm. Its all in worship, when the human heart and divine heart are in concert, there is no limit, "to the joys we share as we tarry there, none other has ever known.

Often I feel like the priest who stood with Elijah on Mount Carmel who kept on praying and shouting and cutting themselves as they were being mocked that maybe their God had gone on holiday or fast asleep.

Our worship services are long and tiresome full of rituals that seem to confuse the spirit. The African Christian must revisit the church program and implement a spiritual agenda rather than a bulletin of social function. Ideally people are here because they seek the face of YHWH.

In the last day the spirit of Elijah will be upon us, this is to make YHWH quick to answer and build a new generation of worshippers who are taught the ways of the Lord.

The key purpose of the program must be to respond to this basic desire from the saints: "That we may see Immanuel the Messiah". There is a Christian Crisis as the African child seeks for his roots. Remember

1. That crisis produces opportunity - Where is God?
2. Opportunity produces ministry - Why are Christians?
3. Ministry produces favor - Does God love blacks? As slaves or masters?
4. Favor produces promotion - Is there something more than church?
5. Promotion produces increase - In what directions should we grow?
6. Increase produces/multiplies responsibility- is this nation becoming better?
7. Responsibility produces rewards- is there benefits in this new Christianity?
8. Rewards produce attack- who is fighting black liberation?
9. Attach creates Crisis[4] - what are the opportunities in liberation?

Our African dilemma, from economics, to politics and agricultural exploitation has presented us an opportunity to look back at the ways of old.

A glance would inform us "it was never like this, it used not be like this." History has robbed and veiled its face in modernity have we been buried in materialism, yet the path in truth, has liberty. Paul also was struggling with the church of his day that could not move to the spiritual platform but were stuck in legalistic rituals of meaningless proportion.

A quick glance at the book of Galatians would reveal the struggle between the physical church and the spiritual hearts.

---

4. Rabbi Ralph Messer, Convention in Nigeria 2011, on Black Histo

i.   Paul apostles not called of man or send by man Yashua Messiah and Elohiym the Father who raised Him from the dead; the introduction is that of power, raising people from the dead. The book of Galatians: to the churches in the region of Galatian These churches included *Lystra, Antioch of Pisidia, Iconium* and *Derbe*, which Paul established on his first journey into Asia. Martin Luther (the reformer) calls it the best book of the bible that he is married to. John Bunyan calls it the book fit for the wounded conscience. Early Christians called it the Crucifixion epistles, to break the thunderbolts of legalism.

ii. Paul the Apostle of the Gentiles writes this letter from the apostolic office as contrasted to the Disciple authority, he cannot claim. There is a difference between theory and practice; the pragmatic application of the gospel as it is reaching new grounds. Apostle Paul argues that the Gospel is a stand alone capable of saving people without extra of *Judaistic* expectations.

iii. The ancient tradition to open a letter the author must appear first so you decide to read or not

iv. The credentials of the author were important to give veracity to what he wrote, by whose authority he wrote and any supporting credentials.

v.   The Churches of Galatia – the Gaul's lived in troubled times with sin and depravity on the increase, immorality rampant and depravity eminent religion offering a solution not relevant and ineffective – the books seeks to deal with guidelines of Christian living victorious lives in a world full of sin.

vi. Key to these observations and comments on Galatians are the following issues to consider about the book:

○ **Its too emotional:** you too will need to find your emotional attachments to the Gospel of Jesus and get emotional about your conviction to avoid dry faith that does not reach you or cause you to do anything

○ **Its Personal:** deal with personal issues and Gospel issues. Be careful not to use your preference as gospel or gloat of ignorance as bliss. Do not be too anxious to agree than differ and avoid confrontation. Faith must reach your personal biases and challenge you to the faith of Jesus of acceptance and understanding

○ **It's too intellectual:** when coming to church please bring your brains with you. Love God with all you MIND and worship God with UNDERSTANDING. Church members must not be lazy to think and stretch their minds into divine search. Be a man who digs for treasure and finds it;

○ **Its too Spiritual:** its not about religion and church but Spirituality. The desire of the book is that we are clear about our new status of spiritual participation, our new status that interacts with God. And use that union as a basis to live and interpret daily issues;

○ **Its too controversial:** the gospel is a two edged sword. Many times we do not want to argue or quarrel but seek for comfort zones. Had it not been for the arguments of:

- Luther we would have been worshiping idols today in Rome
- Calvin we would have been eating the flesh of Jesus
- Charles Wesley purity and Christian walk
- Ellen white eating pigs
- Baptist we would have been sprinkling water on each other
- Pentecostal would have been having dry worship of legalism

THERE ARE PRIMARY AND SECONDARY ARGUMENTS:

- Primary: deal with core values and principles e.g. food to eat and live
- Secondary: is application and relevance e.g. appearance and presentation
- Peter the Disciples with circumcision - wrong
- Paul the Apostle with non-circumcision - right

A PUBLIC CONFRONTATION AT THE CHURCH:

- We lack today man of conviction who will not toy with tact and tolerance but stick your neck up and confront error when you hear it or see it.
- How polite can you be when you notice that there is a hole on the family boat with all on board?
- Heated fellowship and emotional controversial confrontation

THESE LETTERS ARE ONE SIDED:

We do not have the one the church wrote we only hear one side of the story. It is important to always find out what was the motive of the letter, and what issues is Paul responding to.

It would be foolish to think that these were written in a vacuum.

Ask the following questions:

Why was it written?   *Why were you created?*

What were the questions?   *What are your questions?*

What were the problems?   *What are your problems?*

Four cities that shape the academic landscape of Paul

- Alexander – Egypt
- Athens – Rome
- Tarsus – Turkey
- Jerusalem - Gamaliel

Tarsus was the 3rd most important academic city. It was a university town in which Paul was born. He was a Jew by birth with a full Hebrew training in language and culture, but also spoke and wrote Greek. He interacted with many other cultures in this University town from around the word that came here to sharpen their intellect.

He was a tent maker manual laborer to a society that looked down on work in favor of pen pushers. God prepares each worker for his own ministry – all the experience of life is divinely orchestrated to maximize your influence in the gospel field.

The Author is Paul; the date is between 48 and 57 AD. Saul converted Paul of Tarsus the fighter now the defender, declares that he is sent "not of man but of God", to confirm this are the brethren with him

THE BIGGEST ARGUMENT IS "THE GOSPEL PLUS"

They only wanted to improve the gospel by adding to it requirements, new ceremonies and new standards. It is as if they are saying, "We believe in Jesus Christ – but we have something wonderful to add to what you already believe!"

What is at least implied is that the faith that these believers have is not sufficient, "something" more is needed. This is what multiplied meaningless rituals to a fake Christian encounter.

Physicality - worship in the flesh:

This religion I do not need, for it is demonic. The greatest of the social ills have been hidden in the religious department.

The evidence is overwhelming "the conclusion that the Caucasian race is somewhat more aggressive than any other major groups of humanity, then we may legitimately inquire as to whether some ethnic groups within Caucasian race might be characterized by an even higher level of psychological sexual mal-adaptation and therefore have historically manifested consistently higher levels of aggression than most of the Caucasians."[5]

We must stop and ask as a black nation

Why will a church teach about heaven when the very church is a living hell? Will blacks and whites meet in heaven? Is there a black heaven and a white heaven? Is it possible that the church is a breeding ground of racism and segregation?

How much money has the European based churches taken out of Africa? Why are we made to feel guilty over spending our own money and offering and tithe? Can the black-man be trusted with his wealth and resources?

Does God condemn the black church for not returning offerings to America? Are the modern pastors the *Levites* and is the church the temple? Where is the house of the Lord? Is there food in the house of the Lord???

Why are white churches registered as family trusts and black churches are held in white trusts? When will the black-church wake up?

What are the possible solutions to this maze of financial abuse from the west? Do we need the west or they need us. Or have we become an ATM for white owners? Why is it hard for blacks to stand up and talk? Where does the guilt come from when addressing church issues?

Why do fellow Christians demonize those who ask questions? Do black people have pride or we have become slaves and taught never to ask? Is the church allergic to thinking and interrogation? Does the church need our money more than our brains? Who benefits from this division? Are blacks slaves or masters?

Who is the Bible addressing when it says, "slaves obey your masters"?

These are the questions that keep me awake at night when I think about the church. 'Is it access to God or introduction of white Culture?'

Does the church inform politics or politics informs the church.

Who leads us, the Bible or the church; or the Bible leads us to the church.

The church can never lead us to the Bible.

---

5. Michael Bradley, Chosen People from Caucasus, Third World Press, 1992, Jewish Origins, Delusions, Deceptions and Historical, the role of slave trade, genocide and cultural colonization.

Why does the church use political language to cover up evil? Is the church built on racial discrimination? The *black nation* must not enter the temple or church or faith as servants but equal partners, heirs and co-heirs in the gospel feast.

1. A religion that does not hold the word of God as supreme to all biases and traditions

2. The religion that forces me to become like you before I am accepted by Yhwh

3. A religion that reduces you to a slave for an earthly master. If a religion that makes you a slave then you are in bondage at a moment of worship, this is inferiority of the image of God and it soils your value.

4. A religion that robs you of your conscience and gives it to the system. They decide what must bind my conscience. That is idolatry!

5. Fear the system more than you fear Yhwh you are addicted to the system more than to truth. You fear the clergy more than God.

6. A religion that takes away our purpose with God to fulfill the vision of the founder. From what God wants us to achieve to what the church wants to achieve. A religion with no local vision or idea for local community but development of foreign projects.

7. A religion that forces us to maintain the church more than look after our own families and parents is an abomination. The tithe you pay the church is more than the allowances you give your parents.

8. A religion discredits the power of the gospel as food to the poor, freedom to the oppressed, health to the sick. A religion that oppresses people cannot be a true Gospel. Where is abundant life?

9. A religion that stands with the oppressor and manipulates people to worship idols of self or system, worship the structure

10. A religion that is forced on you and compulsory and you worship under fear, is Antichrist

11. A religion that threatens me with demons and sickness and death if I leave them. Or curses me for finding my freedom is colonialism.

12. The religion that alienates people from reality to occult/cult tendencies to deem themselves superior to the rest, a better than thou religion. Remnant religion is a breeding ground of heretics and fanatics.

13. That teaches them as the only means of divine salvation and deems everybody else as lost.

14. A religion that performs fake miracles and Signs to create theatricals rather than introduce me to my savior

15. A religion that is too rigid or too structural. Too physical and not spiritual; or too liberal. The balance is needed between truth and spirit.

16. A religion that cannot translate itself into relevance and allow the progressive revelation of truth. The spirit of YHWH is at liberty to reveal him to every generation. A monument religion that is fake and so, we rather have a movement religion that is relevant.

17. A religion that breaks the Ten Commandments cannot be a true religion. When the institution deliberately violates the prescribed clear expectation of YHWH upon the souls of man.

18. A religion that puts more emphasis on artifacts and rituals. Faith cannot be placed in clothes, foods, or salts and blood of pigeons and waters than emphasis on the cleansing power of the gospel.

19. A religion that teaches the culture of its preachers and insults the indigenous people force them to eat, dress, talk practice the foreign culture. Eating bread and the plastic

20. A religion that takes away the resources of the local people to invest in land affairs. It steals money from local people to serve its own interests. Uses local churches as ATMs to further its own interests.

Where the spirit of the Lord is, there is liberty.

This liberty includes liberty from white traditions and oppressive tendencies of the west to manage "black ignorance" free from fear of hell and the black devil the whiteman has put in hell, free from the white Jesus who blesses the whiteman as he whips the black-man.

SYMMETRICALLY AFRICA HAS BEEN DESTROYED! THIS IS HOW IT WAS DONE.

It is Steve Biko who said, "Black man you are on your own" you are all you have, each other. Here is a step-by-step strategy we need to adopt. Read it with your nation in mind.

This is how we got here and maybe this is our way to get out of here:

1. Whites invaded our territories and displaced us from our homes and land;

2. Then they established themselves on our territory and deliberately

disadvantaged us;

3. Apartheid and oppression build systems (passport, ID. Legislations, schools, currency etc) to maintain their status quo and new lifestyle with no regard to blacks.

4. Colonialisms expanded itself and assisted us to undermine ourselves our culture, our language and traditions for the white traditions "If your enemy wants to burn his house give him the matches"

5. Then ultimately, it perfected itself; the art of oppression is tolerance and voluntary slavery. Because of money, jobs etc. A whiteman can curse you as your boss and you keep quiet.

6. They dominate in arrogance and scare techniques and give fake hope of global village good of humanity where they are the only citizens!

7. *Negropeans*: produce a few blacks that feel better than other blacks. A few black slaves who dress and drive better than the rest and put them into managerial positions (not ownership) to manage. Help contain other blacks. At this stage whiteman can go on holiday while the slave factory continues to function.

This is the maintenance plan. When black now oppresses the other blacks for global fake harmony! "Religion is the organization of spirituality into something that became the hand maiden of conquerors. Nearly all religions were brought to people and imposed on people by conquerors, and used as the framework to control their minds."[6]

If you get angry and feel I am out of order you are a level seven coconut. Brown outside white inside, true color a *Negropean*, coconut skins with white hearts. A watchdog of white culture, cottiers, coterie and mannerisms. A security guard on the door of *dress music*. Language and "civilization".

Note you have called fellow Africans "uncivilized"

Whites knew that the only way they would succeed with the oppression was to enslave our mindset into believing what they thought about us that they are superior to us, by using the very same religion we hold on to.

By giving this religion they bound oppression on our souls, that to think contrary creates internal dissonance. Personal guilt and cooperate guilt were created and church and politics would police your conscience.

Poverty would drive hunger; our appetite for tea with cream would suppress our hunger for land! I need to ask again!

---

6. John Henrik Clark

What's is the character of God? Who rules God?

Who should rule me, when God made us in his image he made us to be ruled by whom, the whiteman?

Are servants made in the image of God?

Is an image of God subject to another human being?

Do the slaves and the masters worship the same God?

Are slaves candidates for heaven?

When slaves get to heaven how do they relate to their masters?

Will the master mysteriously become humble in heaven?

Will the oppressor's character and attitude be transformed quickly to tolerate others and share a room with fellow blacks?

Where in the bible, has God used poor people except as illustrations?

What is salvation? Whose sins must be forgiven?

What is redemption, Redemption from what?

What is restoration? Who needs restoration?

Is there forgiveness of the *whiteman* without the Zacheus model payback the stolen goods four times? When will they pay back the money and bring back the land?

When will they return our stolen treasures and dignity, our art and artifacts hanging in their museums? Our skulls and bones of people they maimed during experiments looking for the soul in a black man?

Are whites human?

If you beat them would they also cry ?

Is it evil for Christians to claim land?

Is it okay for churches to mobilize themselves and claim land?

Are churches interested in alleviating poverty and building communities that are self-reliant? What role does land play to level the economic landscape for equal participation?

What government can rule land without land? Which nation can call itself a nation without its land and resources? Does the church/and African democracy thrive in poverty and non-assertive Christians?

Is it evil to claim our rights from oppressors and demand our dignity?

In whose image are we if we don't exhibit God's character? When God looks at us what does He see? Where blacks created to be slaves of whiteman?

Why do we have white names?

Why do we do white weddings?

Why do whites not do black weddings?

Why do we adopt the Roman Dutch law?

Is this Rome or are we a colony of the Dutch? Did Africa have prisons before colonization? How did we deal with crime? Is it a crime to kill a man who rapes your daughter and kills your wife and makes you bonded slaves? What is the purpose of life without your family structure? Why does the bible teach tooth for tooth? Why did Jesus die if revenge is not allowed?

Was the death of Jesus not revenge to appease God's anger? Who will appease the *blackman's* anger and how? And when will this end and stop? Will the blackman ever wake up again? Has our consciousness been replaced with western ambitions?

Can we not find our roots and stop watering other people's gardens? When blacks prays in English does God Hear them? Then why does he not answer?

Vele! where is God?

We need an African political or cultural manifesto to systematically dismember the monster who sits in our minds and land and banks and classes and courts and prisons. Answers are in social cohesion and respect of indignity.

Till when will blacks continue to endure abuse from whites and their business? When we pray for God to bless us what are we praying for? Is it not idolatry to pray for things a whiteman has? When our ancestors used to pray for the rain, who answered them?

Can we still pray for the rain and it rains? Did we have a God who heard us? Where is he now? Has he left us, or we left him? The new God we have been given does he care about us?

Bob Marley would sing relevance in this generation "emancipate yourself from mental slavery but only ourselves can free our minds," only you can free yourself by freeing your mind, allow yourself to think. Think, yes think. What are the origins of Apartheid? Is it not that whites find its bases from the Bible, the sons of Shem?

Are the white ones the only ones designate to have dominion? Has the *Blackman* become the animal that must be ruled, sheltered and fed, treated controlled and killed? Who shall have dominion on whites?

Is it acceptable for a black woman to make tea for a whiteman? Is it acceptable for a white woman to make tea for a Blackman? There must be religion or the poor will kill the rich. Napoleon Bonaparte

Mother Teresa states that, *"The greatest disease in the West today is not TB or leprosy; it is being unwanted, unloved, and uncared for. We can cure physical diseases with medicine, but the only cure for loneliness, despair, and hopelessness is love. There are many in the world that are dying for a piece of bread but many more die for a little love. The poverty in the West is a different kind of poverty -- it is not only a poverty of loneliness but also of spirituality. There's a hunger for love, as there is a hunger for God."* [7]

The black-man is trapped in the pangs of hunger and white religion has proved to be hard labor and total destruction of the black nerve of spirituality.

THE SIZE OF YOUR POND DETERMINES THE SIZE OF YOUR FISH!

Never trust your dreams into the hands of another man. They will limit you to the capacity of their own potential. Our education system is a factory of black slaves. We are trained to write CVs, not to own industries. The size of your God is equivalent to the size of your church, for the African the whole world is a cathedral, a church without walls.

"He who gives you the diameter of your knowledge prescribes the circumference of your activity. So when your slave master educates you, he does not educate you to be a threat to him." Minister Louis Farrakhan but a servant to his business.

One must ask what is the agenda of the curriculum and church doctrines that moves the poor to dependence or submission.

What will happen when the African is free from these lies? We have no seed how do we pray for the rain. We have no cow how do we pray for grass. We have fields how do we pray for rain!

Wanda Mashabane submits that we must build "African institutions that cultivate African minds because we cannot rely on governments engineered by non Africans."

Genesis teaches us that we must have dominion over birds of the sea and land. Not over each other. "We were created to be a reflection of the divine nature of the universe, of Elohiym as emanated from *Ayn Soph*. We reflect the character, and even movements of the divine, just as a shadow does for that which creates it. It is when we learn we are a self, when we develop 'ego,' that the shadow breaks from the original, we lose our

---

7. Mother Teresa, A Simple Path: Mother Teresa

connection to the divine and the universe, and the Shalom that connection brings."

"Everything was created ached, it is by consciously fostering the illusion of separation that we lose our connection with the Elohiym. Our job is to complete the creation by reducing chaos and imbalance and to reduce the emptiness by 'filling.' We are to utilize our creative faculties to complete the creative process. Where does this wisdom come from? It comes from creation itself."

"We are to journey among all the creatures of the world, learning from them and about them, ascertaining how we can best bring about balance and harmony in the world. It is by becoming part of the natural order that we can understand it and find our proper place within it, while becoming aware of anything that creates disharmony. By doing so, we become the caretakers (rulers) of creation. " [8].

Emphasis is Spirituality (*as Christians*) and citizens, Servants and sons. Ambassadors and Christians. What is our status? Who are we? What do we represent?

What is our maximum capacity and function?

We are created to have dominion, what is dominion and what does it entail and encompass?

What was the function and nature of man before the fall?

How much did we lose? And how do we restore the loss?

The bible is a book about the Kingdom (theocracy) not a republic and Democracy.

We have a difficulty obeying God because we live in a democracy, the opinions of the citizens count (Vote), the people have the power, can remove and put leaders.

There is no democracy in the bible but a king, the citizen's opinions do not count, no vote or referendum. Can't vote the king out. Genesis 1:26 – "we are created as kings and our main job is to dominate and to maintain His (our Father extension) standard on earth".

Denote not only the material but also the spiritual wealth of the universe and its secrets. The loss in Eden was the connectivity in the spiritual realm, which caused struggle and hard work in the physical.

The journey into the spirit will unveil the power to govern the elements.

8. Jeff A.Benner and Michael Calpino: Genesis, Zen and Quantum Physics: A Fresh Look At The Theology of Science of creation. P 89 -90

The human machine needs recalibration in the spirit to access and tap into this realm of real power. The word for sin is rebellion. Going against a government - success is a revolution to be in charge and claim back what is rightfully yours. What the enemy stole from us in the garden must be claimed in the garden of prayer.

A musician thought he could organize a coupe, notes to fight with, fiery darts are his weapons, he fell from heaven like lightning. To find this tool of music and worship the Lord in truth means that we are restored into the high places of divine function and our purpose will be reestablished in our function in the heavenly sanctuary duplicated in our hearts. Genesis chapter 1 clearly shows that God is a spirit Gen1: 2, which he thinks, speaks, wills, and acts (Gen1: 3-4, etc.). Here, then, are the great points of conformity to God in man, namely, reason, speech, will, and power.

By reason we apprehend concrete things in perception and consciousness, and recognize abstract truth, metaphysical, epistemological and moral.

i.   By will we choose, determine, and resolve upon what is to be done. In the will it is unfolded that the freedom of action which chooses the good and refuses the evil.

ii. By speech we make certain acts easy and sensible acts of our own the signs of the various objects of our contemplative faculties to others and ourselves.

iii. There is power in declaration and speech, we are at worship in speech, for through our words we call what is not to be, declare power over the things that are not aligned to align.

iv. By power we act, either in giving expression to our concepts in words, or effect to our determinations in deeds. In the reason is evolved the distinction of good and evil Gen 1:4, Gen1: 31, which is in itself the approval of the former and the disapproval of the latter.

v.   In the spiritual being that exercises reason and will resides the power to act, which presupposes both these faculties - the reason as informing the will, and the will as directing the power. This is that form of God in which he has created man, and condescends to communicate with him.

The kingdom of God is like a man employed to work in the field (Matthew 13) and finds treasure, to which he sells all he has to purchase the land.

That is the Kingdom of God. It's all or nothing.

The woman with a lost coin: search for this treasure until you find it, clean all until you find it, celebrate when the lost human dignity and power has been found.

This virtue is lost in the house and it takes the diligent to place their hands of this priceless treasure Oh what joy when we finally become what the earth (our mother) wanted us to become.

We want power that causes us to cause - Jesus came to earth to extend the Kingdom of Heaven through the agency of humans, sons and not subjects or servants. A family affair reinstates sons. Established a common wealth of citizens, no less rights than the other-all equal.

People treat us the way we treat ourselves we attract those like us. Christ came to restore the family. The program of God is to rule the seen (visible world), from the unseen (invisible world), through the unseen (spirit man), living in the seen (the body), on the seen (earth) and the underworld (the sea and its depth).

The sad part is those who work for the kingdom of darkness understand these dimensions of power while the Christian struggles in the physical space fighting for bread and butter. The Lord wanted His Kingdom to come and His will be done on earth as it is in heaven through His Son and the sons of man.

Earth is supposed to know, experience what heaven is thinking through us. We will become agents of divine intervention upon the earth and cause nature to move at the impulse of our father. Jesus miracle, healing, raising the dead, feeding the hungry. Jesus doing what the Father is doing, in the unseen, there is no sickness because God is always working, and we need to agree with the Father for the manifestation of the spiritual.

By His stripes we are healed. Done already we just need to accept it. Yashua says, "I only do what my father thinks". We have already what is in heaven, we speak things as if they already were, I am Healed now.

Dominion means: To govern; to rule; to control things; to manage: to master something- dominating an area to have Lordship.

King - Rule, means standard, the line separates setting a standard. The Lord is the ruler - sets the standards, the ten points on the ruler-Ten Commandments. Salt means elite standard, when it comes to fashion, working on the job, cooking, and excellent spirit. Daniel, work ethic excellent.

"Only the few will ever become fully conscious. As in the days of the prophets, so in later periods, only a "small remnant" was fully imbued with the lofty ideal. In times of oppression the great multitude of the people persisted in a conscientious observance of the Law and underwent suffering without a murmur. Yet in times of liberty and enlightenment this same majority often neglects to assimilate the new culture to its own superior spirit, but instead eagerly assimilates itself to the surrounding world, and thereby loses much of its intrinsic strength and self-respect.

The pendulum of thought and sentiment swings to and from between the national and the universal ideals, while only a few mature minds have a clear vision of the goal as it is to be reached along both lines of development (p21) **a.** Man's consciousness of God, and divine revelation. **b.** God's spirituality, His unity, His holiness, His perfection. **c.** His relation to the world: Creation and Providence. **d.** His relation to man: His justice, His love and mercy. (34) "[9]

The Africans must be conscious to his divine Genesis; the black man must sit up. Stop making his back transport for the Whiteman. We are not donkeys, but human beings. We must find our domain to have dominion.

How long, oh Lord how long? The Jews were delivered after 490 years. We have been in bondage for 500 years. It's time for our deliverance.

True Christianity must restore the dignity of people not putting soup in our plates. The preacher needs to empower people to occupy and be productive rather than parrots of western agenda. Christianity has failed us. By making us not only to eat the bread but the plastic, which covers the bread. Truth must be separate from western traditions, music, language, fashion, foods, let it be honest we are people not statistics.

He who counts us determines how many of us he needs. Is the statistics for his budget or for our development?

Why does he put us on birth control?

What does he want to control? What will happen if we become more? Our pain is strange to the oppressor. Our poverty is strange to the colonizer. Our politics is strange to the economist.

The way we worship is strange to the Whiteman. Is there any good that Africa can produce but a dance for entertainment? Africa must start writing her own story, her own history, both church and secular. Re-establish cultural respect and simplicity of diet. Get our hands on our natural

9. Dr. K. Kohler: President Hebrew Union College New York The Macmillan; Jewish Theology: Systematically and Historically Considered Company 1918 p 21-22

resources and start making meaningful impact to the society and nation at large. Stop being a charity case.

What I submit cannot be strange except if you are white inside and brown outside: coconuts and *Negropeans* think I have lost my faith.

Is the African banned from accessing his land?

Why is the whiteman afraid to let go the land?

What is the use of fear?

Has the whiteman and the blackman become better people through religion? Why are people afraid of spirituality? Is the intimidation of hell realm? Does fear make Christians? Is there love where there is fear? Africa has sold its soul for a cup of tea.

This religion is fake if it does lead to spirituality or does it connect me with the source, but with the church which wants access to your bank. Seek for the fountain of life and power.

"Religion is for those who are afraid of going to hell. Spirituality is for those who have already been there."[10]

POVERTY

The worst form of poverty is that of the mind, lack of dreams and perpetual mindset of a basket case at the door of the oppressor. Poverty does not produce Christians for religion becomes an ATM and pain killer tablets. The punctuation of prayers is begging for means, sustenance that the Whiteman has in abundance. Has the whiteman become our God who must supply our needs?

How stupid have we become to give up land and accept jobs in offices, only to collect our salaries and buy food, minerals from the same land?

Can't we see the strategy of slavery? Our value is not on our pay slips but surety and land ownership. The key to unlock banking is not a pay slip, but property. It's the ONLY REAL ESTATE - land. Until we are Real in real estate we are poor both in spirit and material. Stop blaming God for your poverty.

The rain falls but you have no seed in the ground. The grass grows you have no cows to eat it. Seasons change, but you have no fruits to harvest. He who has your land eats your blessings. The Lord says I will bless your land not your offices!

10. Vine Deloria, Sioux

He who works the land works with God to charge a premium to the one who sits on his hands.

The lazy man must not eat.

Once written the seed has a life of its own - it can be books, articles.

TV programs, radio shows, movies, art inspiration etc.

"Pay attention to whatever inspires you, for it is "spirit" trying to communicate with you, that's why it's called "inspiration" as "in-spirit". Listen to it, believe it, and act on it."[11]

Depending on the ground there is another harvest awaiting the farmer. Let this generation move from visible material to invisible mental realities that create the visible materials.

All we see is but a creation in someone's mind.

What are you thinking?

How can you change the world?

Where are those thoughts?

Where is the ground you can plant on?

---

11 https://za.pinterest.com/explore/spirituality-quotes/

Real Ministry

"To get what you want in a face to face engagement you need to tell the other party what you want and what they can expect in return. When you start a conversation that will probably lead to a negotiation, there are protocols that should be observed. Set the scene for your advantage"[1]

The bible person and the African both moved in and out of this space to meet and collect answers from the divine for the present.

One element that is familiar is music, the very transport to this celestial space.

1. Kim Meredith, Dealonomics (deal maker), Marlene Fryer; Zebra Press 2013 pp 248

2 Kings 3: **11** But Jehoshaphat said, "*Is there no prophet of the Lord here that we may inquire of the Lord by him?*" So one of the servants of the king of Israel answered and said, "*Elisha the son of Shaphat is here, who poured water on the hands of Elijah.*"

12 And Jehoshaphat said, "The word of the Lord is with him." So the king of Israel and Jehoshaphat and the king of Edom went down to him.

13 Then Elisha said to the king of Israel, "What have I to do with you? Go to the prophets of your father and the prophets of your mother." But the king of Israel said to him, "No, for the Lord has called these three kings together to deliver them into the hand of Moab."

14 And Elisha said, "As the Lord of hosts lives, before whom I stand, surely were it not that I regard the presence of Jehoshaphat king of Judah, I would not look at you, neither will I see you."

15 "But now bring me a musician." Then it happened, when the musician played, the hand of the Lord came upon him.

16 And he said, "Thus says the Lord: 'Make this valley full of ditches.' **17** For thus says the Lord: 'You shall not see wind, nor shall you see rain; yet that valley shall be filled with water, so that you, your cattle, and your animals may drink.' **18** And this is a simple matter in the sight of the Lord; He will also deliver the Moabites into your hand.

19 "Also you shall attack every fortified city and every choice city, and shall cut down every good tree, and stop every spring of water, and ruin every good piece of land with stones."

The antenna of human creation the "hair" can sense and connect with the spiritual presence and send sensitive spasm signals to the nervous system that shivers down the spine.

The passage above shows the easy movement of Elisha between the physical and the spiritual to collect information and interact with God.

Look how he commands the service and enters into the service collects information and comes right back with spiritual information which had physical manifestation.

The reality of the armies, war strategy and victory is all packaged and guaranteed. If this is ministry, then I want this ministry too. Why must our worship services be full of sweat and noise when a simple song with one artist can ship the man of God to the next level?

This is no by far the only modus operandi of divine operation but one of those clear aspects of how music is integrally fused into this theophany encounter.

This question must translate to find meaning for function. Religion is run by the thought police. 'Obey. Listen. This is what you do. Don't ask questions. Go die for your country.' The spirituality says, 'Okay, you can die for your country, but know what you're doing while you're doing it.' [2]

As for the churches that are founded on the prophetic voices, seers, or prophets there is some advise.

Rather than idolize the prophet and lock God in the past.

The question should be, how do we recreate the environment which caused the prophets to move into the realm of God so that He can speak again?

There are rituals and things that the prophets did that caused heaven to move in their favor to evoke that same spirit. We will give the modern church an even louder voice that perpetuates the gift.

Instead of teaching people how to be prophets we teach them to memorize the prophecies – what a shame.

"Until you manifest glory, no one believes you"
"Until you manifest glory, you are on your own"
"Until you manifest glory, you won't be celebrated"

"Until you manifest glory, you won't be noticed"
"Until you manifest glory, no one identifies with you"
"Nobody identifies with Proofless people." [3]
"Creation and animals are waiting for the sons of God to manifest." [4]
"A true worshipper desires the words of this song…"

1. I'm pressing on the upward way,
New heights I'm gaining every day;
Still praying as I'm onwards bound,
"Lord, plant my feet on higher ground."

---

2. Tommy Chong
3. Wole Oladiyun, Anointing for Glory, Printmill Glory Company, 2015, pp 1 you should a carrier of God's glory
4. Romans 8 Nature groans and mourns waiting to be delivered

Refrain:

Lord, lift me up and let me stand,
By faith, on Heaven's tableland,
A higher plane than I have found;
Lord, plant my feet on higher ground.
2. *My heart has no desire to stay*
Where doubts arise and fears dismay
Though some may dwell where those abound,
My prayer, my aim, is higher ground.
3. *I want to live above the world,*
Though Satan's darts at me are hurled
For faith has caught the joyful sound,
The song of saints on higher ground
4. *I want to scale the utmost height*
And catch a gleam of glory bright
But still I'll pray till heaven I've found,
*"Lord, plant my feet on higher ground."*5

UNANSWERED QUESTIONS ON THE HUMAN SPIRIT:

The journey continues into the spiritual realm. The questions asked here I do not have all answers but an introduction to self-introspection and deeper understanding of the critical mass that will force you to move to the ideal. You are spiritual more than you are physical.

1.   Man is flesh and when God puts His spirit he becomes a soul: what does that make us? What does it mean that a human being is a living soul? How does a human being operate? As the body feeds on food what does the spirit feed on? What is the condition of the spirit?

2.   It is not oxygen, because people die with oxygen masks on their face? What is God's element that makes us living souls? How do we develop this spirit man?

3.   Saul goes to a witch and asks for Samuels's spirit, the spirit comes with a prophecy that was true; does the devil know the future?

4.   What is this spirit that Saul called for? Where do these spirits dwell? What impact do they have on the living?

5. Johnson Oatman, Jr., son of Johnson and Rachel Ann Oatman, was born near Medford, N. J., April 21, 1856

5. The spirit of Elijah and the power of Elijah shall be poured upon us in the last days. Does Elijah have a spirit. What does it mean that the spirit can work without the body of Elijah?

6. The man touched the bones of Elisha...was it the Holy Spirit or the spirit of Elisha that touched the man to life? When he asked for the double portion of the spirit of Elijah, what was he asking for? Ezekiel 37. Dry bones hear the word of the Lord. Can bones hear? This spirit that came upon them like a wind, what spirit is that? Where did it come from? What is the spirit?

7. Moses in Numbers 11:17 the bible says the spirit of Moses was put into the 70 elders, what spirit is this?

8. Lazarus come forth, as Jesus calls him to life, *Talita* comes at the resurrection of the small girl, can a dead person hear the voice of the physical except through the spirit?

9. Those people who woke up in Mathew 28, at the death of Jesus, who are they? Where did they go after the weekend?

10. Is it possible that there is a world of the spirit that the human beings are ignorant of? Why does a walk in the graveyard raise your hair at the back? Is the human body able to pick up on spiritual signals?

11. Jesus stops the show.

1 Pet. 3:18-20

18 "For Christ also died for our sins once and for all, the just for the unjust, in order that He might bring us to God, having been put to death in the flesh, but made alive in the spirit; **19** in which also He went and made proclamation to the spirits now in prison, **20** who once were disobedient, when the patience of God kept waiting in the days of Noah, during the construction of the ark, in which a few, that is, eight persons, were brought safely through the water."

1. If the dead know nothing, how did Jesus work with the spirits while he was dead?

2. How did he travel to the prison where the spirits are in his death?

3. Is there consciousness in death that is spirit?

4. Did Jesus preach to demons? OR THE PEOPLE who died before the flood? Where are they and in what condition did he find them and leave them? When he wakes up he says "I have the keys."

5.   Where did He find the keys? What does it mean "He has the keys", what are the advantages when one has those keys?

6.   Did he preach to dead people, if yes? In what condition are those spirits that he ministered to?

7.   If the dead know nothing how did Jesus know where to go? When He returns that the dead shall hear his voice. Can the dead hear? What hears their flesh of their spirit? In the condition of death what is the condition of the human spirit? Which spirit returns to the one who made it? Is it possible that there is a spiritual template for every individual that is like a spiritual fingerprint, which will be given a new body? What is a spiritual person?

8.   Did Jesus tell about his trip to hell after his resurrection or it is Peter's imagination or tradition? If this is true we have a problem, if this is false we have a problem with the veracity of the bible. If it is true, then the state of the dead and spirit must be studied afresh and the position of many churches is at risk.

THE SANGOMA'S STORY BY MELANIE REEDER (BOOK REVIEW)

The calling and practice of Elliot Ndlovu "*are you called into your function*" The purpose of this section is to understand what and how they do their services and get immediate results.

This section seeks to challenge and compare the life of a *saNgoma* to a life of a worshipper and draw parallels. May the Lord lead you as you explore the wide divide in worship how they call on their lord and how we also call upon our God.

What goes into the preparation of worship?

How do you keep in touch with your object of worship?

What is the attitude of a worshipper?

What evokes God to draw near to the place of worship? An open mind is necessary as we review this book of a life of a SaNgoma.

THE LIFE OF ELLIOT NDLOVU

Starts with a "calling", a path to the spiritual realm. This call will not go until he answers it. It caused him great distress and sickness for years.

The voice comes from wise spiritual guides not idols to be worshipped as portrayed by white missionaries settlers.[6]

A. Every worshipper must accept the calling to worship

    i.   Then he had to *twasa* the initiation and subjects the body to a ritual that made him a channel of the spirit. The ultimate goal is to make his body a spiritual temple, and part of daily living. *Take time to undergo training: the battle lines are not for the amateurs, the enemy is well trained while you are sleeping they are sharpening their skills*

    ii.   Training under water with manifestations of apparitions, to familiarize him to the spiritual realm of absurd occurrences. "Water is a place where the physical and the spiritual worlds mingle in both San and Zulu belief.

    iii.   A place of suspension and limbo where the concrete can become fluid and spiritual become manifest. Here in the water the physical body is kept while the spiritual body speaks with the spirit of his ancestors to receive training."[7]

    iv.   The initiate is under the full drive of the *inkanyamba* while undergoing the training.

B. The initiate is flooded with visions, dreams of the supernatural that show him the land of the ancestors, with strange animals that prepare him for a lifetime of interaction with this world.

C. Get to the waters and be baptized, confess your sins and let the old self-die, come out in the newness of life. They also spent time under the water, but you through baptism you receive the power from on high to become a child of the kingdom.

    i.   Change of name, identity from Elliot to Maluleke, a counselor and teacher of others.

D. Let there be a change of name, from the old self to the new self. When Jehovah meets people for a mission he changes their names, for in the name is your mission and destiny. What is your name?

    i.   The *saNgoma* must collect his tool, from dressings, '**ishoba lenkonkoni'**, and bones that he will use in his practice.

---

6. Melanie Reeder, a Sangoma's story (Elliot Ndlovu) 2011, page 11
7. Melanie Reeder, a Sangoma's story (Elliot Ndlovu) 2011, page xxv

    ii.   These are specifically sacred to him as they are set-aside for this purpose.

E. **Identify your tools for work and let them be sacred to you. Consecrate your instruments for the use in the service of the Lord. Dedicate your tools into the work of the gospel. Master your function and polish your skills also, do not offer to the Lord a lame worship with poor playing and mediocrity.**

    i.   A complete intertwined and joined life between the physical and the spiritual into one unit where the spirit of the ancestors is now fully in residents in the life of Maluleke to speak to him and him to speak to them at will.

    ii.   All he needs to do is burn his incense and the conversation begins. Which he then uses for consultation and seeing things ahead of schedule and deal with present issues of clients.

    iii.   The ancestral choices override his personal choices.[8] The ancestors cannot leave his side henceforth, they sit on his shoulders speaking to him all the time. There is no retirement from this, "my body has two lives"[9] Elliot's body was prepared to hear the ancestors talk as they relate messages on the client as he was connected to the spiritual realm.[10]

F. **Move beyond the normal; surrender yourself fully to the indwelling of the Holy Spirit. Do not be afraid to give the Holy Spirit full control over your body and faculties. Let your life die and the spirit is at work. Total occupation: if this service will reach someone and you will work beyond the ordinary, let there be a total surrender of the worshipper to His Worship the Lord of Host until your speech and activities are driven from inside and the Lord is the driver of your activities and life.**

    i.   Ability to perform rainmaking skills, driving evil spirits (very funny that Christianity call them evil spirits, but in their world there are also evil spirits that cause destruction, but the *saNgoma* is under an influence of a good spirit that heals and brings good will to the family and community).

    ii.   The spirits must not be feared by the modern African: the

---

8. Melanie Reeder, a Sangoma's story (Elliot Ndlovu) 2011, page xix
9. Ibid, xxix
10. Ibid, 108

Inkanyamba means that ancestors are near by, then how can the African be afraid of his past? "People must be treated holistically, believing the physical body is not separate from the mind and spirit, a troubled soul can manifest physical illness, both of which need to be treated."[11]

iii.   The *saNgoma* needs to know how to do services and why these services are done. The elements of nature, water, wind, fire, and earth could be manipulated to articulate many things.[12]

G.   You are a healer with song, take it to a hospital of sinners; treat not the symptoms but the root cause. Treat people holistically, from physical to mental to emotional let the service reach the entire person. Be clear to the functions and purpose of elements that you build into the service.

i.   The cleansing of the physical and spiritual channels constantly to keep the path of the spirit clear from obstacles.

ii.   The healer must keep purity of innocence or his medicines will be infected with bad spirit. Anger and bitter roots of the hearts are not conducive for the healer.

iii.   It is not the herbs that heal only, but the power of the ancestors that is in the herbs, the healer uses his hands but the spirit in him fuses with his harvests, mixes and gives the medicine and advises.

iv.   In this lifestyle the *saNgoma* must learn fast to discipline the pure spirit and renew the sense of spirituality.

Elliot had to learn to sit silently, find those moments of being still for hours.

When you are alone, when you have time to contemplate.

Be still, take a simple clay ball in your hands, caress it let it warm slowly to you... think of your planet."[13]

Type of foods to eat (fruits and vegetables) so that we feel the life of the plants inside us. Keep a song in the heart and dance while collecting herbs so that energy is shared.

Then to live in the indescribable sense of "knowing."[14]

Living in constant awareness, to live in the know, do all things with knowledge and room for careless behavior and words. Sober up and keep

---

11. Ibid, 53
12. Ibid, 68
13. Ibid, 180
14. Ibid54

the mind and spirit together. This is a rebirth of the mind as Elliot calls it.

Note that the "physical body and mind need to be emptied of all super-fluity of ordinary life before it could be refilled with the other, more sacred knowledge"[15]

Take time out to refresh from duty and be with nature and refurbish your conscience and clean up the channels of communication between you and your Creator. Watch your diet and keep a song in your heart.

The *saNgoma* must watch the movements in the physical sphere as signs and wonders follow, snakes, rainbows, animals' and nature move to confirm the disapproval of the ritual, *"nature reflects the state of the spiritual guides, animals as representatives of the ancestors and their moods."*[16]

Be sensitive to the movement of the spirit, in nature, in your house and in the worship service. Be alert and flexible to listen to the change of direction should the Holy Spirit see it fit.

It is important to stay alert even during instructions for the evil spirit can interfere, and the spirits also argue among themselves; patiently wait until their voice merge as one.[17]

The voice of conscience must be kept very alert to distinguish spirits.

Lineage must be clear to function and operate. One must be clear when calling names to plug into the right spirit. The spirits (*amadlozi*) are called into space, they are invited into operation, and they are provoked and evoked to draw closer to the *saNgoma*.

Know your story, from your genealogy, have confidence, know who you worship, research the names and His acts so that you can address Him in knowledge and pride. Call on the right name for the right effect and application. At times of war call on the God of War, the One who provides, heals and forgives etc.

"Self-awareness is not self-centeredness, and spirituality is not narcissism. 'Knowing thyself is not a narcissistic pursuit." Marianne Williamson

   o In life the *saNgoma* must respect the abundance of nature, as there is a symbiotic relationship between the healer and the plants. Plants are living and sensitive, they have their own energy that demands to be collected at certain times and seasons for them to work effec-

15. Ibid 58
16. Ibid, 41
17. Ibid 51

tively. Other plants if touched by contaminated people, they lose their strength hence the use of innocent boys and girls to harvest and prepare these herbs to keep their potency. Intuition must be developed to a high level until Elliot would feel the plant as his own life and be aware of the feelings of the plants.

o **Be a friend of nature and find your worship in the midst of nature and listen to other creatures in worship. True inspiration is found when you are in harmony with nature. Record sounds of nature and sing, praise and create music and worship in the midst of nature, tap into the energy of the plants, animals, birds and the movements of clouds, thunder, waves and the wind.**

o There is a song nature sings, put your voice into the universe and let the symphony continue. You are not alone at the moment of worship.

o **The *saNgoma* is a sentinel in an area and he must keep the area away from evil spirit. Occupy the space on behalf of the spiritual community, the mountains and rivers are to be kept in harmony, one cannot afford to have a haphazard life.**

o Secure your territory for worship, come to your sanctuary, temple, church, house and make an altar for worship. Own that place, come here often, early before anybody else and call on the name of the Lord.

o **Cleanse the house for worship, pray for the benches, chairs and shout into the atmosphere as you prepare for worship. Be a sentinel of praise at your post of duty. Create expectation ahead of program, when it happens you must be aware of what you requested.**

o Gratitude forms a very important part of the saNgoma's life. When he receives and is blessed or shown secrets of muti or events, there is need to openly express gratitude, animal sacrifice, offerings or silver coins. These should be done before and after, to welcome or bid farewell, above all the life of a saNgoma is a grateful life.

You cannot come into the house of worship with nothing in your hands. Bring your offering in all its forms.

The attitude of your life must be that of gratitude, carry a song of praise all the time and be a friend of your calling.

Let the worship in your heart never cease to be heard.

Keep your heart in tune with an offering of praise. Worship is an expression of what happens to you all the time. The moment of worship is but an extension of familiar territory.

The Ancestors are not spirits to be worshiped but guides whose opinions and advises are to be respected, it is not true therefore that Africans worship ancestors, but seek for the path that leads them to the creator and solutions to life's challenges, be it misfortune disease and national distress.

Unkulunkulu (God) "controls the bigger picture and has power to throw away all ancestors and all traditional entities…the ancestors are not a religion but part of an extended home."[18]

Mankind is not a lot (it is not good for man to be alone). The senses function at such a level that Elliot can sense the presence of a foreign spirit or other entities.

Have a guide in your worship, "The old prophets would say the angel whom I had spoken to" do you notice a familiar relationship between the prophet and his guide? Often we talk to the air with little clue of impact.

The call is that we become clear to our escort on high places. In the spiritual realm there must be connectivity.

Most religions have names of guides into the supernatural, except that we speak to what we don't know. In the royal house, there is someone who introduces you to the king.

We have come into the presence of God together with thousands of angels in holy convocation. Worship is never alone; join the friends in high places. [19]

Jealousy is another form of witchcraft; it can attract *isinyama* (bad luck).

The love of money was "making people lose their connectivity to older ways of living.

Excess wealth was driving people further and further from the land, from the simple life of fulfilling needs instead of desires."

"Wealth, sciences and technology were distracting many of his clients from the essence of their spirituality and humanity. Modernity was affecting the purity and power of nature and old cultural beliefs were being lost in the process."[20]

---

18. Ibid, 67
19. Hebrews 12 You have come
20. Ibid, 123 & 143

SPIRIT VERSUS THE FLESH (SPIRITUALITY VERSUS CHRISTIANITY)

We must develop spiritual tools to fight spiritual battles. It is not a physical battle but a spiritual one. If you can see it then it's not your enemy.

The battle is what you cannot see. It's not who stole your car, rather who is with the one who stole your car. "For we are not fighting against flesh and blood enemies, but against evil rulers and authorities of the unseen world, against powers in this dark world, and against evil spirits in the heavenly places."[21]

If people fear the Holy Spirit they lose the unseen battle. The spiritual person must fight the spiritual battle not the physical. Surrender your spirit to the spirit. Be possessed with the Holy Spirit, if not full of Him you will be full of demons.

You can't fight an address, a person, or a church, but fear that which is within them! To fear the unknown is to surrender to the spirit. That is the reason in church and during worship people don't want the Holy Spirit, because if it appears we may lose control. So yes, religion is there to control people, not to set them free in the spirit. Churches don't want spiritual people, they are ungovernable.

The system produces slaves, the spirit produces freedom. "You can have religion with spirituality. You can also have religion without spirituality." [22]

The life in the spirit then becomes the reality of all human desire to live above the physical and reach the spiritual with physical acts that evoke spiritual responses. As the saints would cry out:

"Lord, make me an instrument of thy peace. Where there is hatred, let me sow love. Where there is injury, pardon. Where there is doubt, faith. Where there is despair, hope. Where there is darkness, light. And where there is sadness, joy.
O Divine Master, grant that I may not so much seek. To be consoled as to console, To be understood as to understand. To be loved, as to love. For it is in giving that we receive, It is in pardoning that we are pardoned, And it is in dying that we are born to eternal life." [23]

Yes there are demons. And yes there is the Holy Spirit. Our fear of demons has built in fear for angels, fear for the devil has built fear of the Messiah, resulting in physical Christians and not spiritual Christians.

---

21. Eph 6:12
22. Eckhart Tolle
23. Francis of Assisi

The difference of the two is the spirit that drives them and their ability to see beyond the events to spiritual manifestations. People don't want to be possessed (they fear to lose control and be called names) or driven by the Spirit if you are not possessed with God you are fully possessed by demons."It is not good for man to be alone" we need divine company.

1. The emptiness in our hearts will not be filled with material
2. Decisions must be made from the spiritual internal chamber in consultation with the Holy Spirit.
3. The flesh must be subject to the Spirit, not the Spirit subject to the flesh
4. Living in the flesh does not please God but enmity to Him
5. The human being must develop spiritual sensitivity to be able to function within the two spheres and understand physical participation as a servant of spiritual agreements.
6. The scriptures call us to be spiritual not Christian. Buildings are for us. Our hearts are for the Lord. We cannot lock Yhwh in a building.
7. Those who worship YHWH who is Spirit must be Spirit and in the Spirit. There is no condemnation for those who are in the Spirit.

What Spirit drives you?

When you get angry when you see people worshiping ...what Spirit drives you? Marry and Elizabeth met and so did their children. In their bellies greeted each other in the Spirit - the same Spirit. Sense each other to connect with like Spirit. If I offended you today, it is clear, the Spirit in me and the Spirit in you are not the same.

What Spirit drives you?

If not possessed by God then who must possess us?

The breaking point is to fully function at the higher level away from the flesh - run the flesh from the Spirit. Control the lower from the upper.

Conversations of the internal person must guide the activities of the hand on the outside. Inside out.

"Enlightened leadership is spiritual if we understand spirituality not as some kind of religious dogma or ideology but as the domain of awareness where we experience values like truth, goodness, beauty, love and compassion, and also intuition, creativity, insight and focused attention. Spirituality is meant to take us beyond our tribal identity into a domain of awareness that is more universal."

THE WORSHIP EXPERIENCE

Earthen vessels must worship in Psalms and tap into divine power. That moment of connection plugs into the veins of grace and causes movement in the heavenly places and impacts on the lower realms. Psalms are an invocation of the supernatural to inhabit the natural. The sinner is in season when they have washed and cleaned themselves for the moment.

The word is read and the mind is prepared, then prayer begins. There is a presence of God that immediately descends to cover the sinner, transforming them to saints. With a song, a prayer and supplication, access can be granted into the inner chamber where God personally addresses the issues of life.

The heart is moved to know and feel that God has forgiven and that a sinner is not condemned but loved and cared for. The spirit man begins to open to the Spirit of God which "confirms within our hearts that we are the son and daughters of God." This is the same Spirit that resurrected Jesus from the dead it begins to work with the heart.

True worship is an activity and takes no observers and spectators. There are times when one can experience a lifting of the inner man and the soul begins to float into the very presence of God, depending on the season, the sinful man may be thrown into a deep state of sorrow over the sins and the past lived away from obedience. The environment slowly has more of God and less of the one praying, and time cannot be measured as the soul of man begins to seek for the face of God.

At times it's a mixture of pain and laughter, happiness and sorrow. Almost like an out of body experience, like you want to fly away and float into the higher grounds, the attraction is upwards.

Keep the ears open as the Lord begins to impress different messages into your Spirit. Some may become teary with a sense of fragility at times may even cry. "The new spirituality is that it will produce an experience in human encounters in which we become a living demonstration of the basic spiritual teaching.'We are all one.' [24]

It is a supernatural encounter, a meeting and a lifting by the Spirit of truth to the level that new Intel and information can be downloaded into your Spirit. When the sinner has prepared himself enough there is no doubt that God comes down, He has no option but to occupy where He has been evoked and called upon.

24. Neale Donald Walsch

The Lord inhabits the praise of His people. Its sacred ground enters with thanksgiving.

'AfriKan' Theological Perspective

Then we start to talk of natural theology and western theology. "Whatever the Western theology may have taken up and represented as in this way as "natural theology, it was never "natural" and was neither "universally human" nor "immediate".

On a closer inspection "natural theology" always contained knowledge historically mediated from particular intellectual traditions – from the Stoa, from the Plato and Aristotle etc. The common sense which was appealed to always proves to be a common sense that has developed in the history and bears a Western stamp." [25]

It is an insult to sit in the west and discuss and write even pass doctrines on the indigenous without an accurate inculturated and contextual comprehension. Learning is the beginning of wealth. Learning is the beginning of health.

"Learning is the beginning of spirituality. Searching and learning is where the miracle process all begins. "[26]

A glance into the Zulu culture will show the gap of relevance when the west interprets local norms and traditions. There is a vast difference between **"iSaNgoma"** a traditional healer and medium that connects people to familiar spirits. **"Nomtakati"** an upright witch who uses these spirit to destroy and kill people.

The Zulu culture has a **(SA) NGOMA** "healer" – this is a medium spirit. Note the word **NGOMA**, is the same in *Shona* for drum, and song. Therefore, the saNgoma *is* a connector with song. Every worship leader must be a *twasa* full possessed by the spirit to cause the worshippers to connect with the Creator.

In the etymology of the saNgoma is entwined the understanding of how this person operates and there is depth of understanding as to the function of the song in the ceremonies that he/she conducts.

When we come to the churches, we tend to miss this understanding. We have created a pseudo experience when in fact worship must be a spiritual connection rather than a mere physical interaction of the saints.

25 Jargen Moltann, Theology of Hope, Fortress Press, 1993, pp 90
26 Jim Rohn

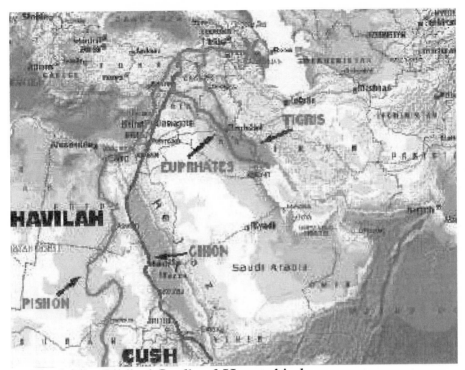

Fig 5: The Biblical Cradle of Humankind.

The people being led in a song have a right to ask where do you want us to go? Music is a tool in the hand of the worshipper to drive people to this realm of solutions and spiritual freedom.

"All people, all over the world, throughout history have shared in common the fact that they belong to a culture of origin. That is a universal reality. Another equally important universal reality is that there are many, many different cultures in the world and each of them is unique."

"The uniqueness of a culture is what gives specialness to its members. The members of a culture are bonded together by their shared culture, which gives them a sense of collective identity."

"We are an Afrikan people," simply reveals that there are values, traditions and a heritage that we share because we have a common origin. The cultural process is naturally ongoing, which allows people to continuously affirm their connectedness through being linked to their origins." However, the continuity of our cultural identity has been interrupted cruelly and unnaturally by the experience of slavery.

We as a people are still suffering from this crime because we have not been allowed to find our way back to the sense of cultural identity and continuity, which would transform us into a unified and whole people.

We have not been able to function in the world with a collective consciousness that naturally imparts a strong sense of cultural roots.

The term "Maafa" (from the book, "Let The Circle Be Unbroken) is a Kiswahili word for "disaster" that we are now using to reclaim our right to tell our own story.

Maafa refers to the enslavement of our people and to the sustained attempt to dehumanize us. Because the Maafa has disconnected us from our cultural origins, we have remained vulnerable in a social order that does not reflect our cultural identity.

We are people of African ancestry living in denial of who we are. We have lost our strength as a people. We are losing our children to systems, which mis-educates them. Our families are disintegrating before our eyes.

Our numbers are growing in the statistics of drug addiction and incarceration.

Responsible national Black organizations are seeking remedies to these problems, but we are not speaking with one voice.

We need to work together as a family who supports its members and responsible for their welfare. We must use the most valuable asset we have - the spirit of our people. It is that spirit that connects us to our Afrikan roots.

Slowly, we are awakening to the need to claim our cultural legacy.

The term "Sankofa" from Akan tradition in Ghana, West Africa tells us to return to the source so that we can go forward with strength and clarity. Culture is a powerful tool for inspiring human beings and bringing them together in a concerted "family" action.

Our cultural roots are the most ancient in the world. The spiritual concepts of our Ancestors gave birth to religious thought. African people believe in the oneness of the African family through sacred time, which unites the past, the present and the future. Our Ancestors live with us.

They created the first civilizations thousands of years ago and they suffered the pain of the Maafa. And yet, they were able to endure the most disastrous and dehumanizing circumstances ever perpetrated against a group of people, only because of the power of the African spirit.

They did not have the freedom to affirm their cultural heritage. We now have that choice.

In the African view of life it is our responsibility to honor their name.

This is perhaps our moment of truth.

We must come together as a family. We must do all that we can do to uplift our people. Otherwise, we are still denying who we are and bringing dishonor to our "family name;" to our Ancestors.

The answer to our social dilemma is the re-socialization of our people into the cultural value-system that affirms our spiritual being. Our Ancestors are calling us "home", back to our cultural selves. We must begin the process of Sankofa." [27]

Sankofa: Akan people of Ghana speak *Twi*, the word means to "Go back and get it" (*san* - to return-look back, reflect; *ko* - to go, intentional movement to a point of advantage*; fa* - to fetch, collect and hold, to seek and take) and also refers to the *Asante*. It also has an *Adinkra* symbol of a bird taking an egg off its back. The expression is utilizing the indigenous knowledge of the past and dealing with present problems using ancient solutions. Going forward while looking backwards.

DOES THE AFRICAN UNDERSTAND THAT THEY ARE EDENITES?

A. Genesis being in Africa : the four rivers mentioned

Civilization Nquaq

B. Etimology (names of days of the week: knowledge of creation)

You will not teach a nation about God as if they did not know him. In the *Shona* language as in many other African languages it is very interesting to note some basic linguistic issues like on the days of the week.

Svondo - Sunday - week

Muvhuro - Monday - day to open

Chipiri - Tuesday - day to offer (kupira)

Chitatu -Wednesday - third day

China-chisi -Thursday - day of the king

Chishanu-gadziriro - Friday - day of preparation

Mugovera - Sabata (us-Sabata) Saturday - day of sharing a not touching work

---

27. Dr. Marimba Any, To Be Afrikan: February 26, 1999 Copyright (c) 1999 Dr. Marimba Ani. All Rights Reserved. Dr. Marimba Ani, an activist in the African Liberation Movement, worked as field-organizer for the Student Nonviolent Committee (SNCC) in Mississippi in the 60s. She has continued her activism through her scholarship. She has created African-centered theoretical concepts that have assisted in the developing of an African Cultural Science. At this time, she is actively involved in retrieving philosophy and in the re-creation of ritual, so that they can be used for the transformation and healing of people of African descent. Currently, Dr. Ani teaches in the Black and Puerto Rican Studies Department of Hunter College in New York. She is credited with writing the scholarly works "Let The Circle Be Unbroken" and "Yurugu: An African-centered Critique of European Cultural Thought and Behavior," as well as articles that have appeared in scholarly journals.

Need we to emphasize the Hebraic element on the *Shona* theology of the week. Though elements have been lost in the history but it is visible that the nation knew about the creation and worship of the true YHWH a monotheistic deity as taught by the scriptures.

C. Hebraic names of God and African names: the African Hebraic Approach

One of the most upheld idea was that and is popularly taught to us over and over is the "myth" that Africans were void of the direct, and true "worship" of God, in the sense that white people are to be perceived as "them" who introduced us to the true worship of "God" through *"Missiology".*

This view has created a serious irreconcilable attitude of "politicians toward Christian scriptures, however there are clear evidences at the brink of the verge namely to black African genetic authenticated original locations. Most of the instructions given by God through Mosses for social control in the book of Leviticus possess the very same internal and inseparable exact fiber with the African.

Social control prior to a written document in our brief examination we will trace norms, and maxims of the Hebraic orient and encapsulate them in the African perspective not forcefully, but as belonging demands. So are the inseparable proceedings of this *"notion".*

Africanism primitively subscribes to the dynamic "Element" of "God" unlike western static views of "God", Africanism especially in my Xhosa culture, it is still popularly upholding as it was in the absence of a "white" man's instructions such as "do not point haphazardly your finger up, because there is (*UQamata*) up there".

All these are "Torah" roots, now (*UQamata*) is from the root 'qa' from words like 'qala' meaning 'begin' the 'm' there supposedly functions as an 'infix' signifying a 'present' state, 'ta' is from words 'like 'Tata'. The idea is that of the 'father', who knew the end from the beginning, the effects of this perception seriously affects all tenses. God, by His presence was known fully in the African context to be the 'affecter' of all tenses not in description format, yet in the functional mode.

Qamata is from the root word *(qa)* having the idea of 'begin, the infix of this word is the 'm' carrying the idea of presents '*ta*' from '*tata*' (father, source of all life) it further means, power and shelter, knowledge of the end beginning.

Tata speaks to the softer side of God, the call of young child to the stronger parent. As contrasted to *Baba*-meaning father. *Tata* is almost a feminine, caring, persuasive warm hand of a parent. Qamata in its phonetic value is pronounced by connecting the tongue to the roof of front teeth, so the observation of this Name is prescribed by the attribute carried by this Name.

First Name that which was popularly embraced in the African black eyes Namely in the 'Xhosa' perspective is *(Qamata)*. In our brief examination we will clearly reveal that Hebraic perspectives and views are foreign to our Western "static thinking".

Hebrew shares its entire fiber with "Africanism", Egyptological notions pretty much confirms that the anthropological "DNA" of the Africans and the ancient Hebrews possessed the same internal (insuline) hence in most of our cultures we seem to be "zealous" to Judaic and Hebraic norms, e.g. circumcision.

In the African cultures, *Xhosas* are the extreme upholders of "circumcision", that which now pretty much relates them to one of the sector of the zealots in the Sanhedrin denomination.

The Name *(Qamata)* is the very same Name *(Yhwh)* and this can be reconciled both in their internal Testimonies, we will carefully examine these Names just to understand fully their internal inseparable fiber in the African perspective.

This Name possesses no difference in relation to the Hebrew Name 'Yahweh'. I mean in the perception of both audiences, Xhosa history records a, number of 'miracles' and 'wonders,' that took place at the provocation of this Name. '*UQamata*' for example, the most popular amongst all, is the humble request of 'rain.' Xhosa people in their early developing communities, if it happens that there is a drought or there is no 'rain' to revive the face of the 'earth', they will set a specific tomorrow in the sense that they will meet with '*UQamata*' to submit their request.

Before this event they had to prepare themselves by washing all their blankets, clothes, and clean their houses properly, and those who were perverted were summoned, and be told to withdraw themselves from evil at the particular moment till '*UQamata*' grants them 'rain'.

Note, white people were not yet occurred. This is prior before the birth of *(nongqawuse)*, who was popularly accused of 'classifying' white people as *(obawo abakhulu, basemanzini)*.

Black people respect the waters, and they believe that there are people therein, since they knew no boats at all. To them seeing white people on boats right in the centers of the waters, *Xhosa Nongqawuse* observed this until she conclusively perceived them as *OBAWO MKHULU*.

This is an old mega deception of "whites" to "blacks". An untold or rather an unrecorded history of a Xhosa man called *"Tsikane".* This man is dated back to as the "black" prophet," before white people put their foot on Southern Africa. *Tsikane* said during his prophecies, he even foreseen, whites' colonial attitude towards blacks in their own native lands. "There is a certain tribe coming from afar, over the seas with hairs likened to that of a maize during its ripen state, they are coming with two things which are the Bible and money."

Tsikane summoned two boys to pour on the ground 20-litre gallons of water. After they were done he requested them again to return the very water they have poured on the ground back into the drum. A simple reply was "we cannot". Then he further said "from the time you've fully developed the love for money, you will be like water, poured on the ground at the impossibility of a return." He was interviewed later, note [*Tsikane*] was powerful and was an entertaining Xhosa dancer.

His face was always arrayed with a substance called [imbola] in Xhosa, after the interview he clearly stated clearly that he had seen *"Qamata"*, in his dreams and visions.

After all he said "I went straight to the waters, to wash this substance called {imbola}, and serve '*UQamata*.' Xhosa history records other things prophesied by *Tsikane* that took place systematically as predicted."

This piece of evidence that which is enough to validate the fact that a whiteman did speak about God to a black man. Africans already knew God before the arrival of Christianity.

The beautiful fact states that everything begun in Africa. Not forgetting to mention that white people indeed talk to blacks about Jesus, whereas blacks already have a black conscious of godly practices, which were later discouraged and classified as evil.

There is clear evidence, short historical traditions of the washing of clothes, blankets and spring cleaning of their houses before ascending the mount for their request of rain, this internally connects with no doubt to Exodus 19:10

Then God said to Moses, "go to the people and consecrate them today and tomorrow, and let them wash their garments, and let them to be ready for the third day, for the Lord will come down, on Mount Sinai". Wow! I don't remember a whiteman telling these folks to consecrate themselves before meeting U*Qamata*.

CIRCUMCISION IN ITS ORIGINALITY

Circumcision is noted to be holding three sections in the sociological acceptable norms, and the popularly upheld one in the postmodern world which is specifically catered for as the attendance of the health section. It is the idea of hygiene and this idea connotes the perception that which appears to be defending, or preventing sexually transmitted diseases, so in this noted section, circumcision is only in the attendance which is designed only for hygiene issues.

The Second notion is the Xhosa people's passion to uphold the culture and practice of circumcision. In the Xhosa context, this ceremony is depicted as an initiation from being a 'boy' to 'manhood'. In the process of this initiation you have to prove yourself a man, by enduring and obeying the assigned procedures and protocols.

After this process you are now accepted as a man distinguished from the 'boys', in this case boys are attributed to 'chaos' while a circumcised man is presupposed to connote order.

This perspective perfectly relates to the same main objectives in the Hebrew orient. It clearly portrays also that the internal Testimony of this ceremony, that which is of the same in both parties by connoting the *separating idea* between the two *elements* which are order and chaos, the idea of the ceremony of circumcision in relation to the commandments is the fact that circumcision separated those who keep the commandments of *Elohiym*.

To those who did not bother themselves to keep them anyway. Now imagine where there are no instructions and no doubt, chaos envelopes the scene.

Let's references our claims on a biblical premise, there is a usage of certain biblical numerals in this ceremony prior to so called white provided document to this account in relation to *'Africanism'* such as seven days, or three days, foundations prior to circumcision properly and spot on in linking Ancient Hebrews to "Africans".

In Genesis 34, after the sister of the "twelve tribes of Israel" was raped in Shechem, by Shechem. After all this drama, Shechem was pleased by this woman up to a point of offering a request for marriage. We have to be very clear, he was sexually pleased with her, and this was picked up by Simon and Levi hence their anger, which was kindled to a point of destroying the whole town of Shechem.

During their journey of circumcision. On the third day, that is where an uproar of anger of these two Hebrew men occurred. The request of circumcision by Simon and Levi connotes the *Xhosa's* zealous passion about this ceremony. So these two men say in the Xhosa ears "*udadethu akanaku-zalela amakwenke angolukanga'.*" On the third day that is when they were killed, so the Hebrew men knew the third day in the context of Circumcision.

In Xhosa culture the third day is generally entitled in the Xhosa context of circumcision as "*ZIYAWHAWAH*" - meaning, that is when pain of circumcision is felt.

While in this state your mind also becomes unstable, imagine you don't have water to drink, or eat only dry food, for the recovery that honors the seventh day as connoting a complete recovery of order to the one circumcised.

The two Hebrew men knew that they were thirsty, hungry and weak. This situation, proceeding to the seventh day is called in Xhosa "*EFUKWNI umkkwetha*" (in a helpless state). Have you noted the connection? Where was a "white" man when all these astounding facts were written?

1. There is a season when these take place (June and December).
2. Cut your clothes, tear your clothes, I die.
3. Sit you down and shave your head and cover you with a red and white blanket at the homestead and you than remain naked and water is poured on you - all hair must be removed.
4. Take you to the mountain, led to the mountain only by the adults
5. Men will surround and sit next to a temporal tent and the spear will come.
6. Then you are circumcised, grab put and cut!
7. Then you must say "I am a man" (live by your word, stand for your word) .
8. Drain the blood out of your wound.
9. They bring dishwater after that '*isicwe*' is applied ku bless
10. The first witness is paper '*shwati*', it is the first covering.

11. Tie the penis, lessen up and tie, every 10 minutes under the proverb that says *"isilonda siphila ngo thunukwa"*, meaning a wound heals when it is frequently touched.

12. On the 3rd day, there is a step '*ziyawhawha*': pain is at its peek, your mind is unstable, you become weak and frail and you are in a state of not eating, drinking (fasting) and not getting out of the temporal shelter, this nuance is called '*eFukwini*'

13. On the last day, which is the 7th day, you are now a man '*Umojiso*', you are requested to sit down, for the elders watch you while you tie yourself without help.

14. And you are given 5 litres of *Umqomboti* (traditional beer), and a sheep is slaughtered as part of the festivities.

15. The first meal is in preparation of the bigger celebration for your home coming as a 'man'. From then on you are accepted as a man amongst men. It is then said, in Xhosa *"uyimele into yakhe"* - meaning "he stood firm for his thing" and is therefore worthy to be called a man.[28]

A quick scan on the continent will show us that the African knew the Creator and even describes Him and His acts with a clear understanding of his attributes and character. If one takes these names and carefully puts them side by side, one will see a thread that Africans have a holistic function of YHWH more clearer than Europeans.

The attributes of YHWH are clearly articulated as described by the names of God in **table 1.1** diagram in the following pages, which makes it clear that you cannot introduce to an African the God he already knows.

Europeans are pagans, we are Hebrews, the text and language says "we knew Him before you spoke about Him."

There are many arguments for the *Yahwistic* knowledge to Africans prior to colonialism. The linguistic argument pleads that Africans have names of YHWH worship and praise.

Let me put it on record, Africans don't worship ancestors, but consult them as conduits to YHWH genealogy, it is used for access to the creation story. Oral tradition traces worship to the source.

There is no African religion that teaches that ancestors created us.

---

28. Coversations with Thembile Ephrat Dyanti : 2016, Johannesburg, on the history and customs of the Xhosa tribes. The sacred ceremonies have a striking resemblance to the Hebraic practices. And if we go in to seek for meaning we will learn the power of history, which connects us.

Monotheism is as old with Africans as our soil. The deities and Trinitarian doctrines are foreign to African theological indignity. For the modern gospel is dual in nature, divided between secular and religious. Forcing us to be Schizophrenic. Christianity struggles to be relevant in daily living by isolating worship to times and places, it misses the opportunity to be experienced on a daily life, ultimately this fake western world-view makes its proponents manifest split personalities.

On the same account in the African culture, life is a continuous expression of spiritual connections. Whether we eat, drink, sleep, die, plant or harvest all of life is a spiritual expression. Let me state that spirituality is lived not taught. In the mind of the African, life is connected with an invisible code, the supernatural is expressed in the natural. Thus theology needs to contextually appreciate the African world-view and not judge our theology with arrogance of western ignorance.

The African is biblical and Hebraic.

These names must make their way into the worship services. The word 'God' has no name but a simple appellation to recognition of the presence of the deity. The names in table 1.1 on the following page will show an experience with this God, who is He and what He has done?

In the true sense of systematic theology *God* has no name but deeds.

In the midst of what He does we know Him.

Einstein admits that "My religion consists of a humble admiration of the illimitable superior Spirit who reveals himself in the slight details we are able to perceive with our frail and feeble mind." - **Albert Einstein**

In looking at who this Spirit is or who God is, we can begin to see details of creation, and trace these elements in all of us. "The new physics provides a modern version of ancient spirituality. In a universe made out of energy, everything is entangled; everything is one." - **Bruce Lipton**

Africans believe The Supreme Creator who is all in all. The Supreme who created everything and causes all to be, He assumes this position because He Created and some of His names suggest that He lives among man and moves within man. He is connected to humans and controls all functions of nature. The African views the mediums and rituals with utter respect for they are the acceptable way to connect with the Creator.

There is no idea of lesser gods, but messengers who carry the message from the throne room. Each messenger has a territory, or dimension or realm that they operate in: Rain, Water, Winds, Fire, and Earth.

Compare this with Hebrew names you will not miss the footprint of YHWH on the continent.

COUNTRY	SOME NAMES FOR GOD
Angola	Kalunga, Nzambi, Suku
Botswana	Modimo, Urezhwa
Burundi	Imana
Cameroon	Njinyi, Nyooiy
Congo	Akongo, Arebati, Djakomba, Katshonde, Kmvoum, Leza, Nzambi
Cote D'Ivoire	Nyame, Onyankopon
Ghana	Bore-Bore, Dzemawon, Mawu, Nyame, Onyankopon
Ethiopia	Arumgimis, Igziabher, Magano, Tel, Yere, Yere Siezi
Kenya	Akuj, Asis, Mulungu, Mungu, Ngai, Nyasaye, Tororut
Liberia	Yala
Madagascar	Andriamanitra, Zanahary
Malawi	Cauta, Chiuta, Leza, Mulungu, Unkurukuru
Mozambique	Mulungu (this is problematic for the whiteman is called murungu) This name is adulterated for it has Christianity giving the White person the Same status with God making whites the Relative of God)
Namibia	Kalunga, Mukuru (in Shona it would mean the big One) Ndjambi, Karunga, Pamba (In Shona Pamba is the one who takes without permission)
Nigeria	Ondo, Chuku, Hinegba, Olodumare, Olorun, Osowo, Owo, Shoko (Interesting to note that the totems of the author are shoko Nigeria and Zimbabwe are connected)

Rwanda	Imana
Sierra Leone	Leve, Meketa, Ngewo, Yatta (in Chichewa Yatta the suggests The ending or Finished)
South Africa	Inkosi, (king) Khuzwane, Modimo, Molimo Mwari, Raluvhimba, Ukulunkulu, Utixo
Sudan	Ajok, Jok, Katonda, Kiibumba, Ori, Rugaga, Ruhanga, Wari (interesting name In Zimbabwe we have Mwari note "Wari" is roots. Are the people Of Zimbabwe and Sudan sharing etymological roots?)
Swaziland	Mvelincandi (the originator), Umkhulumncandi (the great originator)
Tanzania	Enkai, Ishwanga, Kyala, Kyala, Kyumbi, Mulungu, Mungo, Ruwa
Uganda	Akuj, Jok, Katonda, Kibumba, Ori, Rugaba, Ruhanga, Weri
Zambia	Chilenga, Chiuta, Lesa, Mulungu, Nyambe, Nzambi, Tilo
Zimbabwe	Mwari, Unkulunkulu, Nyadenga Musikavanhu, Zame

Diagram: Table 1.1

Human prayers can be answered if the right Priest helps the heart and the rituals are conducted. The Supreme Creator is usually referred to as 'Him', but when it comes to fertility the African has no problem to view 'Him' beyond sex. By the names He has no form and is by far unlimited.

The African believes that life emanates from him - therefore all living things that animate and inanimate possess within them the divine element. A few examples in the table would refresh your mind to the African God we now call 'Him',

In Ghana He is called *Nyame*, the Molder, Giver of Breath and Souls, God of Destiny, One Who Exists of Himself, God of Mercy and Comfort, the Inexplicable, Ancient of Days, the One Who Bends Even Kings, the One You Meet Everywhere, present in the breath of all life.

The *Lugbara* of Zaire and Uganda call Him *Adroa,* which depicts the Lord of the Skies, Deity on Earth, Creator God, River God, the cause of the River to flow. When drawn He is pictured as tall and white with only half of his body visible: to demonstrate that we can only see what He has done but can not put our mind and eyes around who He is. He is present but invisible, not fully understood.

We cannot go over, or under, or around Him. Call Him *Elohiym,*

The *Turkana* of Kenya call him *Akuj* - our Divination to whom all our social ills are cleansed. The restorer of good karma and aura almost suggests that He is our Priest through whom we are cleansed - call him Our Righteousness.

The *Ibo* of Nigeria will call Him *Ala, Anayaroli - Asa* feminizes Mother Nature, the one through whom all morality and well-being is preserved.

The Lord of the harvest and wealth. Call for prosperity.

Chineke *"The first great cause, the uncaused cause", "Creator",* Father of *Ale* - the Earth

South Central Africa (bushman) Kang they simply relate to Him as the Creator God, who shapes, shifts and molds. Chiuta Chuku Mulungu, Mwenco, Wamtatakuya Tumbuka. Creator God, Guinea Famian Rules Over - Protection, health, and fertility

Location: The *Banyarwands Imana Hategekimana, Hashakimana, Habyarimana, Ndagijimana, Bigirimana,* and *"Almighty God."*

Power, goodness, children, planning.

While in the Nile they call Him *Juok, Shilluk,* Supreme God. He created all men on Earth, The Volta call Him *Nyami.*

He brought souls to the Supreme God. The *Ganda* of East Africa, they call Him *Katonda, Lissoddene, Kagingo, Ssewannaku, Lugaba, Ssebintu, Nnyin-iggulu, Namuginga, Ssewaunaku, Gguluddene,* and *Namugereka.* Creator God.

Rules Over: Help, Judgment, aid when the odds are against you, control over spirits, divination, and oracles. Macouas of Zambesi, *Banayis* call Him *Mukuru* the mighty one, the Older one, the Supreme God, creator of everything, Agriculture, architecture, and the harvest. The *Giryama* of Kenya call Him *Mungo,* Rain God.

Masai of Kenya call him *Nenaunir,* The Rainbow Snake, an evil storm God who was linked to the rainbow. Resided in the clouds and was a dreaded spirit. The trauma of the flood never left the African and the rainbow is the great snake that is in the sky. He is the one who rules over the storms.

Nyambe...the one who restores life *Nyambi* creator of everything *Nyame Nyamia Ama*: the Lord in the storm and rain the one who causes it to fall.

The *Nago* and Yoruba of West Africa call Him *Ogun,* Rules Over iron, warfare, removing difficulties, smoothing the path to a desired result, justice, smiths, the God of iron and warfare, hunters, barbers, goldsmiths and steel. *Nupe* of North Nigeria *Soko* (the word) Creator God, (*Soko, Shoko,* is the great *bvudzijena* also the whiteheaded monkey who ruled the mountains, the soko, the word) control of the elements, witchcraft, and communication with the deceased. The word *shoko* also means *word*.

Zulu and Ndebele of Zimbabwe call him, *Unkulunkulu\Nkulunkulu* Great God, bigger than the biggest, the Creator of Earth, God of fertility, organization and order. The One who is bigger and biggest.

The Hottentots call Him *Utixo,* of rain, storms, thunder, harvest and rebirth.

Location - Description: 'Sky', the God who speaks with a voice of thunder.

The Zimbabweans call him, *Mwari, Nyadenga, Zame, Musikavanhu*: the one with no ending, the owner and ruler of the heavens, the base of all beginnings, the maker and founder of Mankind. Compare the names above with the Hebraic ones below.

THE NAMES OF GOD

YWHW: Exodus 20, I AM. *The YWHW-tetragrmaphon.* The divine salvation, the Uncaused Cause, life within Himself, with no need of a chair, food, air or support to live by. In Him life is and without Him nothing that is would have been. All the living find their life and meaning in Him, He holds it all together within Himself.

We lie when we say "my name is" for we are not, our life depends on food, shelter and social status, He is the only true I AM, Genesis 2:4

ELOHIM: Genesis 1:1, Psalm 19:1- meaning "God", a reference to God's power and might - call on power, God in concert with Himself. Let us make man. He creates.

ADONAI: Malachi 1:6 meaning "Lord", a reference to the Lordship of God. The master over all, the ruler over all.

JEHOVAH-YAHWEH: Genesis 2:4, a reference to God's divine salvation.

JEHOVAH-MACCADDESHEM: Exodus 31:13, meaning "The Lord thy sanctifier" the priest who cleans us and gives us access into the presence of God. When beaten by sin and garments soaked in the pools of abomination, God looks at us and says there is a fountain filed with blood, drawn from Emanuel's veins and the sinner plunged will lose their guilt, all in need of cleansing the crimson flood cleanses us whiter than snow.

JEHOVAH-ROHI: Psalm 23:1, meaning "The Lord is my shepherd" makes us sleep in the pastures of divine guidance. When there is too many advises and we seem to have lost our way, the Lord becomes our sherpard, the Roi, the guide in the geography of life. There is a path that we can follow, He is the leader and He will guide us into green pastures, restoring our souls and sitting us besides the still waters.

JEHOVAH-SHAMMAH: Ezekiel 48:35, meaning "The Lord who is present" ever present and helps us in times of trouble. This world has too many voices that pull us apart, we lack the inner peace in the midst of our storms, we come to *Shammah* and He stands on the decks of our ships of worry and anxiety and commands the waves to settle and the winds to keep silent.

JEHOVAH-RAPHA: Exodus 15:26, meaning "The healer" the balm for the broken soul. Modern times have come with multitudes of disease, sicknesses and epidemics, curable and incurable pandemics.

We stop to wonder at times, is there a balm in Gilead? While society is rotting in pain. Yes there is healing in Jesus's name! Our great physician is near the sympathizing Jesus, by His stripes we are healed.

JEHOVAH-TSIDKENU: Jeremiah 23:6, meaning "The Lord our righteousness" making us right with God.

JEHOVAH-JIREH: Genesis 22:13-14, meaning "The Lord will provide" just what I needed.

JEHOVAH-NISSI: Exodus 17:15, meaning "The Lord our banner" the highest point of reference.

JEHOVAH-SHALOM: Judges 6:24, meaning "The Lord is peace".

JEHOVAH-SABBAOTH: Isaiah 6:1-3, meaning "The Lord of Hosts".

JEHOVAH-GMOLAH: Jeremiah 51:6, meaning "The God of Recompense" makes our enemies pay back.

EL-ELYON: Genesis 14:17-20, Isaiah 14:13-14, meaning "The most high God".

EL-ROI: Genesis 16:13, meaning "The strong one who sees".

EL-SHADDAI: Genesis 17:1, Psalm 91:1, meaning "The God of the mountains or God Almighty". The God of the breast he done shaped. The one feeding the infants whose bosom is comfort for the broken, the chest of belonging.

EL-OLAM: Isaiah 40:28-31, meaning "The everlasting God".

An African scholar Michael Matthias Magagula would write a Psalm. See the depth of his understanding of the demonstrations of the Creator.

The intrinsic and extrinsic attribute of YHWH.

The Lord's greatness is unsearchable! (Wisdom)
Blessed is he whose God is the Lord
And he who hath found sweet companion in the Lord (presence)

While the psalmist would praise the Lord
For teaching his hands to war
And his fingers to fight,
I will extol the Lord for His
Mighty acts in my affairs (personal)
The Lord would sustain you while

You hide in a cave (protector)
Even while you wander in a desert
The Lord will sustain you with manna. (Provider)
He taketh from the proud and giveth (justice)
Wealth unto His own
Those whom He hath entrusted with

His Word of life (creator)
God will subdue the mighty under the weak (judgment)
Who daily meditate on His Word?
And frustrate the plans of the strong.
God is a warrior; mighty in battle (War)
And victorious at war

I have seen the war in action,
Therefore will I bless His Name forever and ever? (Eternity)
Every day will I bless the Lord and daily speak of the
Might of His terrible acts.

I will declare Thy greatness O Lord
For I have seen Thy Arrow of deliverance;
Delivering the low and the down trodden.
Uttered prophetic Words of old came true and

Achieved the impossible.
For the Lord confirmed the word of His servants
And performeth the counsel of His messengers.
O gives thanks unto the Lord:
For His mercy endureth forever![29]

SAMPLE OF A PRAYER HOW AN AFRICAN SHOULD APPROACH YHWH

"Meteuro WeChivamnhu, woMunhu Mutema" (A Prayer by an African), sample comparison between calling Jewish Fathers and calling Our Fathers. We have a History with Our creator which the European can not undermine and downplay.

We know our Creator. We are not a dark continent, it is what they called us. This is an attempt to connect back to what our forefathers used to do when they prayed.

It would start with a song and drum, and preparation for *Muteuro* (pouring out praises), which is still being practiced across Africa. When the white men found us doing it they called it paganism, but our Creator heard us pray and answered these prayers.

Ndini Joshua Maponga , Mwana waLazarus,
Mwana waMarara Joshua Munyuki Maponga
Mwana Muchena
Mwana waNduma
Mwana waZibowu

Mwana waNhokwara
Mwana WaDerere
Mwana Chapinduka
Mwana waPfumojena
Vanobva Gujruuswa

---

29. M.M Magagula 2016, Barberton, and Mpumalanga South Africa: In his devotion and reflection about his life and goodness of God in his life.

Mwana WaSvosve
NdiMukanya Chigaramboko Hwiramiti Chiwere Bvudzijena (whiteheard)
Shoko Yembereka Vanopemberea Namachira Machena
Vanomutambo uripamabgwe Makumbo mana mwise ndeweshanu, Phhiri, Skosana,
Kgabo, Mutsweng, Jambase Lisa, Hlati, Mtolo, shoko
Vedzinza ReDzimbabwe muvushe bgwaMunumutapwa
Vana VaNagashe Vana VaKush Vana vaHam (hama dzedu ndiShem naJapheth)

Mwana waNoah, Mwana waMethusela
Mwana waMahalalel
Mwana waSeth
Mwana waAdam
Mwana WaMwari, Mwana WeShoko
Pazvakavambwa, Musikavanhu
Zienda Kuenda Mucheka wakapoterera Nyika

Vanokutii Zame, Mungu, Arumgimis, Qamata, Kalunfa, Nzambi, Suku,
Modimo, Urezhwa, Imana, Njinyi, Nyooly, Akongo, Arebati, Djakomba,
Nyame, Onyakopon, Bore-Bore, Dzemawon, Arungumis, Magono, Nyere Siezi,
Yala, Andiamanitra AZanahary, Chiuta, Gauta, Karunga, Katonda, Lissoddene,
Kagingo, Ssewannaku, Lugaba, Ssebintu, Nnyiniggulu, Namuginga, Ssewaunaku,
Gguluddene, and Namugereka, Pamba Leve, Meketa Ngwewo, Yatta, Mwari,
Raluvimba, Unkulunkulu, Utoxo, Rugaga, Weli, Nyadenga, Enkai, Ishwanga,
Kibumba, Ori, Ondo, Chuku, Hinegba, Olodumare, Olorun, Osowo, Owo, Shoko,
Imana, Imana Hategekimana, Hashakimana, Habyarimana, Ndagijimana,
Bigirimana, Adonai, Jehova Makadesh, Jehovah Jire, Jehovah Rohi, Jehova Nisi,
Jehovah Shalom, Jehovah Rapha, Jehovah Shama, JEHOVAH-TSIDKENU
JEHOVAH-SABBAOTH, Elshadai, El-Olam, YHWH – when His name
is called you evoke His presence.

From here, one can proceed with their prayer requests

SACRIFICIAL SYSTEMS USED TO ACCESS SPIRITUAL STATE

Spirituality is neutral, so power is neutral, it is your heart that either
makes it positive or negative. The use of natural elements such as water,
earth and spirit in harmony with humans will cause movements of the
elements and evoke the spiritual realm.

There is an intrinsic desire of the human beings to interact with the

Divine.

The human body is not only physical but also spiritual with antennas that can connect with the supernatural.

To live life only in the physical is but failure to live life to the full. Like a car that never drives above the second gear, the full capacity of the engine is never felt. Either the driver does not know how to drive or fears the car and the condition of the road.

The African Christian seems afraid to move to his original full function. Civilization cannot allow the search of the spiritual to go on for it will produce people who are ungovernable and powerful.

Education cannot risk allowing people to think and explore their spirituality, as it will render the systems inability to deal with full combination of the 'super natural man'.

The system is designed for recitation more than thinking, we learn to surrender our bodies for work rarely to bring our full minds into life and enhance life through our unique gifts. Only a few people in life have risked moving beyond the visible to occupy the spiritual territory and cause changes in the physical world.

In the beginning, God created the heavens and the earth - the operation of man should be between the two realms with no apology. The human being should embrace the challenge to enhance, to feed and develop the most powerful side of life - **the spiritual.**

The Christian community has not fully moved into the space that will make the believer a vehicle of full divine occupation, but rather a primitive function to be moral beings. The few rituals that the church has kept are on the shallow end of spiritual occupation but mere liturgy for fundraising for structural maintenance. In reality the Christian must manifest the divinity.

Do not talk about God but show of God with the full mind of Immanuel and with ability to perform and do greater things than what the Messiah did. To operate below this is to have a "form of godliness yet denying the power" YHWH instituted a sacrificial system which when done correctly would move the nation from physical to spiritual and allow the entire divinity to create a positive energy and to demonstrate supernatural acts.

In the uprightness of a nation the Lord has appeared to fight and solve complex problems for His people, seas opened, wars were fought, wombs were opened, cities fortified and elements of nature stopped and moved to the advantage of the chosen.

The list below is but a keen observation into the space of spirituality and lifestyle of the "spiritual" people in the bible and from those who perform rituals and evoke the spirits.

○ Building of alters 1 Kings 18:31, evil also builds - do you have an alter

○ Isolation and concentration or meditation

○ Possession and total surrender to the spirit - occupation and sharpening of the spiritual sensitivity

○ Prayer is a tool in the hand of the soul - utterances and evoking of the spiritual world. James 5:16.

○ Do you pray? Do you have a good word you can send Matthew 8:8-10. Centurion says send a word, pass judgments exodus 12:12

○ Fasting and depriving of food, emptying the stomach to fill the mind Matt 6:16

○ Baptism and the use of water in the rituals

○ Working in harmony oh Ps 133:1-3 devils unite also for their things to work

○ Understanding spiritual laws 2 Cor. 10:3-6 the warfare

○ Power of association and contact Act 19:11-12

○ Moving between realms 2 Corinthians 12:2 between the physical and spiritual

○ The application of blood to practice Lev 17:11

○ Then the use of Music in the worship service. Music is the spiritual connection with God.

WATER, WINE OR BEER AND BLOOD ANIMAL SACRIFICES

To the African it is not just blood but life. Rituals of fame, wealth creation, healing, curses, plagues, marriages deaths, and births are all immersed in the blood.

This deep association with sacrifices of birds, animals and human sacrifices all intended to link the mortal with the immortal.

The African is religious by nature, in the sought of gaining access to God has kept a lot of practical forms and practices to communicate with God.

The relationship of an African with the dead is not terminated at death but continues and established by regular offerings and sacrifices *imisebenzi* 'works' to gain favor. These sacraments seek to evoke their dead person to guide and protect, purge for disputes or deal with unresolved issues during a lifetime. Of particular interests is how these festivals and offerings have juxtaposed themselves to the great Easter weekend with the focal point being the blood of the animal.

It must be understood that human beings are spiritual beings. At times of difficulty they will seek to communicate with the unseen through the known spirits. The real meaning is in the Passover, as taught in Exodus 12, the shadow is the sacrifice in the Old Testament and the Cross-is the image.

WASH YOUR HANDS

A Psalm of David. Psalm 24

1 The earth is the Lord's, and all its fullness, the world and those who dwell therein. (Recognize the creation and power of the Lord) **2** For He has founded it upon the seas, and established it upon the waters. (The mind must gather around nature and appreciate the works and mysteries of his handwork.)

3 Who may ascend into the hill of the Lord? or who may stand in His holy place? (There is a question or a desire to come up higher, to draw closer, to be lifted into the holy hill of the Lord, to the presence of the Lord. The human heart desires to go to this hill)

4 He who has clean hands and a pure heart, who has not lifted up his soul to an idol? Nor sworn deceitfully. (Conditions of the hands and heart must be clean. As you wash your hands externally ask God to wash the inside also. The offerings must come from clean hands.

This is a physical act as it is symbolic to clean dealings also in our life. Human preparation for worship verse 1-4 and watch the change as the heavenly hosts respond to the worship, which ascends.

5 He shall receive blessings from the Lord, and righteousness from the God of his salvation.

6 This is Jacob, the generation of those who seek Him, Who seek your face? *Selah (the battle on the banks of a river I will not let you go until you bless me. Stay in the position of worship until He blesses you. The sincerity of the worshipper causes movement in the heavenly realm)*

7 Lift up your heads, O you gates! And be lifted up, you everlasting doors! And the King of glory shall come in. **8** Who is this King of glory? The Lord strong and mighty, The Lord mighty in battle.

9 Lift up your heads, O you gates! Lift up, you everlasting doors! And the King of glory shall come in.

10 Who is this King of glory? The Lord of hosts, He is the King of glory. *Selah*

Melchi-zedek

The African Priest

There are two priestly orders we need to consider and we can use the right channel to access our blessings.

There is the order of *Melchizedek* - the Priest and "King of Righteousness", he is the first man in the Torah to be given and called by the title of KOHEN (priest).

He is predated for five generations before Levi. His life is dated to Abraham, Isaac, Jacob, Levi, Kehoth, Amram and Aaron.

There is *Aaron or Levitical* order that is from the house of Jacob. The Jethro in the wilderness' ordained Ministry as a son of Levi and he had become pagan after the nation was in exile for 490 years.

It is Jethro who recited the oral history of the Hebrews (the Torah) to Moses who could read and write in the 40 years he was in the wilderness.

In the loins of Abraham did Levi and Aaron pay their tithes to *Melchizedek* and the black people should not tithe or worship through Aaron but *Melchizedek* for the priesthood of *Melchizedek* is far much superior to that of Aaron. While Aaron is for the Jews, *Melchizedek* is for the Hebrew.[1]

Melchizedek blesses Aaron and the one who blesses is greater that the one who is being blessed. *Melchizedek* the black priest through whose order the Aronic order is established.

The danger of the Judaic approach and its priesthood is that it glorifies white priesthood instead of Hebraic. The whiteman has idolized himself and fashioned himself and his god alike and therefore presents himself as God's relative with permission to oppress and abuse the black races, and marginalize other nations.

The *Aaronic* ministry is sinful and wicked, it sold and killed the Messiah, whereas the order of *Melchizedek's* sacrifice was once and for all, his blood is his sacrifice. Heb. 7:27 we call on the African Nation to call on the Order of *Melchizedek*. The Aaronic is temporary and cheap and is handed from one generation to another, but *Melchizedek* is from everlasting to everlasting. The order of Aaron works and serves in an earthly office, a shadow, in the copy of the original, and *Melchizedek* functions in the heavenly sanctuary. Heb. 8:5

The Order of *Melchizedek* gives bread and wine to its members while the priesthood of Aaron takes bread and wine from the people. Genesis 14: "This *Melchizedek* was king of Salem and priest of God the Most High. He met Abraham returning from the defeat of the kings and blessed him, and Abraham gave him a tenth of everything" (Heb. 7:1-2).

The Hebrew word '*melek*' means king, and '*tsedek*' means righteousness, *Melchizedek* is *Yashua* the Messiah (*Yashuya Harmashiack*). This mysterious *Melchizedek* is the prototype of Jesus Christ. The Law was designed with the Levitical ordinances but in the order of *Melchizedek* there is perfection and the law is written in the hearts of the people. Levitical order is local, and *Melchizedek* is global. Now that the temple services are no longer in effect the order of *Melchizedek* has now kicked in for direct contact with the office of the Messiah. To worship under the wrong office there gives us but little benefit to link up with our Priest and to know where He is. It gives our prayers a physical address to operate with.

---

1. Heb. 7:4-10)

"Because of this oath, Jesus has become the guarantee of a better covenant" (v. 22). "Therefore he is able to save completely those who come to God through him, because he always lives to intercede for them" (v. 25).

"Such a high priest meets our need," the author says (v. 26). Jesus is exactly what we need. He was human, so he knows our needs (2:14-18), and He can be touched by our infirmities and he is now in heavenly places, in power, so he can effectively intercede for us.

We can therefore be confident to approach the throne of grace to obtain mercy in time of need that we can approach God through him (4:14-16).

He gives us access to God in a way that the Levitical priests could only symbolize.

WHY THE BLOOD?

Christianity is a body of believers who have confessed their faith in the blood of Jesus, which has power to redeem them from their sin. Does God need blood to appease Himself? The center of this faith is the CROSS, which is a pagan symbol of unity for all believers and practices of faith must never lose focus at this event that marks the liberation from shadows to types and anti-types.

The life of an animal is in its blood, sacrifices seek to access this life, but only in worship therefore sing "...Unto Him that loved us and loosed us from our sins by his blood; and he made us to be a kingdom, to be priests unto his God and Father; to Him be the glory and the dominion forever and ever. Amen." [2]

It is significant therefore to look at the death of Jesus Christ as a sacrifice that put an End to all blood sacrifices. All other blood sacrifices were and are still weak; you have to keep on killing, but the true blood sacrifice of Jesus covers it all and leaves no sinner unchanged completely. It is sufficient for all our needs. He died once and HIS death, possessed the power to penetrate into that inner world out of which blood sacrifices have issued.

Hebrews states that, "it actually cleansed the consciences of men while other sacrifices did not avail to cleanse them, that it satisfied the demands of the uneasy consciences of those who were suffering under a sense of their guilt."[3]

2. Revelation 1:5-6
3. Benjamin B. Warfield: Digital Publications Library Theology Christology And Criticism Volume 3; Copyright, © 2003, By Digital Publications, Dallas, Texas, Usa

WHAT ABOUT THE SACRAMENTS?

The mystery of the sacrifice of Jesus is in the bread and wine, which represent the body of Christ. According to Spurgeon, this sacrifice has "the power to excite remembrance consists in the appeal thus made to the senses. The hand touches, the eye can see it, the mouth can taste the bread, allow the entering within. The work of the CROSS takes over to replace guilt with blood - the sacrifice seeks to have this communion."

The wine is sipped - the act is palpable and absorbed into the blood system as to say we now have a new blood that runs in our veins. The ceremony is simple -bread broken and wine poured out the mighty pregnancy of these signs. These emblems are full of meaning.

With Jesus as our Bread breaker, there remains no need to break others but offer us as living sacrifice to God.

With the blood poured out as wine, there remains no need to pour out other peoples blood and animals to have access to God, Jesus has paid it all, remember the blood that now runs in you.[4]

WHAT ARE AFRICANS LOOKING FOR IN ANIMAL SACRIFICES?

The African rituals are soaked into the Semitic or Hebraic rituals with variations due to time and distance from the Torah. These rituals can be traced through our weddings, funerals, harvests and worship services.

"There is a strong sense to evoke the supernatural during all these celebrations and deep understanding of the presence and power of history to shape the future. The living is a mere connecting cable between the two eternities. It is difficult and unfair to remove the African rituals and replace them with western rituals. It is a meaningless cycle of rituals, swapping black gods for white idols. "Men create the gods in their own image." [5]

"And he took the cup, and gave thanks, and gave it to them, saying, Drink ye all of it; for this is my blood of the New Testament, which is shed for many for the remission of sins. But I say unto you, I will not drink

4. THE CHARLES H. SPURGEON COLLECTION: VERSION 2.3 Sermons - (63 Volumes) The New Park Street Pulpit &The Metropolitan Tabernacle Pulpit Making the Words of the Wise Available to All — Inexpensively. AGES SOFTWARE®, INC. Rio, WI USA © 1998-2004
5. Xenophanes, Greek Philosopher, Born: 570 BC, Died: 480 BC

henceforth of this fruit of the vine, until that day when I drink it new with you in my Father's kingdom."[6]

The blood of celebration as seen in the cup of celebration in the meal had wine. People seek to celebrate life but the greatest life to celebrate is that of *Yashua* - the victory that our Savior or the Messenger or Messiah has been born from us and He has come to save us.

The blood of remembrance and the cup of remembrance - these sacrifices are intended to bring to memory and keep them fresh in our memory least they are forgotten. The best we can remember is that Jesus was crucified and rose again on the third day

The blood of forgiveness and the cup of forgiveness - as the blood is spilled the intention is that the wrath of the deceased should see the blood and not kill us. But what a joy to know that Jesus has made us right with God through His blood we all can be forgiven, the vilest offer can confess on that blood and be forgiven. "Come now let us reason together though your sins be as red as scarlet I will make them as white as snow.[7]

The Blood that saves us and the cup of salvation - there is a replacement and substitution of lives here the life of the animal becomes your life and your death is its death.

The Good news is that animals cannot take our place but the Lamb of God that takes away the sins of the world can stand in our place. "Take the cup of salvation and call upon the name of the Lord".[8]

The blood that quenches the thirst for blood and cup of wrath - through the blood we commemorate reconciliation, the coming together of estranged parties. All walls of anger, hostility and animosity are broken as blood flows from Calvary.

The blood brings peace and the cup of peace - now that we have been justified by faith let us have peace with God. By accepting the sacrifice of Jesus our hearts are melted and the bitter root of hatred is broken.[9]

The blood communicates camaraderie – the cup of fellowship. During this sacrifice Jesus stands at each heart and knocks seeking for access to settle the issues at heart. This is the blood that brings in friendships and ministering to one another.[10]

---

6. Matthew 26:27-29
7. Isaiah 1:18 come now lets reason together.
8 Psalm 116: 12-13
9. Colossian 1:20
10. Revelation 3:20 come to the door...

The blood bestows on us blessings-the cup of blessings. At the table of grace we can now wait for blessings knowing that we have made our paths right with Him for this we can raise our voices in thanksgiving.[11]

The blood ushers us into a new life of holiness which comes with the cup of holiness - when you have the blood of a man on your hands you are obliged to live right. The call is that you can be a murderer sinning at will at the cost of other people's lives, you can now worship God in His holiness you have been made right with Him.

The blood places our hands in the promises of God, which is the cup of promises - this is the cup of the new covenant, the covenant of promise that what God promises He will fulfill it.[11] This is eschatology - Jesus promises that He will not drink again until we all sit together in the heavens made new.

As we seek the cleansing from the blood of animals there is a better blood that brings with it blessings, hope and a future at the table with Jesus when all things have been made new. Shall we gather at the table of Grace the feast of the lamb?[12]

The blood gives us admission into that function thus every service must elevate our minds to the bounties that God has in-store for us. Now we see in part, but then we shall see face to face.

So now, my brothers, if you have never in your life before been the subject of any religious conviction, if you have lived up till now an utterly ungodly life, yet if now you will believe that God's dear Son has come into the world to save men from sin, and with unfeigned confess of your sins and trust in him, you shall be immediately saved.[12]

What the blood of animals cannot do Jesus has done through His own blood.

WHAT IS WORSHIP?

Worship |'war sh əp|noun: the feeling or expression of reverence and adoration for a deity: *the worship of God* | ancestor worship.

- o The acts or rites that make up a formal expression of reverence for a deity; a religious ceremony or ceremonies: the church was opened for public worship.

---

11. Proverbs 10:22
12. Revelation 19:9

- o Adoration or devotion comparable to religious homage, shown toward a person or principle: Krushchev threw the worship of Stalin overboard.

- o Archaic honor given to someone in recognition of their merit. [as title] (His/Your Worship) chiefly Brit. used in addressing or referring to an important or high-ranking person, esp. a magistrate or mayor : we were soon joined by His Worship the Mayor.

- o Verb (-shipped, -shipping; also -shipped, -shipping) [trans.]

- o Show reverence and adoration for (a deity); honor with religious rites: the Maya built jungle pyramids to worship their gods.

- o Treat (someone or something) with the reverence and adoration appropriate to a deity: she adores her sons and they worship her.

- o See note at revere.

- o [Intrans.] Take part in a religious ceremony: he went to the cathedral because he chose to worship in a spiritually inspiring building.

DERIVATIVES

Worshipper (also *worshipper*) **noun** ORIGIN Old English **weerth-scipe** [worthiness, acknowledgment of worth] simply put to worship is worth-ship, giving glory to the one who deserves it.

If you want to see how to worship look at how the devil is worshiped. The devil was running worship in heaven and he was the conduit of worship in heaven.

With all the science of taking God to the angels and angels to the Lord, with music as a vehicle to this encounter he was chased away from heaven and this gift never left him.

If there is a department that is run directly by the devil, it is the worship/music department.

It's sad that meaningful music that transports people is deemed evil and that which is empty has become the diet of the saints with little impact.

People walk in and out of worship still empty handed and their souls untouched by the divine.

The *Eurocentric Christian* faith has not moved to the real issues of divine contact (shrine mentality) rather churches are converted into schools of theological nonsense, mass hypnosis and lottery clubs for fundraising.

"Truth is so obscure in these times, and falsehood so established, that, unless we love the truth, we cannot know it."[13] The church is not keen and ignorant about the process on how to move people into spirit for personal spiritual encounters.

People must be possessed by their God, instead churches constantly want to reason God from Eurocentric intelligent of diatonic musical phrases which results in empty worship services.

As an African God is accessible, we don't pray to God, we pray God; worship evokes a presence of Holy Spirit (*mweya mutsvene*).

Now that we have been told about YWHW (God). He must appear during our worship and let the encounter bring change to life, answers to questions, solutions to crisis, identity to citizens and let the day of jubilee arrive.

David cried out "I was happy when they said unto me let us go to the house of the Lord".[14] Those who come to this venue are here to cross over between realms.

The fear of mankind is not the things that threaten him but the move towards the spiritual realm. Materials seem more attractive yet the words of Pharaoh have never been more true.

So Pharaoh said, "I'll let you go to offer sacrifices to the LORD your God in the desert, provided you don't go too far away and you pray for me."[15]

Why are we to remain within the walls of colonial worship? Why do we go to church to look at each other or to look at Yah?

Why does Pharaoh want us within reach?

What is the danger should we move further into the wilderness of our adventure?

Why does he want to control our worship and determine the distance of the experience?

Why must our worship be in his acceptable distance? Is it not the purpose to worship God or make Pharaoh comfortable?

Why does he want us to leave our children and wives and wealth behind?

Will the slave master ever be comfortable with a free worshipper?

---

13. Blaise Pascal: French Mathamatician, physicist, inventor, writer and Christian philosopher. 19 June 1623-62
14. Psalm 122:1-2 our feet shall stand within the gates
15. Exodus 8:28 (CEB)

THE INVITATION OF THE CHOSEN[16]

Jesus spoke to them again in parables: these are earthly stories, which have a deeper heavenly meaning and a message that goes beyond the present audience. *The author of the word is YHWH and He looks at the history of this world in a total sum.* Within each story, there are three periods to consider the present, the past and the future. Each generation is included in the parable.

The question is, "Where are we in this story?"

"The kingdom of heaven is like a king who prepared a wedding banquet for his son." The good news about the gospel is not in the activities and spiritual hype of a service, or donations, tithes and offering, the gospel is about the Kingdom of heaven.

The King is YHWH; the wedding is the event, a celebration of the son coming of age. As Adam opened up on the side and Eve came out of Adam as a wife, so on the cross *Yashua* (Jesus) was pierced on the side allowing for a flow of blood and water; the fountain filled with blood that allowed the sinner to plunge in and lose their guilt and stains.

The church at the cross is claimed as the wife and *Yashua* says "This is now bone of my bones, and flesh of my flesh: she shall be called Woman, because she was taken out of Man."

He sent his servants to those who were invited to the banquet to tell them to come, but they refused to come.

The servants are the prophets, belonging to the king.

What is a messenger without a message?

The King gives out the message, when the messenger receives the message; the office of a prophet is created. It begins with hearing YHWH; and under instruction, the messenger proclaims not his word but the king's word. The content of the message is the INVITATION, to go out to the invited (the JEWS). In his desire, out of His own pleasure, the king choses those He wants.

Who can question the grace and mercy of YHWH, to create vessels of glory and out of the same clay make vessels of common use?

The painful part in the passage is to see the king begging the invited guests "tell them to come," He instructs, and the invited Jews became too busy and preoccupied to attend to the gospel, YHWH's feast; son's wedding banquet. When best invitations come, good excuses do not count.

16. Mathew 22

Then he sent some more servants and said, 'Tell those who have been invited that I have prepared my dinner: My oxen and fattened cattle have been butchered, and everything is ready. Come to the wedding banquet.'

The preparations included the oxen, the fattened cattle, (similar to the prodigal son's welcome: the fattened calf) and everything else. It seems all the King wanted was company for all was prepared and ready for fellowship.

The efforts of the king are divine efforts to prepare fellowship with you, as He had prepared for the Jews, the same is extended to you. The call is to come to the divine feast, "Behold, I stand at the door, and knock. If any man hears my voice, and opens the door, I will come in to him, and will sup with him, and he with me." Revelation 3:20

THE PREOCCUPATION WITH TRIVIAL

"But they paid no attention and went off—one to his field, another to his business". It is more difficult to be lost than to be saved. With an invitation so special, it is sad to note the reluctance of the invited. One can hear YHWH groan with pain, as "they paid no attention".

Our greatest moment of destruction is preoccupation with the trivial things, which squander time, energy and money when free-bonanza-grace-gift-wedding invitation cards linger on the hinges of our sinful - door posts.

If only we knew that the wages of our business is death but the invitation of grace is life, then we would stop our business and attend to the YHWH's invitation.

"The rest seized his servants, mistreated them and killed them." Now this is way out of hand, to refuse to come is acceptable, but why mistreat the messenger, why kill the messenger? The woman who had a parcel of apples and discovered that they were rotten decided to switch of the lights and eat them in the dark. The fact that you cannot see the maggots in your apples; does it make the apples fresh? Darkness provided the comfort, which made maggot protein for consumption.

- The messengers pricked the consciences of the invited, and the Jews killed all the prophets in Jerusalem.
- "The king was enraged. He sent his army, destroyed the murderers, and burned their city."
- There is no way we can mistreat the messengers and not be at war with the King.

The judgment of the Jews and their children has been precipitated by the way they treated the prophets of YHWH. Displacement, wars, scattering of the Jews, and the burning of Jerusalem are directly linked to how the Jews treated the prophets.

Look into your life today, troubles are caused by the reckless way you handle the teachings of the Torah. Divine precepts protect life, and disobedience brings death, I challenge you today chose life! The Torah will teach you Principles that will cast away principalities.

THE NATIONS CAN COME IN

Then he said to his servants, 'the wedding banquet is ready, but those I invited did not deserve to come.' YHWH is never stranded with people, when those invited (Jews) refused to come in, the wedding banquet is not canceled or postponed but through their absence, an opportunity for the gentiles is presented, so that through their absence it can be our presence, as their disobedience has become our obedience. "So go to the street corners and invite to the banquet anyone you find.

So the servants went out into the streets and gathered all the people they could find, the bad as well as the good, and the wedding hall was filled with guests." The call is wide, the places where grace finds us varies, some of us are found in the streets, trading, walking aimlessly, the by ways, the highways, the sanitary lanes are our preoccupation.

"The Good and the bad", we are not saved because we are good, or lost because we are bad, we are invited as we are, the opportunity demands our understanding that we are INVITED. We have been seated on other people's sits, the least we can do is to be careful, humble and comply with the requirements of the wedding feast.

The Gospel - Wedding invitation takes us from the gutters of filth to the tables of grace in the Kings palace. Let us put aside our street behavior, and come in, sit in, and wait on the king. The House of YHWH will be full of guests and you are included in that number, no space for a pin, YHWH works on a full house!

The Question - How did you come in? "But when the king came in to see the guests, he noticed a man there who was not wearing wedding clothes. He asked, 'How did you get in here without wedding clothes, friend?' The man was speechless."

The entrance of the King was to interact with each table, see every guest, and monitor the work of the pastors, popes, bishops, preachers and prophets who run churches, YHWH comes in to supervise the quality of every member seated at the tables. The language of the King is polite as he addressed him "friend", how did you come in without the wedding clothes?

The man had agreed to come, made time to attend, put aside his duties and made way to the palace. The preparation of the king included the oxen, the banquet hall, the tables, the chairs, take note of interest to us are the "wedding clothes, wedding garment, guest robes, clothing of the marriage feast" which appear to be a provided luxury at the entrance of the hall. Sitting on the table was an insult for they had been freely given to all, it was contempt, the guest felt he could sit in his own clothes; he insulted the King who wanted a quality audience all looking well dressed up from his own factory.

Note these attendees had come from the streets and gutters it was the responsibility of the King to give them the clothes intended for the invited, the Jews. The food, the chairs and the honor was guaranteed for these and now become the Kings friends, but "How did you come in without the wedding robes" and you still look poor, wretched, worn and torn when there is such an abundance of provision?

In the banquet hall there is enough to spare all the things that will add to our present comfort and everlasting happiness YHWH has provided, just come in and put on the Hebrew garments provided by the King.

Take advantage of the provision God has made with the House of Israel, and the principles, guidelines on how to access your wealth and health.

The gentile nation, the pagans have heard the call of the Gospel. Here is the GOOD NEWS, the robes that belonged to the Hebrews, we can put them on, the diet meant for the Hebrews we can eat, the tables and chairs meant for the Chosen nations we can sit on, the Torah principles taught to the Hebrews we can now learn. When you come to YHWH's feast, you do not prepare your own meal. The invitation comes as a confirmation that everything is ready, yours is to receive. *The garment of Yashua righteousness is our acceptable robe.*

There is no need to find new ways of accessing YHWH rather than what He has taught the Hebrews, the invited need to understand this principle and stop making noises in churches. Go back to this parable and preach the Gospel in the time. Let the nations walk in, but let the Torah be the guide of our function, activities, dress codes and eating codes.

There is no need to cast out demons (principalities) of disease when we break the principles of diet, put on the robe at the door and your stay in the hall will be disease free, so will the money, the marriages, days of worship, programs for the poor etc.

Go back to the Torah - what is written in the Word? "Then the king told the attendants, 'Tie him hand and foot, and throw him outside, into the darkness, where there will be weeping and gnashing of teeth.' Judgment is passed when mercy is not utilized. To hold YHWH in contempt will result in churches and members' weeping and gnashing of teeth, an awful calamity of negligence, OH YHWH forbid such by your grace!

The Bible; the teaching and instruction, the Torah must be the only rule of faith, to govern all church practices, silence all tongues, and measure every prophecy. *"For many are invited, but few are chosen."*

Today sit and examine yourself and be worthy of the chair YHWH has given you, seek His approval not of man. If you want the blessing of Abraham, Isaac and Jacob, behave like an invited guest and find out if you are putting on the right robe!" [17]

The *Yashua* of the New Testament is the Melchizedek of the Old Testament and Hebrews 8 confirms that Melchizedek is *Yashua*. The African is not a gentile but Royal Priesthood.

WHAT HINDERS WORSHIP? READ THE WORDS OF MOSES AS AN AFRICAN

"Jeshurum grew fat and kicked" As I write this is my prayer for you as you read! Lack of desire and when the stomachs is full of food and the mind is empty of spirit worship becomes a meaningless activity.

The abundance of material possessions is not equivalent to spiritual maturity and content.

We go into worship with our things, not the giver of the things, the mind is preoccupied with what it can see we forget to close our eyes and see the invisible that makes the visible.

There is power beyond the shadows of our materials.

---

17. Kings James Version Torah: the first 5 books of the Moses, which contain the basic Principles on the Hebrew based faith. The entire Bible calls for a lifestyle and the Torah is the key to the Holy Ghost Power of the New Testament. *Yeshua* – the Hebrew name of Jesus -Joshua (YHWH is my salvation) YHWH - the personal name of G-D (I AM THAT I AM)

Moses burst into a song over Israel and for all who are in bondage who await salvation from oppression: "Oh that I may speak and my people will hear me, let the words of my mouth and the meditation of my heart be acceptable to *Hashem*. Let this truth drop like rain on dry ground, the teaching be like distilled dew in the morning on tender plants. Let every precept gently fall like rain drops and shower the vegetation of our imaginations and inclinations of our hearts. Let me shout the Greatness of our YHWH, and give all the glory to Him. He is the Rock, His work is perfect; for all His ways are justice. A God of truth and without injustice. Righteous and upright is He."[18]

We are all witnesses to the corruption of our modern churches; many have not lived in harmony as a family of faith, under the leadership and household of the word, but corrupted themselves with false doctrine to produce a crooked generation.

"Religions have always stressed that compassion is not only central to religious life, it is the key to enlightenment and it is the true test of spirituality.

But there has always have been those who'd rather put easier goals, like doctrine conformity, in place."[19] The brand of Jesus has become a lucrative business model and this holy faith has now become a supermarket of religions. The gospel call is now clouded in the popular sentiments but poor theology.

Slogans and clichés are drummed into the believers too often the worshippers cannot tell if they are listening to the voice of YHWH or their own voices, tainted by carnal desires.

How do we deal with God or how does He deal with us?

Wisdom and discernment have been banished, as congregations opt for childish and senseless sentimental worship services.

Look back is this not the faith that YHWH started at Sinai, which is now being called heresy?

Is it not God who established the principles and says He wants to write these in our hearts, now that we have nailed them to the cross?

Did He not command that "Then have them make a sanctuary for me, and I will dwell among them?"[20]

---

18. Deuteronomy 34
19. Karen Armstrong
20. Exodus 25:8

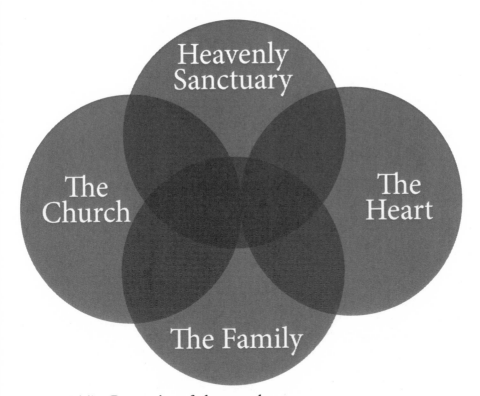

Fig 6: The Dynamics of the temple

The sanctuary Exodus 25:8 "...make me a sanctuary and I will dwell in you." At the intersection of all the temples is the dwelling place of YHWH, to influence the entire community.

Consider the points of contact:

1. *The heavenly sanctuary - the most holy place:* the venue of spiritual interaction between the human and the divine. There true reality and residence of the supernatural.

2. *The church or physical temple - the holy place:* the place of learning and ritual that prepare the human heart for divine occupancy and a venue for encounter, must work like a shadow, type and anti type.

3. *The family or home of residence - the inner court:* the venue of preparation and life interaction of human life, here life is experienced and YHWH loves us through people.

4. *The heart-lifestyle - the inner court (the heart):* the place of decision-making and choices: here the voice of conscience is developed to listen to divine signals, co-operate with family, join the community and access the divine.

When you build a temple it must be from inside out. When you download the software it must be from the most Holy to the outer court. Life must be controlled from the sanctuary.

This must be the locus of control and the citadel of all spiritual connectivity. Build this sanctuary for the Lord to dwell in you. This is the secret to the continuous indwelling of the Spirit of YHWH.

Do you want to live a spiritual life?

Do you want the presence of YHWH to be around you all the time?

Do you want a life above the ordinary?

Then build the Lord a sanctuary and an alter in your life.

There is a declared desire from the Lord to become part of the community of believers.

As a worshipper "Remember the days of old, consider the years of many generations. Ask your father, and he will show you. Your elders, and they will tell you. In His wisdom is all boundaries set and all things are fulfilled in Him."[21]

There history of every nation is twined in the presence of the supernatural. All civilizations have veneration and interaction with the supernatural; music, temples and priests are the relics of preserved history.

Growth is movement towards the space of the glorious and spiritual.

From the Temples of Giza, Peru, Zimbabwe, Greece, China and India, there are traces of people and communities who have moved close to and interacted with power and spirit(s).

Modern faith based organizations have a lot of teachings but little experience.

In the midst of these many activities we seem to have lost the simple connection and plug into the zone of the spiritual to meaningfully harvest the experience and to drive the divine agenda. "But if our gospel be hid, it is hid to them that are lost. In whom the God of this world hath blinded the minds of them which believe not, lest the light of the glorious gospel of Christ, who is the image of God, should shine unto them."[22]

The Apostles would pray and people would be filled with the spirit and this experience was not isolated but the very escort of the gospel. Why is our gospel louder but less powerful - big churches, big public address systems but poor people systems?

21. Psalm 32: 7, Psalm 143:5, Deuteronomy 32:7-9 "Remember the days of old..."
22. 2 Corinthians 4:3-4

Where is the power of "Arise and walk"?

While many are running for popular faiths I recommend that the LORD's portion is His people.

Jacob is the place of His inheritance. True Christian faith "...found him in a desert land and in the wasteland, a howling wilderness. He YHWH, encircled him, He instructed him, He kept him as the apple of His eye. As an eagle stirs up its nest, hovers over its young, spreading out its wings, taking them up, carrying them on its wings, so the LORD alone led him, and there was no foreign God with him."

The Hebrew community was made to " ride in the heights of the earth", that he might eat the produce of the fields. He made him draw honey from the rock, And oil from the flinty rock.

According to the promise made to Moses, Israel was to feed "Curds from the cattle, and milk of the flock, with fat of lambs and rams of the breed of *Bashan*, and goats. With the choicest wheat, you drank wine, the blood of the grapes." This passage moves to the ideas of what true faith must deliver to those who have and practice it.

There is power to live above the labor margin and profit, but the very divine cover that causes things to be beyond the measure of effort. Human beings can do, but when the Lord of Hosts steps into the ordinary wedding banquet simple wine becomes extraordinary. The knowledge of the God must feed us with curds of milk and have the fat of the lambs.

But all the efforts of YHWH resulted in complacency for " Jeshurum (the *Eurocentric church*) grew fat and kicked Him out. He grew fat, he grew thick and he became obese! He had forsaken the God who made him, and scornfully esteemed the Rock of his salvation."[23]

The church today has this stern rebuke. We have this expensive vehicle called religion, which has no wheels. It is ever making noise but going nowhere. "Religion is for people who are scared to go to hell. Spirituality is for people who have already been there." [24]

Oh that my people will see the pain of rejection of truth sinks us in meaningless routines. As much as we desire to go to him during worship our understanding restricts our growth and full participation into an effective encounter of Worship. Our worship services provoke YHWH to jealousy, with foreign gods we meddle, we praise and mention other gods.

23. Deuteronomy 32:15: in the midst of too much food the "upright" forget value, ignored their reputation rushed for perdition than refuge for their souls.
24. Bonnie Raitt

With our lips, we call devils and spirits, this is an abomination that provokes Him to anger. The worshipper must make sure that YHWH is smiling at the service.

There is a high appetite "Sacrificed to demons, not to God but to gods we did not know, to spirits we do not understand and tongues we can not discern. Our generation is in adultery with new gods, new arrivals that your fathers did not fear." The television ministries are championing seemingly new movements in the spiritual realm.

There is a multiplicity of fake miracles and fake happenings to mislead the souls that are seeking. In some cases worship has become a display of magic and gimmicks, show time, entertainment that has no YHWH as a Subject or Object of worship. When you look closely at some of them they only to feed the church with demonic diet that constantly departs from the basic bible based faith.

The divine principles are the standard through which every worship and practice must be tested. In the rush for new trends the church has denied *Yeshua* "The Rock who begot you. You are unmindful, and have forgotten the God who fathered you.[25]

This condition is serious as it has caused YHWH to hide His face from us, and He says "I will see what their end will be. For they are a perverse generation, children in whom there is no faith. They have provoked me to jealousy by what is not God. They have moved me to anger by their foolish idols. But I will provoke them to jealousy by those who are not a nation. I will move them to anger by a foolish nation."

When YHWH retaliates it is to our destructions for He will use others when we show such arrogance. Who can quench the fire, which has been kindled in His anger?

Our wayward teachings away from the Torah to catechism, from Scripture to church manuals, from the bible to denominations doctrines, declarations, from faith healing to commercial healing ministries, from "thus says the Lord" to prophetic movements, it is all a shame. All these shall burn at the lowest parts of hell.

"Why do we harden to listen to?" Thus says the lord, when the Lord has not spoken.

Is this not idolatry at the alter of praise?

Is this not Error which results in sin?

---

25. Deuteronomy 32

Holy fire shall consume the earth with her increase. The Lord will set fire to the foundations of these false mountains. He promises us that He will heap disasters on us, I will spend my arrows on you - literally he will shoot us down one by one.

The list is clear on our path to destruction - "They shall be wasted with hunger, devoured by pestilence and bitter destruction. I will also send against them the teeth of beasts, with the poison of serpents of the dust."

The sword shall destroy the outside - there shall be terror within for the young man and virgin, the nursing child with the man of gray hairs "I will dash them in pieces, I will make the memory of them to cease from among men,"

This is not a permanent move, for the Lord is mindful of our enemies, if He totally destroys us they will scorn and mock Him, for that reason had He not feared the wrath of the enemy, lest their adversaries should misunderstand, lest they should say, "Our hand is high. And it is not the LORD who has done all this. For they are a nation void of counsel, nor is there any understanding in them." Oh, that my people, the Christian community, oh that you would understand this and run away from foolishness and embrace wisdom, Oh that we were wise, that we accept this, truth.

Let YHWH open up our eyes to see and consider the latter end!

YHWH has given us so much power but due to our lack of repentance and absence during worship our lack of appreciation of His word we are being mocked and ridiculed by toothless dogs. "How could one chase a thousand, and two put ten thousand to flight, unless their Rock had sold them, and the LORD had surrendered them?"

Demons are having nature walks in our congregations and we are instilled with fear to run away from things that God has given us power over. "For every demonic system, there is a kingdom and apostolic model, driven by a prophetic process, to counter and replace the demonic system"[26]

---

26. Bishop Tudor Bismarck is an apostolic voice to the nations. From the age of 17 when he began traveling to outskirt villages in the Bulawayo region in Zimbabwe, to the present where he is requested at some of the largest gatherings of Christians around the world, Bishop Bismarck has been known for speaking the gospel. Since 1989, he has been serving as an Apostolic Father and mentor to ministries all over the world. He and his wife, Pastor Chichi Bismarck, serve as the senior pastors of New Life Covenant Church in Harare, Zimbabwe, the headquarters church for Sabula New Life Ministries International. Bishop Bismarck also serves as the Chairman of the Council of African Apostles, a wholly African initiative to bring the key apostolic voices of the African church to bear on uniquely African issues.

The spiritual church is under siege from false western teachings that introduce us to other gods white is not pure "For their rock is not like our Rock, (I speak as an 'Afrikan') even our enemies themselves being judges. For their vine is of the vine of Sodom and of the fields of Gomorrah, their grapes are grapes of gall, their clusters are bitter.

Their wine is the poison of serpents, and the cruel venom of cobras. 'Is this not laid up in store with me, sealed up among my treasures? Vengeance is Mine, and recompense; their foot shall slip in due time; for the day of their calamity is at hand. And the things to come hasten upon them.'[27]

With western civilization the Afrikan child has been introduced to new demons and levels of immorality and greed like we have never seen before, the poison of Sodom is now the diet of the African nation under the guise of civilization.

There is good news for the church today "For the LORD will judge His people and have compassion on His servants. The conditions that finish our strength and rely on His strength, "When He sees that their power is gone, and there is no one remaining, bond or free." In the midst of all our poverty disease and prayers the Lord wants to ask a simple question 'Where are their Gods, the rock in which they sought refuge?

Many ministers are guilty of feeding off the sheep and feeding on the sheep, and the Lord has a word for them too those "Who ate the fat of their sacrifices, and drank the wine of their drink offering? Let them raise and help you, and be your refuge."

Let us turn to the Lord and "see that I, even I, am He, and there is no God besides Me."

The Almighty promises us with His word that it is HIM who kills and gives life: "I kill and I make alive".

If we disobey He says "I wound and I heal, nor is there any who can deliver from my hand. For I raise my hand to heaven," and say, "As I live forever. If I whet My glittering sword, and My hand takes hold on judgment, I will render vengeance to My enemies, and repay those who hate Me. I will make My arrows drunk with blood, and My sword shall devour flesh, with the blood of the slain and the captives, from the heads of the leaders of the enemy."[28]

YHWH will stand and the gentile church will live, " Rejoice, O Gentiles, with His people; [a] For He will avenge the blood of His servants, and

27. Deuteronomy 32
28. Deuteronomy 32 also Ref Exodus 22:24

render vengeance to His adversaries. He will provide atonement for His land and His people".

"Set your hearts on all the words which I testify among you today, which you shall command your children to be careful to observe - all the words of this law. For it is not a futile thing for you, because it is your life, and by this word you shall prolong your days in the land which you cross over the Jordan to possess."[29]

---

29. Deuteronomy 32

In Prayer

Why worship from a distance?

"Leaning on gold while begging for gold" Now PETER and John went up together into the TEMPLE at the hour of PRAYER, being the NINTH hour. [1]

The company to worship - the friendship between the old and the young: Peter the oldest and John the youngest, the parallel comparison of the two is a theme worth exploring in the bible.

The wise and the foolish, the saved and the lost, the rock and the sand, those in the menu and those that are the menu. Here there are those on the gate and the other on the inside, the two disciples make way to the temple.

Worship is powerful in company of the saints. Let the young own our God and let us take them on the road to experience and introduce them to the power in the sanctuary.

The purpose of Worship - Prayer: too often we go to the temple or church or sanctuary to hear people talking, and the Lord said my house would be called a 'house of prayer'.

1. King James Version: Acts Chapter 3:1-20

The Lord must speak and we ought to pray. The major purpose of the temple is Prayer, communion with YHWH. We go to connect with the supernatural. Why waste time talking to ourselves when the object of worship is God. The purpose is to plug into Him, to experience Him, to walk in with problems and reason with Him for solution.

The purpose is to expose ourselves to the one who is outside of us yet working within us to change and make us like Him. Like the prophet and leader of old Moses we walk into the space of instruction and at departure we have the same glory that shines through us. For while we work with Him we start to look like Him. It's a contact that contaminates and rubs off to reflect into our souls and "the less" begins to be like the "much" some of more regulation of grace happens and our carnal flesh and spirits are attracted to the great "I Am".

The purpose of worship is to transport the congregation into this space of no return. When Peter got here he says "it is good that we are here we must build tents and stay here".

Moses says, "If the Lord will not go with us we will not depart from here," the man cleansed of legions of demons says "I will follow you and continue to dwell in the presence."

David says I will dwell in the "house of the Lord forever". There is power in proper worship is the very platform to refuel and recharge the human vessel. We expose the worshipper to the very presence of God and the human littleness is exposed to such power that transformation happens.

The congregation may still have their problems with them after the worship service but note that they have a picture of their God that outshines the challenge. The child is shown the Father, and ego and moral is boosted to deal with the challenges.

WINDOWS OF TIME OR THE TIME OF WORSHIP AND PRAYER

The 9th hour: it cannot be done at anytime: have a look closely at the detail given to us by Dr Luke as he unites the time of miracles (9th hour) and the moments of prayer.

The same time (3pm) Elijah called fire from heaven, Daniel opened his window (3 times of worship synced with times of sacrifices) and faced Jerusalem.

Jesus cried out "In your hands I commit my spirit" and Peter and John come to the house of prayer at the 9th hour - the time of the afternoon sacrifice.

There is time and hour of worship.

These are the set times and the laws of God, moments to access the chamber of grace and whisper the burden and pray for rain in due season.

Observation shows us that these windows position the heavenly sanctuary and the earthly in congruence for effective communication. One cannot ignore this timetable as it has results to those who utilized it.

It seems like at these times that the divine wheel is in direct link with the earthly realm to give quick and easy access to the prayer channel, it is as if at these times YHWH is directly linked with us away from other worlds, though He does not turn.

THE VENUE OF WORSHIP

The best venue is when heaven and nature are used as a cathedral. The Hebrew faith uses the temple and later synagogues, the venue of worship, let them build me a sanctuary and I may dwell among them. Interestingly, the observation of the inside and the outside of the temple, the inner and the outer part of the Temple.

Depending on where you stand, your experience with YHWH will surely be affected by your disposition within the Temple grounds. Quickly on the passage (Acts 3) you can notice three groups, those inside, those outside the courts and those on their way to the house of Worship. **2** "And a certain man lame from his mother's womb was carried, whom they laid daily at the gate of the temple which is called Beautiful, to ask alms of them that entered into the temple…"

THE CONDITION OF THE WORSHIPPER

"And this also, though the word lie heavy upon your hearts: the murdered is not uncountable for his own murder, the robbed is not innocent of the deeds of the wicked and the white handed is not clean in the doings of the felon."

"Yes! The guilty are oftentimes the victim of the injured and still more often the condemned are the burden bearers for the guilt free and blameless, you can not separate the just from the unjust and the good from the wicked, for they stand together before the face of the sun even as the black thread and the white thread are woven together. And when the black thread breaks, the weaver shall look into the whole cloth and she shall examine the loom also."

"Let him who lash the offender look into the spirit of the offended. When you lay an Axe unto an evil tree, let him see to its roots, for the roots of a good and bad tree, the fruitful and the fruitless, all entwined together in the silent heart of the earth. You can not lay remorse upon the innocent neither can you lift from the heart of the guilty."[2]

When we sit on the wrong sit we even lose our identity, and we are called by our condition.

THE CONDITION OF THE WORSHIPPERS

The lame make way to the house of prayer. Here a man who had a name from his family but due to the place he was carried to he ends up being called a certain man. The worshippers come in all forms and shapes, lame, halt, important, blind and an invalid etc. The condition of this man can only be traced to ancestry, from his mother's womb. The father had planted a crippled seed into the womb of his wife and they're by producing a faulty offspring.

These are traditions that we have come to respect as truth and they have limited our level of experience. The children born out of this crippled sperm are crippled worshippers who can but sit at the gate called *Beautiful.*

They are left at the entrance of abundance and never benefit from the power in the house of the Lord. Often worshippers sit at the gate of a decorated worship and instruments only to go back home with nothing but the sense of sounds at a distance of worship.

Note the drama and pain, and the dependency of this man who had to be carried to the place of worship, never to enter but be dumped at the gate.

The faithful carriers would place him near the temple but never inside.

He had short-term solution at the gate that called him to be there everyday, the posture was that of lying down at the temple gate. The condition of the Christian church is painful; we are here at the door of

2. Kahlil Gibran, The Prophet Collection, Axiom Publishing, 2001, pp39-40

the Hebrew faith, but begging for alms at the entrance of abundance. Our plight is such that unless there is help that comes to this gate we will make a profession of alms and reduce ourselves to beggars.

The African Christian when he closes his eyes sees a white God whose relatives are whites and this distorts the experience, as oppression and slavery are still fresh on our minds. The God of the oppressor can never be the same as the God of the slave.

THE VENUE OF WORSHIP IS CONTAMINATED

By pictures, idols of white supremacy, music instrument of oppressors, language of oppression and buildings of oppression - this is what the house of worship has become.

Fig 6: Path of Healing

The four participles of the circle of poverty at the gate:

Worse is the hearts that are heavy with forgiveness.

"Therefore if thou bring thy gift to the altar, and there remember that thy brother hath ought against thee; Leave there thy gift before the altar, and go thy way; first be reconciled to thy brother, and then come and offer thy gift."[3]

While we clap our hands our hearts are crippled, and the spirit cannot move when the hearts are locked in anger for anger contaminates the aura and passage of the spirit.

This fake *Eurocentric Christianity* experience has produced cripples, while the Hebrew people are inside the temple enjoying the blessings of YHWH the rest of the Christian community begs for hand outs at the door of this Hebrew based faith.

Is it true that the Jews own most of the world's wealth and we are begging at their gates? Can you see the pain that Christianity faces at the door of the Jewish Temple.

Two things stand out: leaning on gold, and begging for gold.

In the presence of abundance while in need of provision. Sitting with a blessing, at the entrance of a blessing, to enter into a blessing.

The gate *Beautiful* was built by Solomon; decked with gold and precious stones, this was a venue of the lame, an ideal place to beg.

Solomon had prayed if any men would pray facing the temple please hear them. On that basis let me submit that the man never faced the temple, his back was on the temple and the gate, and his hope was on the people coming to enter into the temple.

What a name, what an opportunity and wasted on a beggar.

Having come all this way, the name of God was mocked as they saw this man on their way in and saw him on their way out, conditions unchanged, instead he was aging at the gate as he had become part of the furniture of the temple throughout all season he had adapted to the gate and secured a permanent venue to beg.

3.Who, seeing Peter and John about to go into the temple asked for alms.

Refer to the four participles of the circle of poverty at the gate:

Attitude of the beggar: in the true spirit of a tried and tested he looked, he saw and he asked for alms. This man was actively involved in the

---

3. Matthew 5:23-24

sourcing of his daily provisions, he relied on the mercy of the worshippers to look at him with pity and place some gifts in his hands.

4 And Peter, fastening his eyes upon him with John, said, look on us, 5 and he gave heed unto them, expecting to receive something of them.

The confidence of the true worshipper: Peter challenges the man to "look at us" have faith in us, trust us, depend on us the participles that appear on this passage can not be ignored, 2 daily, 3 seeing, 4 fastening his eyes, 5. Expecting to receive something.

What a life of daily looking intently with hope and expectation that someone will feel sorry for you. My people stop begging, seek for permanent solutions, the Torah is the only way to Christian liberation.

6. *Then Peter said, silver and gold have I none; but such as I have give I thee: In the name of Jesus Christ of Nazareth rise up and walk.*

"How strange Peter's words must have sounded when he said "Silver and gold have I none; but such as I have I give to thee"; but how exciting Peter's deed when he took the man by the right hand, lifted him up, and through the power of the Holy Spirit healed him. A double miracle occurred that day! The man learned to walk and leap at the very moment he was healed."[4]

The need of the "worshippers": like the beggar at the gate called *Beautiful* the church is full of people who are in need of silver and gold. Financial instability has converted many to African Christian as the pastors are advertising financial break-through, binding the demons that are holding finances, miracle money and debt cancellation - in Jesus' name.

When we discover that silver and gold is not there, God has no money to give us, but wisdom, a God idea that unlocks the finances, wisdom, timing and positioning, giving us what we really need more than what we want. "Success is when opportunity meet preparation."[5] With money we will be here tomorrow again but restoration frees us to live full lives and make our own silver and gold. We cannot give and preach what we do not have, silver and gold have we not, but that which we have we give.

The question is what is it that the church can give?

The preacher can give?

The worshipper can give?

4. Dean Courtier, http://www.sermoncentral.com/sermons/silver-or-gold-i-do-not-have-dean-courtier-sermon-on-evangelism-urgency-70506.asp
5. Hilary Hinton "Zig" Ziglar was an American author, salesman, and motivational speaker.

And I would rather have *Yeshua* than silver or gold.

Like David meeting Goliath, Peter makes a similar remark, in the name of *Yeshua HaMashiack* of Nazareth "Rise and walk." The most powerful words spoken by the disciples to echo throughout the Christian community, ARISE and WALK.

It is a call for the continent to Arise, Africa Arise.

Move away from life at the gate into the very presence of whom you worship. You cannot wait at the gate for them to bring you news of what God is planning for your life.

Put aside your begging clothes and attitude of expectancy and start a meaningful journey into the house of worship, to become "part of" and express your gratitude for YHWHs mercies.

To often we have sat when we must rise, and rise when we must sit. Our resurrection, like that of Lazarus must remove the stones of white tradition. Hear the voice of the Lord, wakeup from our sleep in Bethany the city of figs.

How do we starve in a basket of plenty? We must stand to full health, demonstrate our ability and walk? The church must see this passage as a call to the Christian churches that we need to arise and walk into the realm of true worship that benefits us than a religion that has reduced us to a liability of second hand clothing, food parcels, meals on wheels and soup kitchens.

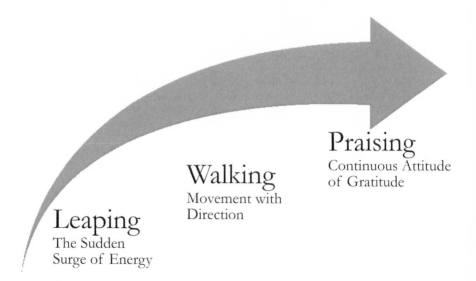

Praising
Continuous Attitude
of Gratitude

Walking
Movement with
Direction

Leaping
The Sudden
Surge of Energy

Fig 7: Dynamics of Healing

How dare we insult YHWH as a nation and make residence at the gate while worship takes place on the inside.

7. *"And he took him by the right hand, and lifted him up: and immediately his feet and anklebones received strength."*

Assist to worship: this news is too good to be true, even when the word is spoken it is very hard to accept it.

We seem to remain seated in disbelief and comfort of our status quo and previous history and common lifestyle. Here is the word of life spoken into our lives that we can arise and walk and still we would not make the move. It took the man of God, Peter an extra effort to reach out with his right hand of fellowship and touch the man, lift him up and give him his first thrust into freedom.

Oh that I may reach and help someone to get up on his or her feet and grasp this power and permanent removal from the gate. The reception from the beggar matured the miracle.

It was already done and agreed in the spiritual realm that today the gate will be empty, the beggar will go to church and home on his two feet. Sad to note that until we reach out our hands to accept that which God has in store for us, we may languish in our poverty.

The condition of this man was not only physical, but mental and spiritual and it took a seasoned man to intentionally make the first move towards his healing, and when he responded by reaching out his hand the bible tells us immediately his feet gained movement, ankle-balance, bones-structure all his limbs for movement were strengthened.

Here is the key, we need power in our feet to walk back to our roots.

8. And he, leaping up, stood, and walked, and entered with them into the temple, walking, and leaping, and praising God. The sudden discovery of a new set of legs and their function created new options, and definitions of worship and praise.

When transport is guaranteed journeys are countless. He could have run anywhere to show off and celebrate. I wonder how the carriers felt when they came to the gate later after the service as usual and found the evidence of the mat and the patient had gone inside to offer a sacrifice of praise.

Never again on his butt would he sit, he had sat long enough. He stood up, and walked, he entered with them, joined the company of the Jews to enter the house of worship.

The nations must never underestimate the value of walking under guidance from the Hebrew rabbis if they believe in the bible then the Torah is the way.

We still have a lot to learn to enter into the worship service of YHWH.

Hold on to the hands of the teachers of the Torah as you enter into the temple.

The entering 'INTO', suggests the man was finally on the inside. Amazing revelation is that, the beggar now the walker, brings in the freshness of worship and changes the entire atmosphere and order of service. The name of *Yeshua* brought a change on his life and there were visible activities around him as he broke many rules of worship to share his testimony.

When the Nations (gentiles) walk in the Jews will be saved, for they will bring with them the freshness and new testimony of what *Yeshua HaMashiak* has done.

The power of the Holy Spirit upon our lives this temple will never be the same when the nations walk in. There will be a new song, and new sound of praise, posture of worship will change and they will know something happened at the gate and now that something is now inside here.

THE STYLE OF WORSHIP

Leaping Worship: define leaping, jumping up and down.

Walking Worship: up and down, he had new legs to test; thank God he was testing them in the temple. It was not very orderly for the senior members who loved their peace and order.

The walking this man considered new then knew all about it and had noting to thank God for. But for this man this was the best day of his life, in the sight of all man he had something to thank God for, from the gate into the temple on my own two legs.

That called for a song!

Praising Worship: the praising was the new songs of what a difference the name had made in his life. The present continuous sense suggests a progressive attitude and verbalizing thankfulness.

At a moment of silence a burst of voice would be heard "thank you Jesus" and all head of concentrating members would turn to find a man standing bouncing from the floor to the ceiling with arms lifted up and a voice of praise.

9. *"And all the people saw him walking and praising God. Visibility of true worship."*

The church has to make a move that the world can see, away from the gate and live lives of "walking and praising God". A continuous celebration of the power of *Yeshua*.

Living in the daily lives.

Transformed "daily", being carried to worship, walking and praising.

A life of thankfulness, imagine going to church not to seek silver and gold but to praise YHWH. The court of the temple will be filled with thanks giving. The people will see and wish to know our God too.

That is what church must be like, not shared poverty, but experienced blessings and a voice of thankfulness.

We must get tired of the life of desperation to the life of abundance. How can we be at the right place and sit at the wrong place? To be able to hear all and benefit from none of it.

Like a knife cutting through meat yet never getting fat. The Hebrew faith calls for our celebrations, we who were once afar off now have been brought near, the goodness of YHWH has been extended to us let us rejoice for the son who was lost now has come home, beggars have finally become worshippers.

10. *And they knew that it was he, which sat for alms at the Beautiful gate of the temple: and they were filled with wonder and amazement at that which had happened unto him.*

They will always remember you for the blunders and sickness you had, they all recognized him as the one from the gate. Their amusement is very interesting, for they knew him in a different condition, when grace changed his status they all wondered of what had happened to him.

Keep them wondering, keep them guessing. When God moves they will marvel as to what has overtaken him. True worship changes status.

11. "And as the lame man which was healed held *Peter* and *John*, all the people ran together unto them in the porch that is called Solomon's, greatly wondering."

The church will participate with the miracle; they will also experience the grace from the gate. As they started to talk about the history of this man they all looked into themselves and found themselves at worship too.

12. And when Peter saw it, he answered unto the people, ye men of

Israel, why marvel ye at this? Or why look ye so earnestly on us, as though by our own power or holiness we had made this man to walk?

True worship leaves spectators in wonder.

The presence of the Lord cannot be doubted for even the skeptic can testify.

Should this not be the marvel of the testimony of those who profess to be in touch with the divine. The question of Peter should be our question, if you work with the powerful, why must you manifest weakness. Flesh gives birth to flesh and spirit gives birth to spirit, glory to glory and dominion to dominion.

13. The God of Abraham, and of Isaac, and of Jacob, the God of Ham, God of *Cush*, God of *Murenga*, God of *Nangashe* our fathers, hath glorified his Son Yashua; whom ye delivered up, and denied him in the presence of Pilate, when he was determined to let him go.

Just as he was given up by the Romans and handed to be crucified, he is still suffering in the hands of the Romans to date through the hands of the European grandchildren. It could be true that while the Greeks were thinkers, the Romans were thinkers.

14. *"But ye denied the Holy One and the Just, and desired a murderer to be granted unto you."*

We have been left to deal with criminals rather than the true Messiah.

These thieves in jackets and ties will reduce us to the scum of this earth, while playing us organ music and calling the name of Jesus. They refuse holiness and drive their own economic agenda on the back of our dignity and conscience.

15. And killed the Prince of life, whom God hath raised from the dead; whereof we are witnesses. They have killed life in us and all hope of what is true and holy. Today we proclaim a resurrection of our true Messiah, the prince of peace, not of war. Has this Jesus been kept alive in African hearts, or He is a dead savior who has left for the heavens awaiting the trumpet sound.

16. And his name through faith in his name hath made this man strong whom ye see and know: yea, the faith that is by him hath given him this perfect soundness in the presence of you all. **17.** And now, brethren, I know that through ignorance ye did it, as did also your rulers.

As Africans accepted this faith in ignorance, but now in knowledge we must seek for the substance, not just the form of worship. **18.** But those things, which God before had shewed by the mouth of all his prophets, that Messiah should suffer, he hath so fulfilled.

19. Repent ye therefore, and be converted, that your sins may be blotted out, when the times of refreshing shall come from the presence of the Lord."

"This time of refreshing is now, when the rains will fall and the mental plants will bud in the beauty of spring will we sing free at last. Free from lies and oppression, free from these white demons some of them in black skins."

The Christian community needs cleansing for now its churches have become a league match of demons and devils with pastors as clowns and idiots on the circus stage of faith.

The farmers of thought will secure new lands for a fresh crop and a bumper harvest.

God's Presence

What is Acceptable Worship?

The battle is on acceptable worship, what will bring YHWH into our presence and bless us with whatever moves our hearts from within.

We, who are coming from the nations into this faith need to understand a few critical points that will bring a complete change in our worship services and usher in the Holy Spirit in full measure.

Like the rich young ruler, yes you have been doing fine, " but one thing thou lackest", this volume seeks to identify that one thing - attitude towards the Torah will desecrate our worship and render us weak in the presence of strength.

There are only two people on earth, the wise and the foolish, those who are in touch and those out of touch.

The wise and the foolish virgins tells us we need to keep our oil and avoid shame on our dignity at the appearing of the groom.

Throughout the scripture an ardent reader cannot fail to see Adam and Eve, Cain and Abel, Sarah and Hagar.

Hagar is second wife but gives birth to the first born in the flesh, and Sarah first wife give birth to second born in the flesh but first born in the spirit. Divine things are for the spiritual, clearly revealed that the ignored will have priority over the chosen by no means do the Jews supersede the genealogical birth right of the Hebrews.

The first birth and the second birth, YHWH loves the second, unless you are born again, of water and of the spirit you will not enter the kingdom of heaven.

The war in the womb of Rebecca, the war between the gentiles (the Nations/Israel) and the Jews (the house of Judah). She was heavy with twins and the older one is Esau, the younger Jacob.

1. The depth of the wisdom of God is baffling, now look the younger was holding the heel of the older one: God says the older shall serve the younger (Romans 9:10).

Esau (Jews) I hated, sold his birth right for a plate of soup, but Jacob (nations) I loved. It is clear that the older will serve the younger, but Jacob must learn from Laban, must be cheated also, look at him with two wives, and idols under his wives seat.

This Eurocentric Christianity (Rachel favorite but evil) has lots of idols that it is sitting on, and claiming to be in her periods.

A little backtrack will show you that Leah is the first wife in the flesh, yet Rachel is the first wife in the spirit. Watch divine wisdom as YHWH switches things around and allows the second wife in the spirit gives birth to the first child in the flesh, and through the second wife (Leah) the plan of salvation is fulfilled and Judah and *Yashua* are born.

It is true therefore to say YAH loves the second. Unloved but productive, here is our African story.

But greater still he stands on the banks of the river on his way home and he fought with God and won, the prayer was, "I will not let you go until you bless me."

---

1. Genesis 25:23: the Lord said two nations are in your womb

Sounds like the prodigal son coming back home.

The return of the nations to their land and true worship.

"Oh what mystery that the Lord hides His things in the simple things only revealed to those who discern."

The father of the 12 nations in the flesh, is the father of many nations in the spirit, for he is the second born, as Esau is the first. All nations that believe in the messiah can therefore call on Jacob as their father in the spirit.

When Jacob blesses the sons of Joseph, he switches the hands between Ephraim and Manasseh, saying that the younger will be greater than the older. Traditions are broken to give priority to divine plan and purpose.

This is not just a physical demonstration: but a deep spiritual manifestation and design of the worlds history through the pen of Hebrew literature. YHWH has not forgotten us or cursed us, the switch is on our heads black people.

This struggle is what the Christian church has to do today before we meet our brother from whom we stole the blessing. The white people have robbed us for too long. This sibling rivalry sums up the total new testament struggle between the law and grace.

The song of Moses and the lamb, the new covenant and the old covenant, they are saved by grace and saved by works, the holy spirit versus mount Sinai. Oh how I pray that the Lord will open up our eyes and give us the victory over this gross blindness and we see the goodness of YWHW and walk in His ways.

The blessings that are in store for us are immeasurable.

When *Yeshua* came and walked on the earth.

He promised us that greater things than this we shall do.[2]

For man and God in harmony is company unlimited.

This is the parable of the olive tree and the nations are grafted on to the main vine. The two thieves reveal those who accepted the gift of salvation and those that cursed it. At the same place others are accepted and others are rejected.

The power of choice is still the greatest gift we have to access this divine gift. To stand with *Yashua* is to be on the Torah – path that leads to life that only a few will find.

---

2. John 14:12-14 Greater things that these shall you do

Christian faith cannot claim success on its prayers and conditions. *Denominationalism* has made churches an end in themselves when there should be path to the throne of YHWH. If our theology is right how come, we hate each other?

The truth of our faith is measured by the quality of the fruit it bears.

The Protestant, Evangelical, Episcopal minister must admit to the members that its not working for all of us, there is something very wrong with our present relationship with the entire Bible and precepts of YHWH.

Even in our prayers there is something missing, our services lack the depth and practical implementation plan on daily living.

We often hear the useless remarks.

God says "Wait, Yes or No many have given up on prayer because of this uncertainty."

HERE IS A RECIPE FOR ANSWERED PRAYER

The principles of the Torah and the Power of the Holy Spirit presents the Christian as unstoppable, this is what *Yeshua* meant when He said we must worship Him in Truth and in Spirit.

In laymen language, we obey and do the principles and the Holy Spirit who is already Spirit will fight the spiritual battles for us.

We do the ordinary and He does the extra ordinary.

We practice the natural and we evoke Him to fight the supernatural.

By physically doing the same, we have activated the Holy Spirit to spiritually start being active in our day and lives.

The Torah gives you the legal right to claim the blessings and the power of divine cooperation.[3]

Basic laws of hygiene, diet, clothing and Shama, give you access to the throne room of YHWH.

The simple formula of answered prayer is Principles - (Torah: the expectation of YHWH on your life) at work in your life will break the Principialities that work against you.

YHWH gave you the Torah so that you can live and work in the blessing.

The principles unblock the flow of divine contact with you.

---

3. Proverbs 10:22 the blessings of the Lord give wealth...

"

Use the Principles to break and cast out principalities. For the principles are stronger than the principalities. Fear not, the principalities have no hold on the principles.

For the Holy Spirit is the voice of the Principles and the devil is the influence of the Principalities.

Obedience is better than sacrifice[4] for HaShem cannot be bought or bribed with acts and gifts from an unconverted heart. The Gentile pain is to try and find new ways to access *HaShem* when He has a clear Hebrew path He introduced to the Jews.

For these blessings to make way to your door post, no one comes to the Father except through Me, Yashua says, "Like the woman with an issue of blood, have faith that your touch at the hem of His garment (Deut 22:12), the five knots on the tallit, the Torah, the five stones of David, **5.** the five loaves of bread, touch the "telos" of the garment, no matter where you are on the four corners or four wings of the world the issues will stop.

The touch of faith on the principles stops the principalities of disease.

The problem has been the Old time religion that built a wall between the Jews and the gentiles. It taught the gentiles the false replacement theology, (that *Christians* have replaced the Jews). No we don't replace the Jews we as the nations the gentiles we are grafted on to the main vine, we are the branches the tree supports, we don't support it, but bear fruit.

The root of this tree (Hebrew faith) is *Yashua*. Every believer must take their rightful place on the tree and eat the sap, and receive nourishment from the root.

---

4. 1 Samuel 15:22, obedience is better than sacrifice: the Lord delights in Obedience more than the sacrifices.

5. 1 Samuel 17:40 David picked up five stones

The fruits of the spirit must be felt from the grafted position. Not away from the vine but on the vine.

No amount of popular sentiments or church slogans, or strikes of the Holy Ghost power, or tongues will grant you victory in your life. The demons will leave for a day and will be back the following day.

How do you break the health principles and then rush to pray for healing: eat right, sleep well and drink right, forgive and have faith and disease will be far from you? The permanent solution is to have the principles govern your life thereby giving God full access to use you.

The great Shama becomes a prayer of evocation, *Shama* Israel, Elohim, YHWH Adonai echad, *"Hear Yea oh Israel the lord your God is one God."*

(Here I am to pray, to listen in obedience to act on faith and hear you Oh God, Be present and active in my life, and in your Oneness, let my scattered life be consolidated into that Oneness. As for today let all that is in store for me from you is ONE with me).[6]

Here is the plain truth for the heart that is searching: the Old Testament gives us the manual of how to work with the Holy Spirit in the New Testament. These are not burdensome commandments, as popularly taught by modern preachers, but lifetime ritual blessings that harmonize our lives with YHWH.

We do them so that it may be well with us, theft, adultery, incest, rape, unfaithfulness in our dealings, slavery, and oppression, marital strive, all these hinder our prayer access to divine blessings.

The Torah is clear on these expectations from Hebrews and the Nations (gentile). Be clear that the African Tribes form the intrinsic fiber of the Hebrew nation, the Europeans are in fact the gentiles and barbarians of the scriptures. The Torah is the path and has never expired, its principles still hold. Let the Hebrew African be proud to meet his History in the Scriptures.

You can not sleep with an animal and say this was nailed to the cross, or eat pig and say it was cleansed by the blood of Jesus, later on poop anywhere without digging a hole and say the holy spirit covers all sins.

Christians wake up and understand our salvation comes from the Jews:

Christianity has Hebrew roots, Hebrew Bible, Hebrew History and language let us swallow our pride and walk back to the main vine. YHWH the nations are blessed. Through them founded the nations of the Jews.

---

6. Deuteronomy 6:4, Hear yea OH Israel the Lord your God is one.

Romans 9: 4 "…for theirs is the adoption as sons, theirs is the divine glory, the covenants, the receiving of the law, the temple worship, the promises. They are the patriarchs and from them we can traced the human ancestry of Christ, who is God over all forever be praised."[7]

Let us walk back to the wilderness and stand as Israel on foot hill of Mount Sinai and here YHWH will build us into a nation of faith to fulfill the promise He made to Abraham, the nations shall be blessed through you.

HERE IS AN INTRODUCTION TO TORAH

Go back to the roots of our Faith, these are our Hebrew roots. Let us be introduced to the God of the Old Testament then we will read and enjoy the New Testament.

The tree of our faith as given in Romans 11: "the branches are the nations (us the gentiles, we don't support the root and the stem but they support us), the stem is the Hebrew faith and the root is *Yashua Harmashiack*. The branches can only bear fruit when attached to the stem and drinking from the roots.

All Christian churches must re-examine their roots in this century and be grafted back into the main vine" - this is the message of the hour.

The olive tree must be grafted as 3-4years (from Sinai to date we are on time for grafting) The nations must come and drink from the tree and benefit from the sap of the tree and bear fruit that is pleasing to HaShem.

YHWH never intended that we look for new methods to approach Him but use the revelation of the Torah to address our issues and interact with Him. The Lord our God changes not. He does not need new covenant to cancel the old, rather understands it as shadow and object.

THE TORAH GIVES US THE BLUEPRINT FOR MORAL, HOLY LIVING

Do we then nullify the Law through faith? May it never be! On the contrary, we establish the Law. (Romans 3:31) When HaShem called a people who did not know Him, He sought to build a new nation that would interact with Him.

---

7. Romans 9: 4

The Torah builds the foundations of all Hebrew faith and faiths, for *HaShem* is making a kingdom of priests to the world. Critical to the Torah is to foretell the coming of the Messiah, *Yeshua HaMashiack.*

If the Jews claim this faith, how do they run the temple services without Levi, who left with the 10 other tribes? Simply put Levitical order is with the nations (Levi), not with the Jews, (Judah)

These principles will guide us into:

- **Knowledge of the mysteries of HaShem (Elohim):**[8] An Illustration, work-board, (as kindergarten learning tools) to the greater truth into the Kingdom of *HaShem.*

- **Christian living:** All who profess the bible today will learn how to live and operate in the Spirit Realm, have a clear picture and plan of what HaShem has done in the past, present and future (the Parousia).

- **Discipline:** holds us together as believers.

- **Detects error:** Only those who are founded in the teachings will be able to see the misuse of Scripture. Look around the church practices today if it is not in the Torah it is wrong. Show me tongues from the Torah, laughing, in the spirit, or people falling in the spirit? Scripture will fortify our faith and circumcise our practice

- **A united Christian faith:** When the Nations (we the gentiles) will accept the foundations of faith as Hebrew will we be able to unite with the Jews and call Abraham our father, thereby eat and access the blessings of Isaac and Jacob.

- **Living in the blessings:** The Jews continue to enjoy the blessings, which Christianity cannot fully access, I advocate for another look at what *HaShem* gave to the Jews as a guideline for lifestyle. Listen from the Torah we are not going to be blessed: we are blessed.

Whether you know it or not, living the Torah will bless you and breaking it will affect you. The Judgments that are stipulated for doing certain acts will follow you, for YHWH is faithful to follow us with blessings and curses.[9]

Some of us are trapped and cursed for incest for the Torah prohibits certain relationships, some of us are poor for the Torah teaches how to bless widows and orphans. Some of us have buried their spouses prema-

---

8. Mark 4:11 to you is given the mysteries
9. Deuteronomy 28:45 I will follow you with curses

turely for the Torah teaches when you laugh at a widow. *HaShem* says I will kill your husband too.

Look at diseases according to Deut. 28 and you will see in your family a curse that lingers. Some families don't get old, other families girls don't get married, others miscarry, yet other murder and have mental conditions (all this happens in the shadow of the power of the cross and Holy Spirit). *HaShem* has promised that He will visit us with blessings and curses and He faithfully causes these to fall of us. Troubles therefore are an alarm at the door of our consciences that announce *HaShem's* desire to dialogue with us and bring us back to His ways.

Let us take our heads out of the sands and look at this subject objectively. Let no man lie to you about the law. You personally look at the entire 613 principles and take a pen and select your guidelines on how you must live your life.

Have a close look at the outline of the Torah, and find the rhythm of worship.

FUNDAMENTALS OF TORAH:

Laws of Character
Laws of Torah Study
Laws of Idolatry and Paganism
Laws of Repentance
Laws of Reading the Shema

Laws of Prayer and Kohanic Blessings
Laws of Tefillin, Mezuza and Sefer Torah
Laws of Tzitzit
Laws of Blessings
Laws of Circumcision
Laws of the Sabbath

Laws of Eruvin (Rabbinical)
Laws of Yom Kippur Rest
Laws of Festival Rest
Laws of Chometz and Matzah
Laws of Shofar, Sukkah, Lulav
Laws of Shekalim

Laws of Sanctification of Months
Laws of Fasts
Laws of Megillah and Chanukah (Rabbinical)
Laws of Marriage
Laws of Divorce
Laws of Yivum and Chalitzah (Levirate Marriage)
Laws of Women
Laws of Sotah (Suspect Wife)
Laws of Forbidden Relations
Laws of Forbidden Foods
Laws of Slaughtering
Laws of Oaths
Laws of Vows
Laws of The Nazir
Laws of Estimated Values and Vows
Laws of Mixed Species
Laws of Gifts to the Poor
Laws of Ma'aser
Laws of The Second Tithe and Fourth Year Produce
Laws of First Fruits and other Kohanic Gifts

Laws of The Sabbatical and Jubilee Years
Laws of Temple Vessels and Employees
Laws of Entering the Temple
Laws of Restrictions Concerning Sacrifices
Laws of Sacrificial Procedure
Laws of Constant and Additional Offerings
Laws of Disqualified Offerings
Laws of Yom Kippur Service

Laws of Misusing Sanctified Property
Laws of Pascal Sacrifice
Laws of Pilgrim Offerings
Laws of First Born Animals
Laws of Offerings for Unintentional Transgressions
Laws of Lacking Atonement
Laws of Substitution of Sacrifices
Laws of Impurity of Human Dead
Laws of The Red Heifer

Laws of Impurity through Tzara'at
Laws of Impurity of Reclining and Sitting
Laws of Other Sources of Impurity
Laws of Impurity of Food
Laws of Mikveh
Laws of Property Damage
Laws of Theft
Laws of Robbery and Lost Objects
Laws of Murder and Preservation of Life
Laws of Sales
Laws of Acquisitions and Gifts (Rabbinical)
Laws of Neighbors (Rabbinical)
Laws of Agents and Partners (Rabbinical)
Laws of Slaves
Laws of Hiring

Laws of Borrowing and Depositing
Laws of Creditor and Debtor
Laws of Plaintiff and Defendant
Laws of Inheritance
Laws of Sanhedrin and Punishments

WHAT ARE THE KEY DEMANDS OF WORSHIP?

1. **Personal prejudice:** when as individuals we have set up our ways and selected a path that seems right in our own eyes, only to find that at the end is a plural arrival at death.[10] This is a result of education and orientation. It is obvious that a collection of wrong education will result in *chatath* (missing the mark), which is sin.

2. **Collective misguidance:** when present church councils formulate statues based on their positions in certain practices, and preference. The souls of people are at stake and the church seeks to protect its position of infallibility. Note that at times the church claims to be a destination, when it should constantly be reminded that it is a station, preparing people to meet their God.

3. **Historical traditions:** It is the inherited church's positions that have perpetrated this error. The roots on which we have fed on

10. Proverbs 14:12 there is a way that seems right to the man but the end of it are ways of death

from the past if by any chance they were bitter the fruit couldn't be sweet.

- *Talents:* The investment of grace. What the Lord has invested in you. This is in you and you are born with, inborn ability
- *Preparation education:* Get knowledge and understand the science of function of your dream. Mentorship and development and growing in the depth of your talent. Develop the skills
- *The anointing hand of the Lord upon your life:* The spirit of the Lord oils the system to operate above average. This brings favor and power
- *Functionality operation:* Find the purpose of life, it is influence and power. Live beyond the ordinary life, have a powerful life full of the Holy Spirit.

THE TORAH ABOVE CAN BE CONSOLIDATED INTO 14 SETS OF PRINCIPLES

Princple1 - The ONENESS of *HaShem*: This principle prohibits Idolatry, which forms the foundation of knowledge into the heart of the believer, let there be light. This light allows the practice of the Torah to happen in the light, as the believer walks on the path that leads to the throne of grace. This is the Book of knowledge

Principle 2 - The commandments of frequent use: The practice of the book of knowledge, to keep the knowledge and memory of Hashem on our minds and lips. These activities include the reciting of the Shema, "Hear Yea Oh Israel the Lord our YHWH is One" YHWH prayer, Tefillin, and blessings, circumcision is included, because it is a sign in our flesh to constantly remind us when we are not in Tefillin or Tzitzit. This is the Book of Love.

Principle 3 - The commandments to be done at fixed times: These are directed at our divine roots and history as creatures from the hand of YHWH—such as Sabbath and holidays – these celebrate the past, appreciate the present and anticipate the future. The Book of Times.

Principle 4 - The commandments on sexual relations: Such as marriage and divorce, and levirate marriage and release from it. There is no need to shy away from the reality of divorce and bind people in abusive and dysfunctional relationships the Torah makes room for divorce and remarriage and clear procedure is taught on how to go about it, than live in guilt and ignorance. This is The Book of Women.

Principle 5 - The commandments on forbidden sexual relations and commandments on forbidden foods: Our food and our sex put us apart, they sanctify us from the nations and separate us as a holy people. Since we are a holy people we are forbidden illicit sexual relations and forbidden foods, "and I have set you apart from the peoples" Lev 20:26 who have set you apart from the peoples" Lev 20). This book The Book of Holiness.

Principle 6 - The commandments by which one undertakes to do and honor the words of their mouths or forbid himself in certain things: For such things as oaths and vows. We as a chosen people don't just talk wind. As we speak, we must do. This book The Book of Promising.

Principle 7 - The commandments on seed of the land: Such as Sabbatical years and Jubilees, tithes and heave offerings, and the other commandments akin to these matters. Every human being is entitled to land they can call their own on which they are to plant their seeds for food. The Book of Seeds.

Principles 8 - The commandments on building the Temple and perpetual public sacrifices: "Let them build me a sanctuary so that I may dwell among them" The Book of Service. From here we can question "Does YHWH expect us to build lots of churches and temples around the world? Are we qualified and commissioned to fundraising and collect people's money in the name of building a sanctuary for the YHWH."

Principle 9 - The commandments on personal sacrifices of the individual. The Book of Sacrifices, the individual has access to YHWH and can call upon Him and do rituals that cleanse him/her at a personal level.

Principle 10 - The commandments on ritual purity and impurity: The things that contaminate us, buildings, people and clothes. As we interact with these, we need to cleanse ourselves, wash hands etc so that we can interact with new things, for a man with clean hands shall see YHWH. The Book of Ritual Purity.

Principle 11 - The commandments on civil relations: Relations in which there is injury at the offset to either property or person. The Book of Injuries.

Principle 12 - The commandments on sale and purchase: The Book of Acquisitions, how to trade and make blessed sales not cursed transactions.

Principle 13 - The commandments on other civil relations in cases that do not have at the outset any injury: This relates to issues such as deposits, and debts, and claims and denials. The Book of Judgments.

Principle 14 - The commandments that are delegated to the Sanhedrin: such as capital punishment, and receiving testimony, and administration of the king and his wars. The Book of Judges.[11]

The human heart searches for something greater and bigger, something more powerful and meaningful. It cannot be church as usual. The worship experience has to give us more than lip service; the worshiping experience needs to be a daily life.

The worshipper (*Asaph*) needs to find the face of God, and worshippers need to bring the sacrifice of praise and the Worshiped need to be called to attend the worship service.

The constant backsliding in modern churches and disinterest of the youth with church can be better understood when we fully realize and take the blame for the weak, meaningless and powerless service that we continue to run.

They want more than just bulletins. Their hearts desire for an encounter with their Creator. Let the worshipper make this possible through the worship service.

Tradition has overtaken contemporary experience, people are not allowed to experience God now, and instead we make them fantasize over historical salvation. Get ready for a change of rhythm in your life, "Oh Lord send a revival and let it begin in me."

COVENANT DEMAND[12]

Worship time is time to visit the covenant: In North African times of Abram there were a number of covenants - salt, water and blood.

The most binding being the blood covenant, which was absolutely unbreakable, guarantee and bound a man to his word. Abram cut a covenant with YHWH to bless him.

It confirmed permanence divine fidelity punishable by death on both parties if broken. To cut a blood covenant you needed the following

11. As taught by Maimonides: 'The Rabbaeiun Moshesh Ben Moimon" a prominent Medieval prolific Spanish and intellectual writer.
12. Pastor Bukki Ajide, Lekki Lagos, Victory Sanctuary: first time I head this word covenant demand taught

o The two families that needed to be joined as one. They bound themselves into one unit. Their weaknesses and strength are fused to form one unit

o The solemn ceremony would require three large animals to be sacrificed. These animals would be cut in half and placed on the ground opposite each other leaving a trail of blood between the two halves "the path or way of blood" to walk here means your blood is your bond.

o The parties would exchange their coats: to declare that I will cover you. "I will protect you", "I will not be in comfort while you are in the cold. My arms are around you when you need shelter. Above all the power and identity, authority that is mine is now moved to yours. (Beslthaezzer, Joseph and his coat, Elisha with Elijah's coat, gave Daniel a coat: the mantle of power. "All that I am and have is now yours, and all that you own and have is now mine".

o They exchanged their weapons, spears, swords or stuffs to declare the sharing of strength, and being a friend to my friends and an enemy to my enemies.

o They would then enter the path of blood with the new coats and weapons, dressed and armed in the new status now "walk the path of blood" and at the center you would then declare the blessings and curses, pledges and promises, loyalties and consequences of default: "entering into a covenant" and stating the demands of that covenant.

o This was the blessing of the covenant that could not be broken and called for full trust and allegiance. All this solemn swearing was done to God, which made him the third party on the agreement.

o They would cut the covenant. The representatives cut their hands and wrists and bound their wrists together so that their blood would intermingle. (Man would it make sense why Jesus was pierced and blood had to flow?)

o With loyalty sworn the two families would join their names and bind themselves to each other forever.

o Lastly the families would have a meal together: bread and wine (flesh and blood) they would chew it, with understanding of being chewed if they did not meet the demands, yet benefit from the sweetness and satisfaction of keeping with the demands.

The African can relate to this even in our marriages and ceremonies killing animals is very acceptable. The sheep, goats, or beasts that are killed during marriages are covenants that we are cutting between families.

The bile that is spilled on us represents that hard times that we will face while eating this meat of marriage. The African child has lost the deeper meaning of this ceremony and has pilled curses upon his head.

During these ceremonies, names are exchanged: coats and blankets are exchanged, blood is spilled and the gods of the families are evoked, in some cultures like the *Nguni* weapons are still carried and exchanged.

"Oh that my people will go home on their holidays and preform these rituals that bind their families together and stop being lead astray by western traditions of useless cakes in town houses."

Bind yourself and your family together and the Lord will bless you. Stand for something and commit your life to purpose and family posterity and watch the miracle.

Many people want to pray, but they are at war with their families, no prayer will unlock your fortune but harmony and peace, covenant with your family. Go back home and make peace, apologise if you erred and find forgiveness, which unlocks your misfortune.

Be careful to honor covenants that you cut and promises you make to your parents. Fulfill them. Stop showing us iPods and cell phones, go home and fix the gate you said you would fix.

Don't become a prayer warrior, instead, confess and be forgiven and the future you desire will open before you. Don't be a fool African child, go home, and get your parents' blessings, get your things sorted. No tree is better than its roots.

African theology: Mikveh, Baptism and Power in the water

The man in John 4 needed a bath (*Mikveh*) that would cleanse him. He needed the water that would wash away his sin, cleanse him from without and give him within.

Here at the pools where people came for their ritual cleansing in the miracle bath and be healed had changed the colonnades into wards with dozens of patience on standby awaiting the waters to be troubles. In this reading the waters will be troubled and you must get into the pool and Lord help us and wash us from within and cleanse us from without. Take away the heart of stone and give us the heart of flesh.

Wade in the water, been to Jordan and been baptized, the crimson tide, have you been washed?

What shall wash away my sin?

Shall we gather at the river?

These are some popular songs that echo the place of the water in the place of worship. There is water that is about to boil out of you, a new song, a new life a new worshipper worth of ministry at the alter of grace.

The earthen vessel is submitted to YHWH to be molded so that you can carry the treasures of the inexhaustible power of Joshua *Harmashiack*. Rabbi Messer introduces the *Mikveh* from the book of Deuteronomy 28.

This is not a quick fix but a long process that kills pride, which makes us sick, broken, unworthy vessels of worship. At the Mikveh service the worshipper must draw a line to wash their hands and body as they prepare for worship. Let your bath be a baptism.

According to Rabbi Messer the "proper way to enter into a *Mikveh* is to first make sure you are already physically clean. First take a shower prior to your immersion. Do not confuse physical cleansing from spiritual cleansing. The immersion is done as evidence that you have already been made spiritually clean and physically represents your change of status - your repentant heart"[13]

The heart is in need of repentance and renewal, dealing with sins of omission and commission, known and unknown, intentional and unintentional sin to enter into the presence of YHWH.

Preparation for worship is critical to the worshipper. Every worshipper must move away from confusion to confidence resulting in stability, to come boldly into the throne room and worship in truth.

As a worshipper you must be healed so that you can heal others. Through worship we usher in the presence of YHWH that heals and cures the congregation. YHWH will break you to take you to a better place.

Depression equals preparation for YHWH is about to change your status. Through your time of confusion look around there is an opportunity at the door. Open the door of your heart and spirit and allow the Lord to make a new thing out of you. He has promised to take away the heart of stone and give you a heart of flesh that can only hear His voice.

---

13. Rabbi Ralph Messer: Simchat Torah Beit Midrash: the Mikveh Process: 2006, pp8

Iniquity is what runs in your blood, your heredity and transgression is what you are doing now as you miss the mark the *Mikveh* will deal with both, for the Lord promises to visit the 3rd to the 4th generation of evil and the 7th generation of goodness. There is a parallel between curses and blessings they are both God's promises.

The devil must not be given too much credit; it is God who "allows curse to come upon us His people due to our transgression." James 4:7-10 we need to submit ourselves to God and submit to the greater hand of God.

Love has power to change things around you. Divine judgments run parallel with blessings and it is in your mouth and hands to change things around for you and your children. You will be set free, you will be forgiven, and you will walk in confidence and YHWH will accept your worship and bring His presence in your testimony and worship.

HOW DO YOU WORSHIP WHEN CURSED?

Messer further breaks down the seven faces of curses as found in the book of Deuteronomy 28 the famous chapter on 'blessings and curses'. The first 15 verses have blessings and the rest is curses.

The word that holds the chapter together is "if", the condition of obedience. The entire religious space and spiritual quests is driven by the factors as described on Deuteronomy 28. People pay their loyalty to a medium priest or pastor who can have solutions. The same black book teaches that obedience is better than sacrifice, yet people sacrifice their salaries, food and time to have a connection with YHWH.

1. *Mental and emotional breakdown: manifesting itself as confusion, depression and an emotional rollercoaster, never emotionally stable as a result relationships are unstable and decision making is sporadic. Deut 28:20*

We have witnessed mental retardation in this world, caused by wars and troubles of this life. From the passage above this has it roots in the presence of evil, occult witchcraft, pagan worship and new age that is found being practiced by individual or family.

YHWH hates those who are involved in necromancy, palm readers, horoscopes a mental diet that promotes violence, sex adultery and casting spells. The Lord visits the family with a curse of confusion (verse 20) in that all the hands touch.

Destruction looms in the air leading to early death. No one has walked away from God and extended their lives. To cut a branch from the tree is the beginning of its death.

The worshipper must go through the *Mikveh* to choose life. Being a minister in the presence of the Lord demands that one rids himself or herself from the filth of the cult, an emotionally and mentally unbalanced person is a broken vessel.

The Lord demands a sacrifice that has no ailment.

2. *Repeated or chronic sickness: Deut 28: 21:22 the Lord will make plagues cling to you.*

The family and person is infected with plagues and disease, the sickness that wastes the body such as anorexia and bulimia, inflammations, scabs, fasting sores, incurable itches, blindness, diabetes, cancer heart disease, incurable tumors and prolonged diseases.

It is not normal that sickness becomes a permanent residence in our homes. What is it that causes these things to "cling" to our genes? True worship needs to visit these strong holds and lose those in bondage.

3. *Barrenness or repeated reproductive problems: Deut 28:18 cursed shall be the fruit of your body.*

The Lord visits the family with curses rooted in bitter judgments, forgiveness, verbal and sexual abuse. In such families there lingers bareness miscarriages and all sorts of reproductive problems.

Let the worshipper look around their family and establish tendencies of irregular menstruation, cramps, frigidity, cysts tumors, prostate cancers, sexually transmitted diseases, anger and rage.

This curse manifests itself in poverty. All these diseases are stored in the blood and are carried over from one generation to the other, the bitter root of judgments bring these things on you. The bitter tongues of racism, gossip and rumors pollute the atmosphere of the soul.

Those who live under this curse have broken the laws of chastity, elusive sex, fornication, pornography, masturbation, abortions, love affairs, running present relationships with ties to the old affairs, unfaithfulness to relationships, drug abuse and deep rooted un-forgiveness to those who have wronged us like molesters etc. Every barren womb awaits a divine negotiation.

4. *Breakdown of marriage and family alienation Deut 28:41 you shall bear children and they shall not be yours.*

YHWH visits these families with a curse and you will find perpetual divorces in the family, poor relationships with parents and grandparents and in-laws.

Abundance of rebellious children, sibling rivalry, spouse or child abuse, jail, neglect and abandonment of children causing orphans, destructive anger and fits of rage. The worshipper must break away from adultery and oaths to foreign gods. All these are painful experiences that must bring us back to God. Pain is intended to put you to your knees and seek for the face of YHWH

5. *Continuing Financial insufficiency Deut 28:17 & 29 Baskets shall be empty, you will not succeed but poverty will haunt you.*

The first and foremost cause of financial instability is divorce and rebellion, religious pride, anger, not honoring parents, lying, cheating and pathological liars.

Look again and you will find that prostitution and drugs will hold your money and cause you not to prosper. Your sin eats your wealth and your basket will be empty, your pocket will have holes. The worshipper needs to be freed from this curse and walk into a blessing.

6. *Being "accident-prone" [14] grope at noonday and not prosper, oppressed and plundered.*

The Lord visits such with wake up calls of high number of accidents, carelessness and impulsiveness. An unnatural impulse to harm self others and animals. The root of this curse is molestation and abuse

7. *History of suicides and unnatural or untimely death [15]*

You may find out that you harbor thoughts of suicide or may have attempted to kill yourself, caused by lack of joy in your life. Look again and you may find out that you harbor a critical spirit and self-hatred.

The Lord visits the family with untimely death, and disease that take life untimely.

These curses are founded in the ties that the family has made with death, occult activities, molestation, abuse and not honoring parents.

How the worshippers cleanse themselves?

Step by step on how to do the *Mikveh*:

---

14 Deuteronomy 28
15 Deuteronomy 28:29

For those who are married this will be your honeymoon.

Do not have sex during your periods, let the body cleanse itself then after seven days wash your body clean and prepare to meet again.

It is a divine program to teach men discipline while the woman sanctifies herself and this allows a couple to have a honey moon once a month. Amen

i. Wash yourself clean first in water in your bath or shower.

ii. After you are clean then fill in the tub with some water and stand in the water. Then open the shower, open the drain and allow water to run over your body and the water drains

iii. As the water is running make your confession: Lord God of Abraham, Isaac and Jacob, I ask you to forgive me of my disobedience, iniquity and transgression. I repent, look at my family and my generations and forefathers, we have not walked in your ways and we turned our backs on your principles. Here today and now I seek for forgiveness and also forgive those that have spiritually, physically, sexually abused me. As this water washed my body I wash away demonic influences that have held on to my family and me. I have given them permission to operate, but today here and now I break those ties and as the wash washes away dirt let the memories and curses that are attached to my practices be washed away. YHWH I open my heart to the filling of the Holy Spirit to operate in my life according to your wisdom and truth take over my life, rule and reign and help me to live and walk in your ways. Make me a vessel of worship in your hands. I ask for the blessings of Abraham rest upon and make a worthy vessel to worship you in the name of *Yashua HaMashiack* Amen.

THE ACT OF INTENTIONAL PRAYER

Prayer is the language of the living soul, to connect with the supernatural, so as to evoke the divine to move on behalf of the human request. The human speaks and desires to have an audience with the Maker.

It is a language of intention that joins the weak to the strong, when the spiritual hand of faith stretches to touch the supernatural hand of divinity to move and change the cause of events, a sinner on his knees can see far much further than a philosopher on his toes.

Prayer is a ladder that extends the dreams of Jacob to join the furniture of heaven and allow the ministration of Angels. Prayer is a tree that "Zacheus" climbs on to see that his height inhibited.

The fact of life is not as physical as Christianity wants us to believe rather it is a spiritual warfare, fighting the unseen that can see us. There are moments of happiness, pain, adversity, darkness and victory. The principalities are at war with the human beings over their divine destiny.

You cannot go to war with rubber bullets and hope to make impact on during the intense encounter with the enemy of your soul. Many of our soldiers in the spiritual warfare are on holiday and pastime with church. Seemingly it's a pleasure excursion and they forget we are at war. It is critical to understand the enemy so that we can prepare sufficiently for combat, for you cannot bring the seen to the unseen. The foe is spirit and we have to learn to move the battle to turf of spiritual combat.

The spiritual preparation demands much more than hymns, tithes and uniforms, rather connection to the source of power. We have the hands sets in our hands (cell phones) but they do not have airtime to make a call so that we can be connected.

As Isaac, and he will tell you "we have the fire, the knives and the wood" but where is the lamb. Programs and protocols are not the reason we are at *Moriah*, what is the critical ingredient of the journey, if not the sacrifice: the lamb.

We have divine promises that must be unlocked through prayer, and by using the word of YHWH we can access His will and demand our victory. Give your time, heart and soul to the season of prayer and intercession and you can employ YHWH to move on your behalf.

Prayer is the supernatural hand in the physical hand.

When done, there is not greater force to move the clock of time in favor of human weakness. How does a human being put God to work? It is through prayer. The season of fervent prayer is a moment of power to claim that victory that only incarnate an honest heart

How the worshipper must claim victory?

How do we confront the sin that attaches itself to our DNA and bones in our generation and that seeks to destroy and render us unfit vessels for worship? Preparation of worship and prayer is critical to have a successful encounter. This preparation must be intentional.

New International Version (NIV): Daniel's Prayer has a format that yielded results:

A. An effective prayer starts with applying the mind to the word and the immediate politics.

Be aware of where you are what is around you, is it a time of plenty, famine, war or disease.

Daniel chapter 9 *In the first year of Darius son of Xerxes [a] (a Mede by descent), who was made ruler over the Babylonian [b] kingdom— 2 in the first year of his reign, I Daniel, understood from the Scriptures, according to the word of the Lord given to Jeremiah the prophet, that the desolation of Jerusalem would last seventy years. 3 So I turned to the Lord God and pleaded with him in prayer and petition, in fasting, and in sackcloth and ashes.*

B. An effective prayer will confess and mediate for the nation, rulers, ancestors and the people of the land. As you see what Daniel did you must do the same. This is the example of a prayer that *Zame* answers. This is important as it aligns your present to your past and map the future. The parent today was a child yesterday and in prayer we come in contact with the acts of God in the past and his intentions for the future. If YHWH was angry with us in the past and made a judgment to the 4th or 7th generation it may affect you directly.

4. I prayed to the Lord my God and confessed: "Lord, the great and awesome God, who keeps his covenant of love with those who love him and keep his commandments, **5.** we have sinned and done wrong. We have been wicked and have rebelled; we have turned away from your commands and laws.

6. We have not listened to your servants the prophets, who spoke in your name to our kings, our princes and our ancestors, and to all the people of the land.

C. An effective prayer is plural and fully recognizes the righteousness of God and the wickedness of man.

7. "Lord, you are righteous, but this day we are covered with shame— the people of Judah and the inhabitants of Jerusalem and all Israel, both near and far, in all the countries where you have scattered us because of our unfaithfulness to you. **8.** We and our kings, our princes and our ancestors are covered with shame, Lord, because we have sinned against you.

9. The Lord our God is merciful and forgiving, even though we have rebelled against him; **10.** we have not obeyed the Lord our God or kept the laws he gave us through his servants the prophets. **11** All Israel has transgressed your law and turned away, refusing to obey you.

> **D. An effective prayer deals with the root cause of the problem: it is informed:**

"Therefore the curses and sworn judgments written in the Law of Moses, the servant of God, have been poured out on us, because we have sinned against you. **12.** You have fulfilled the words spoken against us and against our rulers by bringing on us great disaster.

Under the whole heaven nothing has ever been done like what has been done to Jerusalem.

13. Just as it is written in the Law of Moses, all this disaster has come on us, yet we have not sought the favor of the Lord our God by turning from our sins and giving attention to your truth. **1**

4. The Lord did not hesitate to bring the disaster on us, for the Lord our God is righteous in everything he does; yet we have not obeyed him.

> **E. An effective prayer pleads with God to turn away from anger and appeals for mercy**

15. "Now, Lord our God, who brought your people out of Egypt with a mighty hand and who made for yourself a name that endures to this day, we have sinned, we have done wrong.

16 Lord, in keeping with all your righteous acts, turn away your anger and your wrath from Jerusalem, your city, and your holy hill. Our sins and the iniquities of our ancestors have made Jerusalem and your people an object of scorn to all those around us.

> **F. An effective call for God to hear, to look, to give ear and see: addresses the reality and seeks for God to address Himself to Himself and deal with His name to forgive and act with haste**

17. "Now, our God, hear the prayers and petitions of your servant. For your sake, Lord, look with favor on your desolate sanctuary.

18 Give ear, our God, and hear; open your eyes and see the desolation of the city that bears your Name. We do not make requests of you because we are righteous, but because of your great mercy.

19 Lord, listen! Lord, forgive! Lord, hear and act! For your sake, my God, do not delay, because your city and your people bear your Name."

G. **An effective prayer moves God to intervene and there are a few thoughts to consider in this regard. The Lord of hosts resides in you and his will can manifest in your life. The way to achieve the goals for life is to find purpose of being.**

THE PAST IS PRESENT WITH US.

As you hold a fruit in your hand you are holding a tree and a seed, the past and the future are in your hands. The consequences of the past are locked in the seed in your hand, and the multitude of forests for the future is also trapped in your hand.

All that a tree is in the seed, and all that a seed is - a tree. Now let us talk about human life as a plant in the present with seeds for the future. Until you visit the past to unlock the anger of God the future is trapped in the mistakes of your forefathers.

Understand that your life today is a fulfillment of the promises the lord made to your fathers "I will visit the 3rd and 4th generations, of those that hate me and the 7th generation of those that love me. Go to the graves and ask how they died, there you may find your history in their bones.

Not to speak to the dead, but to have a relationship with your history and find the pitfalls and weaknesses and strengths that are packaged in you. Your true potential could be a vow God took with your father, and your weakness and failure could be a curse they invited by signing covenants with evil.

When a father makes a decision he is shaping his children's future. The African is fully aware to visit his past and make sure all is in order before he tries to solve the problems of today. Daniel 9 is a clear example of this powerful discourse, Daniel and his friends, the nation of Israel in bondage not because of their sin, but the sins of their fathers.

The Lord punished the children, the prayer of deliverance therefore has to visit the past and unlock the anger of YHWH in the past so that the future is a revelation. To remind God of what he vowed and the punishment on our shoulders is wisdom, find out what happened in the past that causes you to be where you are today.

When Daniel confesses the sins of his late fathers and forefathers, ancestors and understood the wrath of YHWH in the past, Heaven moved with expediency to answer and deliver. He can be heard praying, Lord we did not do right, our fathers, and we and out forefathers sinned against you. "Oh Lord forgives, or oh Lord does not delay."

Is it possible that the actions of the presents have been caused buy divine wrath in the past? Have you ever confessed the sins of your fathers? Have you confessed the sins of your ancestors?

Have you gone to the past and dealt with the root cause of the curse in your family? Are you also aware that your actions today will have a direct impact on your children?

Did you know that blessings and curses are in your plan of action and that through you they will be blessed or cursed? History has all the answers to the future you desire. Blessings and curses are all a divine instruction according to Deuteronomy 28, "I will bless you and I will curse you."

The actions of human behavior affect the next generation with either blessings or curses. Daniel has the key; the present tree can be grafted with a different branch to yield a different fruit.

Yes, its possible that you can change the cause of your family history and get a new DNA infused into your family tree then the future generations can harvest for your action and decisions.

Talk about your late fathers, visit their graves and find out what killed them, you will find your future written in your history. Tamper with that history and your solutions will be in your hands.

God of my forefathers, God of my ancestors, the forgiver of all wickedness, look at me and have mercy, rewrite my future for the sake of my children. "Oh Lord forgives, oh Lord Listen", or "Lord act in favor, for your name's sake." 20. While I was speaking and praying, confessing my sin and the sin of my people Israel and making my request to the Lord my God for his holy hill— 21. While I was still in prayer, Gabriel, the man I had seen in the earlier vision, came to me in swift flight about the time of the evening sacrifice.

His prayer was locked in the family, tribe and nation, confession on behalf of the entire nation, and the Lord is looking for people who can stand in the gap on behalf of his people.

National prayers will always find a sweet sport in the heart of the Lord. While still in prayer God intervenes and an answer is given. All prayers have a divine answer and its immediate.

An effective prayer affirms and assures us of our Fathers in heaven.

It is personal, "God told me to tell you that you are beloved"

22. He instructed me and said to me, "Daniel, I have now come to give you insight and understanding.

23. As soon as you began to pray, a word went out, which I have come to tell you, for you are highly esteemed. Therefore, consider the word and understand the vision

WHY BRING TRADITION TO WORSHIP?

John 5 reveals that structure destroys worship. The paralyzed man was healed at a pool full of the sick, the haul, the impotent, the blind, the disabled, and the lame.

Does it surprise you that only one man was healed? The healer came, the dispatcher of angels was at the pool, the great physician and miracle worker stood in the midst of the sick, but lo and behold the attitude of the sick people will make you sick. They still waited for the waters to be trouble when the one who troubles the water was with them.

The Worshipper needs to learn this important lessons that the presence of God creates the experience. All other things can wait, programs and time tables are good, but when the savior stands at the pool, the services of the angels can be suspended, least like the people at the pool the worshippers will still wait for the next service when healing is in the first service.

The question Jesus asks at all services is "do you want to get well?"

WORSHIP IS...

A grand celebration of the miracle of *Mikveh*; the acceptable worship is the intention of the worshipper. Before mouths are opened and worship begin let every worshipper take a bath in the physical water and in the spirit, let the water and the spirit be witnesses, let the worship arise and the people be blessed.

Worship is for God, a moment to swing into the realm of the supernatural and rub shoulders with God in His divine presence.

An act of faith where the worshipper returns an offering of praise and worship. Praise for what God has done. Worship for Who He is.

Worship is a spiritual journey that the saints take to overcome the devil and secure the fellowship and company of angels. In a worship service sickness are healed, sins are pardoned, the sun is made to stand still and like

Elijah in a chariot the worshipper is transported from the physical world, in the spirit to fellowship with YHWH.

Worship is a spiritual warfare and as it is celebration. The worshipper registers audibly their presence in the spiritual realm and announces to God as they are approaching, the condition of the heart of the worshipper is very critical if the worship service must achieve the desired output of putting congregation in touch with the supernatural. It is a ritual of holiness that evokes the Holy Spirit to manifest and become active in the midst of the saints.

When conducted in holiness and purity of heart this is the most powerful part of the worship service for all are prepared to appear and the worship leader guarantees that all are accounted for at the throne of Grace. Worship opens up the skies and windows of blessings and the rain cools the baked ground.

The divine warehouses of blessings are widely open for the saints to carry things from glory, to life they come back with quickened faculties to deal with the physical challenges. It surely brings Glory to God and it is for His pleasure that we receive from His hand.

Worship nourishes the soul as the presence of God is evoked to the place of worship, preparing the saints to move from the type to the anti-type, from the visible to the invisible. A good worship service prepares the pulpit to the throne of God where the word will be spoken and "AMEN" it shall be so.

Worship and prayer can alter the mind of a preacher and tune Him to the great I AM. Worship according to St Chrysostom is potent tool that can subdue the strength of fire. Lions can become vegetarians, wars can be averted and the elements can be controlled.

During the worship service he demons are banished, arrested, and the course of the evil one is stopped.

In the moment of importunate prayer the worshipper is prepared to receive God richest blessings that will not be bestowed in casual prayers.

Worship is the attitude of the soul towards God, this we should all keep watch for it is our duty.

Many souls have been destroyed at the neglect of such a duty. Many times by the time we backslide and fall out of faith the problem is at our secret prayer garden. It is from the private space of communion that the worshipper grows and cooperates with God on His mission.

"Let prayer be the key of the morning and the bolt at night. The best way to fight sin is to fight it on our knees." Phillip Henry.

Every congregation must demand for more out of Worship. What is the best venue for worship? Who makes the best praise and worship team, show me the choir? Define the purpose of worship? "Please if I can't see the object of worship I can't worship!"

Place YHWH in a visible state that all can access Him and adore his marvelous work and worship can be personal.

WHO IS THE WORSHIPPER?

David in the Psalms gives us a hint of his testimony as a worshipper

Psalm 5[a] "these thoughts should fill the mind of the worshipper. David was the chief of worshippers himself and *Leza* calls him the man after my own heart."

FOR THE DIRECTOR OF MUSIC. FOR PIPES. A PSALM OF DAVID

1. *Listen to my words, Lord, Consider my lament.* **2.** *Hear my cry for help, my King and my God, for to you I pray.*
3. *In the morning, Lord, you hear my voice; in the morning I lay my requests before you and wait expectantly.* **4.** *For you are not a God who is pleased with wickedness; with you, evil people are not welcome.*
5. *The arrogant cannot stand in your presence. You hate all who do wrong;* **6.** *You destroy those who tell lies. The bloodthirsty and deceitful, You, Lord, detest.*
7. *But I, by your great love, can come into your house; in reverence I bow down toward your holy temple.* **8.** *Lead me, Lord, in your righteousness, because of my enemies— make your way straight before me.* **9.** *Not a word from their mouth can be trusted; their heart is filled with malice. Their throat is an open grave; with their tongues they tell lies.*
10. *Declare them guilty, O God! Let their intrigues be their downfall. Banish them for their many sins, for they have rebelled against you.* **11.** *But let all who take refuge in you be glad; Let them ever sing for joy, Spread your protection over them, Those who love your name may rejoice in you.*
12. *Surely, Lord, you bless the righteous; you surround them with your favor as with a shield.*[16]

---

16. Psalm 5

The worshipper is according to Psalm 100, "Everybody who comes into worship. The prerequisite is to worship the Lord with gladness and come before Him with joyful songs with a full knowledge that He is God He has made us. We are His people and sheep of His pasture."

With thanksgiving worship, with praise worship, praise His name, celebrate the His goodness and love that endures forever.

Never forgetting His faithfulness that continues through all generations.

The Worshipper, according to McCheyne, must pray for the Pastor. Pray for his body, that he may be kept strong, and spared many years, pray for his soul that he may be kept humble and holy, a burning a shinning light. Pray for his ministry, that it may be abundantly blessed, that he may be anointed to preach good tidings.

Let there be no secret prayer without naming him before your God, no family prayer without carrying your pastor in your hearts to God. The worshipper must be diligent to cultivate holiness and a burning zeal to lead others to Christ[17] makes it the first business of the day.

The worshipper's heart must be in tune with that of the Spirit. According to Psalm 63 you need to earnestly seek God, and your soul must thirst for godliness. The very body of flesh must long for the touch of Grace.

Find a lifetime song to praise God, and lift up your hands in worship. No more sleeping in wrong beds for verse 6 echoes that on your bed you must remember God. The nights should find the worshipper focused on God, and never ending praise in the shadow of His wings.

The worshipper according to John 16:12 is made ready to assume duty by the Spirit of Truth who comes into their hearts and mind to guide the worshipper into all truth. The worshipper will not speak his own things, but speak only what he hears from the Spirit as he brings glory to Jesus and making it know to the saints. Ask and you will receive and your joy will be complete,[18] as you speak to one another, speak in psalms, hymns and spiritual songs. Sing and make music in your hearts to the Lord.[19]

The worshipper sets the temperature of the church, for according to EM Bounds, when the chambers of prayers are closed and entered casually or coldly, then the church rulers are secular, fleshy, materialistic, the spiritual character sinks to a low level and the ministry becomes restrained and enfeebled. There is nothing more fatal to life than a life lived without

---

17. Psalm 5:3,
18. John 16:24
19. Ephesians 5:19

prayer. Watch it even further when you do holy service the neglect of prayer quickly moves you from a relationship with God to systems and religion is powerless without the spirit of truth.

The worshipper who does not pray is like Samson without his locks,[20] (when the glory had departed and yet he says he will wake up as usual).

Time is thin and the devil and his angels work hard to shave of as much of our power as possible. Like Samson, when the Philistines are upon us we can deceive ourselves and say, "We shall wake up as usual", but little do we realize that *Ichabod,* the glory has departed? [21]

The worshipper must prepare for the service and no better word can be found than the sermon of John the Baptist through the pen of Luke 3:4.

Prepare the way so that the king can come in, not a path for mice, or a foot path for pedestrians, not a dirt road for one car at a time, but prepare a Highway, a freeway for there is an entourage of grace on its way to your heart with abnormal loads of blessings to your door post.

The amount of blessing you will receive is equal to the size of the road you prepare. This preparation is very thorough as it calls for the worshipper to make the path straight for the King of Glory to come in.

The low places, low emotions and depressing issues (named here as valleys) must be filled with a song of praise. The mountain egos of self-power and exaltations must be brought low, leveled to allow access of grace. Worshipper help the crooked paths to be made straight and the rough things in your life to be made smooth. On this highway all mankind will see the salvation of God. [22]

The worshipper must have faith.

Faith will grow much faster on the ground where prayer is in abundance. The correct ground to exercise faith is faith ground. Simply put faith activate our prayer and request to work

WHEN IS THE BEST TIME TO WORSHIP?

At the Sanctuary, worship and sacrifice formed the basic functions and these services did not happen at any time but set times, namely the morning sacrifice and the afternoon sacrifice.

---

20. Judges 16:19 "after putting him to sleep, Delilah shaved his head…"
21. I Samuel 4:21 "the glory has departed…"
22 Luke 3:4-6

The times as written in the Bible are the 3rd hour (9am) and the 9th hour (3pm) a close look at these times would reveal the power of the hour as the Lord calls us to ask to rain in due season.

Prayer can be made at anytime but the study below was too compelling to ignore, looks like something extra ordinary happens when the throne of mercy is approached at certain times.

This is a recommendation based on the biblical evidence of times. It is very interesting to note that the detail of time seem to occupy the following passages and encounters.

- *The woman at the well:* (6th hour) 12 pm to fetch water. Seek for water at the right time, on this window of time, *Yashua* awaits you when the world has sidelined you
- *Rebecca came at the 9th hour (3pm):* when your heart is in tune, time will align you with opportunities that shape your destiny.
- *Peter had an encounter at the 6th hour:* the correct dreams and visions are clarified at the right time
- *Cornelius at the 9th hour:* mission is clarified and the lord steps in with a word that changes your disposition
- *Daniel prayed three times:* 9am(3rd hour) 12pm (6th hour) and 3pm (9th hour) correct prayers must be offered on the windows of time. We can't always be praying in emergency.
- *Elijah started to prepare the wood at the 6th hour (12pm) and the prayer was made during the time of the evening sacrifice the 9th hour:* at the time of the last sacrifice he called and the windows of heaven opened with a flame of fire.
- *Peter and John went to the house of worship at the 9th hour (3pm):* when you do not have silver and gold and you have a name to call upon. Call it on time and miracles will follow
- Jesus at the cross spoke at the 6th hour and gave up the ghost at the 9th hour: the universe aligns with divine purpose - Yashua
- 2 Kings 2:16-20

WHERE IS THE VENUE OF WORSHIP?

There are three realities, physical world, the spirit world (demonic world or holy spirit world, and the Presence (in the presence of YHWH) that we

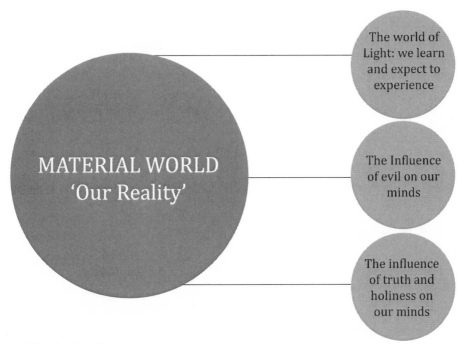

Fig 8: Reality

have to visit constantly to make meaning of our Christian faith.

The worshipper must be aware of these three dimensions to enter during worship services. The instruments and the visible venue is Level One. As the instruments are tuned and voices are raised the worshippers goes into the realm where the spirits, where words and truths are being spoken and sung into the souls of the saints.

Weaknesses are revealed, sin is exposed, power is called upon, desire is expressed and heaven's immediate response is heard as the worshipper carries the congregation into the Holy of Holies and presents them to the Father.

"We have come into this place, gathered in His name to worship the Lord, forget about ourselves and concentrate on Him".[23] Let it be clear that the real venue of worship is level three, "in the presence of Jehovah hearts can mend," [24] and the horizons of separation are extended away from each other, as we draw closer to the Him.[25]

For those who are carnal, the battle is that of using physical weapons

23. Bruce T Ballinger: Published MCA Music Pub. AOD Universal Studio Sound iii Inc 1976
24. Heritage Singers: YouTube 12 May 2010
25. Revelation 4:1 "...come up here and I will show you what will take place..."

Fig. The Realms

to fight spiritual warfare. The weapons of this war are not carnal but spiritual.[26]

The foolishness of education is that it only teaches the realities within the five senses and ignores the spirituality of mankind. Human beings are not only physical but also spiritual and social. The temple model would give us a clearer picture, as the sinner moves from the outer court into the inner and the holy and most holy.

There is a constant interaction between the outer and the inner. The temple on earth is the same type as the one in heaven. The human body is also illustrated on the temple model, as we talk about the outer, it relates to the surroundings of the person, then the inner, represent the mind and the heart, the most holy would refer to the human soul.[27]

All these venues have constant interaction and communication from the priests who conducted services daily at its altars. In a similar way also let me submit the three venues of Christian struggle,

1. The physical sphere (the visible elements of nature)
2. The spiritual sphere, (demonic an angelic realm)

---

26. 2 Corithians 4:10 "…weapons of our warfare are not carnal…"
27. Exodus 25:8 Let them make me a sanctuary so that I may dwell amongst them

3. The divine sphere (where God is resident) this volume seeks to introduce the paradigms of Christian growth.

To only fight in the physical realm is to fight but half of the battle, there is more happening up above the air.

The worshipper must take the service to the real battleground. The spiritual battle must allow the congregation to engage in the death of the physical person and empower the spiritual.

This move will introduce the worshipper to the tools and strategies of warfare. To remain in the physical gimmicks of worship is fake and unprofitable. The twisting of faces and fake spiritual body movements is not worship, for worship is letting God into the room and evoking the spiritual presence of God into the hearts of His people.

Content of worship: While many struggle with the composition of songs, the word of God is the best source of hymnody and for the word is truth and it will accomplish the desires of God. Let the worshipper read the word and see the song

Hebrews: 12:22-24

But you have come to Mount Zion. To the heavenly Jerusalem: taking people to the city. To the city of the living God; taking people to life

To thousands upon thousands of angels in holy convocation; taking people to company

To the joyful assembly: improving attitude

To the church of the first-borns whose names are written in the book of life: positioning them. We have come to God: place their hand into the hand of grace

To the judge of all men. To the spirits of righteous men made perfect: introduce them toe company and comfort.

To Jesus, the mediator of the new covenant; they should touch their salvation. To the sprinkling of blood that speaks better than Abel: experience the forgiveness of their sins: free from guilt and pain [28]

To John, He dwelt among us John 1:14; In Colossians He dwells in Us. John saw it. He saw the glory. He lives in us. Psalm 50

I have come to God so that He may speak

I have come so that I will shine in perfect beauty like Tzion

I have come so that God will be praised (to praise the Lord)

I have come to be have sin devoured

I have come to be judged

I have come as the consecrated one who made a covenant

28. Hebrews 12: 20ff " ...but you have come..."

I have come so that God can speak and He can testify against me
I have come to learn that the problem is not my sacrifice, not my bulls, not my goats,
for all belong to him and He knows the number of birds on a hill
I have come to offer a thanks offering to God
To fulfill my vow to the most high
To call upon the name of the Lord for this is the day of trouble
To be delivers and give honor to God To recite the laws of God

HOW TO PREPARE FOR WORSHIP?

Like a woman in her kitchen who is about to prepare to cook a delicious meal the worshipper must start by cleaning the table and collecting the ingredients that are necessary to cook the meal.

With a clear picture in mind, the goal of worship where the worshippers must be delivered to and experience, the worshipper is clear on the goal of worship. Time spent on each phase, word, and prayer supplication, (physical, mental and emotional and spiritual) the worshipper is in concert with the Holy Spirit as he transports him or her to the throne of grace.

It must be stated that true worship is holistic. It must reach the whole person. Emotions are part of what people are and to leave them out of worship is to offer but a partial offering. Love the Lord your God with all, mind (intelligence of worship), heart (the emotion of worship), strength (the effort and stamina and expression of worship) and soul (spiritual interaction between the human and divinity). Note some issues to consider while in preparation to maximize the depth of worship:

Learn to love divine instruction
To shun away from the way of the thief
To take the divine covenant on my lips and speak it our with confidence
To walk away from adultery/fornication and harness my mouth from evil
To learn how to speak well and love my brother and forgive freely
To be accused on my face
To be torn down and no one will rescue me
I have come to sacrifice thanks offering and honor God
To prepare the way

Come so that God will show me His salvation
Psalm 51 This divine SALVATION is shown when God When God shows mercy and His unfailing love

When He blots out my transgression
When He washes away my iniquity
When He cleanses me from sin
When I repents and recognize his sinfulness
Then Salvation is shown: (the ultimate reality is the visible change of the redemptive
power of God in the life of its worshippers.)

There is truth in my INNER parts
Wisdom in taught in my INMOST PLACE
I am cleansed and I am clean
I am washed and I am whiter than snow
I am crushed and my bones can rejoice
Salvation is shown when:
God hides his face from my sin
Blots out my iniquity
Creates in me a pure heart
Renews the right steadfast spirit within me

I am allowed to constantly be in His presence and not cast away
The Holy Spirit is allowed to stay with me
I experience the joy of salvation
I have a willing spirit that sustains me
Salvation is shown when
A saved sinner preaches to other transgressors
When there is no more blood guilt God has saved me
The tongue can sin to His righteousness
I focus at what God has done more than what I can do and bring.
I come to God with a broken spirit and a contrite heart
In God's pleasure He makes me to prosper
He will build up the walls of Jerusalem.[29]

Then there will be a righteous sacrifice when burnt offerings and bulls sacrificed will be acceptable. The worshipper must call upon the Lord. He must come and pray to the Lord and who promises to listen. Charles Spurgeon admonishes that the goal of prayer is the ear of God, and when prayer fails to reach the ear of God, it has utterly failed.

The uttering may kindle devotion and feeling in our minds. The hearing of it may provide comfort and strengthen the hearts of those with whom

29. Psalm 51

we have prayed, but if the prayer has not gained the heart of God, it has failed in its essential purpose.[30]

The worship service is a desire to seek the face of God and in every prayer meeting the saints should find God when they seek Him with all their hearts, and the saints will find him, declares the Lord.

When the Lord is found he promises to bring us back from captivity.

He will gather us from all the nations and places where He has banished us, declares the Lord and He surely will bring us back to the place from which He has carried us into exile.

There is repatriation in the season of worship taking the people back to their full value, who they are and who they are in Jesus.

What does salvation and the blood of Jesus make of them. We will be transformed from common people to sons and daughters of God, heir and co-heirs together with Christ, sharing with Him in the heavenly things and sitting with him in heavenly places

The worshipper reads Jeremiah 29: 12-14 and this is what they see, "I call upon you oh Lord as I come in prayer. Oh Lord listen. I seek for you with all my heart and desire to find you. I will find you and you will bring me back from captivity."

Joel 2: 12-14: "return to me with all your heart with fasting and weeping and mourning rend your hearts and not your garments return to the Lord your God for He is gracious and compassionate slow to anger and abounding in love and he relents from sending calamity who knows? He may turn and have pity and leave a blessing behind, grain offering and drink offerings for the Lord your God. The worshipper looks at this passage and sees a massage for their souls as they take the word into their souls"

This is how the worshipper takes the word and is able to apply it into their lives, to develop personal holiness there needs to be this internalization of truth and constant interaction of truth between the paper, book and the tablets of the heart.

This is how God writes the words into our hearts.

This is how we convert a filthy sacrifice to an acceptable sacrifice.

Meaningless offerings and services must be baptized into these two Psalms and the leader must visit the in most chambers to establish that there is truth and that God can use and bless the congregation through the assembly.

---

30. Jeremiah 29: 12 -13

It will be sad to continue to worship without the value of divine blessings in our congregations. The leader must come and experience the salvation before leading transgressors and sinners to God.

In the private space the leader must denounce sin and not cast the votes with the wicked, then God will prosper him and rebuild the walls and in "His Pleasure", bring prosperity.

WHO OCCUPIES THE HEART OF THE WORSHIPPER?

In John 1.14 "The Word became flesh and made his dwelling Among Us." We have seen his glory, the glory of the one and only Son, who came from the Father, full of grace and truth. The wholeness of YHWH in the fullness of us, that is occupancy when the human is fully taken over by the divine.

John fully recognizes the gift that God sent to us, Himself; in the full image of the Son. God was born to us, for us, through us, as all of Him and all of us. The mystery of grace to fit a mountain in a teaspoon, and squeeze the sea into a cup. Mingling with divinity, human gift of grace to live with God.

The miracles in how God reduces Himself, to fit in a small venue without bursting the container. How God allows His occupancy to be within when by essence He is without.

There is someone much bigger, more power yet dwelling in the much smaller and make residence in the so weak (Christ in Us, the hope of glory).

How does strength dwell with weakness and not destroy it? How do you store fire in plastic and not melt the plastic? Grace is our insulation.

Someone tell me how does a righteous God come to a sinful nation or heart and make Himself 'one of, one with' without losing Himself. The answer is grace we receive not because we have labored but because He has worked and is still at work in us.

This is clay in the hands of the porter. It is to us a benefit and to Him a duty and gift. Worship is a divine opportunity to infuse more of God in us and empty more of self from us. Sin is resolved in Him for Himself when it touches us it no longer has the sting but the guilt that brings us to repentance. John says God (Jesus) came and dwelt amongst us, as disciples during his time they lived with Him, he was amongst them.[31]

---

31. John 1:14

Then Paul with builds on the thought, to celebrate the reality of the amongst us, Paul pushes the walls on understanding even further when he submits in the book of *Colossians 1: 26-29.*

26. There is a mystery that has been kept hidden for ages and generations, but is now disclosed to the Lord's people. **27.** To them God has chosen to make known among the Gentiles the glorious riches of this mystery, which is Christ in you, the hope of glory.

28. He is the one we proclaim, admonition and teaching everyone with all wisdom, so that we may present everyone fully mature in Christ.

29. To this end I strenuously contend with all the energy Christ so powerfully works in me.

Here is the difference between the writing of John and Paul, to John Jesus is amongst us, to Paul He is in us. The hope of Glory! In simple terms, Glory (God) is hoping on this matter, that through His presence in us would make us experience Glory in the now and see it in the bye and bye.

The only hope we have to reach heaven is with this glory in us. The hope of our glory is Christ in us. To be saved and translated to look like Him is fully depended in Him in us. An opportunity to be with Him in the heavenly places sitting with Him, and behind the curtain with Him, worship transports us to the very presence of our Savior to participate in the heavenly ministry.

The ministry in the heavens is in us as a microcosm. The two temples must all sing *"thy will be done on earth as it is in heaven"*. To us it is not just a going up to Him, it's Him coming down the venue of this union, and that is Worship.

We are preserved from within, magnetized from inside ready to be translated when the big celestial magnet shall be in the clouds "in a moment of a twinkling of an eye we shall be caught up to meet the Lord in the air."

The reality is that worship is a foretaste of this translation.

"The hope of Glory" is the guarantee of our glory in the mystery of giving Christ room in us. When we embrace this truth Glory is waiting to shine in Glory within us.

This is incarnation in its true sense, that we are pregnant with the supernatural, and we birth spiritual things, the first form of "legal fornication" in the bible, Mary full of Spirit and God. So the Worshipper must be full of God while he or she calls the believers to faith.

The worshipper must be pregnant with truth and divine expectation to birth destiny. Mary is in the flesh but carrying the spiritual. There you have the solution, in the world but not of this world. Mary, married to Joseph but carrying the substance of God.

Bound to the earth, but filled with the divine.

We have to understand in the Innermost issue - the heart issue or mind. God desires to sit at the citadel of our thoughts and affection and from the center of us control the things without us, outside of us.

Salvation is not about what we do, but the influence that we have allowed to govern our behavior. The power that makes us do must be broken and God can control the body from the mind, and the mind from the spirit.

The cellphone (the handset) will be configured by the sim-card that you insert. The network service provider governs the behavior of the cellphone handset. It is safe to say do not worry about what you do, but ask who is the service provider. "Spirituality lies in what you do and how you do it and not what result you get."- **Kapil Dev**

Change the sim-card and the handset will automatically download the new software that makes the handset comply with the service provider. When sim-card is changed automatically the handset searches for a new signal in the air and links remotely to the airwaves (there is power in changing the sim-card). God and evil are the air. Let the worshipper find the correct signal and plug the saints to the right frequency of the omnipresent YHWH.

This Trinity concept which is Greco-catholic in nature, seeks to break things apart in order to understand them. The Hebrew says, put things together to understand.

Like a cellphone in your hand, YHWH is the handset and Jesus is the software. The holy spirit is the network that connects us to all networks through which we can reach other places and people more-so, talk to the almighty. "Hear yea oh Israel the Lord your God is One."

The purpose of worship therefore is to enter into the Holy Place, into the very presence of God and participate in the live interaction with angelic company in holy convocation.

This is a spiritual journey and the worshipper must travel in the spirit, into the presence of YHWH who is SPIRIT.

The wisdom of the worshipper is to use physical rituals to access the spiritual realms. Sin cheats us of the opportunity to come boldly, but the spirit of God, when He wins our hearts, encourages us to move with assurance. He takes our prayers and modifies them so that we too can come boldly, with confidence.

The Spirit is our transport into the presence of YHWH. Every Christian must take this trip from the physical, through the Holy Spirit, walk past the demonic realm, into the presence of YHWH.

On the first two levels the physical and the spiritual it's a battlefield.

Have a look at Ephesians 6 in this light "Put on the whole amour."

The devil takes his time to train the initiate, they are shown and taught how to live under water, and move up from earth to mid air, covenants that are done in nakedness with human sacrifices and oaths with demons give demons access into the physical channel, body, and then use the human body as a medium to do evil.

The demon possessed person gives in to the outer powers. Medicine with all its test tubes can argue, but the reality stares us in the face there is more to disease and mental illnesses than tablets. The illusions are real, when the human body is under the control on the demonic forces there is another world and reality that manifests, and this world is a reality.

How dare the Christian? Opting for a powerless faith, weak training that does not challenge the spirit world. We often happily clap hands and shout an empty 'Amen' and 'Halleluiah' which changes and manifest nothing.

These forms of meaningless "isms", collection of doctrines, artificial worship services and workshops have no impact to spiritual warfare. They are physically exhausting yet fear to drive through the barrier of the physical to the spiritual and meaningfully find the hand of the God in the darkness of our souls.

Have you ever walked into a room were there is a witchdoctor and your hair stood on its back? Why? The spiritual nerves stand to tell you that you are now standing on a different ground and your hair is your physical signal antenna that tell you that its catching another frequency.

Have you shaken someone's hand and your spirit is not at ease? Have you felt you stomach turn when in the presence of a person who has inter-action with demons?

Is God not more powerful in us to do exceedingly more than this?

Did Jesus not say greater things than this we shall do when the power has come upon us? Here is how we started, they wanted to stone Jesus and the bible says He walked amongst them and slipped away and they could not touch him. Through our ministry, Jesus demonstrates power over ailments, diseases, sickness, nature, demons, and grave. Look at Phillip who flew from Jerusalem to the Ethiopian eunuch, to baptize him.

Ever thought how God transported him, the bible says and suddenly there sat next to him (eunuch) Phillip and asked him, "Do you know and understand what you are reading."[32]

This is the kind of supernatural power that we should tap into at the moment of worship yet we opt for meaningless recital of verses.

Seek for a true personal faith that will start to deal with issues of depth than formalities. The true worshipper should translate us into the realm of power, that is a spiritual arrival from a journey of physical troubles and pain.

Psalm 19: the two revelations will prepare you for the journey into real worship and fellowship with the supernatural, if you have read the general and specific revelation, then words of our mouths and the mediations of our hearts will be pleasing before our God.

During worship we must join hands with thousands of angels in heavenly places in holy convocation. Faith takes us there to the real venue of worship. The death of Jesus was not only for the forgiveness of sin, but the breaking of the barrier between the holy place and the most holy, so as to give us access in the very presence of God.

This reality unleashes the potential of a Christian to practice their faith at a higher level. There is something very critical that we are missing as Christians that the demonic world takes advantage of. Ministers and worshippers must take us members and move us to the point of interaction with the object of our faith - our God.

Theologians must not over theologize the encounter for it's a reality that the human soul yearns for. Our young people are being lured into the realm of spiritualism, why, because they are looking for something more powerful and meaningful. They seek for depth as the church dishes to them shallow formalities and traditions.

We cannot blame them for we know, but very little and we have settled for less. Our religions have been more towards collecting loyalists rather than warriors of faith.

---

32. Acts 8:26-40 Phillip baptizes the Ethiopian Eunuch

What occupies the heart of the worshippers?

Out of the abundance of the heart the mouth speaks.[33] The worshippers have come from various places with different needs burdens, questions and problems. It is not wise to take them for granted for the sorrows of the heart only God knows.

When the dustbins of evil are full in their lives they need to be emptied at the foot of the cross. Give them a chance to come and pour their prayers (requests) and praise (thanksgiving), for their hearts have an offering of praise that will heal their souls. In the presence of the Lord, burdens are lifted. God wins the hearts to Himself.

Psalm 86 will give the worshipper some light into the lives of other worshippers. David outlines some basic needs in the hearts of the worshippers. In this life that is always asking questions for everyday of the month there are 31 demands the saints have from the throne of grace:

They have come to seek answers for their poverty and needs.

They need protection for their lives they're bombarded with evil demands.

They need salvation for their souls and learn to trust in God.

They seek for mercy in the midst of their blunders. They need continuous assurance that God's ears are next to their lips. They seek for joy and happiness from the creator of satisfaction.

They need to be lifted up for the evil one has pressed their souls with anxiety. They need to taste the goodness of God and abundance of forgiveness. They need to pray to power and have assurance that God is present to do what they ask of Him to do. They need an emergency call to the Lord in the day of their trouble.

They need God to respond with answers. God must show up better than other gods for He is Lord. They need to worship God for who He is and praise Him for what He has done. Their worship needs to bring glory, for the name of God is exalted in their lives. They need to appreciate the goodness of the works of God. They need an education to walk in the ways of the Lord

They need to walk with God in the paths of truth. They need to learn how to serve God with undivided attention.

---

33. Mathew 12:34 you can't speak good things when you are evil: the content of your heart will rhyme with the words of your heart.

They need to fear the Name of the Lord. They need to praise God with all their hearts. They need to glorify His name forever and experience His love towards them. They need to celebrate deliverance from the depths of the grave. They are being attacked by the arrogant. There is a need to feel divine compassion.

They need to enjoy the faithfulness of divine consistency.

They need to feel that Gods face is towards them for mercy. Some are fainting and worship must bring them strength to try again. Yet others feel displaced they need to be servants of the Most High.

They seek for signs from the goodness of God to shame their enemies. They need comfort, help and solid foundations, "OH Lord hear, answer and comfort Selah! Let the worshipper be the source of glad tidings"

Read through Job chapter 38 and you will find words to share.

The encounter is a spiritual union, which brings spiritual remedies to psychological and pathological disorders, dealing with the source of the issues and healing that must come from within.

It does not matter what the saints are going through, the Lord has promised that there are answers in the storms of life. He will answer from the storm and in the midst of darkness, and in the storm there is counsel.

Let the saints brace themselves and stand like man the Lord has questions to ask as the saints have answers to receive.

The worshippers must understand their position in the creation story, "where were you", and there is also a need to appreciate the dimensions and that there are some things that the Lord will not allow to cross over.

The human problem is the Psychology of worship *Doctor Gift Mweemba* attest that human beings are:

A. **Genetically and generally complex by nature:** the human being is a multi dimensional creature of divine origin.

Since worship seeks to address the human being, the worshipper needs to understand psychology and the depth of human sorrow, pain and search in the maze of divine complexity in the "image of God and likeness" of the creature made from the thought and hands of the Eternal God.

The problem asserted is not usually the real problem, there is a deeper need and root cause of the problem. Divorce, finance, disease etc. are challenges that are the external manifestation. They are a cry of human desires, they are not the real problem but fruits of a hidden deeper source of the problem.

Worship therefore must call for the "balm of Gilead" for the people at different realms to the symptomatic reality and plant a solution that heals the disease of the soul.

B. **There are social complexities**: over the period of time the many people have devised plans to intervene the human search and pain. In the midst of it numerous methods have been implemented that makes presence a "socially complexity."

Various cultural and social dynamics must be considered as presenting a maze options. The functionality and comparative nature of solutions, from culture, religion, finance, spirituality and medical; all have their successes and their stories are a benchmark of the nature of the solution given to the worshipper.

People are result oriented; therefore theory of worship must not ignore the pragmatic nature of the human psychology and biological chemistry.

Emotions are not evil they are part of human creation and expression you can't tell people to leave emotions outside, then what do you have, robots at praise?

C. **The solutions are generally complex:** The solutions are complex for there are what we want leading to what we need. Its not praying for a child or rather barrenness being a problem but social status and acceptance at a cultural level and satisfaction on the males side to posterity and continuation of the family name and clan.

The "use" of human meets purpose of the human being as perpetual conduits of past and future. To fail to do this can be classified as failure.

Now how the supply of the child presents a financial obligation, and spiritual health with social demands, which are, by nature problems in their own right. In short "Solutions present more Problems".[34]

To grow people, God has cornerstones of experiences. Remember that, in the midst of the midnight hour the stars will sing and the angels will shout for joy.

The Lord will shut the sea behind the door of affliction when it burst to consume. The clouds will be used to dress up destruction, and affliction has its limits and it will come but not this far. Grace halts the pains and secures our joy.

---

34. Dr Gift Mweemba Interview Bloemfontein Sabbath of June 7, 2014. The Israelite threat of fertility of Baal worship in the land of milk and honey.

Every morning God will give orders to dawn and to shine again, and shake the wicked out of it. All issues that look like mud in our sight God will make the world out it and shape it for our good.

More power is found in knowledge than in the midst of the sea. God has springs that water the sea and recesses in the shadows of the deep. Fear not while your life goes through turmoil and pain, you may gaze into the very gates of death or seen the shadow of death, we have the first born from the dead.

The saints must be overwhelmed by the knowledge that no one has seen the storehouse where God stores the lights and the closet where darkness resides. Be of good cheer when snow and hail fall into your life, for if you could see the storehouse, you will smile.

Your Father, full of kindness, is the dispatch manager and nothing beyond your power will befall you.

The Lord disperses lightning, and sits at the fountains of the eastern winds and scatters the earth. He alone has the remote control that cut off the torrents of the rain.

The wisdom and power of God channels the path of the thunderstorms, why are you afraid when it rains in your life, the hand of Grace has mapped a path for a storm to your door post. Ever thought where God keeps the cooler freezers to turn water to stones, or how He makes snow in the sea. His ways are not your ways; far above the heavens are His plans for your life.

Look up to heaven there is a dominion; God resides over the affairs of this earth. The very nature of our minds is a masterpiece of His handwork. He plants wisdom in our hearts and during moments of worships, He gives us understanding that it is OK. The Lord is the Lord of time; Job 39 gives times for the mountain goats to give birth.

The wild ox cannot be tamed, so there are situations that are out of your control. Like an ostrich in the desert, God has put you like eggs in the sand to hatch. You may feel like you will be crushed on the desert floor, or that some wild animals will eat you up but God watches over His own. The ostrich may treat its young ones harshly like they are not her own but through it all they are safe and protected.

Look at the horse that strikes terror with his snorting ad fiercely paws as he charges into battle. The horse laughs at fear and is afraid of nothing and will never shy away from the sword.

The horse giggles at the clashing of swords and smiles at the blaze of arrows. Let the worshipper prepare the saints for battle and plant in their hearts the triumphant song of the stallion.

When the battle trumpet is blown the horse cannot stand still as he is frenzied with excitement, are we not more than horses?

Like the eagles that sow above the storm let the saints arise to the heights God has for them. Secure their future in the cleft of the rocks on the cliffs and God's pavilions.

Master Servant

Who controls the worshipper?

The modern Christian needs to fully surrender our lives into the hands of God, more than what the witches do and learn how to do battle in the spiritual world.

The devil must be stopped in his tracks, and the evil spirits must be rebuked when they seek to disturb our peace. Even Paul admonishes that when spiritual gifts are present, there needs to be someone who has the spirit to discern spirits. This important so that the as the spirit manifest, the discerner can see which one is the true spirit and which one is evil.

Many churches have settled for the collection of offerings and making members rather than make armies that can wage war in the spiritual realm.

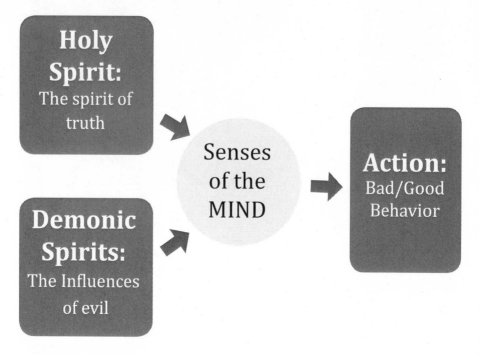

Fig 10: Connect the Spirits

Sadly speaking the duties of ministers has been to teach members how to survive in the physical realm and fight over habits. Always praying that God should remove the cobwebs, but never killing the spider. The root of the problem is the problem of the roots.

The foundation of thought and evil behavior is not in the physical realm but spiritual realm. The demons in the spirit use our minds to gain access to our thinking through visible and subtle communication that lower our moral alertness.

Once the evil idea is planted and compromised then the demons start to work to create opportunities when the ideas would be carried out and sin committed. The intention is not to make us sin, but to grow sin into a lifestyle of rebellion, that will take us away from God and we condemn ourselves in our own guilt.

The final results and action can only verify and confirm whose seed has been planted in our minds, whether God's idea through the Holy Spirit or demons. The result is either works of kindness fruit of the spirit or wages of sin, which is death – fruits of the flesh.

It must be highlighted that the real battles are fought at the physical but at the spiritual level.

Rev 14: The hour of His judgment has come. The word judgment presents as "crisis" with decision making. Therefore every time a decision is made in war and crisis, to who do we give our vote of confidence.

Colossians 1:21 challenges us to align with God, for once we are enemies of God, alienated from God in our minds because of evil and sinful behavior. But now reconciled in Christ in the physical body, continue in such faith and you will be established.

The death of Christ also made a spectacle of the forces of evil, the authorities and the powers were brought to shame.

Colossians 1:15 Let us pose a question to the worshipper who is blessed with VIP treatment. Into the chambers of our thoughts do we manufacture ideas and activities in the body?

Even for those who are claiming to be single, in reality most of them are married to their sex toys. Instead of brining the body under control we take time to please the flesh as we unite our souls with lifeless toys, plastics and electrical gadgets.

The influence of the Holy Spirit will come with a song of praise, hymn of encouragement, a word of prophecy[1] and the power of a worshipper who has been with God will stir the hearts of the congregation to find their places on the circle of divine convocation.

For us to benefit from a meaningful worship service, it must be understood that this takes place within the third level. That's where the blessings and the divine await to cheer the fainting heart.

THERE ARE FOUR VENUES IN THE MODEL OF THE SANCTUARY

1. **Outside of the Temple in the community:** this is social fellowship experienced with the larger community and social space often the worshipper can be in concert or observer and benefit from aesthetic and observation.

2. **The inner Court - Inside but outside, enclosure in the Temple outside:** here the worshipper is involved as a participant and meaningfully contributes to the worship service. In some cases this is duty and because of expectation the worshipper does not

---

1. The Hebrew word for prophecy is passive, —nibba' or hithnabbe', "to be made to speak," or "to bubble forth,"—the Deity being the active power, while the prophet is His mouthpiece

necessarily have to be in it but gives a professional service and can walk away without benefit from the moment of power.

3. **Holy place:** the venue inside: this is when the worshipper begins to allow influence and "takes in" to internalize the worship service and allows the worship service to shine into their souls and as they feed and supplicate as part of the whole and be present to present themselves and the congregation.

4. **Most Holy place - the very chamber of power:** the active role and movement of the divine behind the curtain properly evoked the response is eminent and visible. The worship leader becomes the medium through the service.

5. The people who came for worship meet God who has been looking for them. The worship service becomes the matrimony of and union of the parties.

6. The Worship leader brings God to the people to the centers of human existence "the mental and very soul and spirit of man" and in the depth of their search He (YHWH) incarnates their souls and finds residence in sacred parts and chambers of human life the Most Holy Place is the spiritual realm.

Divinity living in humanity, it is possible for a human being to be filed with the Spirit of the Lord. The desire of YHWH is to make residence in the human heart and the emptiness of the human heart needs divine filling. "I think after time, there won't be anything left to be interesting for mankind. Computers are about to do everything for us. Cellphones are smarter than we are. We'll embrace spirituality because we'll be bored of everything else."[2]

The Spirit is man and infant, and needs to be developed to the extent that it is able to commune with the Creator as was in the beginning.

We have been running away from the soft voice we hear in the garden because we are naked. Genesis 3:1-18, to which the Lord's voice still echoes in the garden, "Where are you?" That innocence we lost in the beginning has been a breeding ground of all religions and cults. On Mount Carmel Elijah was confronted with 400 priests from the temple of Baal whom he allowed to call on their god. At noon Elijah began to taunt them. "Shout louder!" he said. "Surely if he is a god! Perhaps he is deep in thought, or busy, or traveling. Maybe he is sleeping and must be awakened." [3]

2. Damian Marley
3. 1 Kings 18:27

1 kings 18:27 the churches today are the opposite:

Where is our God?

Has he gone on holiday, is he in a deep sleep?

Is he in deep thought?

Why is he not answering?

Why do witchdoctors have a quicker access to their gods and we, who claim to be Christians have no contact with the God we claim to know?

Is evil now closer that righteousness? What is it we must do to break the silence and evoke God to move and speak for Himself? Is it possible that we have a form of Godliness and have denied the power?

What is the use of Churches if they cannot produce spiritual people full of the Holy Spirit instead of Christians empty of divine presence?

You are either full of God or full of demons. The Spirit of the Lord causes Heaven to descend on our offering, ask Elijah

"I will put My Spirit within you and cause you to walk in my statutes, and you will be careful to observe my ordinances.[4] It is impossible to do the work of the Spirit without the Spirit. YHWH in us will enable us to do His will, "for it is God who works in you to will and to act in order to fulfill his good purpose."[5]

"Guard, through the Holy Spirit who dwells in us, the treasure which has been entrusted to you."[6] The Holy Spirit is a faithful watchman on the walls of our hearts who is a treasure and yet also preserves the treasure that we are in Him. The treasure is a preservative that preserves.

A. The Spirit Preserves and assists us to fulfill YHWH's Purpose

"This is the covenant that I will make with them after those days, says the Lord, I will put my laws into their hearts, and in their minds will I write them."[7] The divine movement from the external tablets to the tablets of the heart is the most compelling argument we have on the two covenants.

There are two covenants, the covenant of the flesh versus the covenant of stone. Our hearts are the tablets on which the Lord wants to write his covenant.

B. The Spirit makes the statues of YHWH sync with our hearts

"And Jesus being full of the Holy Ghost returned from Jordan, and was led by the

4. Ezekiel 36:27
5. Phil 2:13
6. 2 Timothy 1:14
7. Hebrews 10:16

Spirit into the wilderness,'[8]. There is no room for emptiness, Immanuel was "full" of the Holy Spirit, and the Holy Spirit was driving Him, directing Him and placing Him at the right venues to be of service.

"Oh how I pray the Lord can drop this in your spirit and live a life that is driven by "higher hands" Oh that the Lord will fully occupy you to move and be an instrument in the hands of grace."

C. The Spirit of the Lord physically leads and takes us places.

We are going places in the spirit! The work of the Lord would move at a much faster pace had we known the formula to appoint those who must work in our midst.

"Therefore, brethren, select from among you seven men of good reputation, full of the Spirit and of wisdom, whom we may put in charge of this task."[9]

D. The Spirit of the Lord gives wisdom, prophesy, teaching and power.

As Micah would declare "On the other hand I am filled with power. With the Spirit of the LORD. And with justice and courage to make known to Jacob his rebellious act, even to Israel his sin."[10]

E. The Spirit gives Power to declare the oracles of YHWH

"I have filled him with the Spirit of God in wisdom, in understanding, in knowledge, and in all kinds of craftsmanship."[11]

The things that YHWH wants done are downloaded into the disks of our hearts through the software of the Holy Spirit we are able to read the mind of YHWH and create physical things that enhance life and make profit for us.

F. The Spirit enhances our talents and gifts.

It makes craftsman out of mere man. "And let them make me a holy place, so that I may be ever present among them." There Physical temple (building) and the Spiritual temple (our hearts) must be constructed well so that the indwelling becomes a reality.[12]

There needs to be an intentional construction of the inner chambers, and external tools to facilitate the inhabitation of the Holy Spirit or Clean spirit.

8. Luke 4:1
9. Acts 6:3
10. Micah 3:8
11. Exodus 31:3
12. Exodus 25:8

G. The Spirit dwells in a venue that has been prepared for divine habitation. *"For he will be great in the sight of the Lord; and he will drink no wine or liquor, and he will be filled with the Holy Spirit while yet in his mother's womb."* [13] Drunkenness fills the heart with emptiness, and sober minds are a favorable place the Lord dwells in. Those filled with the Spirit can birth those that are of the Spirit also.

H. The Spirit fills us to produce the next generation of Spirit filled offspring.

"When Elizabeth heard Mary's greeting, the baby leaped in her womb; and Elizabeth was filled with the Holy Spirit." [14] The presence of the Holy Spirit assists you to identify others who are filled with the same spirit. The software of a spiritual person can read other softwares of the same nature. This is what it means, "they were of the same spirit."

I. The Spirit connects with the Spirit.

"Then Peter, filled with the Holy Spirit, said to them, "Rulers and elders of the people…" [15] Speech must first be baptized in the Holy Spirit before it is baptized in our saliva and mouths. The source of fervent words that are seasoned is the spirit. The Mind should be in connection with YHWH to speak from depth and knowledge of the other.

J. The Spirit is not limited hence the ability to be relevant.

The Spirit will select our words for communication and daily speech.… For we are the temple of the living God, just as God said, "I WILL DWELL IN THEM AND WALK AMONG THEM, AND I WILL BE THEIR GOD, AND THEY SHALL BE MY PEOPLE." [16]

K. The Spirit desires to dwell and fully possess the heart.

As the human body has many physical desires there is a spiritual desire of the human body to function at a spiritual level. *"But being full of the Holy Spirit, he gazed intently into heaven and saw the glory of God, and Jesus standing at the right hand of God."* [17]

The Spirit causes us to see the heavenly things in the midst of physical problems. "And his father Zacharias was filled with the Holy Spirit, and prophesied"[18]

---

13. Luke 1:15
14. Luke 1:41
15. Acts 4:8
16. 2Corinthians 6:16
17. Acts 7:55
18. Luke 1:67

L.   The Spirit gives a word in season.

"And when they had prayed, the place where they had gathered together was shaken, and they were all filled with the Holy Spirit and began to speak the word of God with boldness."[19]

M. The Spirit gives confidence.

"And do not get drunk with wine, for that is dissipation, but be filled with the Spirit"[20]

N. The Spirit can not fill us while full of liquor spirit

"Let this mind be in you, which was also in Christ Jesus." [21]

Through the Spirit we can have a mental transformation."Having been filled with the fruit of righteousness which comes through Jesus Christ, to the glory and praise of God."[22] The Spirit in full occupancy will assist us to realize the fruit of the spirit. "Don't you know that your body is a sanctuary of the Holy Spirit who is in you, whom you have from God? You are not your own."[23]

O. The Spirit in us and makes our hearts shrines of Spiritual contact.

"But if the Spirit of Him who raised Jesus from the dead dwells in you, He who raised Christ Jesus from the dead will also give life to your mortal bodies through His Spirit who dwells in you." [24]

"But when He, the Spirit of truth, comes, He will guide you into all the truth; for He will not speak on His own initiative, but whatever He hears, He will speak; and He will disclose to you what is to come." John 16:13

P.   The Spirit is a teacher of truth and leads to all truth.

The anointing when poured on a life through the Holy Spirit will abide and dwell and control the faculties of thought and action from within.

His anointing teaches you about all things, and it is true and not a lie, and just as it has taught you, and you abide in Him.[25]

The Spirit desires clean vessels and thorough preparation is critical for the manifestation as we unite our spirit with the Spirit of God.

---

19. Acts 4:31
20. Ephesians 5:18
21. Philippians 2:5
22. Philippians 1:11
23. 1Corithians 6:19
24. Romans 8:11
25. 1 John 2:27

As such every believer must consider himself fully owned, occupied and possessed by YHWH through His Spirit. Our Spirits belong to Him and through that nature heaven and earth are united in the physical vessel.

The Scripture highlights the human heart as a 'temple' , 'home', 'house' and 'residence'. Our bodies are therefore "divine shrines", or the "sacred places", in which the Spirit not only lives, but also is daily worshiped, constantly revered, and daily honored. Our thoughts, our speech and actions must be controlled from the temple.

Jacob during the ladder dream, in the morning he woke up "And fear came on him, and he said, this is a holy place; this is nothing less than the house of God and the doorway of heaven."[26] His mind, his spirit, his dream, his encounter had become a doorway of heaven.

There is no better venue and verse that describes the encounter, but we through the spirit have access to the "doorway of heaven". Having access and *"going places in the spirit"* to visit the portals of heaven during moments of worship should be our greatest desire and achievement. Any worship service that does not usher people into this presence would have failed.

All forms of order and liturgy must drive the agenda of taking people to the door of heaven where the Lord says, "behold I stand at the door and knock" if the Lord is not allowed into the inside of our churches then who is with us inside?

"And it shall come to pass in the last days, says God, I will pour out of my Spirit upon all flesh, and your sons and your daughters shall prophesy, and your young men shall see visions, and your old men shall have dreams: And on my servants and on my handmaidens I will pour out in those days, my Spirit; and they shall prophesy."[27]

The manifestation of the spirit can not be limited, as the spiritual people take their place there. The human church cannot control Mwari unless He is an idol. What He promised he will do, He will do.

The season is now, and the times of refreshments are now upon us, the Lord has promised and He cannot lie. The spirit of Elijah will be returned to us and we shall call on the Lord and He will hasten to listen. The Spirit of the fathers will be returned to the sons. There shall be mentorships and handing over of burtons to the next generations.

Mantles of power will be given to the children. There shall be possession with the double portion. Our words and the words of YHWH will be

26. Genesis 28:17
27. Acts 2:17-18

one word. The Spirit of Elijah and the power of Elijah are going to work and make the willing experience the Elijah life, to speak their words like Jehovah's words and live miraculous lives.

Worship should takes place at the four venues. Two words depict worship in *Shona kuteura* and *kunamata*. *Kuteura* is a Shona word for pouring out; emptying of self, it suggests a reckless pouring to the ground like the woman who poured oil on the feet of *Yashua*. It is intentional as it is not careful, liberal distribution of desire. Worship in *Shona* therefore is *Kuteura*.

Kunamata has to do with homage and prayer in a posture of humility.

This is the attitude of those who approach the place of worship.

The Sanctuary or Temple in the Old Testament had four venues that will guide us into the presence of Jehovah.

See the symbols and stations and make this your church, your family and see yourself walking through this diagram to reach the Mercy seat. It is clear on the design that the sanctuary is a meeting place of the earthly and the heavenly, from physical to spiritual.

The utensils in the sanctuary are meant to create in human mind the expectation to approach divinity in Hebraic. The African needs to loon into the sanctuary and see that he has the concept right to access his YHWH.

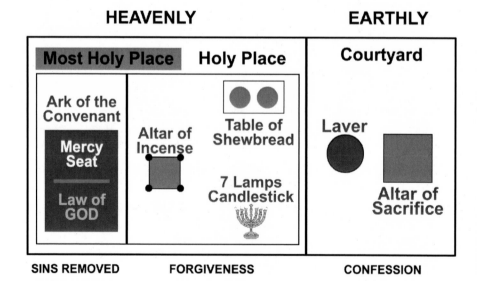

1 Figure 11 : Layout of the Sanctuary

---

1. http://jesuschristinhissanctuary.net/studies_on_the_sanctuary.htm

LAYOUT OF THE SANCTUARY

i.   The outer court:

Have the community in mind where life is lived. This is the worship of the church, group worship and crowds and small groups gather to call upon the Name of *Unkulunkulu (God)*.

The first place of worship is away from the sanctuary but your heart is the sanctuary.

ii.   The outer court/courtyard:

The sacrifice and confession - Like the model of the Temple here you bring your offering and empty your soul as an individual. You touch the innocent to contaminate it with your guilt and you can experience the forgiveness.

Worship cannot begin until the human assumes the posture of humility and admit to their inability to operate in their flesh as ultimate reality. It is when the heart of pride goes down that the spirit goes up.

When you humble yourself the Lord will lift you up to Him.

The washing of hands and feet, where we come from and what we have touched contaminates us, before entrance into the holy place there is a place to get the hands and the feet washed. When sins are confessed, the heart is clean, when the hands and feet are washed the whole body is clean inside and outside.

iii.   The holy place - the word and the spirit of the lord:

With clean hands and feet can you now hold the word or bread and powerful voice of scripture will be audible to your spirit.

Note you enter here into the presence of Light, the oil of the Holy Spirit lights the venue of worship so that you can see.

The combination of the word and the spirit is the true recipe of worship in John 4 worships me in truth and in spirit. The union of your spirit and the Holy Spirit directs your eyes to thee "thus says the Lord" and prepares you for prayer the alter of burnt incense which represents the prayers of the saint from a clean heart.

There is no way YHWH will not listen when you have done your part to approach the throne of grace. The worshipper must come boldly to the throne of grace. The prayers of a spiritual heart reach him like a sweet aroma.

iv.   The most holy place - the meeting with divinity:

The ultimate place we want to be, beyond the curtain, into the presence of Jehovah, and his ways are written into our heart, the miracles of manna are reminded and divine leadership as the rod of Aaron are accepted.

Here at the mercy seat surrounded by cherubim in the presence of glory and gold, power and divine authority is a reality.

The worshipper should not fear to kneel and submit their spirit and flesh to be reprogrammed by grace. The software needs an upgrade and that touch will cause the change as the glory of the "Most holy" becomes transmitted.

This approach brings change. You can't leave the venue of worship the same way you came in. After we have spent time with Leza, then we can walk back to our communities with a new shine on our faces like Moses from the Mountain.

John 17. 15. The worshipper is not of the world. He is one with his congregation as with His God. The Glory that Jesus has is manifested in the ministry of grace.

The worshipper must be sanctified by the truth and sent into the world to overcome by the power of the name. As Jesus has overcome, the worshipper must overcome too by the blood, the word and power of testimony.

Look at John 17: 5. and 6, "With the glory I had before is given as an assurance of the glory to manifest to the world." In verse 22 that same glory has been given, I have given them the Glory.

The unity of the church is not in sin but GLORY makes us one.

Jesus says "I in them and You in Me and that I myself can live in them!" I have given them you; the gift to us is a Glorious nature, through Jesus.

Reality is in the *spiritual realm*. The source of the problem is not physical, it is supernatural. The war is spiritual. In John 16:28 Jesus clearly reveals to us the extent of His glory and does not mince words on the reality of paradigms and realms.

It is clear that He came from the Father, and entered into the world, and that after His death, He will be leaving this world, and returning back to the Father.

Before his death, he spoke to us in figures of speech, but now He announces that we get ready to talk to the Father for ourselves, for if we have loved Jesus the Father loves us too - John 17: 26-27.

CRITICAL INFORMATION THE WORSHIPPER MUST BE AWARE OF:

In order to be a meaningful worshipper, you need to be in the event and not act after the event. Be present during the worship service, be aware of what you are doing and what you want to achieve.

What happens in the Realms?

"

YHWH hears Daniel's prayer and dispatches and answers.

ASK and you have been given. SEEK and you shall find. KNOCK and the door shall be open unto you.

King of the north-demon over Persia (principality-blocks Gabriel: this is where the battle takes place. Evil spirits don't want us to have access to Our Father. The WAR is Spiritual not Physical.

Daniel Seeks YHWH's Face.

Moses and his arms:[28] during the of battle Moses would raise his hands the armies would be winning, and when he put his arms down they would be defeated.

---

28. Exodus 17:12 When Moses' hands grew tired they took stones and put under him and he sat on it. Aaron and Hur held his hands up – one on the other – so that his hands remained steady till sunset.

Aaron and Hur realized the power and mystery of lifting hands (we should also lift up our hands in the moment of worship) battles would be won. The battle was not in the physical but in the spiritual.

Moses was commander in chief of the heavenly host and they responded to his command only as he kept his arms in the air. The team had to support his arm for the whole day and the battle was worn with arm in the air.

You may want to ask who was fighting? The Israelites and spiritual powers were evoked during battle and the army was a physical medium for fighting the spiritual battle. Worship time is a moment to lift each other's hands as the battles of life a waging on.

To break this down, in the New Testament theology, Ephesians 6:10-18 introduces to us a warehouse of our weaponry. The worshipper must not use the moment of worship to advertise sin and push people into the hole of failure and removing hope and joy from the lips of the saints.

The worshippers must be told to be strong in the might of the power of God. When the uniform is put on correctly there should be confidence, as we move and as we cross the bridge from the physical into the spiritual realm and finally into the heavenly realm of our Father's throne.

The devil is presented as a schemer, in the light of all this, let it sink in your head. The battle we fight is not of Flesh and Blood (physical, the sensory world, the actions or done deeds of sin) but we are at war on another level, according to Ephesians.

This dictates that the worship service raise above mere formalities into an intense wrestle in the spirit.

Like Jacob we should be heard crying during our worship *"I will not let you go until your bless me"* why would he need a blessing now, when he had stolen the blessings, he had wealth but no blessing.

There is a difference between blessing and blessings. The blessing is favor, whilst the blessings are results of the divine favor.

WORSHIP IS A WAR-FARE - WE FIGHT

There are good spirits and bad spirits
There are angels and there are demons
There is the Holy Spirit and Evil Spirit
There is Immanuel and Ha-Satan

a. **Rulers** - the devils have territorial rulers, like in the story of Daniel where the chief demon looking over Persia stood in the way of Gabriel to block him from delivering the answers to Daniels prayer

b. **Authorities** - these are powerful beings in the unseen world from the pits of hell who have become reputable authorities in tested methods of destruction over the last 6 000 years of temptation. Their methods have been tried and have worked, they are masters of schemes and the bible calls them authorities of evil.

c. **Powers** - principalities- principal of domains in the demonic realm. It is amazing that within the demonic realm we have such precision and order in terms of dispatch of orders, a direct rebuke to the church today that seem to struggle to recognize the function of ministers in their midst.

d. **Spiritual forces in the heavenly realm** - these are fierce forces that influence and attract towards evil company and sin. This is the marketing division, they major in presenting influences, through media, information that is distorted that allows the mind to start considering the bad practice.

The spiritual forces present the possibilities and when you get interested, you are handed over to the powers that begin to create the situation. From here you are introduced to authorities that are master of manipulation and illusion to perform the act, finally to find yourself under the ruler ship of demons.

Under the rulers the sinners, habit is reinforced into addiction as demons are given access into the your soul to keep you there and start plotting your death. The invisible warfare is a reality. This uniform is spiritual, clothed in psychical reality. Truth, ultimately is experienced in the realm and union of the seen and the unseen, the spirituality of physical manifestation.

Our uniform will protect us, it will make us stand when the enemy comes and will help us stand our ground and when you have done all you can stand.

When you have tried and failed, stand[29]
When you have fasted and answers seem not to come, stand
When friends are gone and the nights are weary and long, stand.
When you have tried all you can, stand,
When demons are dancing on your bed at night, stand,

29. Donnie Mcclurkin: song "Stand"

When your name is on the gutter of utter destruction, stand,
When bills are high and salaries are small, stand,
When husbands are gone and wives have born children from foreign man, stand
When you have tried all you can, stand
When disease eats up you flesh and you bones are dry
When laughter has left your face and pain and gravel is stuck in your teeth

To stand in the posture of submission, and the devil's scheme is to make you desperate, to seek for solutions from him over the problems that he brings. To stand is to be steady and know that your life is in the hand of God, note when you have done all you can. The best thing to do is to stand. When YHWH is coming to meet with Job, He announces that Job must stand and fasten his waist like a man. To stand is to be bold and confident at a post of duty.

A close observation at the passage would reveal the painful truth; the uniform cannot be used in parts, but the WHOLE armor. The exposure of part of the body makes the entire armor useless. It is evil to hear members brag that "my only problem is sex", the small problem exposes the whole body and nullifies the fortifications.

Stand not idly but with a belt of truth – Isaiah 11:5 the messianic dress your loins with truth. Issues of the abdomen need to be held together by a belt of truth, to tie your waist means to discipline your carnal nature so that nakedness is held together with this belt of truth. The areas that cause us shame must be tied with this thick belt of truth.

The whiteman's lies only give us the *white Jesus,* an idol of their imagination. Truth will lead us to *truth* and these lies have dumped us into the abyss of error and meaningless rituals. The battle is in the realm of truth to unmask the "white-lie" that his culture is a better civility that evokes spiritual connection, as opposed to the *"primitive-uncultured African traditions"*, truth must triumph. YHWH created us all and Africans are not a spiritual colony of white supremacy and its religious bigotry.

A. **Breastplate of righteousness** - the breastplate protects all the tender tissues of the body.

Consider also as a worshipper the style of your affection and issues of the heart. These parts must be protected by righteousness, our feelings must be right with God.

The heart is deceitful above all things that know it? If the heart is left vulnerable the no matter how secure the other parts are the battle is lost.

The litmus test of this *Eurocentric Christianity* 'right-doing' simple righteousness - does it teach and practice right-doing? Are the means of righteousness abstinence from African rituals, or justice and mercy?

The blood shed in the hands of democracy and Christianity proves to the contrary. Oppression, abuse, slavery, murder, thuggish behavior reveals that the religion has not entered the hearts of the missionary and preachers. "By their fruits your shall know them"

B. Your feet - the readiness that comes from the gospel of peace.

As contrasted to running barefooted the soldier of the spirit must make sure that their feet run for the gospel and not for gossip.

Did the missionaries bring us peace or a sword? Are we better people with this Christianity or not, have we improved in posterity and health?

Where are we headed? Do we walk into improvement or debasement? Has our feet walked into purity of we have run and lured into corruption and filth?

C. Shield of faith - used to extinguish the flaming arrows of the evil one, the arrows had flames, when the shield was soaked it could be used to extinguish flames and flame tipped arrows.

Faith creates the expected reality, we need to ask Christianity what it believes in? If the whole world become Christian, would this world be a better place? The faith we have been taught is in a false utopia of *European* fantasy and fairytale. Pies in the sky, and our eyes have been moved away from labor, ownership and glory of our land.

Faith must be in YHWH not the gadgets and lifestyles of the whiteman who never sees value in us, more than we can give. What is the faith of an African? What does he desire? What does he want to become? Remember, as a person believes so they behave. The substance of our faith is in our Maker and the glory He has dressed us in.

European civilization is not heaven for us. Has it not made us slaves of the economy and the meaningless religion and idols of mind and statures? Show me your faith Africa!

D. Helmet of salvation – protection of the mind with salvation issues.

The head occupies the greater senses that drive the body and these must be thoroughly guarded. Let the mind be occupied and covered by the helmet of salvation. Think on these things. Saved as opposed to damned? Africa, what have you been saved from?

What has been the price of our redemption? What are we protecting in our minds? What have they put in our minds? How do we think as a people? Are we safe to think as a people? Has this faith improved our minds? Can we think clearly? What tools occupy the processes of our perception?

What is the diet of minds on media and propaganda? What perceptions are on sale to our children? What stories and fairy-tales do they teach our children? What is the color of the dolls our children play with? What picture hangs on the canvas of our inner person? What value do we have in our own minds? See the helmet that is on the Africans head! Has this salvation protected our heads?

E.   The sword of the Spirit - which is the word of God.

The power is in confessing the word and speaking into the realms claiming promises and announcing a new status in Jesus' name. Keep the word of God on the tips of your tongues so that you can do battle in the spirit. Realm weapon on the hand of the mind is the sword of the spirit.

The true word activates the spirit to provoke, cut and battle.

The war is in the mind and only the spirit can govern this estate. The Spirit can invade the mind to change it and direct it towards itself (the Spirit). As situations come your way call on the Lord with a word of prayer-power and your speech salted by truth.

The Word fused in the Spirit will not go out and come back void before it achieves the desired intention. The Spirit causes, for He comes from the Uncaused Cause.

F.   Pray in the Spirit on all occasions with all kinds of prayers and requests - pray with the help of the Spirit or tune your spirit, be in touch with Holy Spirit.

Move away from physical prayer of memorized words that do not reach the heart. Praying in the spirit hints that you must join your spirit with the Holy spirit, surrender your spirit to the Holy spirit and He can hand hold you through the battle lines.[30]

This requires that we change gears to focus beyond the normal but the Spirit, and Go Places In The Spirit. Prayer is transformed into a direct evocation of the Spirit that cause the movement and control over the physical realm.

The weak person has the hand of power in the Spirit. To pray in the spirit as opposed to pray in the flesh, what benefit is the Spirit?

---

30. Romans 8:26

According to Romans 8 the Spirit becomes the filter through which our prayers are presented, for the same Spirit joined with our spirit, searches us from within and presents us above. Prayer must transcend beyond the need for physical things to the spiritual reality. Find the Spirit of the Spirit.

G. Be alert and keep other saints - (mediate-intercessor for others) do battle in the spirit.

As contrasted to slip up and sluggish behavior, be alert at all times of the devils plans around your life. Moving like a roaring lion seeking who he may devour.

Consider the story of Job, in the physical versus the occurrences in the spirit. We fight not small demons. We fight rulers and principality. The worshipper must escalate the warfare from here to the higher ground.

While Job was living and having fun with family there was a discussion in the spiritual realm that affected him in the physical realm. Had he approached the throne "Son of God came to worship" where was Job? He should have been privy to this conversation. For the Lord will not do anything to His people without firstly informing them through His prophets.[31]

He lived after the event.

Where was Job when the discussion was conducted?

Where are you when you name is discussed? The evil people can see you can you see them? When they sit to schemes where are you? Was Elisha not preview to what happened inside the King's bedroom? Did Jesus not tell them what they plotted in their hearts?

Did Peter not see the scheme of Ananias and Safira?

Does the spiritual eye not undress the physical body and its thoughts?

Is there anything that is hidden from the Spiritual eye?

The word of truth cuts and divides even separate the marrow in the bones and lays the heart bear, for nothing is hidden from the Lord.32 Seek the path (Torah) that leads to the Spirit. Train your Spirit to commune with the Spirit and define physical experiences in spiritual dimensions.

It first must be spelled out in the Spirit and then manifest in the physical, from the unseen to the seen. True reality is in the spiritual world, let us march to the city of unlimited exploration and power.

---

31. Amos 3:7 Surely the Sovereign Lord does not anything without revealing his plan to his servants the prophets.
32. Hebrews 4:10 -16

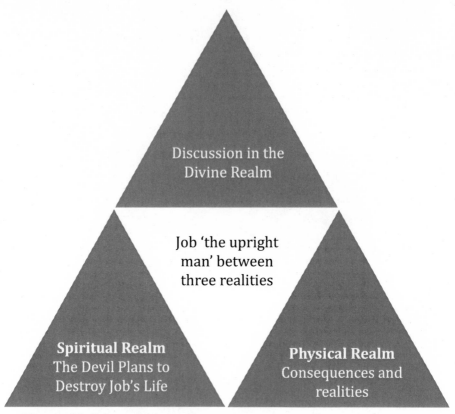

Figure 12: Job and his reality

Is holiness a necessity is it acquired or given?

Hebrews 10 - The demands of the law must be understood in the light that the law is a "shadow of the good things that are coming". It is futile to look at the law as the reality but a shadow of the grand manifestations of the sons of God.

The problem of Hebrews 10 is the nature of repetition to make something clean; they had to keep on sacrificing bulls, sheep and goats. The process in itself lacked the power to make the sinner victorious and "bulls can not take away sins". As in Hebrews 13 the call is that, "We should be holy as our Father is holy, for without holiness no man will see God"

Physical efforts cannot take away sin but acceptance of a gift of grace can. Rituals are a means to an end, not an end in them. That is the gift and the arrival of Christ, holding in His hands not a goat, bull or sheep but His life to do the will of the Father. The first law was set to establish the second, build me a sanctuary so that I may dwell amongst you, but through the sacrifice of Jesus He now lives in us.

That sacrifice is once and for all and in satisfaction He sits on high, the Holy Spirit our connecting cable with the throne room, has been put in our hearts and this law of divine access has to be written in our minds, so that we will not drive the cars of grace with a driving manual in our hands.

This internalization of this truth, Christ in us is a mystery that the cross has brought to us. Please note that in the new dispensation with the access now in place and Christ in us-through the Holy Spirit, Hebrews 10:18 celebrates that "Their sins I will remember them no more and as such we do not need to sacrifice for sin, to sin any longer."

Since the idea is to worship, now that sin is taken care of, Paul then drums it into our heads that we need to come to God with confidence, (come boldly) so that we may enter the Most Holy place, (the chamber of divine interaction). Earlier on, this place could only be accessed once a year by the high priest, but now with Christ in us the mystery and the hope of Glory, we too can enter with confidence.

Speak with your lips and declare the direction of your life henceforth.

We have this confidence on the basis of:

Level 1. Contact with the blood of Jesus - the moment of confession and when you profess with your lips that *Yashua Harmashiack* is Lord; how do you apply this blood into your life? When last did you make a full confession? What is the condition of your heart? Are the issues that cloud your heart that obstruct you contact? Do you have any dirty bones in your closet that need to be emptied?

Level 2. The beginning of a new life with its changes and declare war on addictions. What are your desires? What do you want the Lord to do for you? Do you have expectations during your worship service? What is the reason for your approach? Which battles do you desire to overcome?

Level 3. The open curtain gives us access to another style of life far away from our bodies into His body. Through His priest we live life behind the curtain, we interact in heavenly places and all the decisions to run this flesh are decided behind the curtain. What issues do you desire to control in the spirit? What do you think your spiritual life would look like?

You the worshipper must be sure and guaranteed that as you approach YHWH you are guaranteed acceptance, let us all come with sincere hearts, take the blood of Jesus and sprinkle it on yourself, so that you can be cleansed from the guilty conscience. And then have your bodies washed with pure water (baptism).

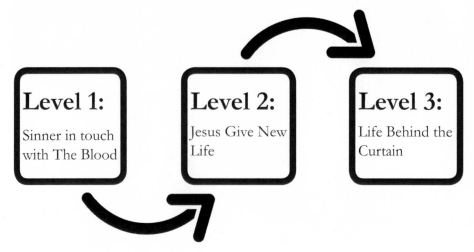

Fig 13: Spiritual Levels

These are the truths that we must hold and never lose for this is hope that the gospel must profess and proclaim. This is the truth that pulpits must echo.

Verse **25** and **26** of Hebrews are key to a victorious Christian life. We come to the body of Christ for encouragement, and sin must not be part of our worship. Sin cannot be a deliberate and casual act, for it destroys our conscience, making it difficult for us to come boldly. Instead we attract judgment through deliberate sinful lives.

The spirit must take us to the place where the Christ in us becomes our salvation. We fall into His grace to receive mercy and grace not judgment and condemnation.

To celebrate the presence of the Holy Spirit Hebrews 10 concludes by reminding us that "Christ in us is a better possession." For that reason we cannot throw away our confidence, for it will be richly rewarded.

Let the upright and those occupied by this truth live in faith, the righteous live by faith, awaiting He who is coming into their situation will come, without delay.

We will not shrink or walk back to the traditions of the flesh, God will not be pleased, instead believe this and you will be saved.

Yes, you can live a victorious life over sin, but when you sin, please hurry to go back to your Father, and let the appetite of the heavenly things kill the taste of raising and garnishing of sin. Everyone who is born of God overcomes the world (chaos, earthliness, carnal nature) this is the victory that has overcome the world. Even our faith.

Who is it that overcomes the world? Only He who believes that Jesus is the Son of God. Coming to us through the covenant of Water, blood and the Spirit is a witness to this truth.[33] That through Him we have a sealed covenant of water, blood and spirit. Through this transaction it can be announced, "God has given us eternal life". To have the Son is to have life. The act of Christ has made us Holy.

Heb 4:1-16 the worship service is an invitation into the presence of God, for without the possibility and ability to enter there is no reason why we should meet. The power of the worship hour is in the entrance in the divine "*menucha sabaitomos*".

The solutions for mankind's restlessness is found in the presence of Jehovah. Worship allows us who cannot rest to find those moments of rest, not because things are done but because He is in our presence. Even the undone can wait in awe of what He has done.

The Sabbath command comes "finished" and when the bigger ones are done the smaller ones are finished too.

The worshipper must make sure that all the worshippers access this "Presence". The worship service must be crafted in such a way that no one should fall short.

The good preaching and sermonizing is worth nothing if it lacks the rest that kills anxiety. What is the use of the gospel it not allow us to enjoy the accomplished work of YHWH. The Jews forfeit this blessing for they did not accept what God had finished, instead they continue in their works and forms of righteousness.

The Pentecostal who pronounces the freedom of the Gospel, fail to benefit from such a powerful gospel for it lacks the Sabbath rest in it. The venue for the blessing is good; the problem is the time to access the blessing. Ask for rain in due season the bible admonishes.

The Sabbath hours are eternally given as the holy hours to access the storerooms of grace as angels worship, the earth can join.[34] And the eternal worship services in Isaiah 66:22 further illustrates that even the heaven that we are going to has a set program of Sabbath worship.

Faith starts here to know that there is a worship service in heaven on Sabbath and by faith we take the earthly worships service and join it with the heavenly one.

---

33. Colossians 5: 4-12
34. Hebrews 12:22.

The worship services must be combined.[35] Faith is the glue between the two services. We, who have believed, enter into that rest; for this is the purpose and the promise of worship. Without faith it is impossible to please Him, for all those who come to Him must believe that God rewards and blesses those that seek him earnestly.[36] Do not worship as if God is yet to do some work. Understand as the leader that God has *been* finished since creation.

Worship recognizes not what God will do but what He has accomplished in Jesus before the creation of the world and that the world finds promises made and fulfilled. Worship celebration unveils these things. He has done marvelous things, Praise the Lord. The miracle is in the seventh day that God himself mentions by His own mouth in Genesis2:4 as a day of rest therefore we can rest. A day when rest was created, so that we can be recreated.

The disobedience of the Jews made it impossible for them to have entrance into the Promised Land but have no rest in it. The foreign armies would continue to harass them while living in the land of the promise. They failed to enjoy the promise although they entered into it. It is for this reason that God set another day called today.

The today of Hebrews 11: 7 is the day of your salvation, that you heard this message, hardening not your heart for your rest can begin today. The voice of God can be heard today, the call to join in the rest is extended to you today, and you can join into this rest. Joshua is mentioned here as the savior into the earthly Canaan.

A parallel is given of what Jesus (the new testament *Yeshua*) makes us do; to enter the Heavenly Canaan. This rest remains, this door is open for all the people of God for we can all come from our own works and enter into the works of Yeshua, through obedience to the Father we have His works cover our works, our disobedience is hidden in His obedience.

Let no one be led astray we cannot save ourselves. Jesus, *Yeshua* has promised us an inheritance into Canaan, to live in houses that we did not build, and harvest in fields that we did not plough, this land flows with milk, nourishment, and honey sweetness.

The worshipper must lead people into such a place of abundance and sweetness of fellowship, let the praises begin. On these issues of rest verse 12 is clear that this is the judgment room of worship, for the word

35. Hebrews 4:2
36. Hebrews 11:6

cuts sharper than a two edged sword. When the word becomes alive, it penetrates into the innermost parts and divides the soul and the Spirit, the joints and the marrow, Hallelujah.

With many of us our souls tired to Spirits, the power of the word penetrates to this level and cut off the *Soul-ties* that are bound to your Spirit.

The writer of Hebrews is fully aware of *man's* ignorance on the forces that are invisible in the spiritual realm and how they bind themselves to our Spirits. The word breaks the ties that bind us to demonic forces and joins us to the Spirit of truth aligning our attitudes and thoughts and inclinations of our hearts towards the throne of Grace.

The worshipper must open up their eyes to the reality that Worship is transparency time, for everything is laid bare, and nothing is hidden from the sight of God.[37] All our lives are uncovered and the truth that the worshipper is giving out also cuts into them.

The judgments of YHWH cut on both sides, the worshippers and the worship leader. We all have come to lay bare our souls at the alter of Praise.

The ritual of worship must be clearly pronounced as a holy ritual, and transformation into the heavenly realm, with Jesus invisible, yet present as the High Priest who officiates over this transportation of people from the seen to the unseen. Jesus is with us, although He has entered into the heavenly sanctuary, behind the veil of faith is the reality of our prayers. The worshippers must hold on to their faith for the High Priest is standing on our behalf. [38]

The beauty of His mediation is that we come weak and feeble yet He is one with us and has experienced our grief and pain, tested in all places like us yet found without fault. He is therefore able to sympathize with us when we fail and fall for He has once stood in our place and is a qualified High Priest.[39]

He is also the True Witness in the Heavenly realm of the reality of life and temptation in the physical and earthly realm.[40]

Let us all therefore come boldly.[41] Walk in power not weakness. Approach in confidence not fear. Come boldly in full assurance to approach the throne of grace courageously knowing that we find help and mercy, forgiveness in

37. Hebrews 4:13 the word is sharper than a two edged sword
38. Hebrews 9:24 He is in behind the veil
39. Hebrews 4:115 We have a great high Priest
40. Revelation 3:14 He is the true witness
41. Hebrews 4: 16 come boldly: receive mercy in times of need

times of need. The worshipper must make it attractive for the worshippers to be confident to seek audience with the Creator and God - our maker.

The blessing is in that we did not receive the spirit that makes us slaves of sin, but we have received the Spirit through which we also can say Abba Father, making us sons and daughters of God.[42] Moments of worship must be declared as children come in time.

There is a difference between the entrance of slaves into the royal presence and that of the children, princes and princesses. Being heirs of the throne means the entrance of heaven is at our feet. You lead this congregation of royalty to the great *I Am*.[43]

Worship is never meant for slaves but for masters. Until we attain this status we remain less of our worth. Many hide and lie under education and a false sense of purity and order and *"disciplined Christianity"*. The nature of the human heart can pretend to be tame at times, but like a tamed tiger, the day it tastes your blood, it will become wild again. Many who think that they are holy are many times shocked when they do things that under normal circumstances they would not do.

The true nature of man does not need window dressings but a full rebirth. If we say we are without sin we lie and the truth of God is not in us, but should we sin we have an advocate with the Father.[44] Good signs of good behavior are not enough to grant us victory. The rotten bones may still be covered by white wash over the tombs of our characters.[45]

WORSHIPPERS BE CONFIDENT

Hebrews 4 gives us the correct tool and venue at which Spiritual lives transcend from the flesh to spirit where the battle tools and strength are found. Christ died so that we can enter through the curtain. Enter the Holy Place to become most holy. The sting of sin is not in the doing but the guilt that it smears our conscience with, which kills our confidence.

Once you lose confidence, the guilt begins to take away more of your confidence, to be helped in a time of need. Getting the divine perfume kills the taste of sin. The time you spend with God changes our taste of life. The book of Galatians introduces these four pillars and they come out as

---

42. Romans 8:1ff NO condemnation for those who live in the spirit
43. Exodus 3:4 I AM that I AM
44. 1John 2:2 We have mediation with the Father.
45. Mathew 23:27 white washed tombs

key to this Pauline writing:

1. **You are holy** - (the imparted and imputed attribute of grace, we stands as He stands in us). Never forget this reality that you are holy, not that you have worked for it, but you have been made holy without your works. The new status that Jesus brings, is holiness. Let confession be heard from you and your status immediately changes.

2. **You are blessed** - (presenting a reality in the midst of absence of things. Work on the Blessing rather than working for the blessing). No more crying and worshiping as if you are a beggar, you are blessed, you are made happy. You might not have it in the physical real, but you are blessed. The problem has never been the giving of God, but your receiving.

3. **Be at peace** - to give the precious gift of presence and attitude. The correct interpretation of the Sabbath is, "Give people rest". People are tired of trouble and pain, let the *Shabbat, shabath, shalom*, stop-rest and have peace with God be a reality in the hour of worship. Let the burdens be lifted at Calvary. You are the vehicle of this experience as a worshipper takes them to the cross and let them find Sabbath-rest. Life starts with rest then labor and creativity. This is the state of creation when the mind is fully in the space of darkness to speak life into death and say "Let there be".

4. **You are children of God** - to give the sense of belonging is by far the best thing that could have happened to us; to be called sons and daughters of God. Through this new status, we, who were far off have been brought near. We enter the palace of God during worship not like strangers or aliens but as children, heirs and co-heirs together with Christ. We have become the one with God.

If through Christ (one person) God planted the church, how much more through us will He not do much more?

God is missing me, the Lord has never left me, but I have walked away from His path. It is the reason and purpose of the enemy to steal, kill and destroy.

God is not affected in that He has resolved the sin problem in the past. The challenge is that sin creates the distance between God and me and after sinning I would have to mend the distance and walk straight to God.[46]

---

46. Zachariah 1:3 Return to me and will return to you

The intention of the devil with sin is that we can no longer approach God and see Him as our father, but angry judge who is waiting to punish us. The painful truth is that the devil will destroy us while God still loves us.

The loss of integrity, credibility, virtue does not reduce the love God has for us. That is why, we ministers, can sin and still do ministry, and fall and God still continues to use us to save others. But when righteousness is gone our salvation is at stake. It must be noted that righteousness is a state of being not an achieved status caused by our action, not what we do or did but what God has done for us through Christ. When the sense of morality is toned down and conscience is silence in sin and after sin, the human soul is in danger!

The Battle of *Soul-ties*, the unifications of two bodies of flesh as they unite they become like each other and cement their spirits, creating access to each other, this is the breeding ground of addiction. The touch, the smell, the look and the memory; all these communicate with the other party and prepares for penetration. People can be away from each other but in each other. At a spiritual level the joining of spirits creates the emotions, love and the desire to own. There is a way that seems right to a man but the end of it thereof are ways of death.[47] These ties are the breeding ground to a multiplicity of sins that will come with protection and serving this evil habit. Adultery is one of the greatest killers of worship as we sin against our flesh.[48]

We bring foreign spirits to the altar of worship. A closer look at this will reveal a few principles that will sober up our thinking. To start with, God is present during a sexual act and He is here for His own pleasure and watches every act with divine interest. The creative force of God is here when clothes are taken off and human beings begin to explore each other's bodies. As you hold your partner you begin to supervise the creation of God and desire to multiply.

Sex is therefore worship: this communion with God as with each other is a creative space for procreation, creation and recreation. Where two are gathered in agreement there the Lord is also as a true witness to the vows and consummations between parties. Never should they be called illegitimate children but instead call the parents, *illegitimate parents*. Children are legitimate. The affection, the desire, the connection, the union the experience, and here the Lord has created nations with the command to be <u>fruitful and mult</u>iply is activated.

47. Proverbs 14:12 "seems" is not as the as "is"
48. 1 Corithians 6:18 immorality is sin against your own body

It is sad that sex has become a center of entertainment for the immoral and creation of bastards, a consummation of sin and ridicule to our generation. But to God here lies the secret of power and the church and the great mystery of how He has positioned Himself as the husband and the church as the wife. Here the Lord undresses Himself. With the church God has stopped being a mystery on the street but a husband in bed.

God seeks access into the chambers of the church and the souls of those who profess His name. There cannot be any secrets between "sheets" parties as bodies are laid bare, God has exposed Himself fully and so must I also come to God with a bare soul and they were both naked and not ashamed.[49]

Have you seen the nakedness of God; then stop being a bag of wheat on the matrimonial bed of grace with fear to explore and enjoy the full extend of God's touch. Let the parties get into each other and get involved in the process that procreates the genes and works of grace.

Out of this encounter God is able to plant Himself in us. Let earth receive Him king. At the worship experience "There is a sweet spirit "in this place" this is the spirit of the Lord. There are sweet expressions on each face as we feel the presence of the Lord. Sweet Holy Spirit, Sweet heavenly dove, stay right here with us filling us with your love. And for these blessings we lift our hearts in praise and without a doubt we know that we will have been revived when we leave this place."[50]

WHAT IS THE DEMON THAT OCCUPIES MANY WORSHIPPERS?

Then sin especially adultery unifies the bodies in sin and the acts meant to create demands in the body that makes it difficult for us to walk back to God, but swim in guilt and avoid intimacy at the moment of worship. The lust level of sin is the struggle in the flesh after God has redeemed the flesh.

The cravings and drive to satisfy the flesh calls for indulgence and continuous acts of Sin. Prayer is necessary for all of us addicted in sex to break the codes of addiction be delivered and saved. The minds must be educated to develop new appetites. The hold of Satan and demons over life must be broken.

---

49. Genesis 2:25 there is no intimacy where there is shame and embarrassment
50. Dorris Akers : Song there is a Sweet Sweet Spirit in this place

These are the strong holds. When the habits of sin become regular, automatic influences and suggestions that become part of life to trigger preset responses to the call of sin. At this point the sinner is rendered weak and ready to sin as and when the enemy calls. There is power to strengthen the soul from the pangs of sin.

The advantage of spending time with God, is that it allows you to collect the smell of the perfume of God's interactions and hugs of grace. Ever smelled the smell of sin, the perfume of an old flame, that makes you hands wet and throat dries up from memories of old ecstasy. The time that we spend with God allows us to walk away with a new smell that is offended by odor of corruption.

Grace works and the spirit makes the mind strong, reformats the senses and tells the body to obey the influence of holiness.

The body needs to be termed and brought into complete obedience of the Holy Spirit.

Bring emotions and addiction to the cross and crucify them on the tree. Let them die with the savior and walk in the newness of life.

Bring the self to subject and the power of Calvary is manifested as a sinner begins a new walk in faith and freedom from the evils that pressed them down. Sin opens the doors and adultery is the clearest form of how a human body can be held bondage when Calvary has cleared.

Christ handles the sin, and you handle the habit and addiction in the spirit as you begin to talk and agree with forces of good that call you to your status with God.

The works of grace makes it possible that after we have fallen into the mud we don't feel comfortable in that state until we are clean at the fountain deep, that "flows from Emmanuel's veins. Sinners are plunged beneath the flood and lose their guilt stains".[51]

Through the death of Jesus we die in Him and we declare that our guilt is his death and His innocence is our life. The cross is the divine exchange of roles and places; as He goes up the cross we are in the hall.

Who do you set free Barabbas or Jesus.

Thank God, we (Barabbas) were set free and Jesus bore our sins now we can declare that His life has become our lives.

Our sins, God has to look for them at the cross with His Son, Hallelujah Amen.

---

51. William Cowper: Song There is a fountain tilled with blood, 1772

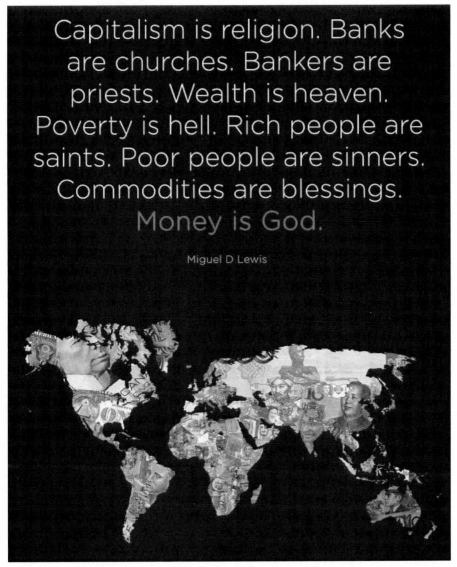

Capitalism is religion. Banks are churches. Bankers are priests. Wealth is heaven. Poverty is hell. Rich people are saints. Poor people are sinners. Commodities are blessings. Money is God.

Miguel D Lewis

In Genesis 3 the devil strikes and bruises our ankles, but thank God for the promise of Calvary, as he bruises our ankles we crush his head.

We have an advantage to kill him when he can, is but hurt us.

Ha-Satan was given power to strike us on the heel; we were given power to strike him on the head. Jesus has done an act that every sinner must enjoy to crush the head of the serpent.

The ancient devil deceiver of the brethren. Victory over sin gives us the full experience of kicking the devil in the teeth and groin as we claim the victory that Jesus' blood has brought.

A foreign God

And The African Problems?

In "primitive" expression of African worship is the total expression of the community and the African worships God with all.

Full expression, dance, stories, history, young and old, education, myths and rituals involve all and bring all to a solution. At the end of the service the community is in agreement of the results they expect.

The ministry for the congregation must be understood so that it will be well placed to reach them. Take note that the poor are here, their struggles as a people of color are clear as they have:

1. **Physical needs on a daily basis:** the bread issues: due to modern economy many of them have been displaced from their homes and turned into town vagabonds seeking for work on street corners that pay next to nothing.

They toil and labor in vain at the hands of their masters; they bring nothing to show for they are deemed as cheap labor.

The worshipper must lift these souls to the throne room of grace and let them be assured that as God watches over the sparrows[1] He surely is watching over them. If God dresses the flowers He will dress them too. Poverty, joblessness and hunger and financial stability

2. **Dealing with demonic forces:** the reality of the spiritual world and the need for divine help.

The African believer is very much aware of the forces in the spiritual realm. There spirit world is a reality to us and there is no need to worship in western naivety of this reality.

The results of ignorance in this regard are seen when the pastors and members seek for the counsel of he witchdoctor on the day of trouble.

For there are some problems we believe "these are the things of the people" and when worship does not address witchcraft, love portions, omens of success, oracles of power, covenants of families and spirits that live in the families inherited and invited worship would have failed our people.

The worshipper must address these snares and minister a liberation of souls that are seeking for solutions in the graveyards, roots, powders, fats of lions and snakes.

3. **Sin, guilt over committed problems and actions:** ultimately the worshipper must address the sin problem. The acts that have been done, the thoughts that have been thought, paths that have been worked.

People come to worship with guilt over sins that they have committed and the moment of worship must be a balm for the weary.

Burdens must be lifted at Calvary and the Son of righteousness must rise with healing it His wings to defend His people.

The gospel call to the cross must be clear and like the thief at the cross let the saints walk out with the full assurance that they will be in the kingdom with Jesus.

---

1. Mathew 6:26 no sparrow falls to the ground without divine notice

4. **Political and social justice:** false government solution and ethnic wars that claim lives and betray confidence in fellow man. The poor politics has plunged people into hopeless souls living from hand to mouth. The same people who oppressed seem to prosper while the black community waits for liberation. Poverty is visible and the gap between the rich and poor is getting wider.

As the African is struggling with the spiritual world he has done and not done certain things that on its own is a problem that creates anxiety and needs liberation and the guilt must be quenched and the freedom to be and worship would be realized.

Seek the face of God. Seek until you feel his presence, until the intensity of the experience evokes the presence of God.

Desire to connect and hear the touch of God and feel His presence. Evaluate your worship service *tools* to assess the worship in your church.

Find your congregation on one of the corners of the following diagram (Fig. 15).

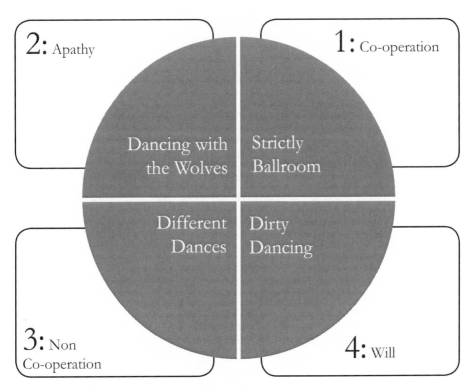

Fig 15: Assessment of cooperation

There are four possibilities of every congregation namely:

A. **Cooperation:** all work in harmony with their wills, volition bound in truth they have become saved and participate in the worship service with sincere hearts.

B. **Apathy:** they participates yet their hearts, like wolves are elsewhere. This state of affairs have lip service members who seem to enjoy the service but God never reaches their hearts to change them with truth, rebuke their sins and call for their repentance. It's a service and nothing more.

C. **Non-cooperation:** there is visible resistance in the worship service, where people sit down and refuse to become members of the worship service. Lack of understanding and protest of methods and dislike of leaders. Many are the causes but ultimately you have a sit in with no cooperation.

D. **Will and non-cooperation produce Dirty dancing:** the will of the members must be arrested to unity of purpose and worship not isolated worship in the body of the whole. The whole body of Christ must worship in unity and harmony. The worshippers can be in the same place yet with different agendas, a sad reality of disunity in the house of the Lord. The dynamics of the congregation must be closely monitored to ensure that at all times God is pleased with our worship.

The African congregation also falls within these frames at this turn of the millennium. We have been moved through the violent acts of the colonialist and there is no way we can cooperate with oppression. The evil that is on our land can not go unchallenged and our people can not forever eat this poison as they lose themselves into second class citizen in the kingdom of grace.

WHO NEEDS DELIVERANCE?

The worshipper and his soul: Deliverance from the powers of evil that we have given access to our lives. Deliverance means resolution, a firm decision to dissociate ourselves from anyone and anything that contributed negatively to our spiritual state.[2] The power of deliverance is in the word that we proclaim with our mouths as we loudly pronounce our resolution in the presence of God.

2. 1 Corinthians 5:9

These new decisions must be guided by the word of truth for to man belongs the plans but from God comes the reply of the tongue.[3] The tongue has the power of life and death and those who love it will eat its fruit.[4]

To work with Christ is life and the path of sin is hard. Jesus breaks the ties and makes the difficult things easy. Jesus came to rescue us from the dominion of darkness and brought us into His kingdom of love, and in Him we have redemption, and the forgiveness of sin. We are blessed with the image of the invisible God that shines on us. We are all claimed heirs, with Christ as the first-born of all creation.

For in Him and through Him all things are created in the heavenly and earthly realm, both the visible and the invisible, he created for Him thrones, powers, rulers, authorities and all things. He is before all things and in Him all things have become, He holds everything together.[5]

The worshipper must declare things in the spirit realm. As Job did in Job 20:28, you need to cancel all the legal rights and the authority that bind you by association and even by word have given the evil spirit of fornication, witchcraft, adultery through which you allowed them access and residence in your soul.

To experience the full delivery the worshipper needs to throw away everything that hinders and the sin that so easily entangles - Hebrews 12:1

The simple definition of *soul-ties* is the consummation of bodies during sex joins to separate bodies and makes them one. By engaging in sexual activities the worshipper must know that they have defiled the body of Christ and united them with prostitutes. For when you commit adultery you unite yourself with prostitutes and you make yourself one with her.

There is a clear call to all worshippers to flee from sexual immorality - 1 Corinthians 6:15-20.

To flee is both in the present and in the past; not only to those who have not started but also even to those you have already united yourself with as one.

How many *"ones"* have you become?

In the mighty Name of Jesus you must name and cancel every agreement and covenant you have made with women and men by word or action and free yourself from their souls living in your soul, this is done by the power of the blood of Jesus.

3. Proverbs 16:1
4. Proverbs 18:21
5. Colossian 1:17 He exist before everything and He holds everything together

HERE IS THE PRAYER FOR DELIVERANCE

I Declare and dissociate myself (1 Corithians 5:9-11) with you_____
(Mention the names) and your spirit
I decree and declare you are not part of my life and you are not yoked together with
me.[6] I am free of your soul and spirit.
Our destinies are not bound together with mine and I break every tie and power that
you have over me In Jesus's Name.
Jesus will keep me from falling and present me before God without fault and with
great joy.
To my God belongs Majesty, power over sin and authority over the elements,
I have a new beginning in Jesus Christ My Lord, now and forever more Amen."

You have started the warfare and therefore beware of the Spirit realm, all the while make these decrees and declarations. You need to make this declaration to the Holy Spirit and He must confirm within your spirit that you are making the legal divorce.

Decisions are for a moment, lifestyle is for a lifetime. The worshipper then needs to make a firm resolution to live a godly life as far as possible, guarding the channels of the soul for signs of temptation.

The ability to resist temptation is not to entertain it and pray for deliverance. The falling away from faith is a result of negligence on this very point, that unless you mean what you say, the demonic forces will not move, as they understand the declaration to be temporary.

These ties must be cancelled and salvation delivered to you. Even African culture understands that when your husband or wife dies you need a time to cleanse the aura before you can start afresh.

The war must be overcome in the body finally as a confirmation of the victory in the spirit, for as Christ suffered in His body, are you also with the same attitude because he who has suffered in the body is done with sin. As a result the body is freed from evil desires and starts to be driven by the will of God.

For you have spent enough time doing what pagans do, living in debauchery, lusts, drunkenness, orgies, carousing and detestable idolatry. The end of all things is near. Therefore be clear minded and self controlled so that you can pray.[7]

6. 2 Corithians 6:14-18
7. 1 Peter 4:1-3 -7

Be a self-controlled worshipper, and alert. Your enemy the devil prowls around like a roaring lion seeking someone to devour. Resist him, stand firm in faith.[8]

What kind of people ought you to be? You have and ought to live holy lives as you look forward to the day of God and speed it's coming. Verse 13-14 keeps in line with His promise, we are looking forward to a new heaven and a new earth the home of the righteous. Make every effort to be found spotless, and blameless and at peace with Him.

Be reminded that the righteousness mentioned in verse 11 is not what we achieve through self-performance and behavior.

2 Corinthians 5:21 – "God made him who had no sin to become sin for us so that we may become His righteousness." The book of Galatians and Romans is clear that this is a work of grace, a Godly lifestyle of the children of God.

Simply put it is the attitude that shuns evil always, according to Psalm[9] "Blessed is a man who does not walk in the counsel of the wicked, or stand in the way of the sinner, or seat with mockers." Worshippers delight in the Lord,[10] and constantly meditate upon His word day and night.

Plant your thoughts and affections besides the streams of water and you will yield fruit in due season. Your leaf of influence will not wither, and in whatever you do you will prosper.[11] Do not be like chaff that is blown away by every wind of temptation. The Lord is watching over you.[12]

No merits are won when you lose or become unrighteous, the prodigal son does not stop being a son because he is in a far country Luke 15.

Spending money with prostitutes and sitting with pigs does not take away his blood status. Let it be clear that righteousness and holiness is our state of being, which is what Calvary has made possible for us.

We have been declared and we have been made holy.[13]

Holiness is a gift we receive when we believe.

The garment of righteousness and holiness is our uniform so that when we approach God, we do so in the confidence of His holiness.

---

8. 1 Peter 5:8-9
9. Psalm 1:1-3
10. Psalm 34:7 …He will give you the desires of your heart
11. Psalm 1:1-6 Blessed is he who does not walk…stand or sit
12. Genesis 28:15 The Lord will watch over you
13. Hebrews 10:10 and by that will you have been made holy through the sacrifice of the body of Christ once and for all.

This is the only way we can come to into His presence, for it is called the Throne of *Grace*[14] most *Holy Place*[15], *Near to God.*[16]

When we approach the Throne of Grace, God is able to reformat our taste buds so that we develop an attitude of prayer and godly lives.

Everyone born of God does not continue to sin,[17] an alarm must be raised on the conscience worshipper that you do not continue to sin deliberately after you have received the knowledge of truth.

There will be no sacrifice left for you except the condemnation that awaits the ungodly Paul admonishes.

Therefore make every effort to be at peace with all men for without holiness no one will see God.[18]

Worshipper, do not miss the opportunity of the grace of God, by coming into the place of worship with roots of bitterness, of hate and grudges. Evil inclinations will grow in your spirit and cause trouble for you and defile many.[19]

Be resolute not to be sexually immoral, least you sell your birth right like Esau who traded long term goals for short-term pleasure. He changed his mind later and sought for it with tears in his eyes and could not find it. He only did not sell his birthright but sold his blessing, and traded his future for a bowl of soup.[20]

When sin lies in wait and the sinner entices you, do not give in, for the complacency of fools kills and seduction of wayward women is a path to the grave, no one goes in her path to return.[21]

Run for your life when lips of adultery drip with honey and with words as smooth as oil. She caresses your ego, the end of fantasy is bitter gall and the pain is sharper than a two edged sword. She is marching to the grave, and her house is the door to the pits of hell.

Do not give your strength to the prostitute. Drink water from your own cistern running water from your own well.[22]

---

14. Hebrews 4:16,
15. Hebrews 10:19
16. Hebrews 7:19; 10:22
17. John 5:8
18. Hebrews 12:14
19. Hebrews 10:26
20. Hebrews 12:1-22
21. Proverbs 2:16-19
22. Proverbs 2:3-15

Words of power *"do not embrace the bosom of another man's wife,"*[23] you will take fire to your chest and not burn, adultery destroys and whoever does it lacks judgment.

Make sure that while you minister your name is written in the book of life, that is where your deliverance is. Be wise and you will shine like the brightness of the heavens. This is the shine of those who lead others into righteousness.[24] You need to purify yourself worshipper and be made spotless and refined. Do not be associated with the wicked who continue to be wicked without understanding, be wise and understand these things.

Note this, Worshipper, that your liberation from the grip of evil is not for the congregation but for you. The one leading others in worship must also worship. The one shouting salvation must also be saved. The doctor cannot prescribe medication to others while he suffers from the same disease.

Drink the balm of Gilead and save your soul, how can you fast on a wedding and walk naked when your Father has garments that cover your shame. You need to engage on this process both academically and spiritually, be fully involved in this process for THIS IS YOUR LIFE. Do not take lightly that the presence of the enemy, he does not only want you to sin, but to literally kill you, and take away your life.[25]

THE POWER OF THE WORSHIPPER

The **Name of the Lord** is a strong tower and the righteous run in for shelter, a mighty fortress a shelter in the times of storm. Tap into the power world. To call upon the name of the Lord evokes His presence within the house of prayer. Of the many things that we can honor the name of the Lord must not be mentioned where there are lies and disrespect, Moses in the book of Exodus admonishes that the name of the Lord must not be taken in vain. For He is excellent and no sin is found in Him.[26]

The power of he worshipper is in the Name of the Lord, for every mention of that name is a revelation of nature character and person of God, and to know the name of a person is to have power in Him. Now that we know who God i,s we can call on Him and He will not be silent.

---

23. Proverbs 5:20, 27-32
24. Daniel 12:3-10
25. Philippians 2:12 work for your salvation
26. Psalm 76:2

These names are a self-revelation as He relates to our situations and us. He is the desire of all ages and with His presence He can address and calm any situation.

God is a difficult subject to deal with, for we cannot name Him or tie Him to what we see and what He has done. He remains way above our thoughts and imagination. He has many names. Through grace, heaven has come down and we can relate to Him as a messiah, brother, savior and friend.

There are three types of His names to consider namely:

Nomina Propia – the proper names of God, *Nomina Essentia* - the essential names of God and lastly *Nomina Personalia* - the personal names of God as Father Son and Holy Spirit.[27]

Of the more personal to *God is Elohim* - Eliyon, first and strong and mighty, fullness of power and highly exalted worship in might.[28] *Adonai* refers to God as the judge and ruler. He remains executor over the affairs of creation and all are accountable to Him. Worship in recognition of what He has done.

On the provision side He appears as *El-shaddai* the God of the mountains or the breast and supply, worship in the abundance of divine supply. The source of blessings and abundance of providence. [29]

Of all that thrills the soul is the unsearchable knowledge of the personal name of God YHWH TSEBHAOTH, God of grace, sacred and different with distinctive qualities of self-existence without the other. The One we can't mention, the I AM that I AM, and I shall be what I shall be.[30] The New Testament has a challenge of Greek deities that seem to be mentioned in the same noun, Theos, pantokrator, Lord Master, Kuros, the possessor, Pater-Father and protector, and creator, the genesis of all things.

These names represent His hand of power able to hear, reach, help, create and recreate. Every time he worshipper calls upon the name they are given access into another side and person of God, names are an address into the abundance of His provisions.

These very names evoke the Spirit of God to draw near to the hearts of the worshippers and answer the requests and fill in their needs.

27. Louis Bekoholf: systematic theology
28. Genesis 14: 19 -20, Isaiah 14:14
29. Exodus 6:2
30. Leviticus 24:16, Exodus 3:14

Music and Worship

What type of music reaches the soul?

The human being is born in natural concert for the very breath is in rhythm and sync with nature.

The first form of music is that which is in unison with the very core of human existence. The beat of the song must attach itself to the human's heart beat. The key must find its worshipper. Each human being is in key, which is comfortable to express self, and worship becomes natural and easy to sing no strain of voice but presenting easy breath of the soul.

Real worship is not forced but naturally finds the worshipper and the body will move without intention.

It's voluntary, natural and honest.

The movement of sound to reach the soul for the education of its virtue. "Give me the music of a nation, I will change a nation's mind."

"If you want to measure the spiritual depth of society, make sure to mark its music.[1] "The music that reaches the soul is soul music. 'Spirituality can release blocks, lead you to ideas, and make your life artful'." Julia Cameron

As the flesh finds the flesh, the spirit finds the spirit and the soul searches for its maker during worship into the union of peace and space of instruction.

It's a mystery we have not fully explored to surrender people into the spiritual realm meaningfully and allow God full access into His vessels. Is this not the upper room experience that they created the venue when the Spirit came down and manifested. Why are pastors and worship leaders afraid of driving into this realm?

MUSIC SELECTION FOR THE WORSHIPPER

The first level in theology and the cognitive space of worship is interested in words and the accuracy of dogma. After that the song must move into humming when the words are no longer an issue but the worshipper does not worry about the structure of the verses but confuse the flow and allow the congregation to begin to unite the words with their experience.

The third level is when the instruments surge in to create dissonance of melody and rhythm and the human soul begins to sing a spiritual song past the mind, when this realm is crossed the human spirit begins to search for The Spirit.

The fourth level is the unity of the spirits. The spirit in the Holy Spirit and us confirm within our hearts that we are sons and daughters of God, heirs and coheirs together with Christ. There is s deep sense of guilt and inadequacy at the encounter, as the less feels heavily weighed by the Holiness of YHWH. The worshipper may be jovial mixed with tears as the waters of life begin to swell in their soul.

Like a flood of water over the soul, the waves of worship take over the service and those in the spirit begin a new expression and dance like David at the arrival of the ark. He danced uncontrollably and lost sight of who he was and where he was. Like a confused and drunk man the disciples burst into languages that the people could hear.

---

1. Plato: the Philosopher born in 427 B.C

The counterfeit is Nebuchadnezzar telling people to fall down at the sound of the instruments. The later is self-evoked while the real is the path of the human soul seeking for God at the moment of worship.

Elisha confronted with the challenge of battle and war, calls on a musician to put him into a trance and cross over the spiritual realm to find a prophecy for the armies at war. The worshipper must not be afraid to cross over and be fully occupied with God.

Why worship in hesitancy when the call is that we come boldly into His Presence, God is Spirit those who Worship Him must know the truth and move spiritually into the very being of God. There must be meaningful interaction and merge of the human seeker and the divine giver. Only then will worship accomplish its basic purpose.

Worship must move people from the shallow waters of Ezekiel to the deep end where people will swim and float in the midst of much water and be carried away, for these waters flowing on the inside are coming from the throne of God. Shall we gather at the river? This is the destination of full surrender and where the worshipper and the congregation are fully under the control of YHWH.

When YHWH is free to speak, to rebuke, to instruct and to empower and manifest Himself with a word, a song and message in due season then worship is in session.[2] Did Isaiah not get here and discovered that he was undone a man of unclean lips living amongst unclean people, did not the Lord burn his lips in the spiritual realm?

WHAT IS THE RECIPE OF A GOOD MEANINGFUL, DEEP, SPIRITUAL WORSHIP SERVICE?

When all things are in place from venue to people and atmosphere of music, they becomes the medium through which people can begin the journey to the other world. People spend too much time philosophizing music. Music is not meant for the physical senses, but spiritual, it is designed by God to by pass the conscience to the subconscious mind and direct the mind to the spiritual.

The music we which has been branded as Christian music is more Eurocentric than Christian. It is fair to submit that. Yes, the bible and proclamation of the gospel came through a missionary vehicle, to the ends

2. 1 Timothy 3:16 all scripture is God breathed well for instruction, rebuke and equip the man for all good works.

of the earth. This meant that the music, the clothes, the culture, the expressions, the food, the medicine, the literature of the masters was drummed and sandwiched the gospel. Our generation has lost sense of being, and cultural awareness that moves the hearts of our people. "Most cultures traditionally link food and spirituality directly with periodic restrictions and celebrations punctuating the year. Abstinence from particular foods or full-on fasting is part of many religious traditions and holidays." [3]

It is very sad to note our people trying to get the spirit through a keyboard and western instruments, and most of the time the praise and worship session and go on for hours without touching the hearts of the worshipper. On the contrary the cultural traditional worshippers do not work that hard to evoke the evil spirits to come. They do not sing as many songs as we sing; yet their worship reaches and connects very quickly.

Their music takes them from the physical to the spiritual realm and when you enter their ceremonies without anyone telling you, your hair at the back of your neck will stand as you sense the presence of the 'other'. What has gone wrong in our services where reverence and presence are not felt. We now have empty churches, which have become dead of God. Is this not the Holy Shrine where God has agreed with His people?

Had the people cleansed themselves before coming here to participate, will we not gain the access we so desperately need. Instead of meeting God we meet each other and refuse to let go and Let God be what He must be.

The building of a sanctuary was that God can tabernacle with us, and if God is not present at our venues why are we at worship? If He is not here then the modern church must answer who is here?

THE CONTENT OF WORSHIP AND THE SONGS OF HEAVEN!

A close look at the book of Revelation will show us the power of repetition, "Worthy, worthy, worthy!", and "Holy, holy, holy!" in the praise of angels. Nature has her songs, human beings, stars have their songs, and angels have their songs, and each group has its own experience to praise God for. The diversity of our tribes must come into play in order to build and design programs and select music that will reach the hearts and connect people with God.

---

3. Marcus Samuelsson

People are looking for depth in worship and too often the diatonic, pop sound of western harmony is too celebratory to achieve the spiritual dimension. The lyrics and poetry of the 16th cannot always appeal to the 21-century world-view. The oriental drums and cymbals, the African drum and groans, the Red Indian chants, aborigines with their pipes monotones all connect.

Is it possible that the Christian church demonized the usage of such sounds in worship to replace it with the hymnody that we now hold as sacred? Is it a coincidence that the five continents, the use of pedal tones, dissonance, humming, and chants evoke spirits than pop diatonic?

The upper room gives us some interesting insights when the Holy Spirit appeared and the remarks that they people said about the disciples and those that were filled with the spirit. They were questioned and viewed as drunk and out of their minds.

There are things that block the manifestation of the Holy Spirit and renders the worship service meaningless. Breaking the Torah - living a life that is in conflict with the principles of YHWH and it manifests itself in

- o **Anger:** Elisha blocks the channels of the spirit to prophesy
- o **Immorality:** sons of Eli – busy sleeping with congregation and engrossed in immorality they lost sight of the venue and "Ichabod" the glory departed yet they continued empty sacrifices void of YHWH.
- o **Sexual Immorality:** Man of Sodom - immoral lifestyle blinded them from the reality of God and His angels who stood in their midst with judgment
- o **False power:** Pharaoh - competition and confidence in his own man blinded him from the presence of a more powerful God who would overpower him with tears and heartache.
- o **Greed:** Balaam - even when God is present you cannot see him worrying about the money. The donkey can see what the human being can not see
- o **Anxiety:** Gehazi - could not see the presence of the angels because he was overwhelmed with anxiety
- o **Presumption:** disciples at sea thought that Jesus was a ghost - when our preconceived ideas blocked the visible miracle
- o **Hunger & pre-occupation:** the man to Emmaus - worried about food and preoccupied with the events of the weekend walked with

Jesus and did not know it

- ○ **Demon company:** Saul, the Holy Spirit can not access our souls when we have given residence to evil spirits
- ○ **Impatience:** when Saul decided to do the sacrifice himself because the prophet was late
- ○ **Lies:** Ananias and Sapphire - at the hour of worship they lied about their offering and forfeited the privileges to worship, they died at the venue
- ○ **Lack of personal testimony:** the seven sons who were beaten by demons after trying to heal like Paul. The demons knew Paul and Jesus but did not know these boys.

In a nutshell, the heart that is preoccupied with sin is blinded at the hour of worship. It is the preoccupation that destructs the heart and mind to lands of corruption and the body can be here but the mind will be in the back rooms of chaos and vice.

How to Worship

2 kings 3:15 - Bring me the harpist, the mystery and let him play for me and while the music was playing the Spirit of the Lord came upon Elisha.

Dan 3 - the plain of Dura also is clear that when the music is played and instruments played, let there be worship. Music must be played and then people will worship

2 Samuel 7:18-22 Temple worship
Genesis 24:62 in the fields meditating
Jacob's ladder the connection between heaven and earth
Bethel the alters of prayer and confession Genesis 13

Hebrew 9 teaches us to worship in the temple Note that the curtain that separated the holy and the most holy place was torn, making the holy place most holy.

Once the worshipper enters the temple they are in the presence of the most holy. Worship is not a means to an end but an end in itself. When we worship we have arrived at the feet of the ancient of days.

Ezra read the book of the law while they were standing and worship took place. The Samaritan woman gives us more insights into worship as two elements come out clearly that they must occupy the venue of worship, in TRUTH and SPIRIT.

The mainstream churches are obsessed with collection of doctrines and training and teaching people to live right.

The Spirit is not taught as the power that equips us and neither is there a service that members go through to accept the Holy Spirit into their lives.

On the contrary the Pentecostal and Charismatic, will spend all sessions calling on the Holy Spirit and doing things in the spirit in the absence of the truth.

The Bible does not teach doing one without the other, but truth and spirit must be the pillars of all Godly worship.

The Samaritan woman acknowledges that she is a descended of Jacob and Joseph, and if the Joseph line is strong then she is a first grade Samaritan for Joseph married an Egyptian and for you to be a Jew you must be born of a Jewish mother. Abraham has lots of his history also around this Mountain and these very fields the patriarch had worked on.

In Genesis 23, the caves of *Macphila* he had bought and buried his wife Sara. This tribe of half Jews lived in Samaria a town rich in history and sites. It is here at Shechem that all man was killed after Dina daughter of Jacob was rapped.

There were many graves here for the whole city was wiped out. Genesis 33:19 - Jacob's well was here also which was in a field that he bought. Jacob, Abraham, and Leah were also in this cave at *Macphila*, which is part Gerizim.

The Samaritan woman claims to be a daughter of Jacob and by so doing show ownership of the ground on which Jesus stood. The amount of her religious knowledge cannot be underestimated as she clearly reveals to us that she knew that the Messiah would come and explain these things.

Worship must find these grounds of experience and knowledge to address the challenges of the day.

The place of worship is a well, therefore all must come with their pitchers and seek for a drink while at the well. The power of this passage rests in the reality that you come to the physical well and walk away with the spiritual water.

You come here looking for water you walk away without a pitcher satisfied with the good news of the gospel. The passage ends up with Christ staying in this town for two days sharing the good news and many more became believers.

5 Questions that will enhance your worship service

Know your audience as you minister and worship! Ask the questions below in singular and plural and establish whom you are dealing with!

A. Book of Genesis: Beginnings – where do you come from?

Remind people about their beginnings, a clear sense of beginning will reveal a clear ending. To have started with YHWH will mean to end with Him.

True worship must take the hand of the worshipper and place it into the hand of His maker and King; here every worshipper is royal.

B. The book of Exodus: The names – what is your name?

Re-affirm their sense of identity, the worshippers must be real, and seek to tap into the image of God in each life and let the mirror of the soul show each worshipper from whose hand they come from. The journey of every life, where are we going?

The entire purpose of colonization was to colonize the image of God on the African soul and mind. The quality of worship depreciates to the value and self-worth of the person. What does an oppressor say when he prays, what does the oppressed say when he prays? Identity is critical for confidence and approach to the throne of grace.

C. The Book of Leviticus: He called – what is your purpose?

Direct them to their purpose, a life of purpose has meaning. Worship must put the hands of the worshipper on the steering wheel of choice and drive on the path of purpose, ask the question, what are you doing here? To be born is one thing to find out why is the reason of life.

Every creation has a reason for its existence. The business of life is to find that purpose. What is your reason for being? To be alive is a blessing, to have a reason to be alive is purpose. If heaven had a meeting to discuss the extension of your life, how will they plead your case?

What difference are you making in this present life? Are you a blessing or a curse? Is the world a better place with you? Does the universe benefit from you?

D. The Book of Numbers: In the desert – where are you now?

Let them know where they are in their situations so they can measure the distance from the real to the ideal.

If they have ambitions and goals, the worship service must awaken the desire to achieve these goals.

The questions are, how far are you from what you want to become? When the Lord called out to the man "where are you" in Genesis, to which the man answered, "I am naked".

Two issues are clear, the things that concern YHWH and that of man are not the same. The Lord is asking geographical location, and man is worried about status and condition in which his sin plunged him. It is of paramount importance that Africa starts asking itself the basic questions of divine positioning, and finds out if we have moved from where we had been placed.

Where are you African man on politics? Where are you on ethics? Where are you on identity? Where are you on religion? Where are you on spirituality? Are you where I put you, have you changed your geography? How far are from your God and how far is He from you? The desert marks the African experience. For a very long time Muslims, Christians and colonization alike have practiced disrespect, arrogance and bullish behavior. They assume that the African has no knowledge or sense of being, nor theology or deity.

E.   The Book of Deuteronomy: The words – is there a word from the Lord?

Worship must bring a word from the Lord that will assist the worshippers to navigate in the wilderness of their problems and challenges. At every point of crisis we need to hear the voice from the Lord as our campus to liberation.

On the sixth day, man must assume power and be in charge of his time space and influence. Those who are prosperous rule the world. He who has the keys to the gate controls those that go in and out of the gate. It is built inside every man to prosper and in as much as it is taught that money is the root of all evil so is the absence of it.

In the book of Genesis there is a clear directive given to Adam to prosper and conquer the world. There are seven spheres of influence, you need to identify your strength and peruse to maximum capacity.

The church for too long has barely entered the arena, we banish our members to the spiritual sphere only, and no wonder the church is without power. The book of Luke 16:8 rebukes us "the children of the world are wiser than the children of the Kingdom".

There are two ways when working with your blessings; either you work for your blessings (then its not a gift) or you work the blessings you already have. The children of the world have mastered the art of working their system so that it benefits them.

The children of the kingdom cannot use the earthly strategy.

God has specified a clear method, which needs to be taught so that the children of the kingdom can withdraw the *Abrahamic, Adamic, Davidic, Aronic,* and *Messianic* blessings, which are given in covenants.

When God saw that all was good, it was good for it to come out of the hand that is Good. And God gave it all to the manager to till and look after the garden. Life is about management and God will entrust you with resources to a better life and influence those that are around you. It is God's desire to make you strong powerful and influential to advance His cause.

The earth must be dominated, not people. Have dominion over the birds of the air, the fish of the sea and the beat of the land not over each other. Leadership must be developed so that the prophecy will be fulfilled "you were faithful in little, come and I will make you faithful over much" Man is created in the image of God, after His likeness, with the entire attribute to run the estate that was given to him. Gen 1:26

At the base of all the mandate is to be "fruitful and multiply and fill the earth and have dominion over all that is on earth."

God planted a garden in the east after the one in heaven and then told man to plant the rest of the world. To subdue the environment, make it beautiful, so that it looks like heaven.

He had to name all the animals also and tender the garden. The dominion mandate will work for any man who puts the principles of the Torah to work. This makes God a partner in your work and "goodness and mercy" pursue, chase after, and follow you the rest of your life.

God is a faithful partner in the business of life. He is interested in your success far much more than you are in your welfare.

1. Abel Gen 4: 2 dominated agriculture
2. Lamech decided to go into women polygamy Gen 4:19 animal husbandry
3. Gen 4: 21 4:20 entertainment industry, Jubal the father of musicians and those who play the harp and flute - entertainment
4. Cain: Gen 4: 16-22 Cain build cities, town planning, engineering, construction and architecture. Politics and government

5.   Gen 4:22 Tubal-Cain forged tools of bronze and iron (mining) tool machinist and tool making

6.   Gen 4: 26 region and worship

The state of man has been lost due to sin and abundance of evil.

In the original plan man was formed as a powerful extension of divinity until the devil robbed us of gold for dust, promising us things that would result in death and loss of our divine clothes.

In Genesis 1:28 "and God blessed them and God said unto them be Fruitful and Multiply and Replenish the earth and Subdue it; and *Have Dominion* over the fish of the sea and over the fowl of the air Andover every living creature that moves upon the earth". The worship service must recognize that it is preparing people for Dominion in the seven major Spheres of influence

A.   **Spiritual and religious:** they seek knowledge and connection - worship must be Spiritual. Those who are Spiritual have the campus of life

B.   **Educational:** want to learn something new - gratification is knowledge. Worship must be educational: seek to get good education that does not make you become but to be. True education is knowledge of self in the plan of YHWH

C.   **Political and government:** how to become influential – strategies of influence. Worship must introduce divine governance. The world suffers when evil men are in power.

D.   **Economy and business:** ways of making profit and encouragement. Worship must address the economics and business of worshipper. To worship God with wealth is to praise Him not to beg for stipends.

E.   **Health and technology:** a breakthrough in this area must be experienced. Worship must bring us into health and breakthroughs

F.   **Culture and sports:** is this relevant to my community. Worship must be culturally correct.

G.   **Media and entertainment:** how to manage influence and use their popularity for the glory of God, for worship must be fun and happy.

The following Figure 16 depicts the water-baptism; the wood-the cross; the fire-purification; the nails sacrifice. Look at the cross and

THE ELEMENTS OF WORSHIP

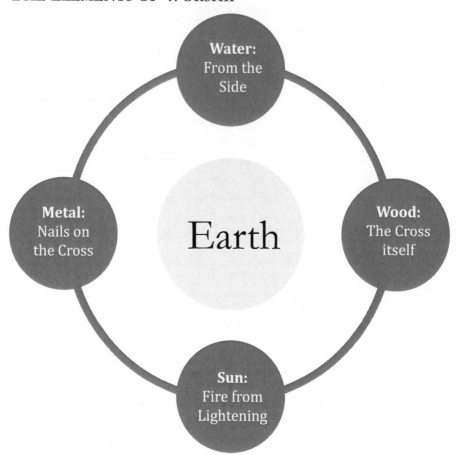

Figure 16: The elements of Worship

you will pray. The worshipper must keep the memories of Calvary clear and fresh on the heart. The elements that make the experience of the cross meaningful will guide the worshipper to find a new dimension in prayer.

The nice part of these circle prayers is that each one of them overcomes the other, so victory is certain at all times, to break forth from the ground, to swallow the floods, break the york that enslave us, quench the fires and melt the situations. The heart is the very ground from where all these elements come from. It is the duty of the worship leader to evoke the hearts of the worshippers to draw from inside their hearts the sacrifice and offering of praise.

All nature, speaks of the glory of the Lord and the heavens are telling the wisdom of God. Nature continues to talk to us of the wisdom and the unsearchable truths that are the foundations of this earth. These elements define our physical world and have been here from the foundation of the earth when God created the worlds and founded it on nothing, calling life out of emptiness and filling the land (soil, earth) with water, vegetation, mineral and light.

A close look at the death of Jesus on the cross we can see the elements of nature being renewed and all nature comes together to witness the salvation and redemption of a fallen race. The water that came from His side, the ground on which the cross was planted, the nails that were in his hands, the lightning and fire, the earthquake that shock the earth, and the wood he hung upon: could this be the meeting place of Christianity and eastern religions?

A. Give your worship enough wood: fire cannot burn where there is no wood.

Wood gives birth to fire, and wood overcomes the earth, and wood conquers of the ground. Prayers of vitality that will shoot forth like the shots of springs with life. When the experiences of life bury us in the ground, these prayers are for a new beginning.

Prayers that overcome the grave of the soil, prayers in isolation bringing forth new plants. You could think this as furniture prayer- for comfort and rest and shelter. Remember Isaac asked the question "we have the fire, we have the wood but where is the lamb." Worship must have its wood, worship must burn something, worship must ask, "where is the lamb?".

B. Let the worship service be grounded with depth to reach the soul.

Earth gives birth to metal and metal conquers wood- these are prayers of pregnancy, incubation of ideas, power and awaiting future revelation.

God is still doing a great and new thing in us, and we can pray that the ground will be conducive, and our hearts can be fertile to yield the fruit desirable to God. The earth prayer takes you back to basics, to the ground. Take me back where I started, back to roots and origins, you ask God to recreate you and make you after His likeness.

The prayer of the prodigal son is an ethnic prayer, going back home, and willing to start at the bottom. Jeremiah encourages us to know that He is the porter and we are the clay, it is safe therefore to fall in the hands of the porter. He can break you and Hallelujah He will make you again.

Worship shouts; let all earth praise the Lord.

C. Nothing beats a warm venue: Fire gives birth to earth, fire conquers wood and earth conquers water as water comes out of metal.

There are times when the fire in our prayers must burn and consume and produce new grounds, new experiences, new testimonies. In these fires of affliction we will come out tested and tried, only the permanent will remain.

This is a warm prayer of power and great heat, the sun shines bright and strong through the firmament, to the righteous and the wicked giving light to the feet.

When the dark night assails, you do a fire prayer and let there be light, at midnight let the sun of righteousness shine in your sorrow. Let direction be visible and you can walk like a child of the light. The spirit of the lord also descended upon them like tongues of fire. And Elijah called fire to come from heaven, as the Lord himself says he is a burning or consuming fire.

D. Let them all wash and be clean in the pure waters of grace.

Water gives birth to wood, water conquers fire. Without fail, at times our prayers are filled with tears, these tears water our wood and make it grow.

Tears wash out consciences and are the language that God understands. Fluid prayer where you want to be where God wants you to be, and you extinguish any doubts in your life. You are pieced on your side, you bleed and water comes out and you can still pray father forgive them for they know not what they are doing.

Lost in the greater love of God you can wash away guilt and shame and absolve others from the pain they have caused you. Look at Calvary and see the water, sweat and blood coming out. It's not easy but for others, but to access it, at times you must die. Have you been to the water and been baptized, are your hands and inner parts cleaned.

E. Design the tools for warfare: Metal gives birth to water and fire conquers metal: brittle warfare weapons are out for change.

Hard and unwavering, this the prayer for wealth and increase, stability and grounding. This is a battle encounter where you are willing to lose flesh, or cut through flesh. You do things because they are right not because they feel right.

Hang your flesh on the tree and suspend it on nails, look at the cross and it will make sense. Use the wood, call upon the fire to burn, the land to give birth, the wind to blow, and metal to cut through.

This is what the Lord used to create us; the ground, and all in us must worship and connect with the creator.

LOOK AGAIN AT THE CROSS AND SEE HOW HE BLEED TO SAVE US

- His genitals at 8 days so that all the male seed bearing tools can be cleansed for use

- He bleeds in the garden: for the lost territory of man, Adam lost it in the garden *Yashua* conquered it in the garden. Shout for victory while you worship the war has been won.

- He bleeds on his back to heal all who are sick, by his stripes we are healed, worship and claim this promise and assure the saints that his blood is sufficient for all our sin and guilt

- He bleeds on the head with a crown of thorns, our cursed ground and thorns have been on his heard and we now cleansed and our thoughts must be those of victory and not of thorns. He put on the crown of thorns so that we can put on the crown of life.

- He bleeds on the side, the church is born from the side as Eve was taken out of Adam. As you worship remind the saints that they are on the side of Jesus to comfort him and be the wife that He died for. Tell them they are bought with the blood.

- The blood also flowed into the inside to deal with our internal pain on the things that eat us from the inside.

- He bleeds on his hands, so that all that we touch can be blessed. The labor of our hands is no longer for death but we now work for life. Tell them their hands are not instruments of righteousness.

- He bleeds on his feet, so that our feet can carry the good tidings, the good news of salvation.

Note the blood fell on to the ground also to redeem the soil and our inheritance. The ground, which was condemned not to produce, would now give forth fruits and harvest. The hearts of the saints need to be sprinkled with the blood of *Yashua* to secure the seed therein.

During the worship service special attention must be paid to release the power of the cross into the heart of the worshippers the new plants must shoot forth from the earth of our hearts.

The fire of the cross must burn within us with the fire of heaven; out of this fire we form the ground and earth on which the seed of the gospel can be planted.

Out of this ground we bring forth the metals of strength, and these metal give us the water that waters other wood. The death of Jesus on the cross cleanses these elements for the human beings to enjoy the material world.

Each worshipper must usher, and have divinity access to their spheres of influence and allow God to be seen through the eyes of dominion. Help the worshippers to recognize God as the consolidated center piece of Dominion and that as we draw closer to God we too can realize our dreams and take our places in the greater plan of salvation.

All nature and its beauty came from the dust, but the creation of man took God part of Himself, "let us make man in our own image after our likeness". Worship restores the Image of God in us. The devil, serpent was given dust for food, and if you do not rise from the things of the flesh you remain as dust and the snake will feed on you.

The image of God could not only mean look and feel, but power and dominion, ownership and ruler ship. As much as the devil has rulers, let the church rejoice for we are also rulers in the house of the Lord. Bringing every thought and imagination under the authority of Jesus, refuse to be ruled by feelings and thoughts that breed sin and push you back to the ground.

Dust yourself like a prince and princess that you are and take your place amongst the saints and declare with your mouth your new status.

Say, " *I am a child of a king, I am a new creation,*

I crucified with Christ, not I who lives but Christ lives in me.

The old things have passed away the new have come, the joy of the Lord is my strength, I do not have the spirit of fear,

I too can say ABBA Father the work that Jesus has started in me, He will not stop until He completes it. Declare, " *I will not die"*

Worshippers struggle with habits and things that seek to take hold of them, but God has given us power to have dominion instead of being dominated.

In the mercy of God Jesus declared for us that in Him we would have peace, so we can all come unto Him as we labor and are heavy laden and He will give us rest - Mathew 11:28.

The coming of Jesus to the world was that we should live victorious lives and have the gift of heaven "life" and have it more abundantly - John 10:10.

It is imperative that the manifestation of the children of God as the Manifestation of Jesus Christ should be that of power and authority over the elements than a cry for help and subordination - John 3:8.

The devil is the master of discomfort and frustration in our lives, stealing happiness and joy through sicknesses and diseases caused by sin.

The entrance of the word opens up the heart to new possibilities of divine manifestation. If the worshipper allows God to take over miracles over poverty, barrenness, death, disease, joblessness, witchcraft, anger, etc. All these will be broken at the blessed hour of prayer. Let the hearts slowly bend to a savior who loves the fainting heart to cheer. In the fullness of His trust, let us lose every care, the moment of prayer is a balm for the weary, it is always sweet to be there.

From the upper room of prayer the saints can walk in the path that is shinning with the glory of the Lord - Proverbs 4:18.

The presence of the Holy Spirit makes each day better than the day before. This presence will increase you not decrease you, grace you not disgrace you, walk you in the light and not in darkness, promote you not demote you, flourish you not diminish you. This is the power of the Cross that makes us live in heavenly places. Our worship services must take us into these lofty places and teach us to interact with holy heavenly beings.

SEVEN DIMENSIONS OF WORSHIP

Theology: the place of *YHWH* on the table of creation and recreation. Where is YHWH in the worshippers?

Worship must focus on the Creator and to acknowledge Him and praise Him draws the human heart into the presence of glory. Worship must not take us to idols and lifeless objects, for what we worship we become like.

Worship in life, worship the giver of life. Worship must be prepared to reach Him, never stop along the way of impurity, but lift our voices until the Lord stands to accept our service.

The divine must be present for worship to take place the human spirit must tap into this dimension to interact be fueled to face the challenges of life.

This is the spiritual nourishment the word works as a means to this end. Worship YHWH in nature with nature.

Anthropology: the nature and value of human beings on the table. Where are the people? Worship must find people. Human beings must be present and directed to their hearts and souls. They must find this God inside the chambers of their hearts and connect the inside with the outside. Worship has to go into the bones and marrow of the person to expose evil and plant righteousness.

The Human being must be present in the midst of worship, and the body, mind, heart, strength and spirit must be at work during this communion. Connect their souls to our creator or nature.

Christology: the priest and the ministry of the Messiah. Can people experience *Yashua* in the worship service. The mediation between creature and creator is in the person of priesthood, there must be a priest who joins and conducts the service. In our religious experience, we confess that *Yashua Harmashiack* in the order of *Melchizedek* is our High Priest.

Full of YHWH full of us. In Him we are all connected, on the cross, He joins the universe to earth and holds humans beings together. The Cross is a great junction and meeting place of all people, races, nationalities, and the ground at the foot of the cross is level, no sinner weaker than the other, or saint greater than the other.

The Priest must minister the ordinances into our hearts during worship, and in the purity of sacrifice and offering, do we all learn to live and offer our bodies as living sacrifices holy and acceptable. Messianic – give people real hope – plant the heart bit of change and power.

Soteriology: the salvation on this table. How are they experiencing salvation today from their challenges? Salvation must be present during the worship service, lift burdens, the human emptiness and shortage meets divine providence and abundance.

People seek the divine for the human experience gives us problems; we need solutions and medication for the sickness of our soul.

Worship is medicine to the human spirit and it is in this service that the human being loses self into something and someone bigger than himself, and allows an invasion of the supernatural, this is salvation to us.

The best form of salvation is when the preservation of the spirit in the body or flesh and get the internal tool calibrated by grace to perform and function beyond the common.

This salvations takes us and preserves us for holy use, it places us all into the hands of the porter for remolding. Like the prodigal son we can walk back to our father with a different message, initially, he said, "give me" and when he returned he says "make me".

In worship we must stop making it a begging session of things and materials but rather a submission to us being made anew. Worship must create in us a new heart and put a right spirit within us.

Ecclesiology: the function and diet of the church. Does the worship service gather people into a community of fellowship? The building and the liturgical paraphernalia that must enhance this experience, from the open field, to the church and closed chambers, whenever you erect an alter church and worship has began.

The real church is in the heart of the worshipper, being aware now that they stand on holy ground, they need to use all that surrounds them to connect. It is a waste of time to go to a house of worship without worship in the inner heart.

Take your church (heart) to church (building). Go inside so that you can go outside. The condition of your heart determines the effect of worship and the acceptability of your offering. Church is a place where we meet God, not a place where we find God. Neither do we leave him there to go home, but he goes home into life with the worshippers.

Church must take care of the poor widows, orphans and foreigners. The tithe must be used for such community work. "When you have finished setting aside a tenth of all your produce in the third year, the year of the tithe, you shall give it to the *Levite*, the foreigner, the fatherless and the widow, so that they may eat in your towns and be satisfied."[4]

Eschatology: the table of preparation for the trumpet to sound. Does the worship service ring a bell in their hearts and breed a sense of the future.

Then hope must break into the presence of despair. Not only hope in terms of the second coming of our Lord and savor, but hope in the return of life and connectivity. Like the spirit of Elijah the hearts of the children are returned to their fathers and the fathers to their children.

Through the worship service, homes must return, children must return,

---

4. Deuteronomy 26: 12 also reference Deuteronomy 14:29. "The Levite, because he has no portion or inheritance among you, and the alien, the orphan and the widow who are in your town, shall come and eat and be satisfied, in order that the LORD your God may bless you in all the work of your hand which you do.

hope must return, laughter must return, joy must return, therefore the redeemed of the Lord shall return.

Come with singing unto Zion and everlasting joy shall be upon their heads, they shall obtain gladness and joy, sorrows and mourning shall flee away. Let there be a return unto me and I will return unto you, worship is a great return, not only God returns, but we too return, come back into our minds and Spirit. We want liberation from depression now, and from sin when he arrives

Pneumatology: Holy Spirit on the table – *Mudzimu Unoyera* (Holy Spirit). Does the worship service connect to the Spirit? Does the service bring people in harmony with the right Spirit? The Spirit seeks Spirit as the flesh seeks the flesh. Let the mind of men find the mind of God. Let the heart of men find the heart of God. Let the Spirit of men find the spirit of God.

Worship is when we join the human with the divine and the Holy Spirit is the communion ground with his ear in the mouth of God and his mouth in the ear of men, to whisper blessed hope and comfort. Worship service must make people hear the word of the Lord. Hear the voice of God echo in the chambers of the soul.

He must speak and we will listen. What is the use of worship if there is no time to hear the word of power from the throne of grace. True worship must not be afraid of the Spirit. Break the entire bible into these clusters. Take dimensions of theology and look at them in this light and see a new light

TRUE WORSHIP – CELEBRATE LIFE AND NOT CHURCHES

Life must be celebrated in its fullness and the worship service must set up this welcome table for the hungry souls to feed.

This table "before me in the presence of my enemies" is not a selfish feast while others starve, but a place of advantage that you can share with your enemies the bounties of divine provision.

The cedar meal (Friday *Shabbat* meal) is a table that has all the elements of *Shabbat* for the worshipper to experience YHWH through a feast and celebration. The community has an opportunity to experience you in full as the lord is working with you and through you. Mugovera (Sabbath), in shona, it is a day of sharing and social cohesion.

Every Sabbath when you sit around your table you have an opportunity to measure the distance between your services, the distance between your bread and wine, bitter herbs, oil and dish etc. This is a special moment to celebrate the past, appreciate the present and anticipate the future.

Look at you ancestors, reflect on those that have gone before you, speak to those after you – your children. Better to be in the house of morning than in a party for a sad face is good for the heart.

The end of the matter is better than the beginning and the hearts of the wise are in the house of morning.

Life in its fullness is not about celebrating all the time but preparation for the change of times.

Life is made out of good times and bad times. Children and the family must be prepared for the change of times.

On a weekly basis the table must supply practical, visible and draw the heart of the saints to that table to participate in the extension of divine grace, prepare your hearts and life for all turns; bitter herbs that balance with the wine and the oil in or next to the bread.

The sound of the *shofar* every weekend is an announcement to join the human song with the divine choir.

The worship in the home or heart joins together with the worship on high. The rituals of eating, sharing and worship in harmony bring good tidings and positive welfare in the home and community. Eating is worship in the Hebraic and African culture – what is worship without drink and food?

Worship and Music

Speaking the Language of God

The world is a field of study for those who seek knowledge; to travel, to look and to learn.

With an open spirit humility will teach you a multitude of things. The universe is open and will unfold itself to the mysteries of infinity, longevity, tenacity of the human body and soul.

You will be shocked to know the use of music in various parts of the world, a wide variety of healing. In the battle fronts there is a song. In private chambers of amusement, public gatherings or community building; music has demonstrated its power to unite people and give energy to life.

The human body as in nature also responds to music and phenomenal realities are altered.

The fish in the ocean, animals on land and birds in the air communicate in supernatural harmony and perfect pitches. The worshipper must be student a of nature in order to be in harmony with the rest of creation.

STUDY TO ENHANCE THE WORSHIP SERVICE:

Biblical Musical Instrument Information: the world of the Hebrew or Black

The ancient Hebrews had a great taste for music, which they used in their religious services, in their public and private rejoicing, at their weddings and feasts, and even in their mourning. We have in Scripture canticles of joy, of thanksgiving, of praise, and of mourning. Also mournful elegies or songs, as those of David on the death of Saul and Abner, and the Lamentations of Jeremiah on the destruction of Jerusalem; so, too, songs of victory, triumph, and granulation, as that which Moses sung after passing the Red Sea, that of Deborah and Barak, and others.

The people of God went up to Jerusalem three times a year, cheered on their way with songs of joy - Ps 84:12 Isa 30:29. The book of Psalms comprises a wonderful variety of inspired pieces for music, and is an inexhaustible treasure for the devout in all ages.

Music is perhaps the most ancient of the fine arts. Jubal, who lived before the deluge, was the "father" of those who played the harp and the organ - Genesis 4:21 31:26-27.

Laban complains that his son in-law Jacob had left him, without giving him an opportunity of sending his family away "with mirth and with songs, with tabret and with harp."

Moses, having passed through the Red Sea, composed a song, and sung it with the Israelites men, while Miriam, his sister, sung it with dancing, and playing on instruments, at the head of the women - Ex 15:20-21. He caused silver trumpets to be made, and sounded at solemn sacrifices, and on religious festivals.

David, who had great skill in music, soothed the perturbed spirit of Saul by playing on the harp, 1Sa 16:16,23; and when he was himself established on the throne - seeing that the Levites were not employed, as formerly, in carrying the boards, veils, and vessels of the tabernacle, its abode being fixed at Jerusalem - he appointed a great number of them to sing and to play on instruments in the temple, 1Ch 25:1-31.

David brought the ark to Jerusalem with triumphant and joyful music, 1Ch 13:8 15:16-28; and in the same manner Solomon was proclaimed king, 1Ki 1:39-40. The Old Testament prophets also sought the aid of music in their services, 1Sa 10:5 2Ki 3:15.

Asaph, Heman, and Jeduthun were chiefs of the music of the tabernacle under David, and of the temple under Solomon. Asaph had four sons, Jeduthun six, and Heman fourteen. These twenty-four Levites, sons of the three great masters of the temple-music, were at the head of twenty-four bands of musicians, which served in the temple by turns.

Their number there was always great, but especially at the chief solemnities. They were ranged in order about the altar of burnt-sacrifices. As the whole business of their lives was to learn and to practice music. It must be that they understood it well, whether it was vocal or instrumental - 2 Chronicles 29:25.

The kings also had their music. Asaph was chief master of music to David. In the temple, and in the ceremonies of religion. Female musicians were admitted as well as male; they generally were daughters of the Levites.

Ezra, in his enumeration of those whom he brought back with him from captivity, reckons two hundred singing men and singing women - 2 Sa 19:35, Ezra 2:65, Neh. 7:67.

As to the nature of their music, we can judge of it only by conjecture, because it has been long lost. Probably it was unison of several voices, of which all sung together the same melody, each according to his strength and skill, without musical counterpoint, or those different parts and combinations, which constitute harmony in our music. Probably, also, the voices were generally accompanied by instrumental music.

If we may draw any conclusions in favor of their music from its effects, its magnificence, its majesty, and the lofty sentiments contained in their songs, we must allow it great excellence. It is supposed that the temple musicians were sometimes divided into two or more separate choirs, which, with a general chorus, sung in turn responsive to each other, each a small portion of the Psalm.

The structure of the Hebrew Psalms is eminently adapted to this mode of singing, and very delightful and solemn effects might thus be produced. Compare Ps 24:10. Numerous musical instruments are mentioned in Scripture, but it has been found impossible to affix heir names with certainty to specific instruments now in use.

By a comparison, however, of the instruments probably held in common by the Jews with the Greeks, Romans, and Egyptians, a degree of probability as to most of them has been secured. They were of three kinds:

A. Stringed instruments:

1. KINNOR, "the harp," Gen 4:21. Frequently mentioned in Scripture, and probably a kind of lyre.

2. NEBEL, "the psaltery," 1Sam 10:5. It appears to have been the name of various large instruments of the harp kind.

3. ASOR, signifying ten-stringed. In Ps 92:4, it apparently denotes an instrument distinct from the NEBEL; but elsewhere it seems to be simply a description of the NEBEL as ten-stringed. See Ps 33:2 144:9.

4. GITTITH. It occurs in the titles of Ps 8:1 81:1 84:1. From the name, it is supposed that David brought it from Gath. Others conclude that it is a general name for a string instrument.

5. MINNIM, strings, Ps 150:4. Probably another kind of stringed instrument used for celebration.

6. SABECA, "sackbut," Dan 3:5,7,10,15. A type of lyre,

7. PESANTERIN, "psaltery," occurs Dan 3:7, and is supposed to represent the NEBEL.

8. MACHALATH. Found in the titles of Ps 53:1 88:1; supposed to be a lute or guitar.

A. Wind instruments:

1. KEREN, "horn," Jos 6:5. Cornet.

2. SHOPHAR, horn, "trumpet," Num 10:10. Used synonymously with KEREN.

3. CHATZOZERAH, the straight trumpet, Ps 98:6.

4. JOBEL, or KEREN JOBEL, horn of jubilee, or signal trumpet, Jos 6:4. Probably the same with 9 and 10

5. CHAIL, "pipe" or "flute." The word means bored through, 1Sa 10:5.

6. MISHROKITHA, Da 3:5, etc. Chaldean name for the flute with two reeds,

7. UGAB, "organ" in our version Ge 4:21. It means a double or manifold pipe, and hence the shepherd's pipe; probably the same as the syrinx or Pan's pipe; or perhaps resembling the bagpipe.

B.   Other Instruments

These instruments gave out sound on being struck i.e. Percussion Instruments:

1.   TOPH, Ge 31:27, the tambourine and all instruments of the drum kind.

2.   PHAAMON, "bells," Ex 28:33. Attached to the hem of the high priest's garment.

3.   TZELITZELIM, "cymbals," Ps 150:5. A word frequently occurs there were probably two kinds, hand-cymbals.

4.   SHALISHIM, 1Sa 18:6. In our version, "instruments of music." "Three-stringed instruments." Most writers identify it with the triangle.

5.   MENAANEIM, "cymbals," 2Sa 6:5, the sistrum. The Hebrew word means to shake. The sistrum was generally about sixteen or eighteen inches long, occasionally inlaid with silver, and being held upright, was shaken, the rings moving to and fro on the bars.[1]

AFRICAN MUSIC

It is a vast passionate expression of voices and instruments, which echoes on every mountainside, and every time you cross a river the rhythm changes.

The African sings in harmony with nature and these oral traditions, songs instruments manufacturing instruments, clothing, dances all form and meet in seasons. Voices can be heard during work, riots, funerals, celebrations, rituals, weddings initiations and festivals.

Key to the music of Africa is the human voice, the percussions, the music instruments which all fuse into a deep rhythm that reaches the soul. Sometimes the drums are so deep that you can feel them on your throat as they alter your heart. There is no barrier between the musician, the dancer and the drummer. The community claps hands and whistles while the ceremony and song is in session. There is no interruption it all comes together extemporaneously. Drums have no key, but fluid to the human soul and enhance personal experience of wholeness and healing.

---

1. Paulette Fortune, Swaziland: a student of the bible and her studies in the biblical use of musical instruments and use in worship. She complied comprehensive study into the history of instruments and expressions of worship, dancing, clapping of hands and prophetic utterances.

They are made of animal skin and wood; by nature drums are material of the past with a song of the present. The fact that they are from the past they carry a message, if not in age but the technology carries the science of spirituality - their use delivers their function.

Drums are powerful, their sound and rhythm vibrates into the bone marrow and flows in the blood stream to create a surge for movement. Like the waves at the community is joined in rhythm and community oneness.

By its very nature 'Ngoma' or drum cleanses the air, to block out all other sounds and create that single sound that allows focus on the event at hand. In this unification a great amount of energy is created that turns the event into a spiritual invitation of divine participation.

As the beat grows it takes people with it, to give into the realm of sound and lose themselves into a spiritual journey. On this path of the spirit sound takes them away, and the drum gives them the pace of the journey.

The movement is not only from the human side but the spirit also comes and the two are bound to meet and the purpose of the ritual is realized.

The fear of western Christianity is that the drum "Ngoma" ushers a realm they can not control and spirits they are not familiar with which come with power (Ngoma - which is healing, prophesy, utterances, prescriptions).

Anything they cannot govern was thus deemed pagan and satanic.

The power that Christianity claims to have therefore must not be afraid of demons but beat the drum past the demons to the Creator, our drums and songs must take us places in the spirit.

Who said in the presence of the Lord there is silence and boredom and in hells there is laughter and celebration?

Who gave us the SONG? Who invented the Ngoma and from where did they get the inspiration? The religion that makes heaven boring and hell exciting is from hell.

Let there be more joy in the presence of the Lord, that monotony and boredom in the presence of YHWH. African must celebrate and experience his worship in his skin and song connects the spirit.

The sounds of the three civilizations of Africa will give you a guide to the true sense of African music.

a. **The Pyramids of Giza**: with the harp and flutes and a strong sense of Arabic influences as it is the bridge between the continents, a very similar melodic modes.

You will find these in the form of *Nyatiti* all around sub Sahara all built for cultural expression and entertainment. Songs are specific to function.

The sharing of our rhythm is sharing our hearts and our heartbeats become the rhythm of the community. It's a great thrill and emotional release that unites communities.

b. **The temples of Timbuktu in 12 century**: the Griots or Jali families who are genealogist, storytellers and historians and the desert kings play to the sound of the winds across the Sahara deserts.

Camels and cow skins are used to make the Kora. Ancient stories and traditions are passed on in form of song to celebrate a past experiences and conquests of kings.

c. **The Great Zimbabwe with the famous Mbira instruments**: by far one of the oldest music instruments, which drive the cross rhythm sounds that evoke the spirits.

You will observe 150 mini ruins around Southern Africa and Central Africa with the greatest being the House of Stone (*Dzimba bgwe*).

This instrument has influence across southern Africa and a mother to Marimba and a dozen other innovations Kalemba etc.

The south has more harmonious melodies and the dances are intense like the Zulu military dances. From central Africa to the South African tip you cannot miss the beauty of rhythm and dance.

The Khoisan being one of the oldest tribes have their fire dances and cyclical groans that turn into trances for worship and celebration.

d. **Western Music**: traditionally this would mean cowboy music, which is folk music.

This is basic guitar, banjo, and harmonica, fiddle mandolin and voices Sentiments of the nation is diaspora that had gone to the state, they would sing as they remember home, hence you find Scottish, and old English, Irish ballads (hillbilly music) and expression in the songs and dances. The music has grown to be called country music.

It is important to highlight that a lot of what we now term Christian music is actually country western music and European hymnody that has its history in European chambers and royal houses.

This music has also migrated from the Monasteries and cathedrals of ecclesiastical expressions.

This is the music of the church fathers, when the Hebraic religion met with the barbarians and gentiles of Europe they adapted the message to their music.

It has grown from the early music, medieval, renaissance, baroque to modern contemporary music. Its typical features would be an orchestra, voices and silent audience who listen very attentively and traditions of when to clap hands and express one.

In post modern era it has now become a culture of the elite, an unfortunately most of them run the religious circles and they have come to deem this music as sacred and clean for it does not evoke lots of emotions but rather intelligent consumption of the intellect.

The African must be taught to acquire the taste like olives and blue cheese for this classic music, later to use it as a standard for worship. The same music Hitler used to kill the Jews.

e. **Middle/Eastern Music:** this region is influenced by Africa greatly from Morocco to India, as the cradle is Mesopotamia.

The traditions of Babel and Nimrod (Iraq) can be traced up to India.

Even with the rise of Islam in the Byzantine era the music has remained grounded on the level of spirituality in it, *maqamat* modes.

These scales are twinned into complex rhythmic structure that have tense vocals and monophonic textures that have the ability to drive the listeners and participants into trances that vibrate into the region of drawing energy levels an cause the body to do "supernatural things."

Maybe it not supernatural but the reality of subjecting the body to the right atmosphere and the body transforms into another form where you can thrust sharp objects into it without breaking the flesh.

The human flesh can walk on hot coals without fear of burning. Did the bible not say "snakes would bite you and not harm you?".

The music sessions can last at times go for more that 3hrs to an applauded climax. There are a wide range of instruments, which range from strings percussions and winds, which are accompanied with dance and unique dress. You will note that this region is influenced by Abrahamic region.

This music is true to its culture and people, aesthetics, ethnicity, and has a unique identity that relates to its historical background.

The people of the east log into the musical zone to move to the higher dimension of wisdom and supernatural acts.

f. **Spiritual music:** this music is above all angelic and is found is chanting and the silence meditation.

From the Temples of Tibet, the Red Indians, the temples of *Voodoo*, *Negro* spirituals and Christian songs that are and were created out of human experience.

As for the Negro in the pain of slavery and smell of death the song kept them going, in the cotton fields and sugarcane plantations you would hear the echo monophonic "I look for that city down where the Jordan roll" songs of liberation and a cry for a better home, "Meeting at the building gonna soon be over" these spirituals are warehouse of oral tradition.[2]

In the broader sense this music is meditational as it is spiritual, new terminology such as Zen music used for meditation, relaxation and the new age ambiance.

The Red Indian and the Aborigines and the Bushman would speak to wolves and eagles in these songs. Their songs often begin slowly and build up with unique instruments and voicing, which call for rain and speak to the heavens and cause the stars to dance.

In the Arctic you also find strong spiritual chants in Mongolia with tense voicing and throat singing a unique form of art found in a few tribes around the world.

g. **Worldly music:** termed circular music a combination of all sounds and music in the world combined together.

A term coined by ethnomusicologist Robert E. Brown. An orchestra of Asian, African, European musicians in song, a world concert of fusion, which is now, termed music has the world, or ethnic folk music.

With technology and movement for the first time people can travel and share their cultures and fuse these together creating unique harmonies like never before.

I had an opportunity to play my *mbira* with a band in Ukraine, we could not communicate in words, yet our music united us and we played all night long. Music reaches were words cant reach.

h. **Worship music:** this is very young on the market roughly sixty years ago new mob worship service have been called "Jesus music" the hippie style, which is also called Christian music, Pentecostal music used widely by charismatic churches.

---

2. Ephesians 5:19 speaking to yourselves in psalms and hymns and spiritual songs singing and making melody in your heart to the Lord.

Of dominance are a synthesizer, keyboards, guitar, bass guitar and vocals. The main emphasis is the Holy Spirit and its desire is to make people encounter the Holy Spirit during worship with a deep sense of individual encounter "I" is a major.

Evangelists use this kind of music for their worship and miracle services. There is a rock element in these genre that makes other religious groups feel that it brings the anarchistic flavor of evil background has been given center stage in worship. Others deem its strong appeal to emotions as evil.

THE PRESENCE OF GOD IN WORSHIP

The human being is emotional, physical, mental, spiritual, and all these elements are present during the worship service.

The scripture would teach that we must love The Lord with all our hearts, minds, strength and souls, which is a holistic experience.

Those who advocate that emotions must be left outside to enhance the mind then spirituality cannot be experienced only at intellect. It is an insult to the creator to tell him that feelings must not come to church. The desire of the worshipper is to lead people to experience YHWH through the service and the entire person must be present.

The Music genres above shows that the landscape of expression is vast, and the type of music will be used to achieve the desired output. The body can worship and the spirit can worship too. The final destination of the song is what is important. Music is worship. Be clear the God you evoke during your worship.

Love, sex, money greed, anger and insight for violence can all be in a song. Music is prophetic, as you sing you are declaring prophecies and calling for things to happen to you and your community and the universe can hear the call and will cause it to pass. Music is one. Music is universal it relates to all people when music is played everyone must here what they want hear. The human body responds, yet the greatest call should be the journey to the spiritual connection.

It is not correct that all people can connect *Mungu* through *murungu* music and the western form of hymnody is being forced down all other nations as the standard of "acceptable worship music". Then you find black people that tortures each other in the singing of notes and that people must respect the cows eye on the staff notation.

Often people are stopped for not singing the proper notes, and the preference of elders has been deemed as religion. Classic music and country music are now deemed as sacred, and African music and instruments are deemed demonic and satanic.

Often not even allowed into church. In some congregation drums must never be seen, but backing tracks, which have drums, can be played. If the purpose is to worship the worshipper must allow that freedom of expression and the let the spirit breath freedom in the presence of the creator. To limit and try and guide the worshipper is tantamount to failure, as you can never tell the heart to sing.

Every person has their song and pain, their joy and tears and the Lord will minister to each one when the purpose is clear the song will unite the experience and guide the worshippers in the throne room on high.

TEMPLE MUSIC OR SANCTUARY MUSIC: THE TEMPLE MUSIC

Upon this the Temple music began. It was the duty of the priests, who stood on the right and the left of the marble table on which the fat of the sacrifices was laid, at the proper time to blow the blasts on their silver trumpets. There might not be less than two nor more than 120 in this service; the former in accordance with the original institution (Numbers 10:2), the latter not to exceed the number at the dedication of the first Temple (2 Chronicles 5:12).

The priests faced the people, looking eastwards, while the *Levites*, who crowded the fifteen steps, which led from the Court of Israel to that of the Priests, turned westwards to the sanctuary. On a signal given by the president, the priests moved forward to each side of him who struck the cymbals. Immediately the choir of the *Levites*, accompanied by instrumental music, began the Psalm of the day.

It was sustained by not less than twelve voices, with which mingled the delicious treble from selected voices of young sons of the *Levites*, who, standing by their fathers, might take part in this service alone. The number of instrumental performers was not limited, neither was it yet confined to the *Levites*, some of the distinguished families, which had intermarried with the priests being admitted to this service.[3]

---

3. http://www.gospelhall.org/bible/bible.php?passage=Psalm+93;&ver1=kjv

THE MYSTERY AND STORIES AND MYTHS OF THE AFRICAN PEOPLE

It is important to start here because you need to see the basis of African faith belief systems; these are a collage from personal observations. Of the things I have heard and seen, I write my testimony as an African child. Migration from wisdom to ignorance the sad story of the African people.

We lived in an era when snakebites were treated by drinking your own urine. The body was its own hospital life was harmony of the inside and outside. The sacred pools and rivers have dried up and the dragon flying snakes have been relegated to the history myths.

Religion cannot function without sacredness "and openly as possible and to build connections with closely associated with ritual, religion and spirituality."[4] It is these pools lured those that would spend months under the water preparing to be healers. These snakes were said to hold water and cause movements in the skies and land. The technologies of calling on the rain have been taken away for entertainment and amusement.

Water has cleansing as soil has feeling and the air has ears. In the olden days when weird birds would visit us to announce change of seasons and sacred rituals. The fighting of chickens announced the arrival of visitors. And the setting of the moon was important to mating and fertility.

The plants have a relationship with us and so is the wind in the making of the rain. African child has demonstrated the ability to tame and influence the elements and cause movements in favor of humanity. A complex matrix of the sacred can be seen below.

The individual must view themselves as a sacred ground, and this is what measures their civility, not education but connectivity to holiness, which then informs his religiosity practices, translated into places and a barrage of spiritual traditions and lifestyle which incubates the supernatural as present in daily living.

Communities live in the shadow of awareness of the supernatural, which is present and can be accessed through activities which draw them near to participate in the "daily" of the living. Sacred is deemed as " individual freedom, well-being, harmony with nature and the self plus a plethora of sacred zones and places, the spiritual sacred."[5]

4. Paul Post, Phillip Nel and Walteer Van Beek, Sacred and contested Identities (space and ritual dynamics in Europe and Africa p 4
5. Ibid, p4

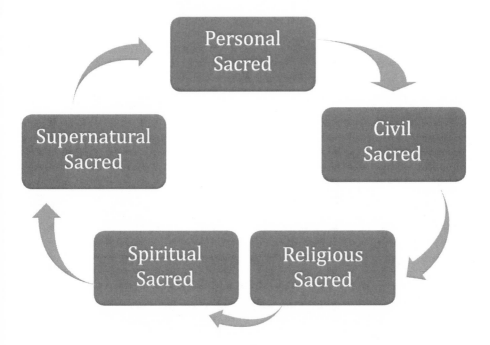

Fig 19: Grounds of Spiritual Interaction

Have you Sang for a lizard and it dances or clapped hands for an eagle and he flaps his wings! Old ladies would close a pregnant woman in a round hut and through massage move the fetus to face the passage of birth.

I never heard of a Bridge and or Caesarian section. Have you seen a child refuse to drink its mother's milk until the mother calls their right totems and call the clan names of their real tribe? Have you seen children named after dead uncles and they take and emulate even mannerisms and scars that their namesake had. This too baffles me.

By looking into the stars the old could tell the future and read fertility and periods of women were paralleled to the moon.

The movement of the upper universe (air), was believed to be locked in the woman's womb, (the low universe blood in womb) ultimately the reality in the depth of the waters (lower universe-water) wisdom was to look outside and know the inside. In simple terms, we have air, then we have blood, and water and life exists in the three realms, the human body is by nature created to be able to live in these three spheres.

There is a cosmos inside every cosmos and there is life in death and there is death in life. When awareness arrives it is the death of death. When ignorance captures the soul its the death of life.

Children were vaccinated by breast-feeding on various mothers and milk was cultured in clay pot and cream was premium oil for cooking. Calabashes were used as cups.

We went heading cattle with nothing but made our own baobab yogurts and chewed wild berries for lunch. We would play games in the Bush until the cattle got lost, then spit in our hand, and strike with a finger, in the direction of saliva we would follow and find our cattle.

The smoke gathered in the grass huts mixed with salt would be used to treat cattle wounds. Food would be dug under ground in harvest time and dug up in summer fresh to be eaten again. Grand mothers knew the season to pick up mushrooms and dry up vegetables and extra fat from sheep for cooking oil.

On our way to school grand ma would ask for your hand and place a spoon of peanut butter and roasted corn to last you till super time. We have moved from knowledge to ignorance. We carry gadgets and have lost the pulse of nature.

The ground has swallowed its beauty and innocent blood we spill has polluted the fertile land. Then came a season of treating animal skins to make ropes for farm use. It started with sparking these animal skins in the riverbed for a few days and then cutting it into thin strips and twist it on the big tree with a clockwise and anticlockwise movement, rubbing it with oil and the result would a tough unbreakable rope. Man living with nature in harmony and our science or indigenous knowledge has melted into plastic products.

Civilization is a funeral of natural knowledge for commercial bondage. Science has become a managing tool for human fear of death and peruse of thrill. True science should seek to explain the mystery of natural wisdom a reality and true power with in- depth observation on nature to interpret it and cause nature obey. Having dominion over the air - birds, the land - animals and fish in the depth of the sea.

Is it by accident that creation challenges us to look upwards, inside and downwards?

Even Jesus in his ministry worked with elements. As of water and its fish; the land and its challenges of food disease and death ultimately the air, walking through walls and finally being taken in the clouds. Who could miss that his birth even the star's moved and the wise man saw the shift and followed. You can follow stars to mystery.

At his death did the Sun not bow down and the earth crust shift and shock and gross darkness covered the earth. In reality the power of the Son of YHWH reveals more than what meets the eye. He spoke to his Father in the night and earlier when they tried to kill him. He walked away from a cliff and they could not touch him.

Power of utterance a word for Jairus' daughter and the wind carried the healing. The African cannot read these events in isolation but see that Faith power to work beyond prayer and hymn. We live and breathe this life of mystery.

The words of the old people did not fall on the ground (*muromo womukuru hauwiri pasi*) their word "caused" and shaped destiny. Their word was as good as their action. Their anger and joy had an impact on the object they blessed or cursed. (*Mvura murongwa haidariki musingwi*) words are ordained; like water, they will not return before they fill up the potholes or achieve the intention. Words will sweep the life like a flood covering every ditch along the way.

The seeds of watermelon were not to be eaten or placed in the mouth if you wanted to plant them. We received gifts from right hand with both hands. Empty hands can receive; empty your hands to receive material or spiritual gifts need a clean soul empty of self.

When eating mealies our uncle's would first take the corn and open a path that lead to our success. Before you gave me water to drink you needed to take the first sip.

If you have poisoned me, we will die together. I wish you all health as it is mine. An affirmation that says I will not give you what will destroy you but we live together even die together. After a funeral we would wash our hands in the same dirty water at the gate to symbolize that we are in this dirt together; we cry together.

It was not for hygiene but to remove the mud in every hand, our community contribution towards each other's pain.

This event reminded us all that our hands are dirty together as we create and destroy each other and when we are dirty together, no one can say my dirt is better or less than yours.

This was community building, community responsibility and community accountability. Moments to forgive each other and share a meal together (*Vukama igasva vunozadziswa nokudya*). We relate better after we have eaten together.

The elders would do water survey with a certain tree they would cut a *v-shaped* branch and walk with the two side twisted to outward. Water that is deep in the ground through the magnetic fields would involuntarily cause the branch to point downward. If you were holding it, you would physically feel the magnetic downward pull to the exact point where a bore-hole was to be sunk.

Depending on the intensity, this would indicate the quantity of water, no need to sink ditches exploring water resources. It was a clean land survey.

MBIRA INSTRUMENT AND AFRICAN WORSHIP

"After all the black man has been through in this world, he can still often reach levels of spirituality the most pampered whiteman cannot touch. Maybe what he's been through is the reason why." [6]

The first *Mbira* song called **Mhemamusasa** seeks to explain that you should build your houses near the *Musasa* trees. The first song you would be introducing yourself to the spirits of the land seeking favor and cooperation.

These trees are good for honey, fiber for thatching. The leaves are fertile ground for mushrooms and the soil is rich in gold and fertile for agriculture. Such music has become entertainment in pubs and wisdom has been flushed down the drain.

THE MBIRA INSTRUMENT IS SACRED

Mbira has been used in spiritual ceremonies since ancient times. The *mbira* players play continuously until night falls and eventually a spirit will enter the body of the medium.

The voice of a bird or a strange cry, like that of an American Indian, is often heard. The medium may convulse or shake as the other participants serve the medium water.

Around the time the sound of the *mbira* is replaced by the sound of a preacher. The sound of the continues till dawn"[7]

Mbira is a traditional instrument of the *Shona* people who have lived in Zimbabwe, Africa from ancient times.

6. Ben Stein
7. http://www.mbirajunction.com/artist/garikai/e_function.htm

The instrument has the ability to contact ancestral souls and spirits (an apparition of a living person) during festivals and ceremonies and is the model for the modern music box."

The word *Mbira* is made up of a number of nouns and to appreciate the Hebraic thought one has to read the letter mbira backwards to grasp the deep meaning of worship.

A – Is the exclamation and Venda tribe has preserved that as an honorable response to the question of life. The Beginning and Alpha, the genesis the creator, the one we cannot give a name to but we just open our mouths in wonder, of surprise "Aaaaa". The Head of an Ox, strength, the word with no sound, the leader in Hebrew and Egyptian hieroglyphics.

This is the Master of the universe, beyond the sun YHWH the uncaused cause. Africans understand that man "A-DAM" is "A" God "Dam". Blood makes the "*Nefesh chayah*" the living soul; human being.

Hence Yashua become the Alpha who took the human flesh with the divine spirit. Phil 2: 6-11. The alpha in the Greek is the source of life, the genesis of all life.

Ra: the incarnate - the son of "A" of the son of the Sun; the ruler of the created world - the sky (air) the world (earth) and the underworld (water and the world of the dead) and believed that man was created from the tears and sweat of "Ra".

From the sun we have warmth, light and all creation grows from the sun. The thought behind this is that the sun is the eye of "Ra" a concrete theology that says we are being watched as the Freemasons have adopted the all Seeing Eye as their symbol. He is worshiped in songs hymns. "A" is the sun and "Ra" is the son of "A"

In Hebrew "Eulogies and the Tephillah. The two Hebrew words for prayer indicate, the one adoration, the other supplication or, rather persuasion and intercession. Both kinds of prayer found expression in the Temple services.

But only after the manifestation of Him, who in His person united the Divine with the human nature, could adoration and supplication be fully called out. Nay, the idea of supplication would only be properly realized after the outpouring of the Spirit of adoption, whereby the people of God also became the children of God as he traveled in the day and in the night. Symbols of head of a hawk, snake or sun disk."[8]

8. http://www.gospelhall.org/bible/bible.php?passage=Numbers+15%3A37-41;&ver1=kjv

Ira "qadash"- holiness, a verb attributed to setting apart, or consecrated, undefiled keep away from common use, and use for holy purposes. Sanctify in the use of it there is cleansing and transmission of holiness.

In modern *Shona* it carries the meaning of "measure", like to prepare you before indulging. "Ira"is sacred that which induces veneration as it is connected to YHWH. Which deserves respect and reverence: this is transmitted to tools, songs, clothes and rituals that are performed in the interaction of the "A-Dam" and "RA" this was Sacrosanct not for common use, but necessary for daily life.

BIRA - THE WORSHIP SERVICE

The worship service where the spirits are called upon for spiritual guidance; a service of intercession filled with music, prayers dancing and clapping of hands to invite the visible presence and manifestation of the supernatural.

It's a healing, problem solving session to call the spirits to possess the living.

The community in the presence of their creator, the human being is willing to succumb to the other world and interact with deity.

Until the spirit arrives the service is music[9] and preparation of hearts to be in sync. The music is the great bridge between the two divides of the physical and the spiritual world.

"Human beings are spiritual beings who are have a human experience. Feelings are sensors that help to pick spiritual signals. They are physical (tactile) stimuli, visual and aromatic stimuli that transmit relevant information to the brain nerve center for decoding and response.

To bottle feelings or hold back the decoded reaction from the senses is tantamount to fraud in the spiritual realm. It's hypocritical. Lets sing in the spirit and with understanding. Music is a communion of spirits. Music evokes spirits to commune with us.

You want to be sure that you are not evoking *evil* spirits, but Holy Spirit.

According to the book of Enoch "the righteous man whose eyes were opened by the Lord, and he saw a Holy vision in the heavens, which the Angels showed to me, I heard and I understood what I saw, not for this

---

9. Berliner, Paul F, The Soul of Mbira and Traditions of the Shona People of Zimbabwe, University Press, 1981.

generation but for a distant generation that will come."[10] There is an inter-action between the physical and the spiritual and music is but an instrument in the hand of the worshipper to access the divine. When worship done properly the "*holy and Great One will come out of his dwelling, to appear with his Host and appear in the strength of his power and heaven.*"[11]

"*Mbira*": the sacred instrument, which is used on a holy, sacred ceremony to talk to "Ra" who has come from "A". This instrument is a physical collection of things created in the hands of the one created (A-dam) to go back to his maker and find solutions.

The wood, (from the bleeding tree, *Mubvamaropa*) the metal, (*Mangu-ra-iron*. From the caves where the ancient kings are buried). The human being all comes together at the ceremony.

Note the intensity of the program and focus at the result; divine inter-vention happens every time the ceremony is conducted. This can go on for a night, or three days or more until the purpose is achieved "*bira*" worship continues

During *Bira* ceremony a pair of maracas (*Makavhu-harvest*) that are used together called "*Hosho*" or shakers. This is made from a gourd, too. The sound from the *Hosho* is very big and unlike the maracas used in music in other parts of the world. The *Hosho* play a main role in driving the beat of *mbira* music. It is added to liven the atmosphere of the *mbira* sound performance, helping the participants enter a trance."

Vocalists of black music such as Soul and Gospel have a powerful vocal style. The vocals of *mbira* music, on the other hand, are more like the blowing of the wind, flowing naturally with the music.[12]

The history of *mbira* begins at the time of "Great Zimbabwe," where the roots of the Shona people are planted. Great Zimbabwe is the *Munhumu-tapwa* Kingdom (bastardized as *monomotapa*), which is said to have appeared in Southern Africa in the 12-14th century.

There is debate if these are the dates of building, establishments or habitation into these exquisite stone walled houses.

The pyramids and stone structures (*Great Dzimbabwe*) still remain the second largest after the pyramids of Giza in Africa. As for the *Mbira* music it is believed that a spirit or angel (an apparition in the true form of a

---

10. The Book of Enoch: A modern translation of the Ethiopian Book of Enoch: SOAS Library at the University of London. Pp 11
11. Ibid pp 11
12. http://www.tinotenda.org/spirituality.htm

living person) came to the earth at this time, and it is believed that this spirit taught the Shona people how to make the musical instrument known as the "*mbira.*"[13]

There were many different "*Mbira*" songs, which the ancestors through oral traditions of the Shona taught over years. *Mbira* may as well be called the mother of the piano, age and dexterity.

These stories and songs are the traditions, the conquests and the history of the people. If you listen carefully you will hear of wars, famines, warriors and epidemics that the nation has gone through. Through this music they celebrate their salvation history to connect to the future they look to the past. This knowledge forms the integral part of daily living for the present generation.

THE SEVEN VOICES OF THE SEVEN THUNDERS

There are seven major tunings according to *Karikoti Garikayi* these are the seven thunders or seven voices of the seven thunders of the book of Revelation chapter 10 *Nyamaropa, Gandanga, Nemakonde, Dambatsoko, Katsanzira, Dongonda, and Saungwane.* Which the musicians as moods, with equivalent of majors, could understand minors, blue scales etc. The *mbira* has all these moods fused into this complex *Mbira* instruments.

The western has **1.** Ionian **2.** Dorian mode harmonica diatonic **3.** Phrygian mode **4.** Lydian **5.** Mixolydian **6.** Aeolian **7.** Locrian these moods are important as they drive a song towards the feelings of the listener.

Each mood reaches the ear and taps a particular response, to celebrate, to cry, to think to worship etc. African music seems to draw us more towards experiencing *Mwari* more than just hearing words about Him in sermons sitting on church benches.

The main root songs or tunings of the Mbira are "*Nhemamusasa-dorian when you open the ceremony or you arrive at a new place*". "Karigamombe-minor-blues, is played when you sacrifice or kill an animal you play this at the kraal". "*Taireva*", "*Mavembe or gandanga/Nemakonde is lower-Phrygian-Bb medium*", Dambatsoko/Mahororo-ionian low E", "*Dongonda/ Nyamaropa-Mixolydian-G*" medium - when you cut the tree that gives the wood for the instrument" are songs that date back to the time of the Shona ancestors. For every ceremony there is a song that evokes the correct atmosphere for worship.

13. http://www.tinotenda.org/spirituality.htm

Note that music is fused into daily living as an expression of the unity between the man and his creation, and his faith and *Mwari* all into a tapestry of living. Life is a continuous worship, not on occasion only but daily participation.

The simplicity of the tuning is: *donki, mombe, mbudzi* (a donkey, a cow and a goat) the phonetics of the sound "donki" gives you your *"doh" mombe* "mi" *mbudzi* etc for the musicians. It is sad to note that the missionaries banned the new converts from playing traditional instruments.[14]

They took away spirituality and gave us *mechanical Christianity* and the African Christian cannot connect to this foreign order of worship; exalting white supremacy – which promotes white capital and religious slavery.

The European music is a square pole being pushed into the round hole of African worship.

These variations in cycles loop into a deep tense ceremony and creates an environment that connects the worshippers to their Creator - *Musikavanhu*. The words sung tap into the human experience and the nature around him, those who hear can relate to the story lines.

There are no spectators in these services as everybody is involved and deeply interested in the solutions, like an atonement service everybody should prepare their hearts for the entrance and arrival of the supernatural.

Death is the passage of the body from the physical to the spiritual realm and a separation of the spirit from the body to a higher world of living spirits.

THE WISDOM OF THE AGES

The wisdom of previous generations can be accessed through these ceremonies. Hence a moment of worship is a moment of connection with life in the past, present and future.

Whereas the western preacher has a bible to refer to, the African has the spiritual world as a library that is accurate and here there is storage of advise, solutions, genealogies and wisdom for the living.

"Ancestral spirits are a source of comfort as well as the cornerstone of religious activity, for the living believe they are protected from worldly harm by their these spirits. Should a sudden misfortune befall a family, they turn first to their ancestral spirits for advice, guidance and protection. In

---

14. http://www.tinotenda.org/spirituality.htm

many cases a family has a special spirit, or *Mudzimu* which, when properly appeased, speaks directly to the family through a living spirit medium. In a lengthy and protocol intensive special ceremony, called Bira or spirit possession ceremony, special songs, selected from a vast repertoire of spiritual arrangements, are recalled to welcome a deceased person's spirit back into the family. Shona prayers, poetry and words of praise are recited." [15]

In this context the *mbira* is played—not simply as music but as a means to communicate with the spirits. Although the *mbira* is the understood medium for calling the spirits, the spirits only join the *bira* ceremony if the *mbira* music so moves them.

So it takes skill and endurance and knowledge of the songs the spirits like for an mbira player to successfully call a spirit to possess a spirit medium. It must be clear that there are spirits (*mashavi*), wandering evil spirits, used witchcraft and bad omens and *Vadzimu* clean spirit that teach *Unhu*, "*ubuntu*" and builds and protect a nation. The same distinction between *Nyanga* or *saNgoma* (healer) and *muroyi* or *umthakathi* (witch) both use *muti*, but one heals the other kills; though they have knowledge of both.

Power is neutral the condition of the heart makes it positive or negative. We can't say when a black hand holds medicine its witchcraft, when a white hand holds medicine it's a doctor.

In these ceremonies Ancestors' spirits listen to the concerns of their living family members as well as impart to them the wisdom, advice, forgotten family customs and protocol to ensure a healthy and successful family or community.

This is the most important religious and spiritual function of the instrument in the *Shona* culture and tradition. These are living tools that call and transport the community into the spiritual realm.

The metal keys are made from smelted iron ore, which is dug out from sacred hills and holy mountains where the *Shona* chiefs and *Shona* statesmen are buried. The keys thus personify the presence of ancestral spirits directly on the instrument. The soundboard, made from a special kind of tree, *Mubvamaropa* (the tree of blood), represents a source of shelter, fuel and basic necessities in everyday *Shona* life.

The resonator gourd or *deze*, into which the *mbira* is mounted and propped as a second level amplifier is a special type of dried squash, called *Nhangatanga* or the first squash, which is a source of food.

15. http://www.tinotenda.org/spirituality.htm

It is also used as a water container, *dende*. In its smaller form and dried, the *nhangatanga* squash is used as a drinking gourd, *mukombe*, and also for *hosho*. The instrument thus symbolizes the basic elements of everyday life in *Shona*.

The *mbira* player adds the final and human dimension to complete a Shona social institution. Thus music is a meeting place of the human and the divine.[16] In simple terms worship takes place in the experience of life.

There is a deep sense of awareness, from dressing to food, to venue and the ceremony there is a call of unity to the human being and nature around him. These elements have a life they bring to the service which the worshippers taps into to experience his faith.

In brief it should be clear by now that the service is a bridge "*zambuko*", (as music is the bridge that joins the two realities). The *mbira* and its player are en-route to another place. This music is meant to function in the realm of the spirit and evoke the spirits to participate in the worship service of the family.[17] We worship to connect, not to entertain.

Made of flat keys beaten from iron bars with a hammer, it is attached to a board of wood with either bolts or a wire. The keys are played with the thumb as well as the forefinger of the right hand. Both hands play the *mbira* at the same time. There is a complex and cyclical music, full of texture and overlapping rhythms, groans and strong rhythm.

When listening closely, it has the potential to be profoundly meditative music with the ability to send a person into a trance. When performed with intention it accomplishes its goal to move the player and listener to another level of worship.

It has an incredibly enchanting and *majestic quality* to it that is like the marching of a king into a place of subjects. Hence the music is a preparation for the arrival of the 'Great one'.

From observations one can have clear insights into the society and its faith. Music is useful for meditation and the healing of a society.

"There exists a multitude of factors surrounding music that play an equally important, if not more important, role in releasing information about a society. One must also consider who plays the music, the repertoire of music played, where the music is played, how the music is passed on, how one learns the instrument, and many more. *Shona* is obsessed with tradition and ancestors to the point of constraining themselves in time.

16. http://www.tinotenda.org/spirituality.htm
17. www.zambuko.com.

When written about, authors illustrate the *Shona* as a very rigid, anti-progressive society. But through a look at *Shona mbira* music, the case will be made that this theme of rigidness and obsession with tradition is taken too far. While the society and music are steeped in tradition, both are open and accepting to variation, newness, and change.

Mbira is one of the most traditional music that exists, but it still relies heavily on variation and change. The same holds true for *Shona* society.

To claim that they don't change or evolve is ridiculous. A cursory glance at their response to colonialism would refute this. It is not only unfair, but it is incorrect to label the *Shona* as an anti-progressive society."[18]

Our dentistry was in two ways, "*Chirovadunguru*" a shrub whose roots would be crushed and dropped into your nose while a strong man is holding you down. The teeth nerves are numbed permanently.

The regular brush with "*mushangura*" and the roots when chewed occasionally cured halitosis and bad breath. For those who have a challenge with nose bleeding, elephant dung would be put on a clay piece and burnt and you will drop your blood on it and the smoke mixed with your blood would clot your problem.

We used to have ankle shakers tied to our ankles while walking in the bush; they say its demonic, but this was a simple deterrent for snakes. The same ankle shakers would be used while you played *mbira* this would be percussion, for music was played when traveling long distances.

It physically reduced the distance. Calling for divine company while on the journey. Forward Kwenda notes, "*the buzz adds depth and context to the clear tones of the mbira keys, and may be heard as whispering voices, singing, tapping, knocking, wind or rain*"[19]

At a *bira*, the *mbira* serves as the "link between the world of the living and the world of the spirits" (Berliner 43).

"When modes of music change, the fundamental laws of the state always change with them (for) this spiritual license, finding a home, imperceptibly penetrates into manners and customs; when issuing with greater force, it invades contracts between man and man, and from contracts goes on to

---

18. http://www2.kenyon.edu/projects/ottenhoff/paper.htm: After coming to some conclusions on what mbira music reveals about Shona society, I compared my conclusions to other authors' views of the Shona. While many of the conclusions are similar, our stands are strikingly different concerning constraint and mobility in Shona society. Much of the literature (primarily Michael Gelfand)
19. Kwenda Forward

laws and constitutions, in utter recklessness ending at last by an overthrow of all rights private as well as public." [20]

THE ELEMENTS OF WORSHIP[21]

In his conclusion Copeland outlines some interesting observations worth sharing when he compares the modern worship and the Old Testament worship.

The simplicity of worship: The worship in the early church was simple, and it was spiritual. The purpose of worship was to encourage the worship of God with the inner man to find their place in the heart of God.

The outward activities were building to lead man to his inside. Let your worship service take people to their souls.

The priority of all worship services must be spiritual, let the spirit of man find the spirit of God and let worship happen when these two have united. A close look at church history will inform that " the first Christians were of too spiritual a fiber to substitute lifeless instruments for or to use them to accompany the human voice,"(**Catholic Encyclopedia**)

The execution of Byzantine church music by instruments, or even the accompaniment of sacred chanting by instruments was ruled out by the Eastern Fathers as being incompatible with the pure, solemn and spiritual character of the religion of Christ."[22]

John Calvin attests that "Musical instruments in celebrating the praises of God would be no more suitable than the burning of incense, the lighting up of lamps, the restoration of the other shadows of the law."

John Calvin continues to say that "The Papists, therefore, have foolishly borrowed this, as well as many other things from the Jews. Men who are fond of outward pomp may delight in that noise; but the simplicity which God recommends to us by the apostle is far more pleasing to Him." [23]

Spiritual worship requires honesty of the flesh (the mechanical program and events done at the worship service) must lead to the spirit.[24]

---

20. Plato the philospher
21. Mark A. Copeland ~ Gospel preacher, Bible teacher: http://executableoutlines. com/back.htm
22. Constantine Cavarnos, Byzantine Sacred Music
23. John Calvin, Commentary on the Book of Psalms, Vol. I, p. 539
24. http://www.ccel.org/contrib/exec_outlines/cjb/cjb_12.htm

Let the people

A = Adoration

C = Confession

T = Thanksgiving

S = Supplication[25]

Finally it must be C=Connection with the source of faith.

A deep feeling that assures and fills the heart with assurance that the service has reached the ears of the Maker.

Worship takes place when human offer, *tevura*, bring with and celebrates with the given blessings hence worship is done in seasons not haphazardly.

African worship is intentional. Seed time and harvest, this is not only about tithe but worship, we need to return a tithe of worship, make time and offer the best of our energy, power, effort, strength and soul and a living sacrifice to the Lord.

Know when to plant so that you can harvest, find a fertile ground to plant your seed. Ask the following questions: is it the right time and place to plant? The needs of the church depend on us. Offers us an opportunity to plant.

Take our seed.

Plant them at the right season and give it time to mature.

The season is right for God to do a new thing for us. Like Achan, I can say its not about you but the sin that lived in my camp. Remind them the covenant made with God cannot be broken, I have pledged my life as an offering in the hand of the Lord.

Here I stand and I make a call that I count those who are with me as we move to do battle for the Lord.[26]

While the earth remains day and night, winter and summer, God has made a covenant with time. Seed time and harvest is not a promise but a covenant. Every year has seasons, and these seasons change. As the yearly seasons change so must you also observe your life and note the correct time to do correct things.

The four seasons are summer, autumn, winter and spring.

Summer: is a time for high and usually the warmest part of the year.

---

25. John Pape, Jr, Five Elements of Worship, http://www.mediatunes.com/bhow/ or http://www.prayway.com/articles/Five_Elements_of_Wor.html
26. Genesis 8:22

The trees and animals are thirsty for water. Veld fires are rife and the soil here in Africa is baking and water is scarce during this season as dry winds blow dust across the landscape. The close of summer is a time for the rains to cool the ground.

Spring: grass is shooting again as seeds. The birds are singing again as flowers flourish. There is a lot of food around.

Autumn or fall: temperatures drop and it cools again. Plants may begin to run short as animals and insects prepare to store some food.

Time for migration to other lands, with lots of celebrations for the harvest.

Winter: it is cold, dark often with frostbites and snow in other lands. Those that hide and hibernate move away from site into exclusive nests and caves as the cold winds freeze the ground.

The trees are stripped of their leaves and time to sink their roots.

The summer time of life, autumn, springtime and harvest, the Afrikan has worship throughout these seasons, as the seasons change the prayer changes and activities all respond to the time and season.

As long as there is day and night there will be seeding and harvest. Let my minister know that God stands on this word. The moments of worship change with the season in the spiritual atmosphere.

Your Pres-ence

Who has come to worship?

The scripture will work to show us to be very clear as a worshipper (the medium *itwasa, isaNgoma* connects people, *svikiro* (shona word for 'medium' spirit). Where spirits arrive, the vehicle through which the spirit can reach the people) that God is present with His angelic host, you are there with your heart ready to minster and the congregation also ready to receive.

It is your duty as a worship leader or worshipper to find that connection and grow to maturity that you can recreate this space for your worship experience.

People have just changed names but we are still the same. The problems in the scriptures will inform us all that the problems of human life are constant and so are the solutions, same God, same faith, same baptism and same Spirit.

Most of the members of today's churches are tired of formalities; they want an experience, they seek the real thing, they need connection and they long and desire for this old faith that worked and performed wonders.

A close look at the bible will inform you that they have come but the conditions of their hearts will vary and the Spirit must impress your heart to minister word to give you.

Nothing is new under the sun, as people were, they remain the same. So a quick look at these characters will open your eyes to your members.

YHWH: lets start by welcoming the owner of the service. Worship is not a means to an end but an end itself. When we worship we talk and adore the Present, welcome the Lord into the service, the Creator of the heavens and the earth, in Him all live and have their being

Eve: who has fallen into sin and left her husband, the woman who has been in a conversation with the devil and has done terrible things that will affect families and future generations. Eve has eaten the forbidden fruit and the sugar juices are still between her fingers. She has been cursed and received a punishment from God. Her home is in conflict.

How will she look at her husband again and every leaf that falls, every animal that dies, and every life that is lost to live and feel that she started it all, the sense of guilt is enormous? At the house of worship point her to the lamb that takes away the sins of the world

Adam: who does not want to take responsibility over his role and kingship and things keep on happening in his home because he is never there. The woman does as she pleases, the children are killing each other, and he is never there. He has lost his garden and he is facing a dark future with thorns and sweat. Assure him that there is a lamb; tell him about the seed of the woman that shall smash the head of the serpent.

Show that where he fell in the garden the Messiah will mourn and cry to claim his victory in the garden of Gethsemane. Connect his garden to the victorious garden in the kingdom made new. The leaves of the tree shall be for the healing of the nations. Tell him its not all lost, through Adam sin has come to all but through the second Adam YHWH will restore the lost garden to the Eden redeemed.

Cain: who has murdered his brother, full of envy and jealousy, he is angry with God and has sought to settle it with his brother. He sits there but he has the blood of his brother on his hands. To this day there are those who are filled with the spirit of Cain. Tell him sin is knocking at your door and you do what is right and the Lord will be pleased with you. The sin that is waiting for you must be conquered, yet after sin the Lord will show mercy and put a sign on you "anyone who will kill Cain I will kill him".

Divine protection is guaranteed even in the midst of sin there is grace that protects us. Lift up his spirit and encourage him to keep on walking.

Lamech: he is struggling with his two wives, a reputable farmer who has broken new grounds by taking two women to him. He too has come to hear a word from the Lord.

Seth: the child who worships in the shadow of his parents' mistake. Constantly seeing the garden at a distance and asks what happened. A severe sense of loss, born to parents who have children but none in the house.

With a brother like Cain who will not end up in church? Seth Worships under a cloud of death and feels his life is a replacement of parental lose. The worship service must minister and help them to find their purpose in life.

Nameless sons and daughters, Genesis 5:4-5: the Bible seems to ignore many other children born in the 930years of his life.

They too have a right to worship though they will appear on the roaster, or do a service, they may never be welcomed as visitors because no one seems to recognize them. They may never sit on the ribbon chairs or be served water by ushers but they too have come. Make them feel they are important in God's sight.

Enoch: Enoch walked with God for 365 years, and by faith he did not see death, for he was taken after it was said he pleased God, Genesis 5:23. Their appearing before the Throne of grace for a walk with God, they have a long experience with God, they are a good influence to the young and source of wisdom and power to the church.

Methuselah: the children of the upright, brought up in a family where the glory of their fathers seem to overshadow their own personalities.

They feel they don't need their surnames because they have their own lives to live. They are blessed with long lives and a good history to share. We all do not need to start in the world and end up in church to share a testimony.

Methuselah comes to church to confirm that you can be born and grow up in the church and still have a testimony of the goodness of God. At the moment of worship give Methuselah a chance to encourage the wayward and establish the youth that "I would rather be a doorkeeper in the house of the Lord"

Noah: mission driven, they have sat with God and they have their blue print of what they need to do with their lives. They have arks to build and things must be done before they die. They come here to gain strength for the task at hand.

They need support and help to accomplish their mission. God has touched their lives and they will live but to do the will of God.

At the place of worship life, Noah preaches and we will know the future and what waits for us in the shadows of the future. A word of prophecy, and word of rebuke and a warning of pending danger.

Cush: the conspicuous one and physically visible as different. Ever thought of how *Cush* felt to have come out of the entire generation of light skinned people and he popped up black? In every church you will find the disabled, the Albinos and other visibly challenged people let them feel welcome and part of the worship service. Because he was the black, modern theologians have taken the curse of Canaan and put it on Cush. Let the house of worship affirm Cush that God did not make a mistake when He created him. Cush is endowed with power and skill, look at the pyramids, look at Nimrod, look at wisdom, it is safely stored in his sockets on the brow of color.

If Cush sits at the front row of your worship service, what would you tell him? "I knew you from your mother's womb, I formed you", and you are creatively different because your father is creative. Nimrod the grand son of Ham the son of Cush, the great hunter is sitting in your audience he has just finished building the city of *Babel, Erech, Akkad, Nineveh, Resen, Rehoboth and Calah in the land of Shinar*. Known as the valley of rich kings. There are those who no longer pray for a house, they can build cities.

He is not mobilizing people to build the tower of Babel because he cannot trust God not to destroy the world with water again. Tell Him there is a rainbow in the sky, and the one who hangs it up there cannot lie.

Terah: Started the journey and when he got to Haran he stopped, camped there and died there before reaching Canaan. They are those who started the journey of faith and have since stopped moving.

They have made temporary structure along the way and have given up going to the Promised Land. They too have come into the house of Worship. The Worshipper must help them to break tents and move to the Promised Land.

Abraham: with all the responsibility of his father's house and cousin the man had a call. His personal needs seem not to be met as God blesses everybody else around him. Do not make a mistake there are those who have done everything right yet they have not yet received their blessing, like Abraham they might even be feeling like their lives are not worth living.

They hold the promises of God which do not feel like ashes in the finger tips, praise the Lord they have come into the house of Worship, point them to the sand of the sea and the stars of the sky. Make alive their hope and help them to hold on a little while longer He who is coming will come and not delay, let the just live by faith.

Sarah: all the servants around her house have children and her husband's house is empty. Sarah is barren she has issues that have kept her down this long and the womb knows sorrow that she can not share. Remember every obstacle in life is God's opportunity to perform a miracle. Sarah needs to be told that God himself is on His way to her house to deliver the parcel personally, in her kitchen.

She needs to live with her mistakes and ill advises but God has not forgotten her. At the moment of worship she must revise her menus and practice lullabies for when God reveals himself, all her sorrows will be swallowed in joy. Tell Sarah that God will eat from her hands and He will spend a night in her tent.

Hagar: she sits there as she has just been forced into Abraham's bed and feels violated. She will not be married or have her own husband but bound to this couple that claims to be driven by divine instruction. She sits here and wonders what this God thinks about her. She is expecting a child from Abraham, and she is confused whether to call Abraham Master or 'hubby', torn with emotions she sits in the pews and waits for a word from the Lord.

Tell her that in the greater events not all things make sense, yet all things come together, they work together for the love the Lord. Tell her that the Lord does not use, or abuse people, she will get her blessing in her tears and pain.

Tell her to be humble and not laugh at the barren mistresses, she must not think that she will substitute the first lady, but that she must be happy and do her duties without arrogance. Hagar; a blessed mistress given an opportunity to sleep with the master and bear him a son.

Those that have been lucky to make it in life, not that they qualified but just happened to be at the right place at the right time and mercy drops fell around them and their status changed. Hagar must be reminded at worship that pride goes before the fall. She stands in borrowed shoes.

Humility will sustain her but through her arrogance she will be banished to desolation.

Hagar will also need tips on how to live with the consequences of her decisions and arrogance, as she has now become a single parent, because of her insubordination. *Ketura* the mother of *Zimran, Jokshan, Medan, Midian, Sihbak* and *Shua*[1] married to the Patriarch Abraham and she hears the husband say, "these children will not eat the inheritance of my son Isaac".

She has witnessed the father pack small gifts and sending her children to the East. Tell *Ketura* that not all is lost, the 'Lord will honor his word the wise man will come from East with gold, myrrh, and frankincense.

Tell the sons not to weep they are the custodians of the Torah and the very Israelites will come back here with no history and their family seemly forgotten as the black race through Median will relate the creation story and set to teach the Israelites how to worship the true YHWH'

Lot: the cousin who felt entitled to Abraham's blessings and competed with his master for portions and grazing land. These spoiled members feel they have a right to pastoral privilege and will always choose the best seats for themselves and they cannot be found to do menial tasks around the house of the Lord.

At the hour of worship remind Lot that his blessings are bound in Abraham, Lot should know that without Abraham he is not. Learn to give honor and be humble to let the man of God eat first and graze his cattle first. Tell Lot that with that attitude he will lose everything that he has saved for his entire life, and will become a husband to his daughters and father his grandchildren of incest with his two daughters.

Mrs. Lot: that which she failed to do inside the city (be the salt of the earth) she became outside the city. Her soul is bound to the luxuries of Sodom and she takes pleasure in choosing sons-in-law for her children. She is the modern miss cosmopolitan. Cannot see her life out in the rural areas and planting vegetables and milking cows.

The farmyard is the grocery shop, far removed from life due to "civilization", Mrs. lot is pulled by grace out of filth but her heart is stuck in the pleasure of Sodom, and she becomes a monument for Gomorrah.

Tell Mrs. Lot that God will destroy everything to save her soul from destruction. "Food for the stomach and the stomach for the food and the Lord will destroy both."

---

1. 1 Chronicles 1:32 the concubine of Abra-Ham

The daughters of Lot: they have done bad things, but it does not make them evil. They slept with their father, they keep in their bosoms of family secrets that cannot be told. Some of these secrets have altered their future and world-view, they are sandwiched by evil and scarcity of resources and a future of incest. They have taken things into their own hands and they have decided to live with their problems, mother and their brothers and sister.

Give them room, for Moab is their tribe and God will empty them from vessel to vessel.

Isaac: Born out of old parents, with high expectations. The future of the tribe rested on his shoulders. He has to obey his old father to the alter of burnt sacrifice. "Isaac come to God to learn to love the Lord your God ." Keep your vow and covenant than the Lord will make you feast on His promises" Deut 12:7.

Ishmael: has come to church, yet he feels his mother was treated unfairly, and by birthright, he feels entitled to the inheritance of Abraham. He is the first-born and he grows up full of hatred over the young boy who is born later to replace and take his place. The disenfranchised worshipper.

Eliazer: the faithful servant, Abraham's faithful servant. He stood in line to inherit the wealth of Abraham but obeys his master to the latter. He is the first man recorded in the Bible who prayed, a trusted servant. Even goes on to find a wife for Isaac.

He demonstrates a deep relationship with God and all his requests God answered. Bless him and tell him that he is setting up a great genealogy of Jesus and the future of the plan of salvation is in his hands. He has come to worship and thank God for a faithful service.

Rebecca: made wrong choices and gave their children advice that will break their homes and chase their children from home. These parents have their favorite children and they breed jealousy amongst the children and drop their ears when man talk and find their own ways to drive their own agenda they started off in faith while watering for the camels and as they grew older they seem to have lost their track of what is right and die lonely lives to regret over the mistakes that have made in the kitchen.

Jacob: the thieves also come to worship, they have gained wealth from theft, swindling and supplanting other people's blessings. They live in constant running and fear of their lives for their problems are always chasing after them. They have cried when others do to them what they have done to others too, *Laban* changes salaries and his wealth if stolen, he get Leah instead of Rachel.

They feel like life has short changed them from the Rachel of their dreams to the Leah(s) of their realization. They are hard workers because of their true love, all the 14 years seemed like a short time for he loves her. Remind Jacob that the blessings were his from birth, he did not need to rob Esau but be still and know that God will bring it to pass.

When he struggles with the angel, then he says "I will not let you go until you bless me": we all thought you had received your blessings in goatskins. Now he knew that the blessings are from God not man. The best thing the Lord would do for you Jacob is to change your name from Jacob to Israel, for now you are more than a conqueror. "We all have the name and nature of Jacob. We all have the tendency to wrestle with life, to take things into our own hands, to set our own agenda, and work things out in our own strength". The result?

The result is much the same; we make a mess of things, which drives us to the river Gorge, the banks of our own Jabbok. Family problems, financial problems, relational problems, no purpose, no sense of destiny, fear of the future, all drive us to the end of ourselves and hopefully into the arms of a God who has revealed Himself in the person of a loving, caring Savior, Jesus Christ. But we must stop wrestling and start clinging! We must surrender our lives, our wills, our dreams and schemes, to the Lordship of Jesus Christ and let Him change us. In Jesus Christ, we can have a new name, in Jesus Christ we have a new nature, in Jesus Christ we have a new destiny, and in Jesus's Mighty name we have a secure future.

Prayer points:

○ *Praise God that He is calling you to trust Him and abide by Him.*

○ *Ask God to forgive you for times you tried to do things in your own strength.*

○ *Pray for spirit of persistent prayer."*[2]

Esau: your appetite of soup will cost you your birthright. Do not sacrifice long-term goals for short-term pleasure. He had his meal of soup when he came back from hunting. It was very sad that the meal he bought he had it for free at super. He was just impatient to wait a little while longer.

Like the sexually immoral youth who would steal from their emotional bag, only to say "I have no pleasure on the marriage bed." Like Esau many youth find themselves making choices that hinder their praise, they forfeit the blessing because they have appointments of corruption and sin after the service.

2. Zodwa Kunene: Women's Ministries Department, SAU, and Southern African Union of the Seventh-Days Adventist Bloemfontein South Africa.

It is sad even at times to discover that they have condoms while praising; the sin that corrupts the soul of the worshippers is adultery. They need to be reminded that the young man must carry the yoke while he is still young. The very things that we sell today as if they are worth nothing, we will cry for these resources and find that even with tears in our eyes they will not return to us.

Remind Esau that God does not rejoice in the worship of fools for whatsoever. A man plants that what he will reap, when you plant the wind you will harvest the whirlwind.

Adah the *Hitite, Oholibamah* the Hivite, *Basemath* the Ishmalite – the wives of Esau. How do you live with a man who is rich but not blessed? The first born who acts like a last-born. The man that has blown up his chances. How do you cook for man who is angry for the mistakes of his youth and carries with him bitterness and pain? How do you comfort a man who is waiting to kill someone and pay back for the loss? The man who loved soup more than his birthright. *Adah, Oholibamah* and *Basemath* had to share Esau and bring comfort to his heart over the pains of youthful impulsive choices.

These women share a man and the Lord build the nation of Edom through them Genesis 36 will show you a battalion of the Edomites, with chiefs, rulers, sons and daughters through it all the Lord still came through to build nations. If these three women would sit in your service what would you tell them? "Though your sins are as scarlet I will make them as white as snow; He who confesses his sins and forsakes them will prosper"

Laban: criminals to the core, schemers of corruption and other men's fall. Always a step ahead of the rest, things must be done their way. Makes his children hate each other forever as he dumps them in the bed of one man, causing jealousy and planting a bitter root between them. Laban never rejoiced in the success of others, but changed the goal post every time they stood to lose. They live for competition and their success must be achieved at all cost. Highly manipulative people who seem to get their way through life. If you take their idols they will bring an army to collect what belongs to them. They have no fear of God, for even when they notice that God is at work their sense of entitlement overshadows their common sense.

Laban has no respect of other people's privacy as he will search for his gods and will even stick his hands into the saddles of another man's wife who is on her periods. He will accuse and curse for those things that they deem important.

He woke up this morning and his gods are missing. Tell Laban not to set up his wealth on earth but in heaven where there are no thieves and moth that eat it. Tell him no to have any other gods except the One in heaven.

Rachel: the beauty of their faces, sexy in body form and stature but sad to note that their outward endowment is not equivalent to the productivity of their loins.

Beautiful thieves who stole the family gods. An Idolater to revenge over the pain caused by their father and positioned herself as a heir of the wealth of Laban: *the one who had these idols would be the rightful heir - she stole the future.*

She placed the whole family in danger at the sword of her father Laban. The lovely and cute but non-productive ladies. They too seek for the face of the Lord, they need to be reminded that life is not all about the mirror and looks. These are the external veneers, God seeks more than beauty of the heart and quite spirit and gentle disposition.

Leah: the ladies who feel unloved but they are blessed with seeds and multiplication through them the house of Jacob will be full of sons and daughters. God has planted in them the greater plans of grace far beyond the reach of the human eyes they have been created to populate the kingdom of heaven. They seem to live lives of the unloved and forgotten, and have fallen into the world of the tolerable other woman.

Too often they do not possess attractive and visible qualities of preferred woman, but a closer look at their future you will find Jesus in their loins. When Jesus calls for his grand mother it is the Leah of affliction not the Rachel of fantasies. Tell Leah that when Jacob dies he wants to be buried next to Leah and she should count her blessings and name them one by one and she will be surprised what God has done.

Zilpha: Asher/Gad servants who are caught up in their master's houses and end up as concubines in the houses of polygamy. She too ended up as the third wife of Jacob. They feel like life is dragging them where they don't want to be and they have no say or power over their destinies.

Dinah: is the innocent girl who like the lost sheep walks in to visit the women of the land. What are you doing in the land when you are a child of kings; the women of the land have men of the land. She too was raped and violated by Shechem Gen 34:1. These ladies sit in the benches of the church breaking apart yet trying to hold it together. At times it feels like their fathers are too busy in the fields while they carry their pain and sit on their grief.

Shechem the Hivite: carries the burden of his son's mistake and negotiates to marry Dinah for his son *Hamor*. It never feels good to discover that the worst of the criminals in the land have been born in your house and at times you sit to imagine how it went wrong for it looked like you had it all together and the day of trouble exposes you to ignorance and fate. Shechem died in the blood of his son's son. He was circumcised old for the evil of his son and died with his tribe at the hands of Jacob's sons.

Hamor: the rapist is in church too; he has done the sin and violated nephews, cousins, sisters and neighbors daughter. The fear of being discovered brings the pain of pending danger.

They are anxious of their future as their sins are chasing them. They will hide behind their powerful fathers to protect them, because they are the most honored of their father's household who end up doing the most dishonorable things that disgrace the dignity.

Tell *Hamor* that the Axe is on the root of the tree, he will not recover from the circumcision, and he has called death the entire tribe. The sin is his immorality get every male child killed, leaving the entire city full of orphans and widows, wealth and livestock will be plundered all because the man could not hold himself in the moment of sexual edge.

The worshipper needs to quicken the hearts of the saints to avoid acts if death and not glory in sin.

Deborah: Rebekah's nurse lived to look after other people. Their history might not be spoken, as their families are unknown. These are our house-maids who live to care for our children and us. They live of the crumbs that fall of from our tables.

Like dogs they live of hand out of unwanted clothes, and spoiled food, from our last week meals. They love the lord and they have come to worship, and seek for the Lord to soften their master's hearts so that they can look at them more tenderly.

Tell Deborah that she will be buried under the oak Genesis 35:4 & 8.

Ever noticed that the same Oak tree where she is buried is where all the gods, gold and silver plundered from *Haran* and *Laban*? Earrings, jewellery, rings and bracelets were buried under same Oak tree. She was rich at her death more than during her life. Even in death God can still reward you for the labor of your hands.

12 sons are here as they sit in your service:

Reuben: they come miserable with curses from their fathers that they will not excel I have seen: but behold the hour of worship the Lord has seen them, "behold a son has been born to me", there is hope for the next generation.

Simeon: unloved, with pain of not being cared for, an instrument of cruelty, cursed anger, violence and wrath scatted descendants. Yet the moment of worship reminds them of "The one who hears", whose ear is not heavy that He cannot hear.

They must be reminded that God has His ear next to the pain. Burdens must be lifted and they need to know that Jesus cares for the broken hearted.

Levi: being attached, they come to worship but fully attached to their things. You cannot separate them from the things that they own, they do not only own things, their things own them too.

They sit in the worship service totally consumed by their possessions like the rich young ruler, Matthew 19.

Tell them the greatest possession is YHWH and to seek first the kingdom of heaven and His righteousness and all these things will be added unto them. Show them the better attachment to the King of Kings and Lord of Lords: Tell them to have Jesus and they will have everything.

Judah: Gen 38- Married Hirah's daughter and the fathered three sons Er, Onam and Shelah. Er who was wicked before the Lord and the Lord killed him having married Tamar. Onam refused to make children for his brother and spilled the semen on the ground and God killed him.

Shelah: was too small to be given as a husband to Tamar. Judah's house is full of drama, extreme disasters and rife in demons of immorality had breakfast in Judah's house. But Judah like some of us has come for blessings, remind him that Jesus will be the lion of the tribe of Judah, for where sin abounds, grace even much more.

Judah: he has come to worship, he has lost his sons to this woman and he has made a promise to make another son for her daughter-in-law. He is confused about his decision and cultural expectation, and the Lord has blessed him with another son and he has not fulfilled his vows, now he has slept with a "prostitute" (daughter-in-law) and has discovered that his stuff and family inheritance is in the hands of the daughter-in-law, he has made his own daughter-in-law pregnant.

Those with complex family issues are here to find a word from the Lord, as Judah sits in your audience tell him that he must fulfill his vows and fulfill his promises even if it is painful. Tell him that the Messiah will be born through his errors and nothing is beyond the reach of grace. The weakest gene in Jacobs line was Judah, yet God associates himself with such abject sinfulness.

Tamar: the widow who has buried two husbands and is in waiting for her young man Shelah to come into her and make a tribe of her. This is glory at its best, God killed two men prior to this and when God has a plan to achieve He will get it done.

The methods of how it is done might seem like a tide of confusion but His ways are too high. Judah through Tamar his daughter-in-law became the father of Perez father of Hezron, and Hezron the father of Ram, and Ram the father of Amminadab, and Amminadab the father of Nahshon, and Nahshon the father of Salmon, and Salmon the father of Boaz by Rahab, and Boaz the father of Obed by Ruth, and Obed the father of Jesse, and Jesse the father of David the king....Luke 3:31-33.

Tamar: do not worry, you may have to dress up like a prostitute, and you may be paid in goats but hold on to your walking sticks. The glory of the Lord will shine upon you as the Lord returns you joy to your tent.

You may have to bring up your children like a single parent and your father-in-law might not like you, he may even despise you, but the Lord is not a man that would forget your tears. He will pay you.

Remind him of his name, and future than the Scepter will not leave his house. His name means "Praise the Lord, praise God". He must praise the Lord in all situations, for when he is weak, that is when God is strong, for the strength of God is demonstrated in his weaknesses. Tell him all things work together for good for those that love the Lord.

Dan: God has judged those that feel that God had dealt with them harshly, remind them that His judgment is His vindication. They do not need to be bitter and carry the poison of vipers in their decision in dealing and judging others.

Naphtali: they sit there and are wrestling with issues, in their silence, they struggle in their lives. Tell them they shall be like a deer and beautiful words and testimonies will come out of their struggles. The Lord has wrestled with them and it will come back to them as a great fortune.

God, the fierce war and military men also come to the service to worship.

These are mighty and strong man of battle, who can handle a gun shield and buckler. With faces that can stare a lion in the face and battle.[3]

---

3. 1Chronicles 12:28, 5:19-22, 2Samule 17:27, 1 Kings 17:1.

Now that they are also in the worship service tell them with precision the treasures will be laid bare and the precious gems will be exposed. Out of their battles the Lord will expose His inheritance.

Asher: he makes me happy, his food shall be rich, they can sing in rejoice in the Lord always and again I say rejoice Philipian 4:4. Happiness brings joy to the hearts of many within the worship service. Their celebration is to the Lord who has made them happy.

It's not always about troubles and sorrows, surely there is a time to be happy in the presence of the Lord.

Issachar: those who know what Israel ought to do, the timekeepers, they have also come for worship. They seek reward, wages that are deserving, a slave of labor. A man burdened with the welfare of others remind them that their portion is with the Lord.

Zebulum: he is my honor, dwelling and living by boats and seeing the fishermen and the sailors are also here, those who are running the fish gate and the economic hub of the cities. The Fish that they control are of the Lord and it is a harvest of creation that they should not forget the Creator in the harvest of creations.

Joseph: may he increase, may he add to my family, he shall be fruitful ,these people when they stand in the worship service and they open their mouths to what God is doing in their lives their dreams make us small and angry.

They could be young and ambitious and the whole world is standing in front of them with endless possibilities of success. Tell Joseph not to share his dreams too often as it breeds jealousy and discomfort with his brothers. There is nowhere in the scriptures where the Lord gave him the dream and asked him to tell people about it.

When you are immature about your dreams you will end up in Pharaoh's house as a slave boy. You will end up running away from your master's wife. The dreams shaped his future. Tell Joseph that his jacket is power and distinction he must wear it with pride. Tell him that the brothers are not scared of him but his dreams. Tell him that the Lord has a better plan in the 30 pieces of silver that he is sold for. Tell Joseph not to sleep with Pharaoh. The Lord would give him his virgin daughter. Tell him not to settle for shrinking flesh the Lord has fresh skin for him.

There are young people who are caught up in relationships with older women who buy them things and make them do things, "sugar mama" as they are known-remind the young people that the Lord will bless the disciplined like Joseph run from evil. You could suffer for the right choices but God will reward you with a palace, a virgin, a crown, power, wisdom and influence.

Benjamin: son of my right hand: Ben-Oni son of my sorrow: a wolf who devours his prey and divides the spoils, son of my right hand: Benjamin-Ben-oni: children born and their mothers died on the delivery beds. These may seem to be the most unfortunate but the grace of God is even more powerful that we can even imagine. Even notice that most of the kings of Israel are from the family of Benjamin. The Lord did not allow Rachel to bring up the boys; maybe for her tendencies of idolatry God opted for an orphan child to breed a tribe of kings. The funeral of Rachel is the birth of a royal seed.

Dinah: Vindicated the only daughter of Jacob, surrounded by 12 brothers: the only flower amongst the thorns

Mrs. Potiphar: she sits here boiling with feelings of the young hunk she is looking at and is busy devising plans to take him to bed. So confused, she is emotionally convinced that the devil has taken hold of her emotions and she cannot control herself, she has made a few attempts and gestures already but seems not to win.

She comes to church today with her mind made up to make her final push and just rape the boy. As she sits at the hour of worship she needs to find a solution and needs a change of heart and mind.

Mrs. Potiphar: married women who are not happy in their homes and are on a spree to capture the market and seize the young boys who work in their houses. They do not have self-control and live to fulfill every earthly passion. There is a fine line between their passion and anger; they will destroy you when they discover they cannot get what they want.

They will rip your jackets apart, female rapists. They also are sitting in the house of worship seeking for the face of God; they still have other boys' jackets in their hands, and have wrongly accused others of acts that are not true. Could it have been in the work place they would file for abuse and harassment when they are the one on the wrong side. Tell *Mrs. Potiphar* that God rewards those that seek for Him with a clean heart.

During that time whisper to her that it could be your son also being abused by another old woman. "Do unto others, as you want others to do unto you." Remind her also to take the jacket back to Joseph and not bear false witness.

Perez: born in a struggle Genesis 38:27-30. There are people who are pushed out of their destiny by events that are beyond their control and blessings seem to miss them. Their strong brothers block their success with their hands. Perez must know that God has a plan of redemption in his loins. Let the heart of anxiety be put at ease, you might seem like you are not making it, but God is merciful and just to push back hands of time and people and give you a descent arrival with an allotted inheritance. Perez you are blessed.

Zerah: those who come to church with their hands. In life they always have a hand out mentality, a collection and give me attitude. They do little investment, but seek more to enrich their hands. Even at birth they stick out their hands before their heads. It takes skilled midwives to slow down the hands and get the heads out. Tell *Zerah* that life is not what is in your hands, but what is in your head.

At the hour of worship *Zerah* must put his hands on his head and ask for the blessings of the Lord to be anointed into his mind. David must sing for him, "thou has anointed my head with oil, the cup in my hand runneth over". Until the Lord blesses and anoints the mind of Zerah the hands will not hold blessings.

The grapes cup bearer, he has forgotten that Joseph is still in prison and he has had his Job restored. Remind him to consider where he is coming from. The Lord will not listen to a man who can not keep his promises. The trust-guard troubled by his dreams from last night that the lord will restore the cup in his hand to minister in the royal chambers. The bread-baker, the Lord visited him with a death revelation of his future, the vultures will eat from his basket, death looms in the air for him. Tell him to put his house in order and prepare to die. The worshipper stands between the living and the dead.

Manoah: she has to worry about her son who is in the reeds and the death that looms in the air should he be found. She has two children missing; the daughter and the son are all at the Nile. She has her mind in the reeds and as she sits here at your service worried about the endangered lives of her children, you need to tell her that the Lord is in the reeds and the crocodiles of the Nile are a creation of God too.

She needs assurance that the Lord will make a way and even if the politics and the times are hard they are not forgotten. Tell her the Lord has a project in her house and is performing a miracle through her to save them all. All situations are divine set ups for bigger and glorious endings.

Moses: the leader, the criminal, the fugitive. He also has come for service, with all his fears and the sins that he has committed. Moses is very educated and well trained, but life has not been "fair" to him, he sits in your service totally confused of what and who he is to himself, to the Israelite family and the Egyptian step parents.

His identity and experience has created trouble in his soul, he is so confused and conflicted to watch his natives tortured and abused by the system/parents that had shown him love and groomed him.

While He sits at your service the Lord calls him to do work but his past and closet is full bones and he has many excuses why he cannot do the work of the Lord.

The worship service must convince him to confront his demons and be a man of war, not fighting external enemies but the internal powers that limit his purpose and render him ordinary when he should be an extra ordinary person.

Aaron: The weak pastor, the pleaser of people, he too has come to church. He must be an example to the rest, and he finds it difficult to stand on his decisions and be counted.

An easy push over who is also trying to make sense of this new faith and its demands. He sits in the service wondering where this God is taking His people. He had accumulated experience in the worship of the wrong God now he must lead the right worship but like his brother Moses, his past seems to overpower his calling.

Let the service establish the covenant that God has set with him that through his loins the lord will minister to the nation forever. The calling of the Lord is upon his life and that his weaknesses are not what God accounts but His calling upon his life. Tell him to stand for the right and be decisive in decisions for these are not his people but Gods people.

Miriam: intolerant sister in- law, who watched the young infant in the reeds and lost time to play with her friends while keeping watch. Now the same boy he changed diapers for has just brought to them a black woman and did not even bother to consult and seek for their advice. He seems to push his decisions on them and force them to accept his choice. The sister in- law who "knows what's best" feels seriously compromised and she detests Mose's choice and openly opposes him.

Miriam is in church today and she is struggling with being taken for granted, the Lord punished her with leprosy and her skin is now wasting away, she too needs a word from the Lord. Give her hope that the Lord will restore her, yet not condone her behavior and condemnation of his anointed.

Bazaliel: the architect, the genius designer and draftsman are at church. The talents God has planted in him are about to be realized as he works on the ark of the master designer and mason. He sits at church today waiting for the Lord to assign him his task and whispers a prayer of power and a keen mind. Tell him that what God has purposed and will He will empower and cause it to happen. His "biddings are His enablings"

Joshua: fear not, the shoes are too big; my servant Moses is dead now I want you to take over. His own mentor had died and the Lord calls him to step in to the role. Joshua is in fear and seeks to pray and while in prayer the Lord appears, let the Lord appear also during the worship service.

He is given comfort by the Kings of Hosts. Fear not I am with thee. Let your worship service assure people that the Lord is with them and they should fear not. Worship must address itself to fear and what is the ability of our God. True love chases away fear.

Caleb: give me the mountain, he has waxed in years and has fought many battles and today he is making requests; give me this mountain. He comes to church with a challenge of working at a huge project at the sunset of his days. He needs support that and encouragement that the Lord will be his strength.

Achan: stolen goods under his bed and has disobeyed the Lord in the course of the week. His mind is in his house where he hid some treasures. He hears of the wars that are being fought and the loss of lives that is taking place.

He knows he disobeyed God and its possible the curse is from his house. But he will not divulge the detail of the goods he had plundered. Achan is busy trying to find other reasons why these disasters happen. He is in church today; tell him that he needs to be committed to the consequences of his choice.

Gideon: man of valor: preparing for war next week and the Lord has given a word to start recruiting and as he looks at his military skills there is nothing to in his name, yet the Lord has chosen him to drive the *Mediates* away. He sits in pews full of anxiety and concerns needing a word from the Lord. Tell him that to work with the lord the biggest tool is willingness to obey. He has the host of the army.

The sophistication of the military strategist in the opposite camp, should not threaten them as the Lord will battle Himself. Calabashes and a few shouts will win the battle.

Tell Gideon and work with the little that can hear the voice of God. Tell him to break his calabash, blow the trumpet and shout; the Lord will deliver victory into his hands.

The Widow of Zerephath: tell her the jars will not run dry: Providence that true Worship offers: THE JAR OF FLOUR AND OIL WILL NOT RUN OUT. I Kings 17:7-16

If we are faithful to the word of God, He will provide for us in moments of need. If we put God first, He will also make us a priority in His schedule of blessings. A time of hunger can be a time of plenty: where God is that is where provisions are.

A. **Brooks dry up at times like these:** what was there is no longer there: the flowing rivers stop and we remain sitting of dry sand: with memories of what used to be a stream

B. **The Word of the Lord is always a source of comfort** when things have gone bad. Stop at every event and listen to what God has to say

C. **The Word sends him to a distant land:** anywhere with Jesus I can safely go.

D. **God prepares things ahead of time.** He had made a plan for the Prophet and prepared a home for him while he sat at the brook. Even at this time God had a plan for the children of brother *Vuyo*, the wife, the band members, friends: fear not God just move in the direction that God is leading and you will meet with your blessings.

E. **A widow was gathering stick:** to make a last meal and die. Gather stick in your life that prepare you for you funeral. Do things with the impact that they could the last things that you do. Have a sense of life: but let the living remember that they shall die. With this in mind whatever your hands find to do: do it with all your might

F. **Bring me water and a piece of bread:** Save God first with all that you have. Be available for service when God is in need of your talent. Don't become too busy and occupied with your own death. Take the service of the Lord as a priority

326 | Decolonizing Christianity

G. **All I have is some dust of flour and drops of oil:** Be truthful in your business. Share your troubles and joys with the Savior. Now let us have a little talk with Jesus and tell Him all about our troubles. He will hear the faintest cry and answer by and by. Just a little prayer will tell that the little fire is burning. A little talk with Jesus makes it all right

H. **After she made for the prophet:** there was enough in the jar for the next 3 years. God will never use you and not fill you up again. There is no one who has obeyed and has been disappointed. There was there will be enough in your hands at the close of your life.

The love of money has made the gospel music a recruiting ground of demons: those who can no longer have a heart to praise the Lord freely first without pay. Save the Lord first and your talent will not run dry. Remember it a gift from the hand of God. Go back to your churches and be useful

If you do not have a church please find a community of faith that will nurture you. In the years of famine and dried brooks the Lord will place you with widows who will keep you.

I was young and now I am old I have never seen the righteous forsaken or their children begging for bread.

THE JAR OF FLOUR AND OIL WILL NOT RUN OUT. Let it be so in your lives.

The Levite and his concubine: judges 19 the Levites who are not living right and have their teeth stuck in food and drink. Tell him not to ignore the statutes of the lord. Remind him that his calling does not protect him from the anger of the Lord. He must get up at once and fulfill his vow as a *Levite* instead of sitting around being bribed by food.

Samson: powerful and mighty: take time of this man for he has many faces. The glory of God has given him and his body and mobile killing machine. One army in one man.

The Worshipper like Samson comes to worship to make battle. But his weakness is that of women and as a result He finds himself in expensive relationships that cost his dignity. Samson comes to church later looking for his eyes and hair that has been shaved off by Delilah. At he conclusion of his life, all he wants is pillars to lean on. Tell Samson to remember his creator in the days. Warn Samson of the dangers of foreign women.

Delilah: they sit in churches looking at every male figure and through body language and suggestions trying to make trophies out of relation-ships. At times they do not even care to a relationship "just if I can sleep with him". They want to find out what makes this man tick and what is he made out of. Without knowing they have become agents of devils in the midst of the saints, through perfumes, dressing in a indecent demeanor they parade availability to the destruction of many.

Deborah: militant ladies who are ready to battle, when men are in hiding they assume the roles of men and take the work forward at the battle front. They mount up horses and roll up their sleeves and skirts at the battle front.

The moment of worship must affirm women that God uses them to do His work and they must place themselves wholly into the hands that will give them strength were they have weakness.

Ruth: those that have lost their husbands and this is all they have, thier future is destroyed and yet they have good hearts and devotion to their commitments and will never break their covenants. All hope is gone of getting this old woman to bear children again yet Ruth hangs on the shoulders.

Tell Ruth that the Lord will not ignore her commitment and troubles and sorrow may linger for a while but joy comes in the morning. The Lord will find for her a redeemer and she will be a grandmother of Jesus.

Naomi: She buried her husband and now she has a new name "widow" ,the widow who was pushed out of her heritage and buried two sons. The pain of loss was great that she looked on the three graves at her homestead with two young daughters in-law looking into her eyes for answers. When calamity strikes the pain is deep but greater still is the blessed assurance that through it all Naomi can learn to trust in Jesus, and be still and know that He is God.

Boaz: he woke up and found a woman at his feet and he is the kinsman. He sits here with a problem and he must be the solution to the nakedness of the woman who deserves justice. Tell Boaz that he is the official grand parent of Jesus. The situation is under control as the Lord is building a new generation through his loins. He must be patient with the prophetic mystery. Tell him that he should marry and not hesitate.

Jesse: all his children are out there at war, he sits here worried about what will become of his generation as all his strength is placed at the edge of the sword. He needs comfort that solutions and salvation will come out of the house of Jesse.

Tell Jesse to trust the Lord and not underestimate his children for the Lord is at work preparing a king from his loins.

David's brothers: those that are defeated at battle and are hearing insults from Goliath, those who have failed to stand up and be counted, daily they take insults from bosses and the strong and feel powerless to do anything as Goliath just seems unconquerable.

Tell the brothers that Goliath is too big to miss; the weakest with faith can conquer the strongest in amour. Tell them that one of them; the anointed and small can achieve what the big, trained and empty cannot achieve. Tell them the "battle is not for the strong, neither is the race for the swift". Tell them "its not by might not by power but by the spirit of the Lord".

David: those that are coming from hot beds of sin still smelling of perfume of Uriah's wife and their hands are still dripping with blood of the husband (Uriah). They too have come with great talent and skills, God has blessed them yet they have soiled their robes. Moments of worship are times for reconnection.

They are open to rebuke and they repent quickly with tears and they still remain people after God's own heart. Tell David to confess his sins and play the harp and offer a clean sacrifice. Tell David to seek for a cleansing with hyssop and the Lord will make him clean.

Tell him "troubles and sorrow will linger for a while but joys comes in the morning"

Jonathan: born of evil fathers and dragged into covenants of death through the foolishness of his father. They are those who are trying all they can to move away from the pain and mistakes of their fathers and they find themselves entangled between loyalty and royalty. Their choice is difficult as it means betraying your father to protect your friend.

Jonathan comes to church with a battle in his heart and a possible loss of his heir ship. Remind Jonathan that earthly treasures are of no value but decisions made in tune with God will last for eternity.

Saul: once a worshipper too, once a king, once ruled in splendor, a head taller than the tallest, when leadership lacks God's lordship it results in a king demon possessed and losing his mind in royal sheet.

How low can you go or king with all facilities from the temple at your disposal or you opt for a witch doctor? Saul feels that God has abandoned him and left him. Remind Saul that God never left Soul; it is Saul who left Him.

He should seek for the Lord with all his heart, and learn to apologize after tearing the prophets' clothes. Worship must minster to Saul to show him that he needs to deal with anger towards others and God, and learn to take his place and not assume responsibilities left for prophets, such activities harden the heart.

Samuel: as he sleeps next to the alter and he is hearing voices as God desires to speak with him. The running up and down and the witness of the all the corruption happening at the temple is preparation for his ministry.

Tell Samuel that it was from this temple that the mother asked for him and it is in this temple that he will minister and be prophet and priest unto the Lord. Tell him the voice he is hearing is the voice of God, he must answer the call and as a servant he must listen.

Abigail: married to a vile tempered and foolish husband, she has to live in constant humiliation and has to follow behind the husband with a mop to clean up all his mess.

A number of times he almost cost them their lives because of his sharp tongue but it is in this service that she will earn her reward as a queen in the palace of David. Those women who feel the same must be encouraged that all is not lost. God will reward every effort and bless every act done in honor of His name.

Hannah: stays around the venue of prayer, it is the message for Hannah. When you feel like you are not fairly treated, arise and find your place at the feet of Jesus and the Lord will visit your problem and bless you with a child. When there are challenges, it is good to remember that you do not seek from men what God can give.

Children are a gift from God not from man, and Hannah knew where to access those blessings and she goes to the source to seek for them. Leave Hannah alone she knows what she wants and the Lord will wipe away all her tears.

Eli: busy with the Lord's work and forgot to bring up his children in the fear of the Lord. The children have become a menace in the sight of God and a reign of terror in the temple courts, even converted the house of worship into a make shift brothel. The father knows better but is strangely silent and paralyzed to inaction.

He sits in the church benches when he knows that his children are the reason for many disasters, pregnancies and ignores it like it's none of his business.

Eli needs to be told that the Lord will break his neck if he keeps silent.

Phenehas and Hophni: when holiness is misused it becomes a funeral policy. The two boys must be reminded that God desires clean hands at His alter, it's a joy to work so close to glory and God demands a better sacrifice.

This is the team that stands and worships with you, standing next to you in your praise and worship. Some of them have forgotten the reason they are here, they now take this as a show and use such platforms to get new girlfriends and men.

Their service has become a catchment arena for their next conquest. Remind Phenehas and Hophni that Ichabod, the glory will depart.

Military generals, Abner, Abshai, Joab: these men have done battle and have killed, can kill and will kill, they are trained killing machines. To them church is about loyalty and the preservation of the throne of David.

These are militant loyalists whose souls have been robed by the system and need a cleansing from the bloodstains on their hands. Tell them to wash their hands and find forgiveness from the Lord.

Michal: Saul's daughter, those that don't believe that people must get carried away in worship and do not allow a full expression of their affection and love for the Lord.

Very educated and taught in the ways of royalty. Always carry themselves with dignity and will never want to be found with their guards down. Often they criticize and condemn those who are "too much". They have cursed themselves with barrenness

Mephibosheth: crippled and forgotten in Lodibar, now at the table of grace he too has a thankful song to sing as he dwells in the house of the Lord.

Bathsheba: she has just lost her son that she had with David, she has lost a husband, all other women in the palace are looking at her and the community knows what she has done. She is broken and in tears as the Lord has dealt harshly with her.

Tell her that Solomon will be born and through her blunders and errors that Lord has identified her as a grandmother of *Yashua Harmashiack*, the Messiah, Jesus of the Greeks will be born from her tears.

Be of good cheer Bathsheba as you left the door open, the church at communion leaves the door open to allow the unseen Messiah to walk in. There are acts of grace in mistakes of man, and prophetic utterances from the foolishness of our choices.

Ammon: those that are obsessed and occupied by demons of fantasy and obsession, they look and talk with their eyes. Their minds are determined to do evil, they come through here on their way to commit sin and nothing will stop them from accomplishing what their hearts have planned.

At the moment of worship such spells must be broken and the worshipper needs to make a call and sound the voice of rebuke that wakes up the sleeping conscience to the voice of God.

Tamar: those that have been abused and suffered rejection at the hands of their loved one. They come to the alter with tears of fresh scars and pain; they cannot explain why the Lord has allowed disaster to fall upon their life. For them even a song of praise says the Lord knows the way through the wilderness and that the later glory will supersede the earlier. He the Lord your God will turn your mourning into dancing and wipe away your tears with laughter and bring joy to you in later years.

Absalom: conspiracy,beauty, hair, anger and murders his brother Amnon.

THEY ARE THREE PEOPLE WHO ARE IN YOUR SERVICE?

The worshipper must recognize that his service is reaching three critical groups of people namely, Prophets, Priests and Kings: Revelation 1: 5 -7 'for every vision there is provision'.

Priests and kings:

- o Priests with vision- stay in the temple
- o Kings with provision- go and do battle
- o Prophets with a message- tell the direction and enhance vision

The anointing to speak into people's lives and the anointing to make wealth. God puts vision into the priest. Communicates the vision to the kings. Not his vision. It's not your provision.

Who are you in the plan of salvation? Kings must be rich in land wealth and power. Financial empowerment.

The unbeatable team. The calling are integrated. Don't try to do the other, stay with your call. Stay in your lane.

Rise up in your anointing 1Chro 22. David prophet, priest and king. David prepared all: 100 billion dollars worth of gold to build the temple, silver brass iron timber debut 20.

Win opportunities and business deals. Priest must approach and say "Confidence". Priests must strengthen your spirit. Make people strong in faith and power. Use 8. 18. Signs and wonders a new day. V2V members are for signs and wonders.

See yourself differently as you approach life you have enough opportunities and no place to hold the blessing (Malachi 3). Test me and see I will open up windows, not doors rather desire to have God open the gates for you.

From your fellow servant, yoke fellow in the work of the Gospel. The sacrifice of blood binds our wills with His divine will and we are all called into this new covenant of blood and ministry of power. To manifest the kingdom of heaven on earth the citizens of the kingdom need to partner with God to achieve greatness.

People need to faint when they see your house car and planes. We have better things in heaven, let's work to share glory on earth. We need all to be in line with the word of God and let the blessings start flowing through us.

Kings and priests, we are as we work for the Lord and Kings went to war to get spoils. Priests minister in the house of the Lord. I am the Priest you, are the Kings and we need a partnership into this kingdom

Matt 6. 21-33 where treasure is there will be your heart also. Before we are saved we are in the kingdom of darkness and we bow to alien spirits. Adam sold us a fruit and thus the devil invaded to have control over and deceive many. Through Birth we are born in darkness through the second birth Col 1. We are moved into the kingdom of light. In darkness you can be in bondage and not know it and my plight is our plight and I have lived below my privileges.

Matt 6. 24 you can work for two masters. Two systems. Mat 4 the temptations of Jesus. Jesus could be tempted, view all the kingdoms and glory if you worship. People are tempted to worship and get that. Jesus was going to be given things. We don't have to serve things. Things should serve US.

Mark 10. What should we do to enter heaven? Gen 14 Abraham got it all back. He meets the priest and the king of Sodom. The King said give me my people and keep the goods. No credit from anybody to make us rich. He gave his tithe to the one he desired. Gen 1 26. Man made in the likeness of God. With dominion own, possess and govern. It's in our hands. God will talk to us to do something on earth

28. Provision. Replenish stock with abundance duplicate Eden replenish, recover former fullness, finish and complete.

Restock the earth with abundance. Get seed from Eden and replant it on the earth. Make ghettos into gardens, blessings that over come the cursed. Joseph was a mobile blessings unit.

YOU are BLESSED

Vision needs provision. For every vision there is provision... PRO-VISION. Provision is for vision. If you want something you never had before give what you never gave before... Abraham gave his son. God is challenged and moved to give more.

To move to another level change your giving. We need to stop surviving and start thriving. Stop hogging resources and manifest abundance.

When we lack provision we lose vision. Eco 16. 16 gather Prov10. 22. The blessings make us rich, he adds no sorrow to it. When you do not know it you will die without it.[4]

You have been paid for.[5] Deceived to buy and look for what is rightfully yours. You don't get an inheritance from labor. As long as a child thinks like a slave he can't have his inheritance. Don't go for things. Things will come after you. Manifest abundance.

When you have enough take care of other people.

Mark 6: Sowing and reaping is a law! Not a church thing. It's a law of harvest and wealth creation. Speaking is a law: The law of confession.

1. **Kingdom benefits:** Being looked after... protection and hedge around you. Open an account with God - to access this you return your tithe.10percent of your profits.

2. **Kingdom blessings:** Offerings - five loaves. God blessed the bread and fish and it multiplied. Invest with God's stock. Only what you bring is multiplied. Blessings are equated to your offering - God gives you ideas that will pay you back a 100 fold. God is waiting for your gifts to feed others.

3. **Kingdom wealth - power and prosperity.** To get it by sacrifice... Psalm 20-1-6. God knows about tithes, offerings and sacrifices... But sacrifices move God to perform. God multiplied your wealth sacrificial giving.

---

4. Gal 4. 1. Gal 3. 29. Rom 4
5. Gen 3 the seed of the woman

Psalm 148. Heavens praise the Lord!

The Space and scope of worship-the Heavens

Praise the Lord from the heavens; (worship in the spiritual space)
Praise him in the heights! (worship in high places)
2 Praise him, all his angels; (worship with angels)
Praise him, all his hosts! (with heavenly bodies)
3 Praise him, sun and moon, (worship in the seasons and nature)
Praise him, all you shining stars! (worship in constellations)
4 Praise him, in your highest heavens, (moving to higher heights)
And your waters above the heavens! (Connecting waters of heaven, earth and body

The content of worship

5 let them praise the name of the Lord! (Do you know the Name?)
For he commanded and they were created. (His power at work in the universe)
6 And he established them forever and ever; (sustainability)
He gave a decree, and it shall not bpass away.1 (divine reliability)
7 Praise the Lord from the earth, (the direction worship)
You great sea creatures and all deeps, (there is life below the sea)
8 fire and hail, snow and mist, (catastrophes and disasters worship)
[g]stormy winds fulfilling his word! (while we cry for disaster nature worships)

Nature in worship

9 [i]Mountains and all hills,
[j]fruit trees and all [k]cedars!
10 [l]Beasts and all livestock,
creeping things and flying birds!
11 Kings of the earth and all people,

People at Worship

Princes and all rulers of the earth!
12 Young men and maidens together,
old men and children!
13 [o]Let them praise the name of the Lord,

Reason for worship

for his name alone is exalted;
[q]his majesty is above earth and heaven.
14 He has raised up a horn for his people,
[s]praise for all his saints,
For the people of Israel who are near to him.
[u]Praise the Lord!

Psalm 82 God in our nature stood,have faith in the Lord, John 10. 31 Jesus to be stoned - I told you that you are gods.

The reality that man is in the image and likeness of His maker, unless we embrace this principle we will die like ordinary man, common man. The worst form of colonization is the colonization of the image of God in us.

God's grace (blessings and favors) is more than enough:

Step: 1 Genuinely accept that Adonai, Jiya Tuscany detest sin, it is very abominable in His sight

Step 2: Openly confess to our High Priest for mercy

Step 3: Put on a new purified self (Christ) without condemnation from your own conscience and thoughts. For God made Him who had to be sin for us so that 'those who have sinned' might become the righteousness of God in 'The Victorious Christ Jesus!' What The Lord begun He has also finished in your life...your birth on its own is evidence of its completion. You were missed in worship by one sacrifice (Christ) has made perfect forever those who are being made Holy. Have a prosperous day

The wilderness was not a home, it was a transit camp, this world is a transit camp, lets look and live to an image. Look at the cross. Have a focused week.

In Jesus name I break every power of darkness that had entangled you. I destroy all the web of satin against you. I loose you from all the powers of darkness against you.

I stand on the word written in Matthew 18:18 and loose you from the powers of darkness in Jesus name, Amen. Please cover yourself with Ps 91. Remember, GOD loves you. God's will is supreme over all rollers, all historical events, and all hostile forces.

He can deliver you in ways you cannot imagine.

Trust his power and love, NO OPPOSITION CAN STOP YOU.

How are you a child of God? Be of good cheer, be confident and have assurance, in Christ you have overcome 'all' your enemies, the authorities, principality, powers and their servants the demons who are using physical bodies against you! In the authority we share in the new covenant in Christ I bind and cast down all the despotism of wickedness and declare peace in your life and descendants, for the Lord has revealed your enemy to me!

I know it's not flesh and blood and believe me we have arrested it and trampled over it in Jesus' name not by the blood of animals but by The Blood of Heaven's Lamb!!!

When your head stops spinning I hope it will be facing the right direction!

God Facing

Is it what we worship or who we worship?

Who we worship is more important than what He has done. The river comes from the sea, and the fruit is not better than the tree.

We don't believe in doctrines but in YHWH, In *Yashua*, Immanuel, "Jesus" the Messiah. Doctrines are a means to an end, not an end in themselves. It is sacrilege to force people to raise hands to a set of man made creeds, the only creed is " do you believe in YHWH?" There is a clear distinction between what the Lord can do and what He is. We can't use pagan ways to worship our Maker.

They worship what he has done, we worship who He is. We believe in Him, not His acts, creation is not for worship, but the Creator.

- The relationship with the created things: how do we relate to the works of his hands?
- How do we respond to the blessings?

AREAS

Suggestions of model worship programs

- ○ This is quality building of the saints: the church will be build by this program as a hybrid that will change the world.
- ○ This program will not only sink their roots into the word but the modern Christian, a venue through which YHWH can tabernacle.
- ○ This brings in understanding and opens the windows of heaven to pouring of the Holy Spirit.
- ○ This creates a venue that YHWH can work with.
- ○ This program offers a better way to teach doctrines and continuity
- ○ This makes the church an extension of the heavenly sanctuary and positions the saints in the direct light with what heaven is doing.
- ○ This builds confidence in the living of a life of faith and power.
- ○ This reduces the work of a pastor as the fathers take up their roles in their families as priests.
- ○ This is a witnessing tool and is very effective to bring and introduce new members to something exciting and meaningful.
- ○ This program can be duplicated to establish a new congregation.

Any elder who will spent three years at your feet with you on this program is qualified to lead a congregation

Psalm 23

Though has laid a table before ME
What is the table?
How do we prepare to partake at the table?
What are the emblems on the table?
Why the table?

The program is to marry the four temples the table on earth must be joined to the table of grace.

Worship must transport people the higher table where the chef Himself is the Ancient of days.

Phase 1: Introduce the emblems of grace

Introduce the people to the emblems on the table of grace so that they can appreciate the works of grace that God has done for us. To help the saints to measure the distance between their emblems.

To correct the thinking that says the table is for food only. The table is not all about bread and wine but full experience.

The saints need to know their seasons on this table and through which they can sit on the table and enjoy the service of the lord in their lives

- The candles - the light in the place of worship
- The dish of water – the utensils for worship
- The Water -the cleansing from without and within
- The Towel – materials that are used for worship
- The horn the chauffer the dead bones make music to the lord, even in death of the body do we still have the breath of life flow through the horn for music – the use of the horns and bones from the previous life.
- The oil of anointing – the use of fat in the worship service
- The bread – food and bread
- The salt – the use of salt in the worship service, covenant of influence and cleansing, a preservative too
- The Lamb with a bone unbroken- the sacrifice and use of lambs blood for transfer the innocence replaced by guilt
- The bitter herbs-the use of herbs, roots, leaves and nature alters the human body to spiritual frequency. This medicine to the physical body
- The belt of the waist- discipline during the moment of worship
- The wine- a celebration as a point of gratitude for the worshipper
- The blessings-the words that are spoken, declarations, oracles, pronouncements that are made
- The participants at the table- involvement, call and response, "*vumani bho*" – the saints must agree
- The chair of Elijah – the witness – recognition of the presence of YHWH during the service

- The Door left ajar: the unexpected arrival of the Messiah – physical expression of the reality of the unseen
- The Posture of eating standing –ready to Go, or siting with Yashua on the Table,satisfaction of work done

Set up the family: establish family order:

- The father- the servant
- The mother – the glue
- The children – the inheritance

Phase 2: Introduce the sanctuary:

The full pack of the mobile temple in the wilderness of life

- The heavenly sanctuary – source - most holy place
- The church – the channel - the holy place
- The home – practice - the inner court
- The heart – individual – lifestyle – outer court

The most holy – the spiritual – the ark of the covenant and the sit of YHWH, the cherubim's and the glory that fills the temple: the curtain of faith that divides the physical and the spiritual

The holy: the mental: the food of the mind: the bread, the lights, information and the oil that burns in the holy place. The alter of burnt incense the place of a prayer from the heart of a fed and enlightened worshipper: how to pray answered prayers, food for the soul and light for the mind is a better way to approach the throne behind the curtain.

The inner court: the physical: the alter of water at the door, *Mikveh* and washing feet and hands before entry. The alter of burnt offering; the sacrifice and value center, the burning place of things that seem important to us, giving our best to the Lord. Feeding of the priests and the flames at the alter that must never go off.

The flames that cook our bread are sacrifice. The flames (coal of fire) that burn our incense are sacrifice. The confessions we must do before we enter the holy place, the lamb we must contaminate with our touch the transfer of sin, from the guilty to the innocent... the ministration of the priest in this court.

Outer court: the world – social- out in the world where the world can see what we have done, when we begin to walk towards the sanctuary they all wonder what has he done.

Keep on walking the work that He has begun in you will not stop until he has accomplished it.

The answers to your problems are found in the enclosure of the sanctuary. This sanctuary is at the center of the community to make sure that every body has direct and quick access to the altars. Once you enter the gates of the sanctuary:

You are covered! Protected... the Lord covers you as He deals with you.

The struggle of life is to work from outside to the inside. The Lord will like to work from inside to the outside.

Phase 3: the feasts on the table of Grace

Marry the emblems with the feasts: the 9 feasts that are on the table. The spirit of worship must be a feast: to celebrate. Make it clear. We are to celebrate what Yhwh has done.

Little of us more of Him, we must go down as He goes up in us. The table will help us commemorate the milestones of divine accomplishments in the lives of Israel as these relate to us in our days. The feast is a celebration a display of victory of Yashua over poverty, sin, slavery, darkness etc.

1. **Identify the 9 feasts and their meaning must be put on the table and the similarities must be build into the emblems on the table.**

The service needs to make sense from the towel and the dressing on to the table and find the meaning of these things

Celebrating the Hanukkah, Yom Kippur etc

The feast of light

Let there be light as the first miracle

There should be lights on the Shabbat table. The presence of the Holy Spirit burning in the substance of oil giving out light

You are the light of the world the city build on a chill cannot be hidden

Let your light shine that all men can see you good works

Arise and shine for the light of the lord has shined upon you

Thy word is a lamp unto my path and a light unto my feet

The feasts are a template of pure worship and they strike a code in the African form and culture and their relevance to the building of man and the community.

a. **Rosh Hashanah/Jewish New Year:** make time to break from the past and find the new beginning. Worship must give people opportunity fresh beginnings. If you have made a mess learn to start again, there is time to begin.

b. **Yom Kippur/Day of Atonement:** the very nature of life is error and the man stand in the pale of God and to build a man he must be taught to forgive as he has been forgiven. This feast teaches that you walk in the light of freedom as a person who has been forgiven, do not carry the baggage of the past, worship is an opportunity to be forgiven as you forgive also.

c. **Sukkot/Tabernacles/Booths:** reduce your appetite for material things. Separate yourself from goods and define your material and your materials should not define you. You add value to them they don't add value to you. Remember that you used to be a slave in Egypt and did not have all this luxury. Luxury must not cause you to forget where you come from. Worship must remind the worshipper of where they come from; it's an opportunity to be reminded.

d. **Pesach/Passover:** Learn to Passover things; blood on the door post secure the living inside. Be dead, claim death on the physical and you can have life on the inside, which is spiritual. Worship is done under the cover of grace - be covered.

e. **Shavuot/Weeks/Pentecost:** occupancy with the spirit of truth and the holy spirit, filled to work in the vineyard and do warfare and call man to glory: worship is the place to be filled with the Holy Spirit.

f. **Hanukkah/Feast of Lights:** be an example, shine and be visible….a city build on a hill can not be hidden; worship is the place to light up our candles of influence and be shinning.

g. **Purim/Feast of Lots - to be tested:** the divine litmus test is on us to prove that we stand; worship allows us to stand and not be consumed like Moses with the burning bush stand without fear.

h. **Simchat Torah/make principle your benchmark:** delight in truth and make it a point of reference: worship gives us new joy in the Torah - Rejoicing in the Torah.

i. **Tisha B'Av /9th of Av: Destruction of Two Temples-** sanctify, identify. Set aside and allocate for holy us. *Worship celebrates our preservation and preserves the sacred so that we can be loyal the royal inside us.*

2. **Marry the feasts to the table and find their meaning in the things we eat. Measuring the distance between the utensils that are on the alter**

The candles and the dish of water

The horn, the chauffer, the dead bones make music to the lord, even in death of the body do we still have the breath of life flow through the horn for music

Water and the oil of anointing
Oil and the bread
The bread and the salt
The salt and the bitter herbs
Bitter herbs and the wine
Wine and the blessings
There is a time for everything under the sun
Time to plant and a time to harvest
A time to gather stones and a time to cast them away
Eccl 3

3. **Break the feasts into seasons on the year, as these are seasons of life and their provisions and what they resurrect in us.**

The 9 feasts are the celebration of life in its totality and the believer needs to constantly be aware of the season they are in the e able to celebrate the past, appreciate the present and anticipate the future

Practical applications of these seasons into the peoples lives – examples:

1. **Adam and Eve's season of creation:** share the power of worship to bring in a new season and change times.

Do not always pass on the blame to others when your fail to be accountable. Take the heat for your failures and mistakes. You should get more involved in the lives of those around you Adam, Eve is with the snake you are not there, the children at sacrifice you are not there, they kill each other you are not there, the question the Lord asked at the beginning must be answered. Adam! Adam, where are you?

2. **Noah's seasons of preparation of destruction:** warn the people during worship of the impending danger and the flood of fire that is coming.

Life is a preparation of the later. Noah's time of building and time of safety. Remind Noah to stay on course, 120 years preaching the same gospel with seemingly no change in the lives of those around him, tell Noah to keep on building and the Lord will honor him with fulfillment. Also remind him to reduce his wine, and stop cursing children while he is drunk. Don't do things that cause your children to laugh at you, or compromise your integrity in the midst of intoxication.

3. **Abraham's season of waiting and developing a wealth based education:** Abraham's time of promise and time of fulfillment ,covenant and reality.

Worship in the power of the divine promise, the promises of the Lord may delay but they will surely come to pass, He who is coming will not tarry, but let the just live by faith.

4. **Lot's time of momentary success and time of loss, gross darkness and perversion fathering his own grand children.**

Remind him that true wealth and joy is found in the company of the saints. Moments of pleasure and city life can cost you.

5. **Jacob's season of making a nation:** remind him there is no need to fast track blessings as the Lord has ordained you to success.

There will be success, no need to pretend to be what you are not in-order to access other people's portions. No need to cook a blessing and spend your life working hard for things the Lord has blessed you with.

6. **Joseph and the season's time of plenty and a time of little:** your dreams will come through.

At times your challenges, victimization, slavery, accusations, temptation, prison while innocent, its all but a set up for the crown. The seasons will change, remind Joseph that The Lord remembers him with a dream, a wife, new clothes and scepter of power.

The old days will not be remembered, remind Joseph to prepare to forgive those that have sinned against him.

- *Ephraim and Manasseh* a time to be old and time to have hands switched on you, the blessings of the Lord are sufficient for the mission at hand. Favor is Divine work in your calling and you have all you need.

- *Job and his season's time of trial and triumph.* The battle is not on the alter of offerings but on the spiritual level, what is happens in the visible realm is planned in the spiritual realm. Tell Job that the Lord will replace all that he has lost with much more; endure your problems and pain the Lord is on your side, even in His silence He will show up with a miracle of long life and restoration.

- *David with his time of persecution and time of inauguration.* Tell David that He does not need to run forever, soon the Lord will place him on the throne and establish a generation of power. Remind David that the Lord calls him a man after His own heart, because of the attitude and spirit of repentance.

- *Samson time of glory and a time of humiliation.* When you are still powerful and you can run, arrest foxes, carry gates and demonstrate power, Tell Samson that he will lose his eyes and, the battle is not for the strong, neither the race is for the swift, remember your creator in the days of your youth before the days evil come nigh when you shall say I have no pleasure in them. The appetite for women and pleasure will leave him on the grinding mill being driven like a donkey. Tell Samson that power is seasonal like mist it will thin in the light of dawn.

- *Nimrod time of power and divine humor, when God laughs at you project.* The adventurous and powerful who build many cities, a mighty hunter before the Lord, ultimately he decides not to trust in God and build his own monument, remind him, the Lord does not bless projects of foolishness. The moment of worship must bring sanity to madness.

- *Isaac a time to be a son and a time to be a sacrifice and a time to be a father and a blessing.* In sunset of your days you may be doped by your children and spend your old age in darkness.

Tell Isaac it's all in the plan.

- *Esau a time to sell blessings a and time to seek for them with tears,* tell him not to sell the valuable during the time of hunger, careful you don't sell the long term goals for short term pleasures.

- *Pharaoh a time of pride and a time of divine visitation.* Tell Pharaoh that arrogance and magic do not stand on the way of God who wants to redeem his children. If you enter a contest with powers you do not understand, you are bound to sacrifice your children and throw nations into distress. Tell him that he is not god, but mortal.

- *Aaron, a time of learning and a time failure.* In worship Aaron must be taught that his life is that of support, to the leadership of Moses. A position he has to stand in to bring the nation into worship of YHWH and not idols.

- *Miriam, a time to babysit and a time to let go.* You fail to accept his choice and killed yourself early. To mock other people's choices using derogative language of race are an early disease and death application. She sings like an angel, yet curses like a devil, the Lord will not remember your praise when your mouth is full of bitterness and racial discrimination.

- *Moses, a time of royalty and a time of peasantry.* 40 years you will learn to be somebody, then 40 years you will learn to be a nobody, and 40 years you save everybody, seasons and changes for leadership. Keep your channels of importance at bay, and do not consider your present position as a final destination, there is work to be done. Tell Moses the lord is waiting for him on Mount Sinai.

- *Zipporah* the wife of a great man, who circumcised her own children and stood in the gap, when the Lord would have killed Moses, tell her to cover for her husband and stand in the gap. Tell her that the sister-in-law, Miriam may not like her and ridicule her, she should not soil her garments in anger, the Lord will fight for her.

- *Jethro, a time of seeming rejection,* when your inheritance was given to Isaac, and you were banished away with tokens but there is a time of restoration as you teach Moses (the grand child of Isaac) the ways of YHVH. You are strategically positioned to restore a nation.

- *Joshua, a time to learn and a time to lead.* While you walking behind a great man learn to learn, and position yourself as a servant of the people. The journey is long but the Lord prepares the heart to occupy tand lead the people into the Promised Land.

- *Achan, a time to disobey and a time to face up with consequences.* He has stolen goods that are in his house and the Lord has clear instructions that these must not be kept or taken. The nation is in pain because of the sin of Achan, battle is being lost, families are burying their loved ones and every turn of repentance is blinded by the love for treasure. Tell Achan that the Lord is watching, His eyes miss no details, the pursuit of greed will burry his family in the rumble of stone.

- *Samuel, a time to be lonely in the temple and a time for divine visitation.*

- *Absalom* a time to be the most handsome man with hair and beauty and a time to hang out there

- *Ahimaz* a time to be the best announcer and time to let Cush do it

We talking seasons and a change of time. The place to apply breaks and see the other side of life. Create your own worshippers, use the bible as a guide to find people and where they are in life, people are the same, it's just the change of names but human characters are still the same.

The purpose of worship is for the people to find themselves, find others and find their God. Human characters and weakness must be exposed and the disease of the heart must be brought into the surgery of grace, our darkness must come to the light and our sin to forgiveness.

It is a moment to lift up hearts and burdens at the foot of the cross and learn to crucify our shame for his Glory.

The Covenants in at the table

1.   They asked me tell us about the Covenants:

Edenic Adamic ADAM and Eve (Gen 1-2; although the word "covenant" is not used, some divine promises are made) Life on Earth: "Be fruitful and multiply; fill the earth and subdue it..." (1:28)

Vegetarian Diet: "I have given you every plant... and every tree with seed in its fruit... for food" (1:29) Male and Female: "It is not good that the man should be alone" (2:18; cf. 1:27)

Disobedience and Death: "...but of the tree of knowledge of good and evil you shall not eat" (2:17

2.   Noahdic NOAH and his Family (Gen 6-9)

Life: God saves the family of Noah (6:18), telling them to be fruitful and multiply, and fill the earth (9:1-7)

Diet: they may now also eat animals, but may not eat/drink their blood, and may not shed human blood (9:2-6)

Covenant: God promises not to destroy the whole human race again through a flood (9:8-11)

The "sign" of this covenant: the rainbow set in the clouds each time it rains (9:12-17)

3.   Abrahamic ABRAHAM and his Descendants (Gen 12, 15, 17)

His descendants will be numerous and will become a great nation (12:2; 15:5; 17:20; 18:18; etc.)

They will inherit the "promised land", later called the land of Israel (12:1; 15:18-21; 17:8; etc.)

All other nations shall be blessed in him (12:3; 18:18) or through his offspring (22:18; 26:4)

The "sign" of this covenant: the circumcision of all male descendants (17:9-14, 23-27; 21:4; etc.)

4.   Mosaic MOSES and the Israelites (Exo 20-34; Deut 5-11)

Monotheism: "Hear, O Israel: The Lord is our God, the Lord alone" (Deut 6:4; cf. Exo 20:1-3)

Torah: the Law given on Mount Sinai, or Mount Horeb (esp. the Ten Commandments: Exo 20:1-17; Deut 5:1-21)

Reciprocity of relationship: "I will be your God, you will be my people" (esp. Exodus 6:7; Lev 26:12)

The "sign" of this covenant: the stone tablets on which the Law is written (Exodus 24:12; 31:18; etc.)

5.   Davidic DAVID and the Kingdom (2 Sam 7

God will establish forever David's "house" = the royal dynasty through his descendants (7:11-16)

David's son (Solomon) will build God's "house" = the first temple of Jerusalem (7:4-7, 13)

The "sign" of this covenant: the descendants of David (1Kings 1-3) and the temple itself (1Kings 5-8)

6.   The "New" or "Renewed" Covenant: salvific JEREMIAH The Lord will make "a new covenant with the house of Israel and the house of Judah" (Jer 31:31)

God's Law will be within people, written on their hearts (Jer 31:34)

This text is also quoted in the New Testament in Heb 8:8-12

7.   Messianic JESUS

At the Last Supper: "This cup that is poured out for you is the new covenant in my blood." (Luke 22:20; cf. 1 Cor 11:25)

The Letter to the Hebrews calls Jesus "the mediator of the new covenant" (Heb 9:15; 12:24; see also 8:1-13) Paul also speaks of Christian leaders as

"Ministers of a new covenant" (2 Cor 3:6)

Phase 6: the Introduction of the New Testament

The grafting of the wild branches to the tame vine
The two trees the wild olive and the tame one (Romans 9-11)
The witnesses (Revelation 10)
The two covenants (the lamb and the Savior)
The two seasons (evenings and mornings)

Law and grace

Notes:

Offertory reading: 12: the principles of seed and harvest:

Sowing into the 4 parts of the sanctuary:

- The most holy – give to God
- The holy place – give to yourself – educate and develop you
- The inner court – give sacrificially – give to your priests
- The outer court- give to the community

Procedure at the house of worship

o Come into sanctuary or alter silently and confess your mistakes and clean up you bad feeling before entry into the house and space of worship.

o The ladies to light up the candles/lights and say the prayers to secure the house

o The dressing and usage of Sabbath clothes to be encouraged and Hebrew emblems. The members need to appreciate the new testament as an old covenant

o The communion table is set every week and people should participate

o The quality of the people you want to develop, can relate to charismatic prayer life, to catholic emblem, to Islamic rituals and SDA doctrine.

o Create a world-class worship center that is not limited by denominationalism.

o The homes must start implementing these in their daily lives

DECLARATIONS

201/7 the year of completion...The spirit of harvest!

The work of a progressive believer is to understand the set times and the laws of nature. The rain falls to wet the land, the early rains, then we plant, and we grow plants, it rains to ripen and finally later rains to harvest. The divine cycles of 7 years cannot be ignored.

7 years of plenty and bumper harvest and 7 years of drought and starvation. Investments and harvest do not happen in the same season... Neither is every rain for harvest.

For those who have been planting for the past 6 years I declare 2017 as the year of completion. The spirit of harvest!

The book of Enoch suggests that when the wind blows through **6.** "And through the second portal in the middle comes what is fitting, and from it there comes rain and fruitfulness and prosperity and dew...And through the middle portal next to it there come forth fragrant smells, and dew and rain, and prosperity and health...."

11. "And from the middle portal comes in a direct direction, health and rain and dew and prosperity. **12.** And from the middle portal comes forth dew and rain, and prosperity and blessing.".

The rain that has fallen clearly reveals that we are in the portal of a blessing upon our land.

My grandfather could tell from the blowing wind what season we would experience...This is geography and science at its best. Should we apply our minds to this apocalyptic synopsis and find the relationship between spirituality and geography/weather patterns we stand a chance to know what Israel ought to do at this season.

I therefore decree and declare 2017 as a year that you complete all your tasks and seasons of lack...
I decree a season that the judgments put on your life expire.
I declare complete healing and liberation I decree the waters to rain on your physical and spiritual land.
I declare a dew season on your relationships and let your social ground bring forth fruit.
I decree and declare this is a season of abundance, blessings, health, prosperity and dew. I declare a season of fragrant smells and fruitfulness.

It's your season the winds are *blowing onto your land...let there be a bountiful harvest.*

For extra reading refer to the book of Enoch LXXVI. The Twelve Windows and their Portals. Look at the following streams of theology:

- Protestants or Charismatic theology
- Mainstream systematic hermeneutics
- Reformation theology and apologetics
- Cross over into Judaism
- World religions
- African philosophy and thought

What must we be doing and how must we think as a nation. The truth is that we have a continent of beliefs and a sea of abuse, we have to swim and begin to contribute our theology to the western world.

Africa is a continent of free people, let us be. Now world science and classics. The journey of faith continues to find truth and apply to life. Africa cannot constantly be recycled by other people's thoughts. The search for God will not cease.

I am looking for God! I bought and read myself these gifts this year and that's how we farm thoughts; spending thousands on Christmas with an empty head. With a stomach full of food and a head full of wind! The mouth dishes gravel. Celebrating pagan holidays with no clue of divine expectations.

Who are you Blackman?

How did you get here?

Where is your God and who created you?

Who is teaching you?

Is the god of the master and slave the same?

What is the spirit?

Does our present worship usher us into the presence of God?

Are modern churches now ATMs of western master?

Whose idols have you made your gods?

Who is harvesting your thoughts and land?

These are the questions that drove me to read these books.

Personal reflection!

To find out what's next! ...

Yes life must go on!

No one can see the wind.

But we all can tell when the trees move...

Oh that we may trust the unseen.

The uncaused cause...

He that causes all to happen moves invisible...

Yes his works that can doubt.

Revela-tions

A Spiritual Conclusion

Worship in truth learn and understand what you are doing, information must lead to practice, learn the right and truthful and your worship will be guided by knowledge not theatricals of emptiness.

Worship has to invite God into the house, the physical house must be occupied by the presence of the Lord.

"Let there be" thorough preparation of the entrance of the Holy One.

Worship must give the congregation or community the ability to invite the Holy One into the hearts of those who are present.

Worship in Spirit: let the hearts of the worshippers find the heart of God and the union of the spirits is what worship is all about.

The worshippers must move to the battlefront in the spiritual world and break through that barrier to the presence of the Lord.

Worship must call us to come boldly, if the "sinners" have confidence when they approach their god, why will those who profess to possess truth be timid and fearful to approach the throne of grace?

Worshippers must experience the filling in of the Holy Spirit. To have a service, the internal person must be ministered to by the Holy Spirit or Holy One

Worship must collect the word and information from the presence of the Holy One to deal with challenges in the present age. Troubled lives must come here and find solutions and their issues solved.

Worship must accord us the opportunity to dwell in the presence of the Lord, an experience we should have every time we come to worship. There is no taking chances, it is a practical desire of the worshipper to find the presence of the Lord.

Master the art to drive to this venue in every worship service.

Worship must become the way of life so that the worshipper can make this an integral part of life.

Worship stops being when the building begins to be at the heart as a daily conversation of the community so that we can manage the outside from inside.

Worship teaches us to develop the voice of conscience so that the Voice of the Holy Spirit is louder each day as you learn to distinguish internal voices.

Remember that inside there are voices: Your voice, the evil voices and the Holy Spirit's voice. Worship must join your voice with the Holy Spirit voice to deal with the evil voices.

Worship must be a tool to an impact in the world as a light of the world. An immediate solution is present when a believer is here. The instructions are audible and spiritual decisions will be made.

The presence of a believer becomes the presence of YHWH; their word (God and Man) is one with power to transform the physical world.

Like the man from Emmaus the people will say "did not our hearts move within us when He ministered in our midst".

The Old Testament with the Old African had worship: Look backward; you will see the future of true spirituality. [1]

Fear not and do not despair as the tears are of a woman in labor, it's for a moment, than the smiles of an infant will melt the sorrows of the night. Once we have hope all is possible, the sweat of our pain will yield its fruit and rewards of glory.

There is a bright future for my people. Look backward and see ahead, the night has whispered wisdom to the day. Look ahead and see honor and reward for our patience. Had it not been for the religion our hands will be full of blood of fools. Come stand with me the sons of Cush. The mighty tribe of Ham. You are great, as you were once great, history will dine with your future.

I go for a while to the land of my fathers. For a little while you see me and for a while you will see me no more.

I will return to you and you with believe.

Too long we have given ear to the hogwash of oppression that pacified our indigenous knowledge. We have worshiped the redundancy of imperialism. The time has come for Africa to arise. Look at the sunrise, glance across the horizon and waters of despair.

The tree was not uprooted but pruned. There shall be showers of blessings. There shall be a season of refreshing. It will shoot again and the birds and beasts will return to the meadows of pride. I see the grand entrance and return.

The restoration of Africa and her glory is in site. Africa Arise. It's not where and what they say you are but who you are.

I have dreamed of a Shona elder enedevu ezinde ezimhlophe (with a long white beard) and with rare dark skin so complex to liken.

Stood between a huge stone and an enormous river, with red eyes, he said to me "I know your father".

He didn't wait for me to answer he proceeded strongly by saying once again, "you humans can't even honor yourselves, you owe yourselves honor before being honored, now how can you foolishly expect honor?"

As I was gazing at him, I discovered that on his head was an enrolled animal skin, and a long rod on his right hand, as I turned to look around me, it was only me and him who were present at that moment.

---

1. Subscribe to #FarmersOFThought - Maponga J III
https://www.youtube.com/watch?v=wi6p1R90Q9I&feature=youtu.be

He continued by saying "the Spiritual space does not honor people who have no honor for themselves, sufficient self-honoring connotes external honor, the secret code of the spiritual realm is self-honor.

It is the proper guide and conduct, the spiritual world honors not dis-honest, honor yourselves for it is the channel to honor you in any strength and how, anywhere you provoke", then he dis-appeared!

The desire of my soul is to live above the world.

EUROCENTRIC CHRISTIANITY AND AFRICA

The honorable guest of honor, professionals, ladies and gentleman.

The age of truth has risen upon us, in infancy we accept everything, in adolescence we question everything, in maturity we question the question and bring order to chaos. Madness is relative, and normality is a myth, the human being is twined with spiritual influences that can cause physical dysfunction.

Christianity is not a qualified doctor to diagnose all such maladies as demonic as some of these are mere psychiatric disorders that have pharmaceutical solution.

The madness of the individual mind, the madness of a nation is catastrophic, in the absence of sanitized teaching, the African child has become a patient in the *Eurocentric-Christian* ward, infested with mental fungi and moral decay. The mind of the so-called "normal" are locked in the prison of the "*white-masters*" and they will do all they can to maintain the status quo.

These *Negropeans* (*Negros* on the outside and white on the inside) are watchman at the door of reason to keep as many locked in this sewage plant of the mind. Africa has become a dumping site of European spiritual waste that has been taught and pushed on our plates as a delicacy.

If Christianity is the best form of worship, why are the Europeans no longer Christian?

The fable of civility is a fairytale of degradation, an allegorical lore of depravity, which teaches that the concrete jungle of modernization will usher civility, it is a pathetic mythos.

When Africa is now New York in construction, fully Urbanized, will we have clean water, forests and animals?

Will we not look back and wish for the "primitive" which we are now?

To live in harmony with nature is the true definition of being civilized, to eat real food, and leaves and roots for medicine is being educated.

If the whole world will be Christian, will this place be a better place? Will we have more land, and live healthy lives? Is there a benefit, which we will realize with the *Christianization* of our names and drinking acids and putting on plastic clothes? Why is the whiteman keen and eager to make the blackman a Christian? Is this Christianity we practice now the real Christianity of the book of Acts chapter 2?

THE PHASES OF CHRISTIANITY IN THE AFRICAN PEOPLE

1. The apostolic in the shadow of the Messianic revelation and ministry is an age of spirit power and manifestations. Active inter-actions between faith and practice

2. The roman era of popularity in the ambit of the Pontiff Maximas built bridges between Judaism based Christianity and pagan Rome. An age of idols and adulteration, crucifixes, indulgences, saints, doctrinal creeds, worse of all canonization of scriptures. On the business front slavery was rife during this period and Christians where the merchants and scriptures were used to justify these hideous trades

3. The reformation era: that of protests, revolts and a clarion call of change: lead by Luther, Zwingli's, Kelvin and the mother of all protestants: as in protesting against roman paganism masquer-ading as Christianity. The New world was a result of the migration and persecution of Europe and people found comfort in the Red Indian land now called USA.

4. The missionary or mercenaries era: the events of the late 1700's into the 1833's, the sun turning black, the falling stars, meteoroids, the moon turning red and references to scripture moved people into an *eschatological* frenzy to "spread the gospel and the end will come".

Adventism, later day saints, Jehovah's witnesses, and other prosaic churches were formed during this era. Africa was considered a dark continent. Two groups of people left Europe, the missionary and the mercenaries both carried the bible canonized by Rome to the Africans they gave the gospel. The criminals/colonialist had champions in slave trade like Willie Lynch letter - *The Making of a Slave*

It was the interest and business of slave holders to study human nature, and the slave nature in particular, with a view to practical results. I and many of them attained astonishing proficiency in this direction.

They had to deal not with earth, wood and stone, but with men, and by every regard, they had for their own safety and prosperity; they needed to know the material on which they were to work. Conscious of the injustice and wrong, every hour they were perpetuating and knowing what they themselves would do.

If this method is installed correctly you will control the slaves for at least 300 years, part of the strategy was to brand himself the whiteman as God, or colonize the very space of worship, so that for the slave to fight the whiteman will be equal to fighting god: hence put the fear of God in the slave.

"Given time, nature will find us again and justice will triumph over evil. As for those who throw arrows in the air they must have metal helmets."

a. As parchments of the new testament as of Matthew,Luke and John

b. Later they printed the entire New testament

c. Then they also included the book of Psalms and proverbs

d. Ultimately the entire Old and the New Testament

The era of Truth requires the entire sacred scriptures to be pulled from the archive in totality and the African to apply mind to text and dissect and interpreted for local consumption.

It is here in these omitted works that we find the nature of the beast call *Eurocentric Christianity* that ignores maladies and the use of medications to chase away evil spirit? Quote the book of Tobi and the woman who had demons and she killed her 7 husbands. The liver of a fish burnt on hot coals was used to cure the woman. A very interesting account that resonates with African Practice.

Finally we are in the Age of Truth and modern Scholarship has to content with two juvenile ideologies Christianity and Democracy both as products of the New Age and the intention being to bulldoze, override, undermine and be forerunners of colonial oppression and economic suppression of the African people. There is truth in the scripture, but the plastic that wraps it is dirty and the African is forced to eat both the plastic and the bread.

The painful truth is that the soul of the African has been sold for a plate of food and demonic education that fragments the social fibers.

Three words are critical for consideration in pursuit of that truth:

Contextualize: all texts must have contexts or they remain a pretext

Indigenization: the people must practice theology not theorize it, it must be a pragmatic praxis of indignity, song, clothes, food, art all must be harvested from the indigenous person

Enculturation: is the warehouse of social truth, and truth must find the culture of the community, symbols of deity and it's understanding and therein finds longevity into daily lives.

The western (*Eurocentric Christian* is schizophrenic by nature, as the practice of Christianity needs a venue, time, place, and person who is a custodian of the body of "truth" ministers of priests.)

The African does not separate between sacred and secular, rather life is a continuous religious expression of life itself, to eat, marry, plough are all religious expressions. Therefore worship takes place in the canopy of nature and creation.

The blackman has been drugged to hate himself and in the desire to be like the whiteman he has torn his soul and veiled his eyes from the reality of the prison of the mind. Christianity must be decolonized, as the god of the master and slaves cannot be same. This white god is scared of our drums and clothes which makes him foreign to us, and he can not be omniscient for the black culture is unknown to him. Why must we be white first before we are accepted into faith? Why change names to be white?

How come he only responds to pianos and organs and not *mbiras, koras* and drums? This is Fanon's anger and pain as expressed in the works *"black skins, white masks"*. It is the silent scream of all those who toil in abject poverty simply to exist in the hinterlands and vast conurbations of Africa. It is the anger of all whose cultures, knowledge systems and ways of being that are ridiculed, demonized, declared inferior and irrational, and in some cases, eliminated.

This is not just any anger. It is the universal fury against oppression in general, and the perpetual domination of the Western civilization in particular. The whiteman is the most violent on the face of the planet and the cause and reason of all wars in this generation.[2]

I am fully aware that to speak a language of the whiteman is to take on a world, a culture and movement into enslavement. Are you aware that our enemy is the teacher? The blackman is to say No to those who attempt to build a definition of him.

---

2. Michael Bradley, Chosen people from the Caucasus.

The reason we here today is to assist the black person to overcome his feeling of insignificance, "What does the black man want?" is a question posed by Fanon in his book *"Black Skin, White Masks"*. In this work the black person has to champion his own journey of discovering his dignity through an interrogation of his own 'Self' a journey that will not be unfamiliar to all those who have been forced to endure western civilization.

Here are some few pointers to the young minds from an old doctor of the mind

1. Is the whiteman not a measure of life?
2. How should a black man talk to himself in private and in public?
3. Are you aware and passionate about denouncement of colonial racism that sits in your mind?
4. what is the definition of your blackness, do you use white tools or black tools to define yourself?
5. Are you aware of the intellectual ferment, social decay setting into your life constantly, which is moving you away from your truth to the "utopia of civilization"?
6. Are you aware that Most of the Europeans are racists and that by accepting European culture we become racist also with deep seeds of inferiority, for black will never be white and white does not desire to be black?
7. What measures have you taken to deal with the psychology of colonialism and its effects upon your soul, have you detoxed your spirit of anger and inferiority? Do you feel more cultured when you comply to white expectations? How do you feel when you go to worship in your cultural clothes? Is it easy to sing in your own language? psychoanalytic deconstruction....*Ngugi wa Thiong* in Decolonising the Mind (1986).
8. In what manner do you as a black person emulate the oppressors?
9. Do you as an educated black person thinks or feel that your uneducated people no longer understand you? That this self-division is a direct result of colonialist subjugation and is beyond question.
10. Have you considered "the black problem", that "civilized society" does not like uncomfortable truths and naked honesty here is a clarion call against complacency? *"The whiteman has told you heaven is in the sky and hell under the ground and he* (the whiteman) *takes every-thing in the middle..."*[3]

3. Mohammed Ali

In this life it is the black war for white justice. The reality idealized Africans have become the noble savage. If we do not stand now are all being transformed into a mighty white river into which all other histories and cultures flow and merge as mere minor and irrelevant tributaries. Beside phylogeny and ontogeny stands sociogeny - the individuality of each community must be preserved.

Hate is not inborn; it has to be constantly cultivated….worm- eaten roots of the structure. While The black man wants to be white.

The whiteman slaves to reach a human level…White men consider themselves superior to black men.

While we waste our time trying to be white… the whiteman is improving to conquer the universe. Is it true that for the black man there is only one destiny and that is to be white? Psycho-existential complex, an inferiority complex has been created by the death and burial of local cultural originality.

"What does the black man want?" We too must ask ourselves this question..

Ask yourself the question of existence why are you here? To convey the master's orders to your fellow men, and so that you can be promoted as guard and be put in a position of honor on the table of slavery?

Religion essentially has imprisoned our anger and limited our dreams. We live with oppressors because the bible says "though shall not kill". But the same says "do unto others what you want others to do unto you", can we also do the whiteman what he did to us?

Our picture of heaven overshadows our responsibility on earth to occupy and dominate. The rewards will be delivered by God and we must wait for God to bring justice: this argument and faith based notion remains trapped solely on the physiological foundation…"the fact is rapture has not saved anybody" Fanon admits.

When this whiteman's religion addresses us as Africans it behaves as an adult who talks to a child. This *Eurocentric Christianity* behaves as if the African has no culture, no intellect, no civilization, no language, no ethics, no God, no morals, no "long historical past." Africa has to wear the slavery clothes that the whiteman has sewed for him. Our continent is running a castrated psychological, academic, spiritual and economic system that produces *Afropeans or Negropeans.* Our dignity has been patronized and we are witnesses of this wicked mental rape in the continent.

So the first thing that the black man wants is to say 'NO'.

No to degradation of man.

No to exploitation of man.

No to the butchery of what is most human in man: freedom.

And, above all, no to those who attempt to build a definition of him. Fanon *"black skin white masks"*.

In conclusion human beings are created equally and dignity is not me fitting into a white cast and eating at the table of a whiteman, but BEING. Being myself? Being the participle of continuous self-improvement in the comfort of myself. My skin is no measure of my intellect.

To the African I say:

Find your voice and speak........Find your feet and walk

Find your hands and work ....Find your mind and think

Find your spirit and connect to the Creator who has no shame in what you are

The 'Afrikan' Dream. Our people free to be themselves without fear or ridicule. Our land to produce food, water and minerals for us and our children. Foreign people to respect our culture and way of life

There would be no prison, but that our people would respect and learn the ways of the past.

Our schools to teach our history not when we were oppressed Our old people live and die in dignity full of years Our economies exploit indigenous knowledge and be proud of our roots. That we stop speaking in English to look educated but in proverbs and 'Afrikan' languages.

I dream of Afrikan leaders who would love people and their land more than profit. Oh that we can stop buying Chinese hair and products and manufacture our own products

That we can get rid of democracy and find Afrikan governance models that work for us. Oh! That the creator of the universe would replace these foreign gods who take our money and declare us sinners with no dignity.

Every child born will see the sun and sing to the moon, swim in the rivers and climb trees for fruits.. I dream of Africa our homeland not a dumping site of western toxins

Soil air and water (SAW) the trinity of life. The three natural resources from which everything we have comes from. It is the combination and manipulation of these elements that produces the entire human invention and livelihood is hinged on their purity.

Industry must be careful in how it exploits nature for when these three elements are not respected the quality of human life is greatly compromised.

Whoever has access to these elements controls human life and can charge a premium to the masses. We have those who sell air time, water and refuse others land to live on. It is true when human beings are clustered in high density suburbs that violence is rife where there is clutter.

The making of location was a deliberate move to dispose the Blackman access to clean air, clean water and fertile land. Whoever owns your land owns your life.

The Blackman cannot sit and feed on hand outs as if he cannot farm for himself. Before the whiteman came to Africa we were not dead. They did not find us starving, sick, and poor, but vibrant societies. Without calling for war, we say we want clean water, clean air, and clean soil. It is not too much to ask, it is a human right.

Our land can not be raped as our minerals are suggesting leaving mountains of cyanide and big holes for tourists.

If Democracy does not deliver to it's three basic elements then it's an enemy of our very existence. The appetite of the West and East in our mineral resources cannot be quenched by destroying our home.

Africa is not a solution to their problem, for in solving their problem, we are creating our own problems, some of these resources cannot be replaced. Stop and think, after they have depleted the resources we remain with ghost towns.

I call for sustainable development strategies that have ecological intelligence money can not be the only factor that drives Civilization, restoration and rehabilitation of our habitat needs precedence.

Why do banks want land as collateral? Because land is the only Real estate! Saw soil, air and water. These old problems need new solutions. Jeremiah 31:29 "The parents have eaten sour grapes, and the children's teeth are set on edge."

When those who have start to pray? What are they praying for? They need protection from who? Are they holding stolen goods?

Are they asking God to protect them from those they stole from?

What is the right prayer? Will sharing be a better solution?

Will God answer these prayers?

How long will it be before they repent of their greed?

Are they really convinced that they own the land and they are rightful beneficiaries of colonialism?

Why is Christianity a shelter for such thugs?

Does Jesus attend such meetings to listen to oppressors praying and seeking for power to oppress us some more?

Why did they not pray over racism and apartheid now they pray for currency? Are they affected by the present political changes? The time has come we must speak or we die. Next time when a whiteman prays for you do not close your eyes Blackman.

Africa Arise!

Glossary

Apartheid: a religious organization that teaches segregation based on "biblical false doctrine" that the white race is superior to all other races. An insensitive mantra that makes the white-man a relative of god and all others slaves. It is perfected into an economic system that offers privileges to whites first, Colored (the mixture of white and other), Indians and lastly local Blacks. In South Africa it manifested as a government that oppressed the southern African nations and still continues to drive the agenda through business and commerce.

Africa/Afrika: a continent trapped between the two thieves like Jesus on the cross the West and the East. The continent of he Hamites or Black races, their home and the cradle of humankind. The richest continent and the poorest.

African: a people of the soil of Eden, people of color with origins and a relationship with the ground of Africa. Language and culture flow in their veins and consider the continent as their home of birth and death.

Afrikan: South Africa is the only country on the African continent whose name is defined by its geographic location. Therefore, the Afrika spelled with a 'k' represents a redefined and potentially different Afrika, and also it symbolizes a coming back together of Afrikan people worldwide. Oct 21, 2014[1]

---

1. An African dating an Afrikan - Africa on the Blog: www.africaontheblog.com/

Christianity: A Faith established by Yashua at the turn of the century and inaugurated in the book of acts, driven by the Holy Spirit. A social change based of love for neighbor as equivalent to love for self.

It's a powerful faith based system that connects with YHWH and performs miracles using the access of Yashua the Messiah of Nazareth, son of man and Son of God.

It's a none sexist, none racial as it mandate states "go yea to all the nations, be a Jew to the Jews and a gentile to the gentile. The Europeans and the Jews killed the Messiah; through His death (human sacrifice/ a divine gift) the nations have been reconciled to YHWH, with a promise of a second coming and establishment of a new system in paradise.

It encourages people to prepare to meet Him when He shall return and graves be opened with a mass resurrection of the righteous to meet the Lord in the air.

Christological experiential anthropology: a study that seeks to give the believer a path to god, and is grounded in the personal encounter of person and maker. It is meant to be experienced and the observation of the other who experiences too. There are not spectators here but participants. Spirituality must be experienced and connection established with expected outcomes.

Colonization: the process of making colonies, taking peoples land by force and subjecting them to the powers of your monarch and political systems. It's a total take of the social structure to introduce the white ways of life.

Eurocentric Christianity: a religion of the 21st century that is forced on the entire nation as it comes as a pioneer of democracy and colonial imperialism. A form of belief system that has "whitened" all Hebraic culture to European.

It comes with its own gods understood as the "holy trinity" and messiah. In recent times it has so many varieties and has been a prison for the nations of the world.

It is enforced white culture, which totally disregards other cultures and seeks to place white culture as superior.

A Judeo-based faith form, it is what people are "called", a belief system that seeks to make people bible based, yet does not fully believe in the scriptures as all inspired. It's a worldwide movement of a divided group of interpreters of the bible with the West as the main drivers.

Through this system people have been Christianized and their names and cultures vandalized to worship the bible characters and the god of the slave masters. Christianity is religious colonization. It is a form of societal Schizophrenia that makes people worship on a day and become something else in the week. It has been the cause of many wars from 538 Ad to date.

From Pagan Rome to Papal Rome, to Reformation and now Protestantism, orthodox and Indigenous churches which more than 35 000 churches around the world and more being formed everyday.

Its biggest commodity is Jesus, not of Nazareth but some white Caucasian with blues eyes, summed up as the colonization of the image of Jesus.

Eurochristian syndrome: a 21st century disease that is viral, it manifests itself with social paralysis and African cultural hate. It builds a pseudo family/sub culture and financial "break-through" with a weekly doze of motivation, followed by financial donations to MOG (man of god)

Hebrew: the collection of the 10 tribes and mixtures with the rest of the nations of the world

Idolatry: the worship of inanimate things, giving veneration to creatures instead of creator.

Imperialism: the expansion policy of a country to control land and local people, it a systematic process of making local structure weak while you enslave them and build industries that support your home country.

Jews: the two tribes of Israel that remained how to represent the nations of Israel, (discount the children of *Khazar* in modern Israel) they are not Jews, they claim to be.

Khoisan: the indigenous people of the south that have been pushed into extinction due to civilization. They are called "bushman", but they are Khoi-Khoi, or Koi San.

These are Bantus, their last home is the Kalahari Desert where a few groups remain to date.

Lemba/Remba: Hebrew tribe in South Eden, which practices Hebrew faith, and by genes is more Jews than the 'Jews'. They are found around Zimbabwe (Mberengwa and Lowveld areas and South Africa, Venda in the Limpopo Region)

Mudzimu Unoyera: (Holy Spirit,) the greatest ancestor in the African worships the one who connects us directly with YHWH. The same spirit that links every tribe to the original ancestry of heaven. Our families and tribes are but branches that link us up to the original parent; through this spirit we have access to divinity.

Materialism: new demon that occupies people who chase after vanity, those who find meaning in what they own, more than what they are. Labels and brands don't make you a person of quality, but your heart, spirit and the internal content.

Mashavi: *Shona* word for evil spirits, the dead people have roving spirits and have not found a home where they can dwell. These are demons fused with the spirits of wicked people who have died.

Mtakhati: a western definition of a person who uses traditional herbs and powers for destructive purposes

Mbira: an ancient music instrument of worship, which incubates the theology and practice of the *Shona* tribes and the tool for divine connections.

Mudzimu: the *Shona* word for Spirit, used to depict both the forefathers/ancestors and Spirit, with Unoyera (holy) meaning the Holy Spirit. In the Shona culture therefore the Holy Spirit is intertwined with the ancestors their voice of right is one.

Murungu: a violent race of Caucasians who have positioned themselves as relatives of God. Murungu also in some cultures deemed as God, the missionaries who branded God in His image and has created an idol in his likeness and travels the world forcing people to bow and pay homage to this idol. An intolerant race of people that does not respect other people and deems "civilization" as an agenda to redeem people from primitive ways. Only to discover that industrialization vandalizes the very nature that primitive people preserved. A race complicated people who kill animals for pleasure and trophies.

They advocate for human rights that destroy the fiber of indigenous societies and have an economic imperialistic agenda to the world to turn our societies into a village where they will function as modern economic chiefs.

Negropeans: these are black people who are now saturated with white habits so much that they have become a new form of colonization of blacks. They have been told by the white "you are not like them". It's a psychological defective syndrome that hates what it looks like and it likes.

Spirit: the God factor in the physical person. The center of connection where the divine and the human interact to work beyond the flesh; the locus of control and moral platform and center of moral soundboard.

SaNgoma: medium who uses music to cross over between two realms, the physical and the spiritual to find solution for the present life, a healer.

Ubuntu: core values of African community developments, the unwritten ground rules of African living, respect, honor, locked up in myths and fables to pass on the oral traditions. Ubuntu is the reason of existence and loving your neighbor as you love yourself, being naturally friendly and useful for the well being of human kind.

West: a world view of whites that thinks that technology and its inventions make people civilized as opposed to indigenous people as primitive and backward. A form of movement that is raping the resources of the world to advance its cause. It comes with its education, medicine and forms of governance that obliterate the social fiber to build a new system that idolized their technology as the best form of life. It sets new standards of wealth and beauty that have turned local people into Christmas trees.

Worship: a gathering of a community for the purpose of seeking the face of their God.

Worshipper: the one who leads and conducts worship, with an intention of linking them to deity and higher powers. They use music and speech to evoke people to find their spiritual connections.

Zambuko: is the bridge between two divides, used here to bridge the physical and the Spiritual world, and music being that bridge.

Yashua: YaHshua, Yehoshua, Y'shua, Yeshua, Iesous, Iesus, or Jesus The Sacred Name or Yahshua, Yehoshua, Y'shua, Yeshua, Iesous, Iesus Or Jesus.

THE SACRED NAME OR TRUE NAME

There has been much controversy about what the True Name or Sacred Name of the Messiah is, with all sorts of speculation and conjecture being taught as fact. Below are some statements that I have heard over the years:

"The name of **YAHshua** has been replaced by the names of G-Zeus (Jesus), and Ea-zeus meaning healing zeus (Iesus, and Iesous) which are pagan in origin." "Now that we know that his real Hebrew name is **YAHshua**, we can't use Jesus any more in good conscience.

"I prefer to use the Hebrew name **YAHshua**, instead of His Gentile nickname Jesus. "As true believers we need to refuse the blasphemous Talmudic moniker of Yashua and use his true name **YAHshua**."

"The name Baal means "Lord" in Hebrew. The church translators replaced the true name of the Messiah, **YAHshua** with the title "Lord". When people use that title, they are unknowingly worshiping a pagan idol, and that is why it is so important that we restore the true Hebrew name **YAHshua** back into the English translations."

"Jesus" is nothing more than a pseudo substitute for the true name **YAHSHUA**." "You should not use the name Ge-sus because the Ge means earth or soil in Greek, and the sus means swine or pig in Latin, so you are saying, "earth pig".

"Jesus is a corrupted name derived from the Greek IESOUS. Ies, or iysh in Hebrew means man, while sus -soos means horse, so when you speak that name, you are referring to the Messiah as "man horse" or "man beast"."

"The name **IESOUS** or "hey-soos" means "hey horse". Just look at this example: Ps.33: 17, "A horse (Heb. hey-soos/Grk. Iesous/ Eng. Jesus) is a vain hope for safety; neither shall he deliver any by its great strength.""

Many in the Hebrew roots and sacred name circles have continually and fervently expressed the sentiment outlined in the above statements.

Some of the popular sacred name bibles have even reinforced the Jesus/ zeus fallacy by supplying supposed scholarship to demonstrate this in the explanatory notes section of their translations.

It has been stated by some that the Name Jesus is a false Hellenic (Greek) name that was conspiratorially created by the early church, in an attempt to give glory to Zeus and the Greek goddess Iaso while intentionally censoring the "true name" of Messiah which they say is **YAHshua**. Some have said, that since the Name of Jesus shares the same letter sigma (V) or "s" from the end of the Greek god Zeus' name, that at the very least, it constitutes a pagan connection with the Name of Jesus.

This would be the same as saying that all Greek masculine nouns that have the added sigma as a case ending are somehow related to Zeus.

If this were factual, which it is not, it would make for an incredibly long list of supposedly pagan names. One excellent example would be John 1:1 where **Theos** (God) and **Logos** (word), which are both masculine nouns end with a final sigma.

We should also note that when the name **Iesous** is rendered in the genitive form of Iesou there is no final sigma, so in this case according to the theory, would the pagan connection then be eliminated?

The same elimination of the final sigma also happens with the name Zeus in Acts 14:12. Amazingly, I have seen it claimed by some that Jesus is the name that actually represents the person of the anti-messiah, and is an indicator of the far greater evils being promoted by traditional Christianity.

Iesou (Ihsou) and **Zeus** (zeu) are not related, and have two completely different spellings. The first letter from Zeus (zeta) is vocalized with a 'dz' sound, and the dipthongs eu (zeu) and ou (Iesou) have a totally different vocalization. The final sigma (V) or "s" added on at the end of Iesous occurs in the standard transliteration of the proper masculine noun from Hebrew to Greek. Greek nouns and names almost always have case endings, so the sigma (V) or "s" is added at the end of the word to distinguish that the name is the masculine form, and also makes it declinable. There is absolutely no relation between these words, and the most basic scholarship can easily prove this.

If we take the same logic used in the Jesus/zeus fallacy, and apply it to a Hebraic context, then people could never name their children Nathan or Jonathan, because those names have the same ending as Satan. Of course we all know that those are scriptural Hebrew names (Nathan and *Yehownathan*).

Because of the many errant allegations that have been used to create fear, and other so called scholarshipS many have been falsely led to believe that "**YAHshua**" is the original Hebrew name for the Messiah. In order for **YAHshua** to be an actual name in Hebrew, it would need to be spelled in Hebrew as *Yod-Hey-Shin-Vav-Ayin*. [2]

---

2. Htt://www.seekgod.ca/htname.htm

Music Notes:

BIBLICAL TEXTS REFERENCING MUSIC AS PRAISE WITH INSTRUMENT ACCOMPANIMENT:

2 Chronicles 5:11-14: **11** And it came to pass, when the priests were come out of the holy place: (for all the priests that were present were sanctified, and did not then wait by course: (present: Heb. found)

12 Also the Levites which were the singers, all of them of Asaph, of Heman, of Jeduthun, with their sons and their brethren, being arrayed in white linen, having cymbals and psalteries and harps, stood at the east end of the altar, and with them an hundred and twenty priests sounding with trumpets:)

13 It came even to pass, as the trumpeters and singers were as one, to make one sound to be heard in praising and thanking the LORD; and when they lifted up their voice with the trumpets and cymbals and instruments of music, and praised the LORD, saying , For he is good; for his mercy endureth for ever: that then the house was filled with a cloud, even the house of the LORD;

14 So that the priests could not stand to minister by reason of the cloud: for the glory of the LORD had filled the house of God.

Nehemiah 12:44-47

(The Importance of Music Directors and Leaders in Worship Service) **44** And at that time were some appointed over the chambers for the treasures, for the offerings, for the first fruits, and for the tithes, to gather into them out of the fields of the cities the portions of the law for the priests and Levites: for Judah rejoiced for the priests and for the Levites that waited. (Of the law: that is, appointed by the law) (For Judah...Heb. For the joy of Judah) (waited: Heb. Stood)

45 And both the singers and the porters kept the ward of their God, and the ward of the purification, according to the commandment of David, and of Solomon his son. **46** For in the days of David and Asaph of old there were chief of the singers, and songs of praise and thanksgiving unto God. 47And all Israel in the days of Zerubbabel, and in the days of Nehemiah, gave the portions of the singers and the porters, every day his portion: and they sanctified holy things unto the Levites; and the Levites sanctified them unto the children of Aaron

Psalms 33:1-5

1 Rejoice in the LORD, O ye righteous: for praise is comely for the upright. **2** Praise the LORD with harp: sing unto him with the psaltery and an instrument of ten strings. **3** Sing unto him a new song; play skillfully with a loud noise. **4** For the word of the LORD is right; and all his works are done in truth. **5** He loveth righteousness and judgment: the earth is full of the goodness of the LORD

Psalms 98

1 A Psalm. O sings unto the LORD a new song; for he hath done marvelous things: his right hand, and his holy arm, hath gotten him the victory. **2** The LORD hath made known his salvation: his righteousness hath he openly showed in the sight of the heathen. (Openly or revealed) He hath remembered his mercy and his truth toward the house of Israel: all the ends of the earth have seen the salvation of our God.

4 Make a joyful noise unto the LORD, all the earth: make a loud noise, and rejoice, and sing praise. **5** Sing unto the LORD with the harp; with the harp, and the voice of a Psalm. **6** With trumpets and sound of cornet make a joyful noise before the LORD, the King.

7 Let the sea roar, and the fullness thereof; the world, and they that dwell therein. (The fullness or all it contained) **8** Let the floods clap their hands: let the hills be joyful together **9** Before the LORD; for he cometh to judge the earth: with righteousness shall he judge the world, and the people with equity

Psalm 100

1 A Psalm of praise. Make a joyful noise unto the LORD, all ye lands. (Praise: or, thanksgiving) (all the earth) **2** Serve the LORD with gladness: come before his presence with singing.

3 Know ye that the LORD he is God: it is he that hath made us, and not we ourselves; we are his people, and the sheep of his pasture. (And not... or, and his we are)

4 Enter into his gates with thanksgiving, and into his courts with praise: be thankful unto him, and bless his name. **5** For the LORD is good; his mercy is everlasting; and his truth endureth to all generations. (To all, to generation and generation)

Psalms 149

1 Praise ye the LORD. Sing unto the LORD a new song, and his praise in the congregation of saints. (Praise..Heb: Hallelujah) **2** Let Israel rejoice in him that made him: let the children of Zion be joyful in their King. (In him and in his Makers)

3 Let them praise his name in the dance: let them sing praises unto him with the timbrel and harp. (In or with the pipe) **4** For the LORD taketh pleasure in his people: he will beautify the meek with salvation. **5** Let the saints are joyful in glory: let them sing aloud upon their beds.

6 Let the high praises of God be in their mouth, and a two-edged sword in their hand and mouth and throat **7.** To execute vengeance upon the heathen, and punishments upon the people; **8** To bind their kings with chains, and their nobles with fetters of iron;

9 To execute upon them the judgment written: this honor have all his saints. Praise ye the LORD.

Psalms 150

1 Praise ye the LORD. Praise God in his sanctuary: praise him in the firmament of his power. (Praise ye...Hallelujah) **2** Praise him for his mighty acts: praise him according to his excellent greatness.

3 Praise him with the sound of the trumpet: praise him with the psaltery and harp. (Trumpet: or, cornet) **4** Praise him with the timbrel and dance: praise him with stringed instruments and organs. (Dance: or, pipe) **5** Praise him upon the loud cymbals: praise him upon the high sounding cymbals. 6Let every thing that hath breathes praise the LORD. Praise ye the LORD.

1 Chronicles 15: 16-24

15 And the children of the Levites bare the ark of God upon their shoulders with the staves thereon, as Moses commanded according to the word of the LORD. **16** And David spoke to the chief of the Levites to appoint their brethren to be the singers with instruments of music, psalteries and harps and cymbals and sounds by lifting up the voice with joy.

17 So the Levites appointed Heman the son of Joel; and of his brethren, Asaph the son of Berechiah; and of the sons of Merari their brethren, Ethan the son of Kushaiah; **18** And with them their brethren of the second degree, Zechariah, Ben, and Jaaziel, and Shemiramoth, and Jehiel, and Unni, Eliab, and Benaiah, and Maaseiah, and Mattithiah, and Elipheleh, and Mikneiah, and Obededom, and Jeiel, the porters.

19 So the singers, Heman, Asaph, and Ethan, were appointed to sound with cymbals of brass; **20** And Zechariah, and Aziel, and Shemiramoth, and Jehiel, and Unni, and Eliab, and Maaseiah, and Benaiah, with psalteries on Alamoth;

21 And Mattithiah, and Elipheleh, and Mikneiah, and Obededom, and Jeiel, and Azaziah, with harps on the Sheminith to excel. (On the... or, on the eighth to oversee)

22 And Chenaniah, chief of the Levites, was for song: he instructed about the song, because he was skillful. (Was for the carriage: he instructed about the carriage) (Song: Heb. lifting up) **23** And Berechiah and Elkanah were doorkeepers for the ark.

24 And Shebaniah, and Jehoshaphat, and Nethaneel, and Amasai, and Zechariah, and Benaiah, and Eliezer, the priests, did blow with the trumpets before the ark of God: and Obededom and Jehiah were doorkeepers for the ark.

1 Chronicles 15: 28-29

28 Thus all Israel brought up the ark of the covenant of the LORD with shouting, and with sound of the cornet, and with trumpets, and with cymbals, making a noise with psalteries and harps. **29** And it came to pass, as the ark of the covenant of the LORD came to the city of David, that Michal the daughter of Saul looking out at a window saw king David dancing and playing: and she despised him in her heart.

Exodus 15: 20-21

20 And Miriam the prophetess, the sister of Aaron, took a timbrel in her hand; and all the women went out after her with timbrel and with dances. **21** And Miriam answered them, Sing ye to the LORD, for he hath triumphed gloriously; the horse and his rider hath he thrown into the sea.

2 Samuel 6:5

5 And David and all the house of Israel played before the LORD on all manner of instruments made of fire wood, even on harps, and on psalteries, and on tumbrels, and on cornets, and on cymbals.

1 Chronicles 23: 1-5

1 So when David was old and full of days, he made Solomon his son king over Israel. **2** And he gathered together all the princes of Israel, with the priests and the Levites. **3** Now the Levites were numbered from the age of thirty years and upward: and their number by their polls, man by man, was thirty and eight thousand.

4 Of which, twenty and four thousand were to set forward the work of the house of the LORD; and six thousand were officers and judges: (set... or, oversee) **5** Moreover four thousand were porters; and four thousand praised the LORD with the instruments which I made, said David, to praise therewith.

2 Chronicles 29: 25-30

25 And he set the Levites in the house of the LORD with cymbals, with psalteries, and with harps, according to the commandment of David, and of Gad the king's seer, and Nathan the prophet: for so was the commandment of the LORD by his prophets. (Commandment of the LORD: Heb. commandment by the hand of the LORD) (By: Heb. by the hand of) **26** And the Levites stood with the instruments of David, and the priests with the trumpets.

27 And Hezekiah commanded to offer the burnt offering upon the altar. And when the burnt offering began, the song of the LORD began also with the trumpets, and with the instruments ordained by David king of Israel. (When: Heb. in the time) (The instruments: Heb. hands of instruments) **28** And the entire congregation worshipped, and the singers sang, and the trumpeters sounded: and all this continued until the burnt offering was finished. (Singers: Heb. song)

29 And when they had made an end of offering, the king and all that were present with him bowed them, and worshipped. (Present: Heb. found) **30** Moreover Hezekiah the king and the princes commanded the Levites to sing praise unto the LORD with the words of David, and of Asaph the seer. And they sang praises with gladness, and they bowed their heads and worshipped.

2 Samuel 6: 12-16

12 And it was told king David, saying, The LORD hath blessed the house of Obededom, and all that pertaineth unto him, because of the ark of God. So David went and brought up the ark of God from the house of Obededom into the city of David with gladness.

13 And it was so, that when they that bare the ark of the LORD had gone six paces, he sacrificed oxen and fatlings. **14** And David danced before the LORD with all his might; and David was girded with a linen ephod. **15** So David and all the house of Israel brought up the ark of the LORD with shouting, and with the sound of the trumpet.

16 And as the ark of the LORD came into the city of David, Michal Saul's daughter looked through a window, and saw king David leaping and dancing before the LORD; and she despised him in her heart. "And David danced before the Lord,"

Refer-
ences

1. The Bible
2. Louis *Bekoholf: Sytematic* Theology
3. Michael Bradley: Chosen People from the Caucasus. (Jewish Origins Delusions, Deceptions and Historical Role in the salve Trade, Genocide and Cultural Colonization.) Third world Press, Chicago, 1992
4. Willie Lynch letter: The Making of a Slave: This speech was delivered by Willie Lynch on the bank of the James River in the colony of Virginia in 1712. Lynch was a British slave owner in the West Indies. He was invited to the colony of Virginia in 1712 to teach his methods to slave owners there. The term "lynching" is derived from his last name. From Brown America, The story of a New Race by Edwin R. *Embree.* 1931 The Viking Press.

5. Desmond Mpilo Tutu, Hope and Suffering, *Skotaville* Publishers, 1983, pp x

6. The Book of Enoch: A modern translation of the *Ethiopean* Book of Enoch: SOAS Library at the University of London. Pp 11

7. Prof *Evangelos Nikolaidis:* Islamic Fundamentalism and Terrorism 2016, Alpha – Omega Agency. Attacking innocent people is not courageous. A professor of Business Ethics, Corporate Governance and stakeholder Management

8. Kahlil Gibran, The Prophet Collection, Axiom Publishing, 2001, pp39-40

9. Dr. K. Kohler: President Hebrew Union College New York The Macmillan; Jewish Theology: Systematically and Historically Considered Company 1918 p 21-22

10. Benjamin B. Warfield: DIGITAL PUBLICATIONS LIBRARY THEOLOGY Christology And Criticism Volume 3; COPYRIGHT, © 2003, BY DIGITAL PUBLICATIONS, DALLAS, TEXAS, USA

11. Mark A. Copeland ~ Gospel preacher, Bible teacher: http://executableoutlines.com/back.htm

12. THE CHARLES H. SPURGEON COLLECTION: VERSION 2.3 Sermons - (63 Volumes)

13. The New Park Street Pulpit &The Metropolitan Tabernacle Pulpit Making the Words of the Wise Available to All — Inexpensively. AGES SOFTWARE®, INC. Rio, WI USA © 1998-2004

14. Yurugu: An African-centered Critique of European Cultural Thought and Behavior," as well as articles that have appeared in scholarly journals.

15. Edited by Andrew Burnet: Book of Great Speeches 2013: Chambers Harrap Publishers Ltd (makers) a comprehensive guide to the inspired and inspiring speeches that have shaped the world we live in.

16. Dean Courtier, http://www.sermoncentral.com/sermons/silver-or-gold-i-do-not-have-dean-courtier-sermon-on-evangelism-urgency-70506.asp

17. Hilary Hinton "Zig" Ziglar was an American author, salesman, and motivational speaker.

18. Jeff A.Benner and Michael Calpino: Genesis, Zen and Quantum Physics: A Fresh Look At The Theology of Science of creation. P89-90

19. Dr. Marimba Any, To Be Afrikan: February 26, 1999 Copyright (c) 1999 Dr. Marimba Ani. All Rights Reserved. Dr. Marimba Ani, an activist in the African Liberation Movement, worked as field-organizer for the Student Nonviolent Committee (SNCC) in Mississippi in the 60s. She has continued her activism through her scholarship.

20. Lewis R. Gordon, Africana Philosophy and Philosophy in Black

21. Lewis R. Gordon, The Black ScholarVol. 43, No. 4, The Role of Black Philosophy (Winter 2013), Published by: Taylor & Francis, Ltd.

22. Kwame Gyekye (born 1939) is a Ghanaian philosopher, and an important figure in the development of modern African philosophy. Gyekye studied first at the University of Ghana, then at Harvard University, where he obtained his Ph.D. with a thesis on Græco–Arabic philosophy. He has been a Fellow of the Smithsonian Institution's Woodrow Wilson International Center for Scholars, and is a life-time Fellow of the Ghana Academy of Arts and Sciences. He was educated at Mfantsipim School

23. http://www.philosophybasics.com/general_african.html

24. African Traditional Religions, Worldmark Encyclopedia of Religious Practices COPYRIGHT 2006 Thomson Gale

25. Jacob K. Olupona is Professor of African Religious Traditions at Harvard Divinity School, with a joint appointment as Professor of African and African American Studies in Harvard's Faculty of Arts and Sciences. A noted scholar of indigenous African religions, his books include African Religions: A Very Short Introduction, City of 201 Gods: Ilé-Ifè in Time, Space, and the Imagination, Òrìsà Devotion as World Religion: The Globalization of Yorùbá Religious Culture, co-edited with Terry Rey, and Kingship, Religion, and Rituals in a Nigerian Community: A Phenomenological Study of Ondo Yoruba Festivals. In 2007, he was awarded the Nigerian National Order of Merit, one of Nigeria's most prestigious honors.

26. The Book of Enoch: A modern translation of the Ethiopian Book of Enoch: SOAS Library at the University of London. Pp 13

27. Dennis Healey; English Politician born in 1917. Chambers Book of Great Speeches, Edited by Andrew Burnet, Chambers Harrap Publishers Ltd 2006, 2013.

28. Xenophanes of Colophon was a Greek philosopher, theologian, poet, and social and religious critic. Xenophanes lived a life of travel, having left Ionia at the age of 25 and continuing to travel

throughout the Greek world for another 67 years

29. Bruce T Ballinger: Published MCA Music Pub. AOD Universal Studio Sound iii Inc 1976

30. Rabbi Ralph Messer, Torah Law or Grace, Simchat Torah Beit Midrash Publishing, 2011. Pp 161 kingdom Principles to live by

31. Rabbi Ralph Messer: Simchat Torah Beit Midrash: the Mikveh Process: 2006, pp8

32. Melusi Ndhlalambi: Co-Founder/Executive Producer at Melvee Video Productions

33. Dr Gift Mweemba Interview Bloemfontein Sabbath of June 7, 2014. The Israelite threat of fertility of Baal worship in the land of milk and honey.

34. Wole Oladiyun, Anointing for Glory, Printmill Glory Company, 2015, pp 1 you should a carrier of God's glory

35. Bukky Adije: Victory Sanctuary: Lekki Lagos

36. Norman Solomon, Judaism, Oxford University Press, 1996, pp 59.

37. Cicero, Roman Orator 7 November 62BC (Catilina your hopes must obviously be at an end)

38. Coversations with Thembile Ephrat Dyanti : 2016, Johannesburg, on the history and customs of the Xhosa tribes. The sacred ceremonies have a striking resemblance to the Hebraic practices. And if we go in to seek for meaning we will learn the power of history, which connects us.

39. M.M Magagula 2016, Barberton, and Mpumalanga South Africa: In his devotion and reflection about his life and goodness of God in his life.

40. Bishop Tudor Bismarck is an apostolic voice to the nations. From the age of 17 when he began traveling to outskirt villages in the Bulawayo region in Zimbabwe, to the present where he is requested at some of the largest gatherings of Christians around the world, Bishop Bismarck has been known for speaking the gospel.

41. Paulette Fortune, Swaziland: a student of the bible and her studies in the biblical use of musical instruments and use in worship. She complied comprehensive study into the history of instruments and expressions of worship, dancing, clapping of hands and prophetic utterances.

42. Francis of Assisi

43. Plato: the Philosopher born in 427 B.C

44. Eckhart Tolle

45. Bruce Lipton
46. Damian Marley
47. Albert Einstein
48. Deepak Chopra
49. Neale Donald Walsch
50. Jim Rohn
51. Kim Meredith, Dealonomics (deal maker), Marlene Fryer; Zebra Press 2013 pp 248
52. Plato: the Greek Philosopher 427 B.C
53. Screen Kierkegaard, Dannish Philospher born 1813
54. Friedrich Nietzsche: German Philosopher 1844
55. Paul Post, Phillip Nel and Walteer Van Beek, Sacred and contested Identities (space and ritual dynamics in Europe and Africa p 4
56. Gcina Nhlapo, 29 March 2016 Interview on Music. He is a musician and Worship leader as Cities of Refuge Johannesburg. The power of African worship and praise is in their experiences, which they have not been allowed to express fully.
57. Charles Forster Kent, Judaism, Sterling Innovation, 2010 pp 273
58. Jo Thobeka Wreford Working with Spirit (experiencing Izangoma Healing in contemporary South Africa, epistemologies of healing)
59. Edwin W Smith: The Christianity of Africa in the golden stool, Hilbron Publishing House, p 173
60. Oscar Wilde, The Soul of Man and Prison Writings: The Soul of Man Under Socialism, and Selected Critical Prose, Oscar Final O'Flahertie Wills Wilde, October 16, 1854, Dublin, Ireland Irish.
61. Paul Post, Phillip Nel and Walteer Van Beek, Sacred and Contested Identities (space and ritual dynamics in Europe and Africa p 43
62. Vaclav Havel: Television and Radio interview from Prague, 1990 Czechoslovakia. "The contamination as a sin we committed against ourselves".
63. Credo Vusamazulu Mutwa, Indaba, My Children (AfricanTribal History, legends, customs and religious beliefs) Blue Crane Books, 1964 pp xix-xx
64. Richard Sauta: Brigadier General: Zimbabwe Nation Special Forces an independent thinker and military strategist
65. Juegen Moltmann, Theology of Hope, Fortress Press, 1993, pp 319
66. Paul Post, Phillip Nel and Walteer Van Beek, Sacred and contested Identities (space and ritual dynamics in Europe and Africa p 5

67. Nhlanhla Shabangu, an ardent student of History and Hebraic literature. Interview Johannesburg 2016. He is a heritage fundi Egyptology, Ethiopian and Kermit Continent a lover of the darker races an activist of social change.

68. As taught by Maimonides: 'The Rabbaeiun Moshesh Ben Moimon" a prominent Medieval prolific Spanish and intellectual writer.

69. Apostle I.N Sithole, Oasis of Life Family Church, Daveyton Johannesburg, Interview 2015

70. Rijk van Dijk, Ria Reis and Marja Spierenburg, Ngoma, The quest for fruition therough Ngoma, p 39

71. Aryeh Kaplan, Maimonides's Principles (fundamentals of Jewish Faith), Olive stone Publishing Services 1984, pp 37

72. Aneneas Chigwedere, The Mutasa Manyika Dynasty 1695-2000, Mutapa Publishing House 2015, pp 159

73. William Cowper: Song There is a fountain tilled with blood, 1772

74. Zodwa Kunene: Women's Ministries Department, SAU, and Southern African Union of the Seventh-Days Adventist Bloemfontein South Africa.

75. Berliner, Paul F, The Soul of Mbira and Traditions of the Shona People of Zimbabwe, University Press, 1981.

76. http://www.gospelhall.org/bible/bible.php?passage=Numbers+15%3A37-41;&ver1=kjv

77. Grace to You: Unleashing God's Truth, One Verse at a Time The Critical Elements of True Worship Scripture: Romans 12:1-2 http://www.gty.org

78. http://www.rantlifestyle.com/2014/08/13/21-reasons-why-religion-is-wrong/

79. http://www.tinotenda.org/spirituality.htm

80. http://www2.kenyon.edu/projects/ottenhoff/paper.htm: After coming to some conclusions on what mbira music reveals about Shona society, I compared my conclusions to other authors' views of the Shona. While many of the conclusions are similar, our stands are strikingly different concerning constraint and mobility in Shona society. Much of the literature (primarily Michael Gelfand)

81. http://www.mbirajunction.com/artist/garikai/e_function.htm

82. http://jesuschristinhissanctuary.net/studies_on_the_sanctuary.htm

83. Miyamoto Musashi, The Book of the Five Rings, Bantam Books 1982, pp 9 the master must guide the student as the outcome is

on him changing into enlightenment The student must understand that he is the object and primary beneficiary of education.

84. Twitter: @giles_fraser

85. http://www.theguardian.com/commentisfree/belief/2013/may/31/wickedness-allied-truth-religious-belief-heinous

86. Rabbi Ralph Messer, Convention Tapes in Nigeria 2011, on Black History.

87. John Calvin, Commentary on the Book of Psalms, Vol. I, p. 539

88. http://www.ccel.org/contrib/exec_outlines/cjb/cjb_12.htm

89. John Pape, Jr, Five Elements of Worship, http://www.media-tunes.com/bhow/ or http://www.prayway.com/articles/Five_Elements_of_Wor.html

90. Subscribe to #FarmersOFThought - Maponga J iii https://www.youtube.com/watch?v=wi6p1R90Q9I&feature=youtu.be

About the Author

Maponga Joshua III

Joshua Maponga is a Leadership Development Facilitator, Life Coach and Speaker.

Maponga Joshua has spent years in the corporate, religious and social space - a time that has made him own the title, 'a creative powerhouse'. There are those who think in the box, there are those who think outside the box and then those who break the box and think.

He lives and breathes change; his dynamic thinking has surely broken social, religious, economic, national boundaries. Maponga is the CEO of the institute Farmers Of Thought, who's core business is to build a consciousness and improve the quality of human experiences.

He is a pragmatic African citizen with a global view, "think globally and act locally", as he says it. He plays a dozen musical instruments in addition to being a writer, speaker, life coach and social entrepreneur - indeed he is a man of no limitations.

Maponga is a graduate of Andrews University (Berrien Springs Michigan USA), he holds a Degree in Philosophy (BA theology) and Personal Ministries, with a variety of Outcome-based qualifications from international institutes such as ILO (International Labor Organization). He has a wide range of experience in branding, banking, non-profit organizations and the project management space with multinational companies such as Vodacom, SAPO, Absa World Vision, PRASA, SALGA, Milpark College and SAPS, to mention a few.

His involvement in the corporate space includes motivation, crisis management, business negotiations, strategic sessions, change management, material development and turn-key solutions in consultancy.

The birth of his two daughters and their growth has inspired him to develop tools for youth development and parenting. His latest book, "Shopping Skills" has been received well and comes after his other book, "So You Want To Be The Master" became a bestseller.

He has also written, developed, produced, presented and anchored on TV Programmes; Joshua Show, Behind Gospel, One Gospel, Late debate, Education Channel "ED" and others. He challenges all who live mundane lives to move beyond cocoons of human limitations to excellence.

Made in United States
North Haven, CT
17 May 2024